Wiley's Level I CFA® Program 11th Hour Final Review Study Guide 2022

Thousands of candidates from more than 100 countries have relied on these Study Guides to pass the CFA® Exam. Covering every Learning Outcome Statement (LOS) on the exam, these review materials are an invaluable tool for anyone who wants a deep-dive review of all the concepts, formulas, and topics required to pass.

Wiley study materials are produced by expert CFA charterholders, CFA Institute members, and investment professionals from around the globe. For more information, contact us at www.efficientlearning.com.

Wiley's Level I CFA® Program 11th Hour Final Review Study Guide 2022

WILEY

Contents

Foreword	VII
Quantitative Methods (QM)	
Study Session 1: Quantitative Methods (1)	1
Study Session 2: Quantitative Methods (2)	15
Economics (EC)	
Study Session 3: Economics (1)	41
Study Session 4: Economics (2)	81
Financial Statement Analysis (FSA)	
Study Session 5: Financial Statement Analysis (1)	109
Study Session 6: Financial Statement Analysis (2)	117
Study Session 7: Financial Statement Analysis (3)	139
Study Session 8: Financial Statement Analysis (4)	177
Corporate Issuers (CI)	
Study Session 9: Corporate Issuers (1)	189
Study Session 10: Corporate Issuers (2)	201
Equity Investments (EQ)	
Study Session 11: Equity Investments (1)	215
Study Session 12: Equity Investments (2)	239
Fixed Income (FI)	
Study Session 13: Fixed Income (1)	261
Study Session 14: Fixed Income (2)	295
Derivatives (DR)	
Study Session 15: Derivatives	313
Alternative Investments (AI)	
Study Session 16: Alternative Investments	329

Portfolio Management (PM)

Study Session 17: Portfolio Management (1)   335

Study Session 18: Portfolio Management (2)   357

Ethical and Professional Standards (ET)

Study Session 19: Ethical and Professional Standards   389

Foreword

Wiley's Level I CFA® Program 11th Hour Final Review Study Guide 2022 is a concise and easy-to-understand review book that is meant to supplement your review for the CFA® Level I Program Exam. It becomes extremely difficult to go through the entire curriculum in the last few weeks leading up to the exam, so we have condensed the material for you. You must remember, though, that this book is not meant to be a primary study tool for the exam. It is designed to help you review the material in an efficient and effective manner so that you can be confident on exam day.

About the Authors

Wiley's Study Guides are written by a team of highly qualified CFA charterholders and leading CFA instructors from around the globe. Our team of CFA experts work collaboratively to produce the best study materials for CFA candidates available today.

Wiley's expert team of contributing authors and instructors is led by Content Director Basit Shajani, CFA. Basit founded online education start-up Élan Guides in 2009 to help address CFA candidates' need for better study materials. As lead writer, lecturer, and curriculum developer, Basit's unique ability to break down complex topics helped the company grow organically to be a leading global provider of CFA Exam prep materials. In January 2014, Élan Guides was acquired by John Wiley & Sons, Inc., where Basit continues his work as Director of CFA Content. Basit graduated magna cum laude from the Wharton School of Business at the University of Pennsylvania with majors in finance and legal studies. He went on to obtain his CFA charter in 2006, passing all three levels on the first attempt. Prior to Élan Guides, Basit ran his own private wealth management business. He is a past president of the Pakistani CFA Society.

There are many more expert CFA charterholders who contribute to the creation of Wiley materials. We are thankful for their invaluable expertise and diligent work. To learn more about Wiley's team of subject matter experts, please visit: www.efficientlearning.com/cfa.

STUDY SESSION 1: QUANTITATIVE METHODS (1)

THE TIME VALUE OF MONEY
Cross-Reference to CFA Institute Assigned Reading #1

Interest rates can be thought of in three ways:

- The minimum rate of return that you require to accept a payment at a later date.
- The discount rate that must be applied to a future cash flow to determine its present value.
- The opportunity cost of receiving money today as opposed to saving it for a certain period and earning a return on it.

Interest rates are composed of the real risk-free rate plus compensation for bearing various risks.

- The real risk-free rate is the single-period return on a risk-free security assuming zero inflation. With no inflation, every dollar holds on to its purchasing power, so this rate purely reflects individuals' preferences for current versus future consumption.
- The inflation premium is added to the real risk-free rate to reflect the expected loss in purchasing power over the term of a loan. The real risk-free rate plus the inflation premium equals the nominal risk-free rate.
- The default risk premium compensates investors for the risk that the borrower might fail to make her payments on time in full.
- The liquidity premium compensates investors for any difficulty they might face in converting their holdings readily into cash at close to the most recent market price. Securities that trade infrequently or with low volumes require a higher liquidity premium than those that trade frequently with high volumes.
- The maturity premium compensates investors for the higher sensitivity of the market values of longer term debt instruments to changes in interest rates.

Present Value versus Future Value

- Present value (PV) is the current worth of sum of money or stream of cash flows that will be received in the future, given the interest rate.
  - For a given discount rate, the *longer* the time period till the future amount is received, the *lower* the present value.
  - For a given time period, the *higher* the discount rate, the *lower* the present value of an amount.
- Future value (FV) is the value of a sum of money at a specified date in the future.
  - For a given interest rate, the future value *increases* as the number of periods *increases*.
  - For a given number of periods, the future value *increases* as the interest rate *increases*.

Since PV and FV are separated in time, remember the following that we can add sums of money only if they are being valued at exactly the same point in time.

Annuities

- An annuity is a series of recurring periodic level payments.
- An ordinary annuity is an annuity where the cash flows occur at the end of each compounding period.

- An annuity due is an annuity where cash flows occur at the beginning of every period. Problems relating to annuities due can either be solved in [BGN] mode or by converting the value of an ordinary annuity to that of an annuity due.

$$PV_{\text{Annuity Due}} = PV_{\text{Ordinary Annuity}} \times \ (1 + r)$$
$$FV_{\text{Annuity Due}} = FV_{\text{Ordinary Annuity}} \times \ (1 + r)$$

Perpetuities

A perpetuity is a never ending series of level payments, where the first cash flow occurs one period from now (at t = 1).

$$PV = \frac{PMT}{I/Y}$$

The Effects of Compounding Frequency

- As the number of compounding periods *increases*, the future value of the investment *increases*.
- As the number of compounding periods *increases*, the present value of the investment *decreases*.
- The effective annual rate *rises* as compounding frequency *increases*.

Loan Payments and Amortization Schedules

Loan amortization is the process of retiring a loan obligation through predetermined equal monthly payments. Each of these payments includes an interest component, which is calculated on the principal outstanding at the beginning of the period, and a principal repayment component. The principal component increases with the passage of time, and the interest component declines over time in line with the decreasing amount of principal outstanding.

The principal outstanding at any payment date equals the present value of the remaining payments discounted at the periodic discount rate.

The Cash Flow Additivity Principle

The additivity principle states that the present value of any stream of cash flows equals the sum of the present values of the individual cash flows. If we have two streams of cash flows, the sum of the present values of the two streams at any point in time is the same as the present value of the two series combined by adding cash flows that occur at the same point in time. The cash flow stream can also be divided in any desired manner, and the present value of the pieces will equal the present value of the series.

ORGANIZING, VISUALIZING, AND DESCRIBING DATA
Cross-Reference to CFA Institute Assigned Reading #2

Types of Data

- **Numerical data** can be measured or counted.
- **Categorical data** indicate a quality or characteristic of a group of data.
- **Cross-sectional data** examines the same variable at a specific time for multiple observational units.
- **Time series data** examines the same variable at different points in time for the same observational unit.
- **Panel data** uses cross-sectional data over time, typically represented in a *data table*.
- **Structured data** can be easily organized and presented as arrays of variables or dimensional data tables.
- **Unstructured data**, on the other hand, do not follow conventional organization approaches.
- **Absolute frequency** describes the number of observations.
- **Relative frequency** divides the number in each group or interval by the total number of observations to provide a normalized comparison.
- A **contingency table** summarizes two or more categorical variables into a single table with one variable as rows and the others as columns.
  - **Joint frequency** represents the number of variables observed at the intersection of a row and a single column.
  - A **marginal frequency** represents the number of variables observed as the total across a row or down a column.

The chi-square test of independence can be used to determine whether membership in a row or column affects the number of variables. A test statistic greater than the chi-square distribution value at a particular level of significance, the null hypothesis of independence is rejected, and the variables have a statistical relationship.

Presenting Data

- A **histogram** is used graphically to represent the data contained in a frequency distribution.
- A **frequency polygon** also graphically illustrates the information in a frequency distribution. The coordinates or points of a frequency polygon are the frequency of each interval plotted against the midpoint of the interval.
- A **cumulative frequency distribution** plots the cumulative frequency of each interval against the upper bound of the interval.
- A **bar chart** is like a histogram, but for categorical rather than numerical data.
  - A Pareto chart is a bar chart with categories ordered by descending number of observations.
- A **tree map** consists of colored rectangles that represent categories or intervals of data.
- A **word cloud** represents textual data with the value of observations represented by the size of the words and the category or the sentiment represented by the color of the words.
- A **bubble chart** is a frequency polygon representing multi-dimensional data.
- A **scatter plot** represents x- and y-axis data as would be common in a linear regression.
- A **heat map** assigns different colors indicating the magnitude of the variable.

Measures of Central Tendency

- The **arithmetic mean** is the sum of the observations divided by the number of observations.
    - The **trimmed mean** includes only some percentage of the middle of the values.
    - The **winsorized mean** replaces outliers to the highest or lowest observation in some percentage of the middle data.
- The **median** is the middle value of the data once arranged in ascending or descending order.
    - The advantage of the median is that it is not sensitive to extreme values and is useful for asymmetrical distributions.
- The **mode** is the most frequently occurring value in a data set.
    - For grouped data, the mode is the interval with the greatest number of observations.

Alternative Concepts of the Mean

The **weighted mean** is calculated by assigning different weights to observations in the data set to account for the disproportionate effect of certain observations on the arithmetic mean. The arithmetic mean assigns equal weights to every observation in the data set, which makes it very sensitive to extreme values.

The **geometric mean** is used to average rates of change over time or to calculate the growth rate of a variable over a period.

$$R_G = \sqrt[n]{(1 + R_1)(1 + R_2)...(1 + R_n)} - 1$$

The arithmetic mean provides the best estimate for a one-period growth rate because it is the average of all the periodic growth rates over time. Geometric mean, however, indicates how the periodic returns are linked to the total value change over time.

- The geometric mean is always less than or equal to the arithmetic mean.
- The geometric mean equals the arithmetic mean only when all the observations are identical.
- The difference between the geometric and arithmetic mean increases as the dispersion in observed values increases.

When the variable is a rate or a ratio, the **harmonic return** presents a better picture of central tendency. It may be viewed as a special type of weighted mean where the weight of an observation is inversely proportional to its magnitude. It is used in the investment management arena to determine the average cost of shares purchased over time.

Harmonic mean:

$$\overline{X}_H = \frac{n}{\sum_{i=1}^{n}(1/X_i)} \text{ with } X_i > 0$$

- Mathematically, unless all the observations in the data set are identical (equal in value), the harmonic mean will always be less than the geometric mean, which itself will be less than the arithmetic mean.

- The harmonic mean reduces the tendency of extreme outliers to pull the mean in that direction.

Quintiles

A quantile is a value at, or below which a stated proportion of the observations in a data set lie. The positional location, L, in an ascending array of the value below which y% of observations lie is:

$$L_y = (n+1)\frac{y}{100}$$

Quantiles may be visualized by a **box-and-whisker plot**, which shows whiskers at the highest and lowest values and boxes for the middle quartile ranges. To better identify outliers, the boundaries of the IQR +/− some percentage will be applied to establish the whiskers. Outliers will appear outside the whiskers.

Measures of Dispersion

The range represents the difference between the highest and lowest values in a data set.

$$Range = Maximum\ value\ -\ Minimum\ value$$

The **mean absolute deviation (MAD)** is the average of the absolute values of deviations of observations in a data set from their mean.

$$MAD = \frac{\sum_{i=1}^{n} X_i - \overline{X}_i}{n}$$

The variance is the average of the squared deviations around the mean. The standard deviation is the positive square root of the variance. While the variance has no units, the standard deviation has the same units as the random variable.

Sample variance $= S^2 =$
Sample standard deviation $= S =$

If the series is returns over time the relationship between the geometric and arithmetic means is:

$$X_G = \overline{X} - \frac{S^2}{2}$$

Target downside deviation, also known as **target semi-deviation**, measures dispersion of observations below the target rather around the average.

$$S_{Target} = \sqrt{\frac{\sum_{\substack{for\ X_i \leq B}}^{n} (X_i - B)^2}{n-1}}$$

The coefficient of variation is a measure of relative dispersion. It represents risk per unit of return.

$$CV = \frac{S}{\overline{X}}$$

Asymmetric Distributions and Data Correlation

$$skewness \approx \left(\frac{1}{n}\right)\frac{\sum_{i=1}(X_i - \overline{X})^3}{S^3}$$

- A positively skewed distribution has frequent small losses and a few extremely large gains.
- A negatively skewed distribution has frequent small gains and a few extremely large losses.

$$K_E \approx \left[\left(\frac{1}{n}\right)\frac{\sum_{i=1}^{n}(X_i - \overline{X})^4}{S^4}\right] - 3$$

Table 3-1: Kurtosis Properties

Kurtosis	Excess Kurtosis	Distribution	Description
Kurtosis > 3	$K_E > 0$	Fatter tails	Leptokurtic
Kurtosis = 3	$K_E = 0$	Normal distribution	Mesokurtic
Kurtosis < 3	$K_E < 0$	Fatter (skinny) tails	Platykurtic

$$COV_{XY} = \frac{\sum_{i=1}^{n}(X_i - \overline{X})(Y_i - \overline{Y})}{n-1}$$

PROBABILITY CONCEPTS
Cross-Reference to CFA Institute Assigned Reading #3

- A random variable is one whose possible values or results are *uncertain*.
- An outcome is the observed value of a random variable.
- An event could be a single outcome or a set of outcomes.
- Mutually exclusive events are events that cannot happen simultaneously. The occurrence of one precludes the occurrence of the other.
- Exhaustive events cover the range of *all possible outcomes* of an event.

A probability is a number between 0 and 1 that reflects the chance of a certain event occurring. A probability of zero means that it is impossible for the event to occur, while a probability of 1 means that an event will definitely occur and the outcome is not random.

There are two basic defining principles of probability:

1. The probability of any event, E, is a number between 0 and 1.
2. The sum of the probabilities of mutually exclusive and exhaustive events equals 1.

Methods of Estimating Probabilities

An empirical probability estimates the probability of an event based on its frequency of occurrence in the past.

A subjective probability draws on subjective reasoning and personal judgment to estimate the probability of an event.

An a priori probability is based on formal analysis and reasoning.

Probabilities Stated as Odds

The odds *for* an event are stated as the probability of the event occurring to the probability of the event not occurring. Odds for an event, E, are stated as $P(E)$ to $[1 - P(E)]$.

If the odds *for* are given as "a to b" then:

$$P(E) = \frac{a}{(a + b)}$$

The odds *against* an event are stated as the probability of an event not occurring to the probability of the event occurring. Odds *against* an event, E, are stated in the form of $[1 - P(E)]$ to $P(E)$.

If the odds *against* are given as "a to b" then:

$$P(E) = \frac{b}{(a + b)}$$

- Given the odds for an outcome, the odds against the outcome are simply the *reciprocal* of the odds for.

- Given the odds against an outcome, the odds for the outcome are simply the *reciprocal* of the odds against.

The Dutch Book Theorem states that if the probabilities reflected in the stock prices are not consistent, they give rise to profit opportunities. As investors take positions to take advantage of such opportunities, the inconsistency is eventually eliminated.

Conditional versus Unconditional Probabilities

Unconditional or marginal probabilities estimate the probability of an event irrespective of the occurrence of other events. They can be thought of as stand-alone probabilities and answer questions like "What is the probability of a return on a stock above 10%?" or "What are the chances of getting a 3 on a roll of a die?"

Conditional probabilities express the probability of an event occurring *given* that another event has occurred. The questions answered are like "What is the probability of the return on a stock being more than 10%, *given* that the return is above the risk free rate?" or "What is the probability of rolling a 3, *given* that an odd number is rolled." Conditional probabilities are computed using joint probabilities.

- A *joint probability*, P(AB), answers questions like, "What is the probability of *both* A and B happening?"
    - If A and B are mutually exclusive events, the joint probability P(AB) equals zero. This is because mutually exclusive events cannot occur simultaneously.
    - If A is contained within the set of possible outcomes for B, P(AB) = P(A)

Mathematically, conditional probability is expressed as:

$$P(A|B) = \frac{P(AB)}{P(B)} \text{ given that } P(B) \neq 0$$

The multiplication rule for probability calculates joint probabilities using a conditional probability.

$$P(AB) = P(A|B) \times P(B)$$

The addition rule for probabilities is used to calculate the probability of A or B occurring.

$$P(A \text{ or } B) = P(A) + P(B) - P(AB)$$

Given that A and B share some outcomes, if we simply add P(B) to P(A) we would be double counting the shared outcomes. Therefore, we subtract the joint probability from the sum of the probabilities of A and B.

If the events are mutually exclusive, the joint probability of A and B, P(AB), equals zero, so P(A or B) would simply equal P(A) + P(B).

Dependent versus Independent Events

With two dependent events, the occurrence of one is related to the occurrence of the other. For example, the probability of doing well on an exam is related to the probability of preparing well for it.

Two events are independent if the occurrence of one does *not* have any bearing on the occurrence of the other. For example, the probability of doing well on an exam is unrelated to the probability of there being 5 trees in the park nearby.

When two events are independent:

$P(A|B) = P(A)$ or equivalently, $P(B|A) = P(B)$

- With independent events, the word *and* implies multiplication, and the word *or* implies addition.

$$P(A \text{ or } B) = P(A) + P(B) - P(AB)$$

$$P(A \text{ and } B) = P(A) \times P(B)$$

The Total Probability Rule for Unconditional Probabilities

The total probability rule expresses the unconditional probability of an event in terms of conditional probabilities for mutually exclusive and exhaustive events.

$$P(A) = P(AS) + P(AS^C)$$

$$P(A) = P(A|S) \times P(S) + P(A|S^c) \times P(S^c)$$

The probability of Event A, P(A), is expressed as a weighted average in the total probability rule. The weights applied to the conditional probabilities are the probabilities of the scenarios. For example, the weight attached to the conditional probability, P(A|S), is the probability of scenario S, P(S).

Expected Value

The expected value of a random variable is the probability-weighted average of all possible outcomes for the random variable.

$$E(X) = \sum_{i=1}^{n} P(X_i)X_i$$

$$E(X) = P(X_1)X_1 + P(X_2)X_2 + \ldots P(X_n)X_n$$

Variance

If variance is zero, there is no dispersion in the distribution. In this case, the outcome is certain, and the variable is not a random variable.

$$\sigma^2(X) = E\{[X - E(X)]^2\}$$

$$\sigma^2(X) = \sum_{i=1}^{n} P(X_i)[X_i - E(X)]^2$$

Standard deviation is the positive square root of the variance. The variance has no units while the standard deviation is expressed in the same unit as the expected value and the random variable itself.

Total Probability Rule for Expected Value

Similar to the total probability rule for stating unconditional probabilities in terms of conditional probabilities, the total probability rule for expected value states (unconditional) expected values in terms of conditional expected values.

$$E(X) = E(X|S)P(S) + E(X|S^c)P(S^c)$$

$$E(X) = E(X|S_1) \times P(S_1) + E(X|S_2) \times P(S_2) + \ldots + E(X|S_n) \times P(S_n)$$

Covariance

Covariance is a measure of the extent to which two random variables move together.

$$Cov(R_i, R_j) = E\{[R_i - E(R_i)][R_j - E(R_j)]\}$$

The covariance between the returns on Asset I and Asset J can also be calculated as:

$$Cov(R_i R_j) = \sigma(R_i)\sigma(R_j)\rho(R_i, R_j)$$

Properties of Covariance

Sample covariance, which is computed using a sample of historical data about the two variables, is calculated as:

$$Cov(R_i, R_j) = \sum_{i=1}^{n} (R_{i,t} - \overline{R}_i)(R_{j,t} - \overline{R}_j)/(n-1)$$

- Covariance is a similar concept to variance. The difference lies in the fact that variance measures how a random variable varies with itself, while covariance measures how a particular random variable varies with another.
- Covariance is symmetric, i.e., $Cov(X,Y) = Cov(Y,X)$.
- Covariance may range from positive infinity to negative infinity. Variance on the other hand, is always positive.
- The covariance of X with itself, $Cov(X,X)$ equals the variance of X, $Var(X)$.

Interpretation of Covariance

- When the covariance of returns of two assets is *negative*, it means that when the return on one asset is above its expected value, the return on the other tends to be below its expected value. There is an *inverse* relationship between the two variables.
- When the covariance of returns of two assets is *positive*, it means that when the return on one asset is above its expected value, the return on the other also tends to be above its expected value.
- Covariance of returns is zero if the returns are unrelated.

Limitations of Covariance

- Because the unit that covariance is expressed in depends on the unit that the data is presented in, it is difficult to compare covariance across data sets that have different scales.
- In practice, it is difficult to interpret covariance as it can take on extreme large values.
- Covariance does not tell us anything about the strength of the relationship between the two variables.

Correlation Coefficient

The correlation coefficient measures the strength and direction of a linear relationship between two random variables. It is obtained by dividing the covariance between two random variables by the product of their standard deviations.

$$\text{Corr}(R_A, R_B) = \rho(R_A, R_B) = \frac{\text{Cov}(R_A, R_B)}{(\sigma_A)(\sigma_B)}$$

A shortcoming of the correlation coefficient is the fact that it does not specify which factor or variable *causes* the linear relationship between the two variables.

Correlation Analysis

- The correlation coefficient can have a maximum value of $+1$ and a minimum value of -1.
- A correlation coefficient greater than 0 means that when one variable increases (decreases) the other tends to increase (decrease) as well.
- A correlation coefficient less than 0 means that when one variable increases (decreases) the other tends to decrease (increase).
- A correlation coefficient of 0 indicates that no linear relation exists between the two variables.

Correlation is different from the slope or gradient of a line. The slope of a line (on which all the data points lie) can take on any value, but if the slope is positive, the correlation between the two variables would equal $+1$ as long as the points lie on a straight line.

Limitations of Correlation Analysis

- Correlation is a measure of linear association.
- Correlation may be an unreliable measure when there are outliers in one or both the series.
- Correlation does not imply causation.
- Correlations may be spurious in that they may highlight relationships that are misleading.

Expected Return of a Portfolio

$$E(R_p) = \sum_{i=1}^{N} w_i E(R_i) = w_1 E(R_1) + w_2 E(R_2) + \ldots + w_N E(R_N)$$

Variance of a 2-Asset Portfolio

$$Var(R_p) = w_A^2 \sigma^2(R_A) + w_B^2 \sigma^2(R_B) + 2 w_A w_B Cov(R_A, R_B)$$

$$Var(R_p) = w_A^2 \sigma^2(R_A) + w_B^2 \sigma^2(R_B) + 2 w_A w_B \rho(R_A, R_B) \sigma(R_A) \sigma(R_B)$$

Variance of a 3-Asset Portfolio

$$Var(R_p) = w_A^2 \sigma^2(R_A) + w_B^2 \sigma^2(R_B) + w_C^2 \sigma^2(R_C)$$
$$+ 2 w_A w_B Cov(R_A, R_B) + 2 w_B w_C Cov(R_B, R_C) + 2 w_C w_A Cov(R_C, R_A)$$

To calculate the variance for a portfolio containing *n* different assets we would require *n(n-1)/2* unique covariances.

Finally, the expected value of the products of uncorrelated random variables equals the product of their expected values.

$E(XY) = E(X)E(Y)$ if X and Y are uncorrelated.

Bayes' Formula

By using Bayes' formula, we can reverse the "given that probability" P(A|B) and convert it into P(B|A) using P(A) and P(B). Bear in mind that you will probably have to use the total probability rule to calculate P(B).

$$P(B|A) = \frac{P(A|B) \times P(B)}{P(A)}$$

$$P(\text{Event}|\text{Information}) = \frac{P(\text{Information}|\text{Event}) \times P(\text{Event})}{P(\text{Information})}$$

Counting Problems

- Factorials are used when there is only one group and we are simply arranging a given set or group of n items. Given n items, there are n! ways of arranging them.
- The labeling formula is used for three or more groups of predetermined sizes. Each item must be labeled as a member of one of the groups.
- The combination formula is used when there are only two groups of predetermined sizes and crucially, the order or rank of labeling is NOT important.
- The permutation formula is used when there are only two groups of predetermined sizes and the order or ranking IS important.

COMMON PROBABILITY DISTRIBUTIONS
Cross-Reference to CFA Institute Assigned Reading #4

Discrete versus Continuous Random Variables

- A discrete random variable is one that can take on a countable number of values. Each outcome has a specific probability of occurring, which can be measured.
- A continuous random variable is one for which the number of possible outcomes cannot be counted (there are infinite possible outcomes) and therefore, probabilities cannot be attached to specific outcomes.

The **probability distribution** of a random variable identifies the probability of each of the possible outcomes of a random variable.

A **probability function p(x),** expresses the probability that "X," the random variable takes on a specific value of "x." A probability function can also be stated as $P(X=x)$.

A **probability density function (pdf),** which is denoted by $f(x)$, is used to determine the probability that the outcome lies within a specified range of possible values. It is used to interpret the probability structure of continuous random variables.

A **cumulative distribution function (cdf)**, or distribution function, expresses the probability that a random variable, X, takes on a value *less than or equal to* a specific value, x. It is the sum of the probabilities of all outcomes that are less than or equal to the specified value, x. A cdf is denoted by $F(x) = P(X \leq x)$.

The Discrete Uniform Distribution

A discrete uniform distribution is one in which the probability of each of the possible outcomes is identical. The best example of a uniform distribution is the probability distribution of the outcomes from the roll of a fair die, for which the probability of each outcome is 1/6.

The Continuous Uniform Distribution

A continuous uniform distribution is described by a lower limit, *a*, and an upper limit, *b*. These limits serve as the parameters of the distribution. The probability of any outcome or range of outcomes outside this interval is 0. Being a continuous distribution, individual outcomes also have a probability of 0. The distribution is often denoted as U(*a,b*).

The probability that the random variable will take a value that falls between x_1 and x_2, that both lie within the range, *a* to *b*, is the proportion of the total area taken up by the range, x_1 to x_2.

$$P(x_1 \leq X \leq x_2) = \frac{x_2 - x_1}{b - a}$$

Remember that $P(X \geq x)$ is the same as $P(X > x)$ or this distribution because it is a continuous distribution where $P(X = x)$ equals zero.

The Binomial Distribution

A binomial random variable is the number of successes (X) from a Bernoulli trial that is carried out "n" times. A Bernoulli experiment is an experiment that has only 2 possible outcomes which are labeled "success" and "failure." Further, these two outcomes are mutually exclusive and collectively exhaustive.

The probability of x successes in *n* trials is given by:

$$P(X = x) = {}_nC_x(p)^x(1 - p)^{n-x}$$

- The **expected value** of a binomial random variable (X) is given by:

$$E(x) = n \times p$$

- The **variance** of a binomial random variable is given by:

$$\sigma^2 = n \times p \times (1-p)$$

Binomial Trees

Binomial trees may be drawn to illustrate possible stock price movements. Binomial stock price models are extensively used in option pricing.

The Normal Distribution

- It is completely described by its mean and variance.
- It is symmetric about the mean (skewness = 0).
- Kurtosis = 3.
- Any linear combination of jointly, normally distributed random variables is also normally distributed.

Skewness and the Binomial Distribution

- If the probability of success is 0.50, the binomial distribution is symmetric.
- If the probability of success is less than 0.50, the binomial distribution is skewed to the right.
- If the probability of success is more than 0.50, the binomial distribution is skewed to the left.

Tracking Objectives, Tracking Errors, and Portfolio Risk

Tracking error is a measure of how closely a portfolio's returns match the returns of the index to which it is benchmarked. It is the difference between the total return on the portfolio (before deducting fees) and the total return on the benchmark index.

$$\text{Tracking error} = \text{Gross return on portfolio} - \text{Total return on benchmark index}$$

Calculating Probabilities Using the Standard Normal Distribution

This **standard normal distribution** is a normal distribution that has been standardized so that it has a mean of zero and a standard deviation of 1. To standardize an observation from a normal distribution, its standardized value or *z-score* must be calculated. This is done by subtracting the mean of the population from the observed value of the random variable, and dividing the result by the standard deviation.

$$\text{z-score} = (\text{observed value} - \text{population mean}) / \text{standard deviation} = (x - \mu)/\sigma$$

Essentially the z-value represents the number of standard deviations away from the population mean, an observed value of a random variable lies.

Confidence Intervals

A confidence interval represents the range of values within which a certain population parameter is expected to lie in a specified percentage of the time.

Shortfall Risk and Safety-First Ratio

Shortfall risk is the probability that a portfolio's value or return, $E(R_P)$, will fall below a particular target return (R_T) over a given period.

Roy's safety-first criterion states that an optimal portfolio minimizes the probability that the actual portfolio return, RP, will fall below the target return, R_T.

The safety-first ratio (SF Ratio) is similar to the Sharpe Ratio. The Sharpe Ratio is a special case of the SF Ratio, where the threshold level is the risk-free rate.

$$\text{Shortfall ratio (SF Ratio) or z-score} = \frac{E(R_p) - R_T}{\sigma_p}$$

Portfolios with *higher* SF Ratios are *preferred* to those that have a *lower* SF ratio; *higher* SF Ratio portfolios have a *lower* probability of not meeting their target returns.

The Lognormal Distribution

A random variable, Y, follows the lognormal distribution if its natural logarithm (ln Y) is normally distributed. Three important features differentiate the lognormal distribution from the normal distribution:

1. It is bounded by zero on the lower end.
2. The upper end of its range is unbounded.
3. It is skewed to the right (positively skewed).

The lognormal distribution is frequently used to model the distribution of asset prices because it is bounded on the left by zero.

Discretely compounded returns are based on discrete or defined compounding periods, such as 12 months or 6 months. As the compounding periods get shorter and shorter, the effective annual rate (EAR) rises. With continuous compounding, the effective annual rate is given as:

$$EAR = e^{r_{cc}} - 1 \quad r_{cc} = \text{continuously compounded annual rate}$$

The expression for calculating the continuously compounded rate, r_{cc}, is given as:

$$r_{cc} = ln(EAR + 1)$$

Student's t-Distribution

- It is symmetrical.
- It is defined by a single parameter, the degrees of freedom, (df), where degrees of freedom equal sample size minus one (n − 1).
- It has a lower peak than the normal curve, but fatter tails.

As the degrees of freedom increase, the t-distribution curve becomes more peaked, and its tails become thinner (bringing it closer to a normal curve). Therefore, the confidence interval for a random variable that follows the t-distribution will become narrower when the degrees of freedom increase for a given significance level.

The t-distribution is used in the following scenarios:

- It is used to construct confidence intervals of a normally (or approximately normally) distributed population whose variance is unknown when the sample size is small (n < 30).
- It may also be used for a non-normally distributed population whose variance is unknown if the sample size is large (n ≥ 30).

Chi-Square and F-Distribution

Chi-Square Distribution

- The chi-square distribution is asymmetrical.
- The chi-square distribution with k degrees of freedom is the distribution of the sum of the squares of k independent standard normally distributed random variables. Therefore, like the t-distribution, the chi-square distribution is a family of distributions.
- The chi-square distribution does not take on negative values.

F-Distribution

- Like the chi-square distribution, the F-distribution is a family of asymmetrical distributions bounded from below by 0.
- Each F-distribution is defined by two values of degrees of freedom, called the numerator and denominator degrees of freedom.
- If χ_1^2 is one chi-square random variable with m degrees of freedom and χ_2^2 is another chi-square random variable with n degrees of freedom, then $F = \left(\chi_1^2/m\right)/\left(\chi_2^2/n\right)$ follows an F-distribution with m numerator and n denominator degrees of freedom.

Like student's t-distribution, as the degrees of freedom of the chi-square distribution increase, the shape of its pdf becomes more like a bell curve.

For the F-distribution, as both the numerator (df_1) and the denominator (df_2) degrees of freedom increase, the density function will also become more bell curve–like.

Simulation

Monte Carlo simulation generates random numbers and operator inputs to synthetically create probability distributions for variables. It is used to calculate expected values and dispersion measures for random variables, which are then used for statistical inferences.

Investment Applications

- To experiment with a proposed policy before actually implementing it.

- To provide a probability distribution to estimate investment risk.
- To provide expected values of investments that can be difficult to price.
- To test models and investment tools and strategies.

Limitations

- Answers are as good as the assumptions and model used.
- Does not provide cause-and-effect relationships.

Historical simulation assumes that the distribution of the random variable going forward depends on its distribution in the past. This method of forecasting has an advantage, in that the distribution of risk factors does not need to be estimated. However, it faces the following limitations:

- A risk factor that was not represented in historical data will not be considered in the simulation.
- It does not facilitate "what if" analysis if the "if" factor has not occurred in the past. Monte Carlo simulation can be used for "what if" analysis.
- It assumes that the future will be similar to the past.
- It does not provide any cause-and-effect relationship information.

SAMPLING AND ESTIMATION
Cross-Reference to CFA Institute Assigned Reading #5

- **Probability sampling** gives every member of the population an equal chance of being selected. It therefore creates a sample that is representative of the population.
- **Non-probability sampling** depends on factors other than probability (e.g., a sampler's judgment or access to data). As a result, there is a significant risk of creating a non-representative sample.
- In a simple random sample, each member of the population has the same likelihood of being included in the sample.
- In systematic sampling, every *k*th member in the population is selected until the desired sample size is reached.
- Stratified random sampling: Stratification is the process of grouping members of the population into relatively homogeneous subgroups, or strata, before drawing samples. The strata should be mutually exclusive and collectively exhaustive. Random sampling is applied within each stratum and the size of the sample from each stratum is based on the size of the stratum relative to the population. This often improves the *representativeness* of the sample by reducing sampling error.
- **Cluster sampling** divides the population into clusters, where each cluster is a mini-representation of the entire population. It then selects certain (entire) clusters using simple random sampling.
  - In one-stage cluster sampling, all the members in each sampled cluster are used.
  - In two-stage cluster sampling, a subsample is randomly selected from each selected cluster.

Cluster versus Stratified Random Sampling:

- In **cluster sampling**, the entire whole cluster is considered a sampling unit and only (selected) sampled clusters are included.
- In **stratified random sampling**, all the different strata are included and only specific data points within each stratum are selected as sampling units.

Cluster sampling offers the most time-efficient and cost-effective probability sampling plan for analyzing a vast population. However, it can result in lower accuracy because a sample from a chosen cluster might not be very representative of the entire population.

Non-Probability Sampling

Non-probability sampling methods rely on a researcher's sample selection capabilities (not on a fixed selection process).

Convenience sampling selects elements based on ease of access or convenience, which limits sampling accuracy. However, it allows quick data collection at a low cost. It is typically used in small-scale pilot studies as a cost- and time-efficient sampling method

Judgmental sampling hand-picks elements from the population based on the researcher's knowledge and professional judgment, allowing the study to focus directly on the target population of interest. However, judgmental sampling is susceptible to biases and skewed results. It is typically used (1) in circumstances where there is a time constraint, or (2) when the specialty of researchers is critical to select a more representative sample than by using other probability or non-probability sampling methods.

Sampling error is the difference between a sample statistic and the corresponding population parameter.

$$\text{Sampling error of the mean} = \text{sample mean} - \text{population mean} = \bar{x} - \mu$$

The Central Limit Theorem

The important properties of the central limit theorem are:

- Given a population with *any* probability distribution, with mean, μ, and variance, σ^2, the sampling distribution of the sample mean x, computed from sample size n will approximately be *normal* with mean, μ (the population mean), and variance, σ^2/n (population variance divided by sample size), when the sample size is greater than or equal to 30.
- No matter what the distribution of the population, for a sample whose size is greater than or equal to 30, the sample mean will be normally distributed.

$$\bar{x} \sim N\left(\mu, \frac{\sigma^2}{n}\right)$$

- The mean of the population (m) and the mean of the distribution of sample means are equal.
- The variance of the distribution of sample means equals σ^2/n, or population variance divided by sample size.

Standard Error of Sample Mean

The standard deviation of the distribution of sample means is known as the standard error of the statistic (σ_x).

When the population variance is known, the standard error of sample mean is calculated as:

$$\sigma_{\bar{x}} = \sigma \big/ \sqrt{n}$$

Practically speaking, population variances are almost never known, so we estimate the standard error of the sample mean using the sample's standard deviation.

$$s_{\bar{x}} = \frac{s}{\sqrt{n}}$$

Point Estimates versus Confidence Intervals

A **point estimate** involves the use of sample data to calculate a single value that serves as an approximation for an unknown population parameter. For example, the sample mean, x, is a point estimate of the population mean, μ.

A confidence interval uses sample data to calculate a range of possible (or probable) values that an unknown population parameter can take, with a given probability of $(1-\alpha)$. α is called the level of significance, and $(1-\alpha)$ refers to the degree of confidence that the relevant parameter will lie in the computed interval. For example, a calculated interval between 100 and

150, at the 5% significance level, implies that we can be 95% confident that the population parameter lies between 100 and 150.

A (1-α)% confidence interval has the following structure:

$$\boxed{\text{Point estimate} \pm (\text{reliability factor} \times \text{standard error})}$$

Desirable Properties of an Estimator

- Unbiasedness.
- Efficiency.
- Consistency.

Characteristics of Student's t-Distribution

- It is symmetrical.
- It is defined by a single parameter, the degrees of freedom, (df), where degrees of freedom equal sample size minus one (n − 1).
- It has a lower peak than the normal curve, but fatter tails.
- As the degrees of freedom increase, the shape of the t-distribution approaches the shape of the standard normal curve.

As the degrees of freedom increase, the t-distribution curve becomes more peaked and its tails become thinner (bringing it closer to a normal curve). Therefore, the confidence interval for a random variable that follows the t-distribution will become narrower when the degrees of freedom increase for a given significance level.

The t-distribution is used in the following scenarios:

- It is used to construct confidence intervals of a normally (or approximately normally) distributed population whose variance is *unknown* when the sample size is small (n < 30).
- It may also be used for a non-normally distributed population whose variance is unknown if the sample size is large (n ≥ 30).

When the population is *normally* distributed we:

- Use the z-statistic when the population variance is known.
- Use the t-statistic when the population variance is not known.

When the distribution of the population is *nonnormal* the construction of an appropriate confidence interval depends on the size of the sample:

- If the population variance is known and the sample size is large we use the z-statistic. This is because the central limit theorem tells us that the distribution of the sample mean is approximately normal when sample size is large.
- If the population variance is not known and sample size is large, we can use the z-statistic or the t-statistic. However, in this scenario the use of the t-statistic is encouraged because it results in a more conservative measure.
- This implies that we cannot construct confidence intervals for nonnormal distributions if sample size is less than 30.

When Sampling from a:	Small Sample n < 30	Large Sample n > 30
Normal distribution with known variance	z-statistic	z-statistic
Normal distribution with unknown variance	t-statistic	t-statistic*
Non-normal distribution with known variance	not available	z-statistic
Non-normal distribution with unknown variance	not available	t-statistic*

* Use of z-statistic is also acceptable

Resampling

Resampling is the process of repeatedly drawing samples from the original observed data sample in order to infer population parameters.

Bootstrapping is very similar to the process of using random sampling to construct the sampling distribution of the sample mean. However, the difference here is that we have no knowledge of what the population looks like so a sample with size n is repeatedly drawn from the population, and the sample is treated as if it is the population. Note that each item drawn is placed back in the sample for the next draw so some items may appear several times in the resamples, other items may not appear at all.

The **jackknife** also selects samples repeatedly, but leaves out chosen observations from subsequent resamples (i.e., they are not replaced). The jackknife is often used to reduce the bias of an estimator, and other applications include finding the standard error and confidence interval of an estimator.

- The jackknife produces similar results for every run, whereas bootstrapping usually gives different results.
- For a sample of size *n*, the jackknife usually requires *n* repetitions, whereas with bootstrapping, the number of repetitions is more subjective.

Sample Biases

Data-Snooping Bias

Data snooping is the practice of extensively searching through a data set for statistically significant relationships till a pattern "that works" is discovered. In the process of data snooping, large numbers of hypotheses about a single data set are tested in a very short time by searching for combinations of variables that might show a correlation.

Warning signs that data snooping bias might exist are:

- Too much digging warning sign.
- No story, no future warning sign.

The best way to avoid data-mining bias is to test the "apparently statistically significant relationships" on "out-of-sample" data to check whether they hold.

Sample Selection Bias

Sample selection bias results from the exclusion of certain assets from a study due to the unavailability of data.

Some databases use historical information and may suffer from a type of sample selection bias known as **survivorship bias**. Databases that only list companies or funds currently in existence suffer from this bias.

Another variation of selection bias is backfill bias. When a new hedge fund is added to an index, its past performance is backfilled into the index's database. Typically, new funds are added after a period of good performance, so adding the fund's instant history into the index database may inflate index performance.

Look-Ahead Bias

An analyst may not have complete information at the time of testing. Look-ahead bias arises if the analyst uses an assumed figure instead. The actual figure may be different from the one used in the study. One solution to mitigate look-ahead bias is to use point-in-time (PIT) data when possible.

Time-Period Bias

Time-period bias arises if the sample data is drawn from a certain time period. The results obtained from the study of such a data set will be time-specific.

HYPOTHESIS TESTING
Cross-Reference to CFA Institute Assigned Reading #6

Steps in Hypothesis Testing

- State the hypothesis.
- Select the appropriate test-statistic.
- Specify the level of significance.
- State the decision rules.
- Calculate the sample statistic.
- Make a decision regarding the validity of the hypothesis.

Null versus Alternative Hypotheses

- The null hypothesis (H_0) generally represents the status quo, and is the hypothesis that we are interested in rejecting. This hypothesis will not be rejected unless the sample data provides sufficient evidence to suggest otherwise.
- The alternate hypothesis (H_A) is the statement that will only be accepted if the sample data provides convincing evidence of its truth. It is the conclusion of the test if the null hypothesis is rejected. *The alternate hypothesis is essentially the statement whose validity we are tying to evaluate.*

One-Tailed versus Two-Tailed Tests

Under one-tailed tests, we assess whether the value of the population parameter is either *greater than, or less than* a given hypothesized value. Hypotheses for one-tailed hypotheses tests are structured as:

- $H_0 : \mu \leq \mu_0$ versus $H_a : \mu > \mu_0$; when determining whether the population mean is *greater* than a hypothesized value.
- $H_0 : \mu \geq \mu_0$ versus $H_a : \mu < \mu_0$; when determining whether the population mean is *less* than a hypothesized value.

> When we want to ascertain whether the population mean is *greater* than the hypothesized mean, we compare the test statistic to the *positive* critical value.

The following rejection rules apply when we are trying to determine whether the population mean is *greater* than the hypothesized value.

- Reject H_0 when:
  Test statistic > Positive critical value

- Fail to reject H_0 when:
  Test statistic $\leq$ Positive critical value

The following rejection rules apply when we are trying to determine whether the population mean is *lower* than the hypothesized value.

- Reject H_0 when:
  Test statistic < Negative critical value

- Fail to reject H_0 when:
  Test statistic $\geq$ Negative critical value

Under two-tailed tests, we assess whether the value of the population parameter is *simply different from* a given hypothesized value. Hypotheses for two-tailed hypotheses tests are structured as:

$H_0 : \mu = \mu_0$

$H_a : \mu \neq \mu_0$

The following rejection rules apply for two-tailed hypothesis test

- Reject H_0 when:
  Test statistic < Lower critical value

  Test statistic > Upper critical value

- Fail to reject H_0 when:
  Lower critical value $\leq$ Test statistic $\leq$ Upper critical value

> When we want to ascertain whether the population mean is *less* than the hypothesized mean, we compare the test statistic to the *negative* critical value.

Type I versus Type II Errors

- Type I error: Rejecting the null when it is actually true.
- Type II error: Not rejecting the null when it is actually false.

The significance level (α) represents the probability of making a Type I error. A significance level of 5% means that there is a 5% chance of rejecting the null when it is actually true.

If we were to fail to reject the null hypothesis given the lack of overwhelming evidence in favor of the alternate, we risk a Type II error—*failing to reject the null hypothesis when it is false*.

Sample size and the choice of significance level (probability of Type I error) together determine the probability of a Type II error.

The power of a test is the probability of *correctly* rejecting the null hypothesis when it is false.

$$\text{Power of a test} = 1 - P(\text{Type II error})$$

Errors in Hypothesis Testing

Decision	H_0 is True	H_0 is False
Do not reject H_0	Correct decision	Incorrect decision **Type II error**
Reject H_0	Incorrect decision **Type I error** Significance level = P(Type I error)	Correct decision Power of the test = $1 - P(\text{Type II error})$

- The *higher* the power of the test, the *better* is it for purposes of hypothesis testing.
- An *increase* in the power of a test comes at the cost of *increasing* the probability of a Type I error.
- The only way to *decrease* the probability of a Type II error given the significance level is to *increase the sample size*.

Confidence Intervals versus Hypothesis Tests

- In a confidence interval we state that the population parameter lies within the interval, which represents the "fail-to-reject-the-null region" with a $(1 - \alpha)$ level of confidence.
- In a hypothesis test, we examine whether the population parameter lies in the rejection region, or outside the interval, at the α level of significance.

P-Values and Hypothesis Tests

The p-value is the smallest level of significance at which the null hypothesis can be rejected. It is the probability of obtaining a critical value that would lead to the rejection of the null hypothesis.

- If the p-value is *less* than the required level of significance, we can *reject* the null hypothesis.
- If the p-value is *greater* then the required level of significance, we *fail to reject* the null hypothesis.

Summary of Hypothesis Tests on the Mean of a Single Population

Type of test	Null Hypothesis	Alternate Hypothesis	Reject Null if	Fail to Reject Null if	p-value Represents
One-tailed (upper tail)	$H_0 : \mu \leq \mu_0$	$H_a : \mu > \mu_0$	Test statistic > Critical value	Test statistic $\leq$ Critical value	Probability that lies above the computed test statistic.
One-tailed (lower tail)	$H_0 : \mu \geq \mu_0$	$H_a : \mu < \mu_0$	Test statistic < Critical value	Test statistic $\geq$ Critical value	Probability that lies below the computed test statistic.
Two-tailed	$H_0 : \mu = \mu_0$	$H_a : \mu \neq \mu_0$	Test statistic < Lower critical value Test statistic > Upper critical value	Lower critical value $\leq$ Test statistic $\leq$ Upper critical value	Probability that lies above the positive value of the computed test statistic *plus* the probability that lies below the negative value of the computed test statistic.

The t-statistic for hypothesis test concerning the mean of a single population is:

$$t\text{-stat} = \frac{\bar{x} - \mu_0}{s/\sqrt{n}}$$

In a t-test, the sample's t-statistic is compared to the critical t-value with degrees of freedom (n-1) at the desired level of significance.

The z-test is used to conduct hypothesis tests of the population mean when the population is normally distributed and its variance is known.

$$z\text{-stat} = \frac{\overline{x} - \mu_0}{\sigma/\sqrt{n}}$$

The z-test can also be used when the population's variance is unknown, but the sample size is large.

$$z\text{-stat} = \frac{\overline{x} - \mu_0}{s/\sqrt{n}}$$

In a z-test, the z-statistic is compared to the critical z-value at the given level of significance.

Significance of a Test in the Context of Multiple Tests

A Type I error captures the risk of rejecting a true null hypothesis. Stated differently, it is a false positive test result (the null is rejected [a positive test result], when the null is actually true). The expected portion of false positives is referred to as the **false discovery rate (FDR)**.

So, for example, if we were to run 1000 tests with a 5% level of significance, we would expect to get 50 false positives, on average. This reflects what is known as the **multiple testing problem**.

Under the false discovery approach to testing, p-values from the various tests are ranked from lowest to highest, and then adjusted. As a final step, a simple comparison is made to eliminate false positives.

Hypothesis Tests Concerning a Single Mean

The t-test is used when the variance of the population is unknown *and* either of the conditions below hold:

- The sample size is large.
- The sample is small, but the underlying population is normally distributed or approximately normally distributed.

Hypothesis Tests Concerning the Mean of Two Populations

Population distribution	Relationship between samples	Assumption regarding variance	Type of test
Normal	Independent	Equal	t-test with pooled variance
Normal	Dependent	N/A	t-test with paired comparisons

Hypothesis Tests Concerning the Variance

Hypothesis tests for the variance of a normally distributed population involve the use of the chi-square distribution where the test statistic is denoted as χ^2. Three important features of the chi-square distribution are:

- It is asymmetrical.
- It is bounded by zero. Chi-square values cannot be negative.
- It approaches the normal distribution in shape as degrees of freedom increase.

The chi-square test statistic with n − 1 degrees of freedom is calculated as:

$$\chi^2 = \frac{(n-1)s^2}{\sigma_0^2}$$

Hypotheses related to the equality of the variance of two populations are tested with an F-test. This test is used under the assumptions that:

- The populations from which samples are drawn are normally distributed.
- The samples are independent.

The test statistic for the F-test is given by:

$$F = \frac{s_1^2}{s_2^2}$$

Features of the F-distribution:

- It is skewed to the right.
- It is bounded by zero on the left.
- It is defined by two separate degrees of freedom.

The rejection region for any F-test, whether it be one-tailed or two-tailed, always lies in the right tail. This unique feature makes the F-test different from other hypothesis tests.

Hypothesis Test Concerning	Appropriate Test Statistic
Variance of a single, normally distributed population	Chi-square stat
Equality of variance of two independent, normally distributed populations	F-stat

Hypothesis Test Concerning the Correlation Coefficient

Parametric Tests of Correlation

H_0: $\rho = 0$
H_a: $\rho \neq 0$

This would be a two-tailed t-test with n − 2 degrees of freedom.

Test stat = t

Note that the value of sample correlation, r, required to reject the null hypothesis, decreases as sample size, n, increases.

Non-Parametric Test of Correlation

When the population under consideration is not normally distributed, we can use a test based on the **Spearman rank correlation coefficient**, r_S. The Spearman rank correlation coefficient is essentially equivalent to the usual correlation coefficient but is calculated on the ranks of the two variables within their respective samples.

Test of Independence Using Contingency Table Data

When faced with categorical or discrete data, we must use the chi-square test to test whether there is a correlation between the variables.

Parametric versus Nonparametric Tests

A parametric test has at least one of the following two characteristics:

- It is concerned with parameters, or defining features, of a distribution.
- It makes a definite set of assumptions.

A non-parametric test is not concerned with a parameter, and makes only a minimal set of assumptions regarding the population. Non-parametric tests are used when:

- The researcher is concerned about quantities other than the parameters of the distribution.
- The assumptions made by parametric tests cannot be supported.
- When the data available is ranked. For example, non-parametric methods are widely used for studying populations such as movie reviews that receive one to five stars based on people's preferences.
- When there are outliers.

Statistically versus Economically Meaningful Results

Even though a trading strategy that is being studied provides a statistically significant return of greater than zero (based on the hypothesis test) it does not guarantee that trading on this strategy would result in economically meaningful returns. The returns may not be economically significant after accounting for taxes, transaction costs and risks inherent in the strategy.

INTRODUCTION TO LINEAR REGRESSION
Cross-Reference to CFA Institute Assigned Reading #7

Calculating and Interpreting the Correlation Coefficient

In order to calculate the correlation coefficient, we first need to calculate covariance. Covariance is a similar concept to variance. The difference lies in the fact that variance measures how a random variable varies with itself, while covariance measures how a random variable varies with another random variable.

Properties of Covariance

- Covariance is symmetric i.e., $\text{Cov}(X, Y) = \text{Cov}(Y, X)$.
- The covariance of X with itself, $\text{Cov}(X,X)$ equals the variance of X, $\text{Var}(X)$.

Interpreting the Covariance

- Basically, covariance measures the nature of the relationship between two variables.
- When the covariance between two variables is *negative*, it means that they tend to move in opposite directions.
- When the covariance between two variables is *positive*, it means that they tend to move in the same direction.
- The covariance between two variables equals zero if they are not related.

$$\text{Sample covariance} = \text{Cov}(X,Y) = \sum_{i=1}^{n}(X_i - \overline{X})(Y_i - \overline{Y})/(n-1)$$

$n = $ sample size
$X_i = i$th observation of Variable X
$\overline{X} = $ mean observation of Variable X
$Y_i = i$th observation of Variable Y
$\overline{Y} = $ mean observation of Variable Y

The numerical value of sample covariance is not very meaningful as it is presented in terms of units squared. Covariance is standardized by dividing it by the product of the standard deviations of the two variables. This standardized measure is known as the sample correlation coefficient (denoted by r) and is easy to interpret as it always lies between -1 and $+1$, and has no unit of measurement attached.

$$\text{Sample correlation coefficient} = r = \frac{\text{Cov}(X,Y)}{s_X s_Y}$$

$$\text{Sample variance} = s_X^2 = \sum_{i=1}^{n}(X_i - \overline{X})^2/(n-1)$$

$$\text{Sample standard deviation} = s_X = \sqrt{s_X^2}$$

Computed correlation coefficients are only valid if the means and variances of X and Y, as well as the covariance of X and Y, are finite and constant.

Linear Regression with One Independent Variable

Linear regression is used to make predictions about a dependent variable (Y) using an independent variable (X), to test hypotheses regarding the relation between the two variables and to evaluate the strength of this relationship. The regression computes the line of best fit that minimizes the sum of the regression residuals (the sum of the squared vertical distances between actual observations of the random variable and predicted values of the variable based on the regression equation).

$$\text{Regression equation} = Y_i = b_0 + b_1 X_i + \epsilon_i, i = 1,....,n$$

b_1 and b_0 are the regression coefficients

$b_1 = $ Slope coefficient

$b_0 = $ Intercept

$\epsilon = $ The error term that represents the variation in the dependent variable that is not explained by the independent variable.

Classic Normal Linear Regression Assumptions

1. The relationship between the dependent (Y) and the independent variable (X) is linear in the parameters, b_1 and b_0.
2. The independent variable, X, is not random.
3. The expected value of the error term is zero: $E(\epsilon) = 0$
4. The variance of the error term is constant for all observations ($E(\epsilon_i^2) = \sigma_\epsilon^2, i = 1,...,n$). This is known as the homoskedasticity assumption.
5. The error term is uncorrelated across observations.
6. The error term is normally distributed.

An unbiased forecast is one where the expected value of the forecast error equals zero.

Cross-Sections versus Time-Series Regressions

- A **cross-sectional regression** uses several observations of X and Y over a particular period of time.
- **Time-series data** use many observations from different time periods for the same subject.

Classic Normal Linear Regression Assumptions

- The relationship between the dependent variable (Y) and the independent variable (X) is linear and the independent variable, X, is random.
- The variance of the error term is constant for all observations. This is known as the **homoskedasticity assumption**.
- The observations (pairs of X's and Y's) are independent of each other. This implies that regression residuals are uncorrelated across observations.
- The regression residuals are normally distributed.

The Standard Error of Estimate

The standard error of estimate (SEE) is used to measure how well a regression model captures the relationship between the two variables. It indicates how well the regression line "fits" the sample data and is used to determine how certain we can be about a particular prediction of the dependent variable (Y_i) based on a regression equation. The SEE basically measures the standard deviation of the residual term (ϵ_i) in the regression. The smaller the standard deviation of the residual term (the smaller the standard error of estimate), the more accurate the predictions based on the model.

$$SEE = \left(\frac{\sum_{i=1}^{n} (Y_i - \widehat{b}_0 - \widehat{b}_1 X_i)^2}{n-2} \right)^{1/2} = \left(\frac{\sum_{i=1}^{n} (\widehat{\epsilon}_i)^2}{n-2} \right)^{1/2}$$

The Coefficient of Determination

The coefficient of determination (R^2) tells us how well the independent variable explains the variation in the dependent variable. It measures the fraction of the total variation in the dependent variable that is explained by the independent variable.

Calculating the Coefficient of Determination

1. $R^2 = r^2$
    The coefficient of determination equals the correlation coefficient squared. This calculation only works in linear regression i.e., when there is only one independent variable.

2. $$R^2 = \frac{\text{Explained variation}}{\text{Total variation}} = \frac{\text{Total variation} - \text{Unexplained variation}}{\text{Total variation}}$$

    $$= 1 - \frac{\text{Unexplained variation}}{\text{Total variation}}$$

Analysis of Variance in a Regression with One Independent Variable

Analysis of variance (ANOVA) is used to evaluate the usefulness of the independent variable in explaining the variation in the dependent variable.

The F-statistic is used to test whether the slope coefficient in the regression equals zero (H_0: $b_1 = 0$ versus H_a: $b_1 \neq 0$). It equals the ratio of the average regression sum of squares to the average sum of the squared errors.

$$F = \frac{\text{MSR}}{\text{MSE}} = \frac{\text{RSS}/k}{\text{SSE}/(n-k-1)}$$

Degrees of freedom (numerator) $= k = 1$

Degrees of freedom (denominator) $= n - k - 1 = n - 2$

The F-test is a one-tailed test. The null hypothesis is rejected if the F-stat is greater than F_{crit}. Rejection of the null hypothesis means that the independent variable significantly explains the variation in the dependent variable.

- If the independent variable does not explain much of the variation in the dependent variable, the *F*-stat will be relatively small.
- If the independent variable does a good job of explaining much of the variation in the dependent variable, the *F*-stat will be relatively high.
- For regression analysis with only one independent variable, the *F*-test duplicates the *t*-test. In such a regression, the *F*-stat (F) equals the *t*-stat (t_{b1}) squared.

ANOVA Table for Simple Linear Regression ($k = 1$)

Source of Variation	Degrees of Freedom	Sum of Squares	Mean Sum of Squares
Regression (explained)	1	RSS	$MSR = \dfrac{RSS}{k} = \dfrac{RSS}{1} = RSS$
Error (unexplained)	$n - 2$	SSE	$MSE = \dfrac{SSE}{n - 2}$
Total	$n - 1$	SST	

Figure 1: Components of Total Variation

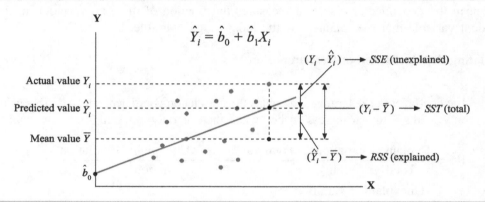

- SST measures the total variation in the dependent variable.

$$SST = \sum_{i=1}^{n} (Y_i - \overline{Y})^2 \rightarrow \text{Total variation}$$

- RSS measures the variation in the dependent variable that is explained by the independent variable.

$$RSS = \sum_{i=1}^{n} (\widehat{Y}_i - \overline{Y})^2 \rightarrow \text{Explained variation}$$

- SSE measures the variation in the dependent variable that is not explained by the independent variable.

$$SSE = \sum_{i=1}^{n} (Y_i - \widehat{Y}_i)^2 \rightarrow \text{Unexplained variation}$$

Testing the Significance of the Correlation Coefficient

H_0: $\rho = 0$

H_a: $\rho \neq 0$

This is a two-tailed t-test with n-2 degrees of freedom.

$$\text{Test-stat} = t = \frac{r\sqrt{n-2}}{\sqrt{1-r^2}}$$

Reject H_0, if t-stat > $+t_{crit}$ or if t-stat < $-t_{crit}$

Hypothesis Tests of the Slope Coefficient

Test stat =

$$t = \frac{\widehat{b}_1 - B_1}{S_{\widehat{b1}}}.$$

Standard error =

$$S_{\widehat{b1}} = \frac{S_e}{\sqrt{\sum_{i=1}^{n}\left(X_i - \overline{X}\right)^2}}.$$

Hypothesis Tests of the Intercept

Test stat =

$$t_{intercept} = \frac{\widehat{b}_0 - B_0}{S\widehat{b}_0} = \frac{\widehat{b}_0 - B_0}{\sqrt{\frac{1}{n} + \frac{\overline{X}^2}{\sum_{i=1}^{n}\left(X_i - \overline{X}\right)^2}}}.$$

Standard error =

$$S_{\widehat{b0}} = \sqrt{\frac{1}{n} + \frac{\overline{X}^2}{\sum_{i=1}^{n}\left(X_i - \overline{X}\right)^2}}.$$

Variation in independent variable =

$$\sum_{i=1}^{n}\left(X_i - \overline{X}\right)^2 = \frac{\sum_{i=1}^{n}\left(X_i - \overline{X}\right)^2}{n-1} \times (n-1).$$

Indicator Variables

Indicator variables (or **dummy variables**) in regression models help analysts determine whether a particular qualitative variable explains the variation in the model's dependent variable to a significant extent.

- A dummy variable must be binary in nature (i.e., it may take on a value of either 0 or 1).
- If the model aims to distinguish between n categories, it must employ $n-1$ dummy variables. The category that is omitted is used as a reference point for the other categories.
- The **intercept term** in the regression indicates the average value of the dependent variable for the omitted category.
- The **slope coefficient** of each dummy variable estimates the difference (compared to the omitted category) a particular dummy variable makes to the dependent variable.

Test of Hypotheses: Level of Significance and p-Values

- The choice of significance level is a matter of judgment. A lower level of significance increases the absolute value of t_{crit}, resulting in a wider confidence interval and a lower likelihood of rejecting the null hypothesis.
- Increasing the significance level increases the probability of a Type I error but decreases the probability of a Type II error.
- The p-value is the lowest level of significance at which the null hypothesis can be rejected. Note that the p-value that is generally reported by statistical software packages as part of the regression results applies to a null hypothesis that the true population parameter equals zero, versus an alternative hypothesis that the true population parameter does not equal zero (given the estimated coefficient and standard error of the coefficient). For example, a p-value of 0.007 tells us that we can reject the null hypothesis that the true population parameter equals zero at the 0.7% level of significance (or with a 99.3% level of confidence).
- The smaller the standard error of an estimated parameter, the stronger the results of the regression and the narrower the resulting confidence intervals.

Predictions and Prediction Intervals

There are two sources of uncertainty when we use a regression model to make a prediction regarding the value of the dependent variable.

1. The uncertainty inherent in the error term, ϵ.
2. The uncertainty in the estimated parameters, b_0 and b_1.

Given that the parameters of the regression must be estimated and that their true population values are not known, the estimated *variance* of the prediction error, s_f^2, of Y is calculated as:

$$S_f^2 = S_e^2 \left[1 + \frac{1}{n} + \frac{(X_f - \overline{X})^2}{(n-1)S_X^2} \right] = S_e^2 \left[1 + \frac{1}{n} + \frac{(X_f - \overline{X})^2}{\sum_{i=1}^{n} (X_i - \overline{X})^2} \right].$$

The standard error of the forecast is:

$$S_f = S_e \sqrt{1 + \frac{1}{n} + \frac{\left(X_f - \overline{X}\right)^2}{\sum\limits_{i=1}^{n}\left(X_i - \overline{X}\right)^2}}.$$

Note the following:

- The better the fit of the regression model, the smaller the standard error of the estimate (s_e) and, therefore, the smaller standard error of the forecast.
- The larger the sample size (n) in the regression estimation, the smaller the standard error of the forecast.
- The closer the forecasted independent variable (X_f) is to the mean of the independent variable ($\overline{X}$) used in the regression estimation, the smaller the standard error of the forecast.

Prediction interval: $\widehat{Y}f \pm t_{critical\,for\,\alpha\,/\,2} s_f$.

Functional Forms of Linear Regression

1. In the **log-lin model**, the dependent variable is logarithmic, but the independent variable is linear.
   - The slope coefficient in this model is the relative change in the dependent variable for an absolute change in the independent variable.
2. In the **lin-log model**, the dependent variable is linear, but the independent variable is logarithmic.
   - The slope coefficient in this regression model provides the absolute change in the dependent variable for a relative change in the independent variable.
3. In the **log-log model** (or **double log model**), both the dependent and independent variables are logarithmic.

STUDY SESSION 3: ECONOMICS (1)

TOPICS IN DEMAND AND SUPPLY ANALYSIS
Cross-Reference to CFA Institute Assigned Reading #8

Demand Concepts

Demand is defined as the willingness and ability of consumers to purchase a given amount of a good or a service at a particular price.

The law of demand states that as the price of a product increases, consumers will be willing and able to purchase less of it, and as the price decreases, they will be willing and able to purchase more of it (i.e., price and quantity demanded are inversely related).

The **demand function** uses quantity demanded as the dependent variable in capturing the relationship between own-price and quantity demanded. The **inverse demand function** makes price the dependent variable in capturing the relationship between own-price and quantity demanded. The **demand curve** is based on the inverse demand function.

The slope of the demand curve equals the coefficient on quantity demanded in the inverse demand function. The slope of the demand curve is also the reciprocal of the coefficient on own-price in the demand function.

Changes in Demand versus Movements along the Demand Curve

- When own-price changes, there is a **movement along the demand curve** or a **change in quantity demanded**.
- When there is a change in anything else that affects demand (i.e., a change in any of the factors assumed constant in the demand function), there is a **shift in the demand curve** (because the intercept term in the inverse demand function changes) or a **change in demand**.

Demand Elasticities

The own-price elasticity of demand is calculated as:

$$ED_{Px} = \frac{\%\Delta QD_x}{\%\Delta P_x}$$

$$ED_{Px} = \frac{\%\Delta QD_x}{\%\Delta P_x} = \frac{\Delta QD_x / QD_x}{\Delta P_x / P_x} = \left(\frac{\Delta QD_x}{\Delta P_x}\right)\left(\frac{P_x}{QD_x}\right)$$

> Slope of demand function
>
> Coefficient on own-price in market demand function

We look at the absolute value of own-price elasticity of demand when classifying how sensitive quantity demanded is to changes in price:

- If own-price elasticity of demand equals 1, demand is said to be **unit elastic**.
- If own-price elasticity of demand equals 0, demand is said to be **perfectly inelastic**.
- If own-price elasticity of demand equals ∞, demand is said to be **perfectly elastic**.
- If the absolute value of price elasticity of demand lies between 0 and 1, demand is said to be **relatively inelastic**.
- If the absolute value of price elasticity of demand is greater than 1, demand is said to be **relatively elastic**.

While the slope of the demand curve remains constant along a downward-sloping linear demand curve, the ratio of price to quantity is different at each point along the demand curve (unless the demand curve is perfectly elastic or perfectly inelastic).

- At relatively low prices (relatively high quantities), the ratio of price to quantity is relatively low so own-price elasticity of demand (absolute value of ED_P) is low and demand is relatively inelastic.
- At relatively high prices (relatively low quantities), the ratio of price to quantity is relatively high so own-price elasticity of demand (absolute value of ED_P) is high and demand is relatively elastic.
- Demand is unit elastic at the midpoint of the demand curve, relatively elastic above the midpoint, and relatively inelastic below the midpoint.

Factors That Affect Price Elasticity of Demand

Availability of close substitutes: If a consumer can *easily* switch away from a good, her ability to respond to a price increase (by reducing consumption of the good) is *high*, and demand for that product would be *relatively elastic*.

Proportion of income spent on the good: If a relatively *small* proportion of a consumer's income is spent on a good (e.g., soap), she will not significantly cut down on consumption if prices increase. Demand for such a good will be *relatively inelastic*.

Time elapsed since price change: The *longer* the time that has elapsed since the price change, the *more elastic* demand will be.

The extent to which the good is viewed as necessary or optional: The *more* the good is seen as being necessary, the *less elastic* its demand is likely to be.

Own-Price Elasticity of Demand and Total Expenditure/Total Revenue

- If demand is relatively elastic, a decrease in price will result in an increase in total expenditure, and an increase in price will result in a decrease in total expenditure.
- If demand is relatively inelastic, a decrease in price will result in a decrease in total expenditure, and an increase in price will result in an increase in total expenditure.
- If demand is unit elastic, a decrease or an increase in price will result in no change in total expenditure.

Total Expenditure/Revenue Test

- If the price cut *increases* total revenue, demand is relatively elastic.
- If the price cut *decreases* total revenue, demand is relatively inelastic.
- If the price cut *does not change* total revenue, demand is unit elastic.

Total Revenue and Price Elasticity

- If the demand curve facing a producer is relatively elastic, an *increase* in price will *decrease* total revenue.
- If the demand curve facing a producer is relatively inelastic, an *increase* in price will *increase* total revenue.
- If the demand curve facing a producer is unit elastic, an *increase* in price will *not change* total revenue.

Note that no producer would knowingly set a price that falls in the inelastic region of the demand curve.

Income Elasticity of Demand

Income elasticity of demand measures the responsiveness of demand for a particular good to a change in income, holding all other things constant.

$$ED_1 = \frac{\%\Delta QD_x}{\%\Delta I} = \frac{\Delta QD_x / QD_x}{\Delta I / I} = \left(\frac{\Delta QD_x}{\Delta I}\right)\left(\frac{I}{QD_x}\right)$$

$$E_1 = \frac{\%\text{ change in quantity demanded}}{\%\text{ change in income}}$$

If income elasticity is *greater* than 1, demand is income elastic, and the product is classified as a **normal good**.

- As income *rises*, the percentage increase in demand *exceeds* the percentage change in income.
- As income *increases*, a consumer spends a *higher proportion* of her income on the product.

If income elasticity lies *between* zero and 1, demand is income inelastic, but the product is still classified as a **normal good**.

- As income *rises*, the percentage increase in demand is *less* than the percentage increase in income.
- As income *increases*, a consumer spends a *lower proportion* of her income on the product.

If income elasticity is *less* than zero (negative), the product is classified as an **inferior good**.

- As income *rises*, there is a *negative* change in demand.
- As income *increases*, the amount spent on the good *decreases*.

When income changes, there is a shift in the demand curve (change in demand).

Cross-Price Elasticity of Demand

Cross elasticity of demand measures the responsiveness of demand for a particular good to a change in price of *another* good, holding all other things constant.

$$\text{ED}_{P_y} = \frac{\%\Delta QD_x}{\%\Delta P_y} = \frac{\Delta QD_x \big/ QD_x}{\Delta P_y \big/ P_y} = \left(\frac{\Delta QD_x}{\Delta P_y}\right)\left(\frac{P_y}{QD_x}\right)$$

$$E_C = \frac{\%\text{ change in quantity demanded}}{\%\text{ change in price of substitute or complement}}$$

For **substitutes**, the numerator and denominator of the cross elasticity formula head in the *same* direction. Therefore, cross elasticity of demand for substitutes is *positive*.

- A *high* value for cross elasticity indicates that the two products are very *close* substitutes.
- For substitutes, an increase in the price of another good results in an increase in demand (shift in demand to the right).

For **complements**, the numerator and denominator of the cross elasticity formula head in *opposite* directions. If the price of one good increases, demand for the other falls. Therefore, the cross elasticity of demand for complements is *negative*.

- A *high* absolute value for cross elasticity indicates that the two products are very *close* complements.
- For complements, an increase in price of another good results in a decrease in demand (shift in demand to the left).

Substitution and Income Effects

The law of demand states that when the price of a good falls, quantity demanded increases, and when the price rises, quantity demanded decreases. There are two main reasons for this:

The substitution effect: If the good becomes cheaper compared to other goods, more of the good gets substituted for other goods in the consumer's consumption basket. The substitution effect always goes in the opposite direction of the price change.

The income effect: If the consumer's real income increases (in terms of the quantity of goods and services that can be purchased with the same dollar income), then, if the good is a normal good (which most goods are), the increase in real income (due to the decrease in its price) leads to an increase in quantity purchased.

Normal Goods

For normal goods (e.g., restaurant meals, which most people tend to buy more of when their incomes rise), the substitution and the income effects reinforce one another.

Inferior Goods

If a good is an inferior good:

- The substitution effect of a change in price will be the same as for a normal good (i.e., a decrease in price of the good will cause the consumer to buy more of the good).

- However, the income effect will be the opposite of what it is for a normal good. For an inferior good, the increase in real income resulting from a decline in the good's price will cause the consumer to buy less of this good.

Overall, for an inferior good (e.g., margarine, which most people buy less of as their incomes rise), the income effect mitigates the substitution effect of a price change.

Note that:

- The substitution effect of a change in the price will always go in the direction opposite to that of the price change. If the price increases, less will be consumed, and if the price decreases, more will be consumed.
- The income effect of that same price change, however, depends on whether the good is normal or inferior.
  - For a normal good, the income effect reinforces the substitution effect, both leading to a negatively sloped demand curve.
  - For an inferior good, the income effect and the substitution effect work in opposite directions.

Giffen and Veblen Goods

For Giffen goods and Veblen goods, the demand curve is actually upward sloping.

A **Giffen good** is a special case of an inferior good where the negative income effect of a decrease in price of the good is so strong that it outweighs the positive substitution effect. Therefore, for a Giffen good, quantity demanded actually falls when there is a decrease in price, which makes the demand curve upward sloping.

Note the following:

- All Giffen goods are inferior goods because the income effect and substitution effect work in opposite directions.
- However, not all inferior goods are Giffen goods.
  - For inferior goods, the income effect partially mitigates or offsets the substitution effect.
  - For Giffen goods, the income effect outweighs the substitution effect.

With status goods such as expensive jewelry, the high price itself adds to the utility from the good, such that the consumer values the item more if it has a higher price. Such goods are known as **Veblen goods**.

Giffen Goods versus Veblen Goods

- Giffen goods are **inferior goods**. They are not status goods. An increase in income would reduce demand for them (due to negative income elasticity of demand).
- Veblen goods are **not inferior goods**. An increase in income would not lead to a decrease in demand.

Supply Analysis: The Firm

Short Run versus Long Run

- In the **short run**, at least one factor of production is fixed. Usually we assume that labor is the only variable factor of production in the short run.
- In the **long run**, quantities of all factors of production can be varied.

Total, Average, and Marginal Product of Labor

Total product (TP) is the maximum output that a given quantity of labor can produce when working with a fixed quantity of capital units.

- TP provides insight into the company's size relative to the overall industry.
- It does not show how efficient the firm is in producing its output.
- In the initial stages, total product *increases at an increasing rate*. Later, as more units of labor are employed to work with the fixed quantity of capital, total output *increases at a decreasing rate*, and the slope of the TP curve becomes *flatter*.

Marginal product (MP) (also known as **marginal return**) equals the increase in total product brought about by hiring one more unit of labor, while holding quantities of all other factors of production constant.

- MP measures the productivity of the individual additional unit of labor.

Average product (AP) equals the total product of labor divided by the quantity of labor units employed.

- AP is a measure of overall labor productivity.
- The lower a firm's AP, the more efficient it is.

Relationship between MP and AP

- MP intersects AP from *above* through the *maximum point* of AP.
- When MP is *above* AP, AP *rises*, and when MP is *below* AP, AP *falls*.

Note the following:

- Total product is simply an indication of a firm's output volume and potential market share.
- Average product and marginal product are better measures of productivity, as they can reveal competitive advantage through production efficiency.
- Average product is the preferred measure of productivity when workers perform tasks collectively, as in that case individual worker productivity is not easily measurable.

Breakeven and Shutdown Analysis

Accounting Profit versus Economic Profit

Accounting profit (also known as **net profit**, **net income**, and **net earnings**) equals revenue less all accounting (or explicit) costs. Accounting costs are payments to nonowner parties for goods and services supplied to the firm, and do not necessarily require a cash outlay.

> Accounting profit (loss) = Total revenue − Total accounting costs

Economic profit (also known as **abnormal profit** or **supernormal profit**) is calculated as revenue less all economic costs (economic costs include explicit and implicit costs). Alternatively, economic profit can be calculated as accounting profit less all implicit opportunity costs that are not included in total accounting costs.

> Economic profit = Total revenue − Total economic costs
> Economic profit = Total revenue − (Explicit costs + Implicit costs)
> Economic profit = Accounting profit − Total implicit opportunity costs

Normal profit is the level of accounting profit that is required to cover the implicit opportunity costs that are not included in accounting costs.

> Accounting profit = Economic profit + Normal profit

Note that:

- When accounting profit equals normal profit, economic profit equals 0.
- When accounting profit is greater than normal profit, economic profit is positive.
- When accounting profit is less than normal profit, economic profit is negative.

Total, Average, and Marginal Revenue

Revenue	Calculation
Total revenue (TR)	Price times quantity (P $\times$ Q), or the sum of individual units sold times their respective prices; $\Sigma(P_i \times Q_i)$
Average revenue (AR)	Total revenue divided by quantity; (TR/Q)
Marginal revenue (MR)	Change in total revenue divided by change in quantity; (ΔTR/ΔQ)

The Demand Curve in Perfect and Imperfect Competition

- In **perfect competition**, each individual firm faces a perfectly elastic demand curve (i.e., it can sell as many units of output as it desires at the given market price).
- In **imperfect competition**, the firm has at least some control over the price at which it sells its output. The demand curve facing the firm is downward sloping, so in order to increase units sold the firm must lower its price.

Total, Average, and Marginal Revenue under Perfect Competition

- MR always equals AR, and they both equal market price.
- If there is an increase in market demand, the market price increases, which results in both MR and AR shifting up and TR pivoting upward as well.

Total, Average, and Marginal Revenue under Imperfect Competition

- As quantity increases, the rate of increase in TR (as measured by MR) decreases.
- AR equals price at each output level.
- MR is also downward sloping, with a slope that is steeper than that of AR (demand).
- TR reaches its maximum point when MR equals 0.

Note that MR equals price plus Q multiplied by the slope of the demand curve.

> MR = P + Q(ΔP/ΔQ) or MR = P + Q $*$ Slope of demand curve

- Under perfect competition, the slope of the demand curve is zero. Therefore, MR = P
- Under imperfect competition, the slope of the demand curve is negative. As a result, MR is less than price.

Total, Average, Marginal, Fixed, and Variable Costs

Cost	Calculation
Total fixed cost (TFC)	Sum of all fixed expenses, here defined to include all opportunity costs
Total variable cost (TVC)	Sum of all variable expenses, or per unit variable cost times quantity; (per unit VC $\times$ Q)
Total cost (TC)	Total fixed cost plus total variable cost; (TFC + TVC)
Average fixed cost (AFC)	Total fixed cost divided by quantity; (TFC/Q)
Average variable cost (AVC)	Total variable cost divided by quantity; (TVC/Q)
Average total cost (ATC)	Total cost divided by quantity; (TC/Q) or (AFC + AVC)
Marginal cost (MC)	Change in total cost divided by change in quantity; (ΔTC/ΔQ)

Characteristics of Total Cost Curves

- TC and TVC increase at a decreasing rate at low levels of output, and increase at an increasing rate at higher levels of output.
- The difference between TC and TVC equals TFC.

Characteristics of Average Cost Curves

- As output levels rise, AFC continues to fall at a decreasing rate as total fixed costs are spread over more and more units.
- The ATC curve is U-shaped. It falls initially as fixed costs are spread over an increasing number of units. Later, however, the effect of a falling AFC is offset by diminishing marginal returns (increasing AVC) so ATC starts rising.
- The vertical distance between the AVC and ATC curves equals AFC. The vertical distance between the AVC and ATC curves gets smaller as output increases.

Average Cost and Marginal Cost Curves

- MC intersects ATC and AVC from *below* at their respective *minimum* points.
- When MC lies below AVC, AVC falls, and when MC lies above AVC, AVC rises.
- When MC lies below ATC, ATC falls, and when MC lies above ATC, ATC rises.

Short-Run Marginal Cost (SMC) versus Long-Run Marginal Cost (LMC)

- SMC is the additional cost of the variable input (labor) that must be incurred to increase the level of output by one unit.
- LMC is the additional cost of all inputs necessary to increase the level of output, allowing the firm the flexibility of changing both labor and capital inputs in a way that maximizes efficiency.

Marginal Product and Marginal Cost Curves

- A firm's MP curve is linked to its MC curve. Initially, as more labor is hired, MP rises and MC falls.

- At the point where MP reaches its maximum, MC stands at its minimum.
- As output expands further, MP falls and MC rises.

Average Product and Average Variable Cost Curves

- A firm's AP curve is linked to its AVC curve. Initially, as the firm hires more labor, AP rises and AVC falls.
- At the point where AP reaches its maximum, AVC is at its minimum.
- As the firm increases output further, AP falls and AVC rises.

Costs are directly related to input prices and inversely related to productivity.

- If the wage rate were to rise, costs would also rise, but if labor productivity were to improve, costs would fall. This relationship can be captured by the expression: $MC = w/MP_L$.
- Similarly, if wages rise, AVC also rises, but if labor productivity were to improve, AVC would fall. Therefore, $AVC = w/AP_L$.
- As the firm benefits from increasing marginal returns, MP_L increases and MC declines. However, as more and more labor is added to a fixed amount of capital, diminishing marginal returns set in and MP_L falls, causing MC to rise.

Marginal Revenue, Marginal Cost, and Profit Maximization

Profits are maximized when the difference between TR and TC is at its highest. The level of output at which this occurs is the point where (1) marginal revenue equals marginal cost (MC = MR), and (2) MC is not falling.

- When MR > MC, the firm should increase production, as the last unit produced added more to revenue that it did to costs.
- When MR < MC, the firm should reduce production, as the last unit produced added more to costs than it did to revenue.
- Recall that $MC = w/MP_L$, so if MC is falling, MP would be rising. If an additional unit of labor causes MC to fall, the firm would want to add that unit of labor until MC is upward sloping.

Perfect Competition

- The firm's profit-maximizing quantity is the output level where MR (which equals P and AR) equals MC while MC is rising. If P is greater than ATC, the firm makes economic profits. Economic profits are possible in perfect competition only in the short run. In the long run, more firms will enter the industry, taking market prices down to a level where they equal ATC.

Monopoly

- A monopoly faces a downward-sloping demand curve. As a result, the MR and demand curves are not identical. The profit-maximizing level of output occurs at the point where MC equals MR while MC is rising. Once the profit-maximizing level of output has been determined, the optimal price is obtained from the demand curve. If P is greater than ATC, the monopolist earns positive economic profits, and these can continue in the long run due to high barriers to entry.

Breakeven Analysis

A firm is said to break even if its TR equals its TC. At the breakeven quantity of production, price (or AR) equals ATC. This is true under both perfect and imperfect competition. Breaking even implies that the firm is covering all its economic costs (total accounting costs and implicit opportunity costs), so, while it is not earning positive economic profits, the firm is at least covering the opportunity cost of all its factors of production, including capital. In other words, the firm is earning **normal profit**.

The Shutdown Decision

- At price levels below AVC, the firm will not be willing to produce, as continued production would only extend losses beyond simply total fixed costs.
- When price lies between AVC and ATC, the firm will remain in production in the short run, as it meets all variable costs and covers a portion of its fixed costs.
- To remain in business in the long run, the firm must break even or cover all costs (revenues should meet total costs).
- Once prices exceed ATC, the firm makes economic profits.

Short-Run and Long-Run Operating Decisions

Revenue-Cost Relationship	Short-Run Decision	Long-Run Decision
TR = TC	Continue to operate	Continue to operate
TR = TVC but TR < TC	Continue to operate	Exit market
TR < TVC	Shut down	Exit market

Economies and Diseconomies of Scale

A company's **production function** shows how different quantities of labor and capital affect total product.

- Short-run ATC curves are U-shaped.
- The larger the plant, the greater the output at which short-run ATC is at its minimum.

The **long-run average cost (LRAC)** curve illustrates the relationship between average total cost and output when all factors of production are variable. The LRAC curve is also known as a *planning curve* because it shows the expected per-unit cost of producing various levels of output using different combinations of factors of production.

- **Economies of scale** occur in the downward-sloping region of the LRAC curve. They result from mass production and specialization of labor.
- **Diseconomies of scale** occur in the upward-sloping region of the LRAC curve. They result from bureaucratic inefficiencies as effective management, supervision, and communication become difficult.
- In the horizontal portion of the LRAC curve, when an increase in production does not result in any change in average costs, a firm realizes **constant returns to scale**.

Also, note that:

- The **minimum efficient scale** is the smallest quantity of output at which long-run average cost reaches its lowest level.
- In the long run, all firms in perfect competition operate at their minimum efficient scale, as price equals minimum average cost.

THE FIRM AND MARKET STRUCTURES
Cross-Reference to CFA Institute Assigned Reading #9

Perfect Competition

Characteristics

- There are a large number of buyers and sellers.
- Each seller offers an identical product for sale.
- There are minimal barriers to entry.
- Sellers have no pricing power.
- There is no non-price competition in the market.

Demand in a Perfectly Competitive Market

- The **market demand curve** is downward sloping.
- The relationship between MR and price elasticity can be expressed as:

$$MR = P[1 - (1/E_P)]$$

Optimal Price and Output in Perfectly Competitive Markets

Each firm in perfect competition is very small compared to the size of the overall market. The actions of any firm do not impact market equilibrium. Each firm can sell as much output as it desires at the equilibrium market price.

- Therefore, the demand curve faced by an individual firm is perfectly elastic (horizontal).

Average revenue equals price and marginal revenue. $AR = P = MR$

The law of diminishing marginal returns dictates the "U" shape of SR cost curves.

Firms always maximize profits at the point where MC equals MR.

- Total revenue equals price times quantity sold.
- Total cost equals AC times quantity sold.
- The positive (negative) difference between the two equals economic profit (loss).
- If the two are equal, the firm only makes normal profit.

In the short run, a firm in perfect competition can make economic profits, economic losses or normal profit.

- In each scenario the firm produces the output level at which MC equals MR.
- Whether it makes a profit or a loss depends on the position of the demand curve relative to its average cost at the profit-maximizing quantity.
- If $P > AC \Rightarrow$ Economic profit
- If $P = AC \Rightarrow$ Normal profit
- If $P < AC \Rightarrow$ Economic loss

In the long run, all firms in perfect competition will only make normal profit.

- In the LR, $MC = MR = P = AR = \min AC$

Schumpeter's Take on Perfect Competition

Joseph Schumpeter suggested that perfect competition is more of a long-run type of market structure. In the short run, companies develop new products or processes that give them an edge over competitors but in the long run, as competitors adopt those new products, perfect competition prevails.

Monopoly

Characteristics

- There is a single seller of a highly differentiated product, which has no close substitutes.
- There are high barriers to entry.
- The firm has considerable pricing power.
- The product is differentiated through non-price strategies (e.g., advertising).

Factors that Give Rise to Monopolies

- Control over critical sources of production
- Patents or copyrights
- Non-price differentiation leading to pricing-power
- Network effects, which result from synergies related to increasing market penetration
- Government-controlled authorization

Demand Analysis in Monopoly Markets

The demand curve faced by the monopoly is effectively the industry demand curve. It is downward-sloping.

- The AR curve is the same as the demand curve.
- The MR curve and the demand curve have the same y-intercept.
- The slope of the MR curve is two times the slope of the demand curve.
- The x-intercept of the MR curve is half of that of the demand curve.
- The MR curve is the derivative of the TR curve with respect to quantity sold.

Supply Analysis in Monopoly Markets

- The monopolist does not have a well-defined supply function that determines optimal price and output.
- The profit-maximizing output level occurs at the point where MR = MC.
- The price is determined from the demand curve (based on the profit-maximizing quantity).

Optimal Price and Output in Monopoly Markets

The profit-maximizing output level equals the quantity at which:

- MC = MR; and
- Profit is unaffected by changes in quantity: $\Delta\pi/\Delta Q_D = 0$

The profit-maximizing level of output always occurs in the relatively elastic portion of the demand curve. Given its cost structure and price elasticity of demand, a monopoly can use the following equation to determine the profit maximizing price.

$$P[1 - (1/E_P)] = MC$$

Natural Monopolies

A natural monopoly is an industry where the supplier's average cost is still falling even when it satisfies total market demand entirely on its own.

Regulation of Natural Monopolies

- Marginal cost pricing forces a monopoly to charge a price that equals its marginal cost of production. Under marginal cost pricing, the monopoly makes an economic loss, which the government must subsidize. Alternatively the government may allow the monopoly to discriminate on prices or to engage in two-part pricing to offset losses. Marginal cost pricing is also known as **efficient regulation**.
- Average cost pricing forces a monopoly to charge a price that equals its average cost of production. This allows the monopoly to earn normal profits.

Price Discrimination and Consumer Surplus

First-degree price discrimination occurs when a monopolist is able to charge each individual consumer the highest price that she is willing and able to pay.

Under **perfect price discrimination**:

- The MR curve equals the demand curve.
- The profit maximizing level of output increases.
- The entire consumer surplus is eaten up by the producer.
- There is no dead weight loss.
- The more perfectly a monopolist can price discriminate, the more "efficient" the outcome.

In **second-degree price discrimination**, the monopolist offers a variety of quantity-based pricing options that induce customers to self-select based on how highly they value the product (e.g., volume discounts, product bundling).

Third-degree price discrimination can occur when customers can be separated by geographical or other traits. One set of customers is charged a higher price, while the other is charged a lower price (e.g., airlines charge higher fares on one day roundtrip tickets as they are more likely to be purchased by business people).

Factors Affecting Long-Run Equilibrium in Monopoly Markets

An **unregulated** monopoly can earn economic profits in the long run as it is protected by substantial barriers to entry.

For **regulated** monopolies, such as natural monopolies there are various solutions:

- A marginal cost pricing structure. However, the firm must be provided a subsidy in this scenario.
- An average cost pricing structure.
- National ownership of the monopoly.
- Franchising the monopoly via a bidding war (e.g., selling retail space at railway stations and airports).

Monopolistic Competition

Characteristics

- There are a large number of buyers and sellers.
- The products offered by each seller are similar, but not identical. They serve as close substitutes to each other.
- Firms try to differentiate their product from the competition through advertising and other non-price strategies.
- There are low barriers to entry and exit.
- Firms have some degree of pricing power.

Demand and Supply Analysis in Monopolistically Competitive Markets

Demand:

- Each firm faces a downward sloping demand curve.
- Demand is relatively elastic at higher prices and relatively inelastic at lower prices.

Supply:

- There is no well-defined supply function.
- Neither the MC nor the AC curve represent the firm's supply curve.
- The firm will always produce at the output level where MC = MR.
- The price that is charged is derived from the market demand curve.

Short-Run versus Long-Run Equilibrium

- In the **short run**, a firm in monopolistic competition produces the output level where MC equals MR, and charges the maximum possible price that buyers are willing to pay for its product (determined by the demand curve).
- In the **long run**, firms in the industry make normal profits, there is no incentive for new firms to enter, or for existing firms to exit the industry.

Monopolistic Competition versus Perfect Competition

- A firm in monopolistic competition generally produces *lower* output and charges a *higher* price than in perfect competition. In perfect competition, price *equals* marginal cost, while in monopolistic competition, price *exceeds* marginal cost. This excess of price over marginal cost is known as *markup*.
- For a firm in monopolistic competition, in the long run, the profit maximizing output level occurs at a point where demand is tangent to the average cost curve, but at a stage where average costs are *still falling*. In perfect competition in the long run, each firm produces an output level where average cost is at its *minimum*, or at its efficient scale of production. Firms under monopolistic competition therefore, have *excess capacity*.

However, monopolistic competition enjoys some support because it offers consumers options to choose from. Product innovation, advertising and brand building are crucial to a firm's success in monopolistic competition.

Oligopoly

Characteristics

- There are a small number of sellers.
- The products offered by sellers are close substitutes for each other. Products may be differentiated by brand (e.g., Coke® and Pepsi®) or be homogenous (e.g., oil).
- There are high costs of entry and significant barriers to competition.
- Firms enjoy substantial pricing power.
- Products are often differentiated on the basis of quality, features, marketing, and other non-price strategies.

Demand Analysis and Pricing Strategies in Oligopoly Markets

Pricing interdependence (kinked demand curve model): The demand curve has two contrasting shapes. It is relatively elastic above current prices, and relatively inelastic below current prices. This results in a kink in the firm's demand curve and a break in its marginal revenue curve. This break in the MR curve implies that it would take a significant change in costs of production to change the firm's profit-maximizing output level.

The **Cournot assumption** asserts that each firm determines its profit-maximizing level assuming that other firms' output will not change. In equilibrium, no firm has an incentive to change output. In the long run, prices and output are stable (i.e., there is no possible change in output or price that would make any firm better off).

Game theory: Nash equilibrium is achieved when none of the firms in an oligopoly market can increase profits by unilaterally changing its price. Each firm tries to maximize its own profits given the responses of its rivals. Each firm anticipates how its rival will respond to a change in its strategy and tries to maximize its profits under the forecasted scenario. As a result, the firms in the market are interdependent, but their actions are non-cooperative: Firms do not collude to maximize profits.

The **Stackelberg model** (also known as the **dominant firm model**) assumes that decision-making is sequential. The leader or dominant firm determines its profit-maximizing level of output, the price is determined from the demand curve for its product (the dominant firm is the price-maker) and then each of the follower firms determine their quantities based on the given market price (they are price-takers).

Factors Affecting Chances of Successful Collusion

- There are fewer firms in the industry or if one firm is dominant. Collusion becomes difficult as competition between firms in the industry increases.
- The firms produce similar products.
- The firms have similar cost structures.
- Order size is small and orders are received more frequently.
- There is minimal threat of retaliation from other firms in the industry.
- There is minimal external competition.

Supply Analysis in Oligopoly Markets

- The supply function for a firm in an oligopoly is not well-defined because optimal quantity and price depend on the actions of rival firms.
- The firm produces where MC = MR.
- Equilibrium price comes from the demand curve.

Optimal Price and Output in Oligopoly Markets

There is no single optimal price and output that fits all oligopoly market situations.

- In the kinked demand curve model, the optimal price is the prevailing price (at which the demand curve kinks).
- In the dominant firm model, the leader produces an output level where MC = MR. Followers have little or no power to influence price.
- In the Cournot assumption, each firm assumes that rivals will have no response to any actions on their part. Each firm produces where MC = MR.
- In Nash equilibrium, firms continue to respond to changing circumstances with the aim of maximizing their own profit. Since there is significant interdependence between firms, there is no certainty regarding an individual firm's price and output.

Identification of Market Structure

Econometric Approaches: Estimate the price elasticity of market demand based on time series analysis or cross sectional regression analysis.

N-firm concentration ratio: Computes the aggregate market share of the N largest firms in the industry.

- It does not quantify market power.
- It is unaffected by mergers in the top tier.

Herfindahl-Hirschman Index (HHI): Adds up the squares of the market shares of each of the largest N companies in the market.

- The HHI equals 1 for a monopoly.
- If there are M firms in the industry with equal market shares, the HHI will equal $1/M$.
- Does not account for the possibility of entry, nor does it consider the elasticity of demand. However, it is more useful than the concentration ratio.

AGGREGATE OUTPUT, PRICE, AND ECONOMIC GROWTH
Cross-Reference to CFA Institute Assigned Reading #10

Aggregate output refers to the total value of all the goods and services produced in an economy over a period of time.

Aggregate income refers to the total value of all payments earned by the suppliers of factors of production in an economy over a period of time.

Aggregate expenditure refers to the total amount spent on the goods and services produced in the domestic economy over a period of time.

Gross Domestic Product (GDP)

- **Output definition**: GDP is the market value of all final goods and services produced within an economy over a period of time.
- **Income definition**: GDP is the aggregate income earned by all households, companies, and the government in an economy over a period of time.

Criteria for Inclusion in GDP

- Only goods and services produced *during* the measurement period are included.
    - Transfer payments and income from capital gains are excluded.
- Only goods and services whose value can be determined by being sold in the market are included.
    - The value of labor used in activities that are not sold in the market is excluded.
    - By-products of production processes which have no explicit market value are not included.
    - Activities in the underground economy are not included.
    - Barter transactions are not included.
- Only the value of *final* goods and services is included in the calculation of GDP. The value of intermediate goods (that are resold to produce another good) is excluded because the entire value added during the production process is reflected in the selling price of the final good produced (**value-of-final-output**). GDP can also be measured by summing the value added at each stage of the production and distribution processes (**sum-of-value-added**).

Nominal versus Real GDP

$$\text{Nominal GDP} = \text{Quantity produced in Year t} \times \text{Prices in Year t}$$

$$\text{Real GDP} = \text{Quantity produced in Year t} \times \text{Base-year prices}$$

GDP Deflator

The **GDP deflator** broadly measures the aggregate change in prices across the overall economy. Changes in the GDP deflator provide a useful measure of inflation.

$$\text{GDP deflator} = \frac{\text{Value of current year output at current year prices}}{\text{Value of current year output at base year prices}} \times 100$$

$$\text{GDP deflator} = \frac{\text{Nominal GDP}}{\text{Real GDP}} \times 100$$

The Components of GDP

$$\text{GDP} = C + I + G + (X - M)$$

Expenditure Approach

$$
\begin{aligned}
\text{GDP} = \ & \text{Consumer spending on goods and services} \\
& + \text{Business gross fixed investment} \\
& + \text{Change in inventories} \\
& + \text{Government spending on goods and services} \\
& + \text{Government gross fixed investment} \\
& + \text{Exports} - \text{Imports} + \text{Statistical discrepancy}
\end{aligned}
$$

Income Approach

$$
\begin{aligned}
\text{GDP} = \ & \text{Gross domestic income (GDI)} \\
= \ & \text{Net domestic income} + \text{Consumption of fixed capital (CFC)} \\
& + \text{Statistical discrepancy} \\
\text{Gross domestic income} = \ & \text{Compensation of employees} \\
& + \text{Gross operating surplus} \\
& + \text{Gross mixed income} \\
& + \text{Taxes less subsidies on production} \\
& + \text{Taxes less subsidies on products and imports} \\
\text{Household disposable income (HDI)} & \\
= \ & \text{Household primary income} - \text{Net current transfers paid (net taxes)}
\end{aligned}
$$

The Equality of Expenditure and Income

$$S = I + (G - T) + (X - M)$$

Based on this equation we can say that domestic private saving can be used for:

- Investment spending (I);
- Financing government deficits (G – T); and/or
- Building up financial claims against overseas economies by financing their trade deficits (lending the domestic economy's trade surplus, X – M).
- If an economy has a negative trade balance, foreign savings will supplement domestic savings and foreigners will build up financial claims against the domestic economy.
- If the government runs a fiscal surplus, the surplus will add to domestic savings.

$$(G - T) = (S - I) - (X - M)$$

A fiscal deficit occurs when government expenditures exceed net taxes (i.e., G − T > 0). In order to finance a fiscal deficit:

- The private sector must save more than it invests (S > I); and/or
- The country's imports must exceed its exports (M > X ⇒ trade deficit) with a corresponding inflow of foreign saving.

Generating the Aggregate Demand Curve

The **aggregate demand (AD)** curve shows the combinations of aggregate income and price level at which the following conditions are satisfied:

- Planned expenditures equal actual (or realized) income/output.
- There is equilibrium in the money market.

The first condition gives rise to the **IS curve**, while the second gives rise to the LM curve. By combining the IS and LM curves, we obtain the **aggregate demand curve.**

Deriving the IS Curve: Relationship between Income and the Real Interest Rate

- Consumption varies positively with income, but negatively with taxes.
- Investment expenditure varies positively with income, and negatively with real interest rates.
- Government expenditure does not vary with income. Taxes vary positively with income. Therefore, the government's fiscal balance varies negatively with income.
- Net exports vary negatively with income, and negatively with domestic price levels.

$$S - I = (G - T) + (X - M)$$

- The **fiscal balance (G − T)** and the **trade balance (X − M) decline** as income rises.
- The **saving-investment differential (S − I) increases** as income increases.

The point of intersection between these two lines defines the point where aggregate expenditure and aggregate income are equal.

Changes in the level of real interest rates (r) cause shifts in the line representing the saving-investment differential. If the real interest rate falls (rises) the point of intersection between the (S − I) and the (G − T) + (X − M) curves occurs at a higher (lower) level of income.

This **inverse relationship between income and the real interest rate** is referred to as the **IS curve.**

The LM Curve

The LM curve shows the combinations of interest rates and real income for which the money market is in equilibrium. Equilibrium in the money market requires that real money demand (M_D/P) equals real money supply (M/P).

Demand for real money (RM_D or M_D/P) is a positive function of real income and a negative function of interest rates. Given the real money supply, an **increase** in real income (which would lead to an increase in real money demand) must be accompanied by an **increase** in interest rates (which would lead to a decrease in real money demand) so that demand for real money remains the same and equilibrium in the money market is maintained.

Therefore, if real money supply is held constant, we can infer a positive relationship between real income (Y) and the real interest rate (r). This **positive** relationship between real income and the real interest rate is illustrated by the LM curve.

Changes in real money supply cause shifts in the LM curve. If real money supply increases (decreases), the LM curve would shift to the right (left).

The Aggregate Demand Curve

If money supply is held constant, the only variable that affects real money supply is price. A **decrease** (increase) in the price level leads to an increase (decrease) in real money supply. The **increase** (decrease) in real money supply leads to a rightward (leftward) shift in the LM curve so the point of intersection of the IS and LM curves now occurs at a **higher** (lower) level of income.

The inverse relationship between the price level (P) and real income (Y) is captured by the aggregate demand curve. IS-LM analysis also suggests a positive relationship between the price level and real interest rates.

Slope of the AD Curve

The steepness of the slope of the AD curve depends on the relative sensitivities of investment, saving, and money demand to income and real interest rates. The AD curve will be flatter (small changes in price cause relatively large changes in quantity demanded) if:

- Investment expenditure is highly sensitive to the interest rate.
- Saving is insensitive to income.
- Money demand is insensitive to interest rates.
- Money demand is insensitive to income.

Interest Rates and Aggregate Demand

- If the increase in aggregate demand is caused by an increase in money supply, interest rates fall.
- If the increase in aggregate demand is caused by any other factor (with real money supply, M constant) interest rates will rise.

Aggregate Supply

Aggregate supply (AS) represents the quantities of goods and services that domestic producers are willing and able to supply at various price levels.

- The very short-run aggregate supply curve is horizontal.
- The short-run aggregate supply curve is upward-sloping.
- The long-run aggregate supply curve is vertical.

In the long run, wages, prices and expectations can adjust but capital and technology remain fixed. This condition is relaxed in the very long run.

The LRAS curve basically defines the potential output of the economy. The potential output of any economy does not vary with the price level. When an economy operates at its potential output level, all its resources are fully employed and it is said to be working at **full employment**. At this output level, unemployment is at its **natural rate**.

- **Structural unemployment** results from structural changes in the economy, which make some skills obsolete and leave previously employed people jobless.
- **Cyclical unemployment** is the unemployment generated as an economy goes through the phases of a business cycle.

Short-Run versus Long-Run Equilibrium

- The point of intersection of the AD curve and the LRAS curve defines the economy's **long-run equilibrium position**. At this point, actual real GDP equals potential GDP.
- The point of intersection of the AD curve and the SRAS curve defines the economy's **short-run equilibrium position**. Short-run fluctuations in equilibrium of real GDP may occur due to shifts in either or both the AD and SRAS curves. Short run equilibrium may be established at, below, or above potential output. Deviations of short-run equilibrium from potential output result in **business cycles**.
  - In an **expansion**, real GDP is increasing, the unemployment rate is falling and capacity utilization is rising. Further, inflation tends to rise during an expansion.
  - In a **contraction**, real GDP is decreasing, the unemployment rate is rising and capacity utilization is falling. Further, inflation tends to fall during a contraction.

Impact of Factors Shifting Aggregate Demand[1]

An Increase in the Following Factors	Shifts the AD Curve	Reason
Stock prices	Rightward: Increase in AD	Higher consumption
Housing prices	Rightward: Increase in AD	Higher consumption
Consumer confidence	Rightward: Increase in AD	Higher consumption
Business confidence	Rightward: Increase in AD	Higher investment
Capacity utilization	Rightward: Increase in AD	Higher investment
Government spending	Rightward: Increase in AD	Government spending a component of AD
Taxes	Leftward: Decrease in AD	Lower consumption and investment
Bank reserves	Rightward: Increase in AD	Lower interest rate, higher investment and possibly higher consumption
Exchange rate (foreign currency per unit domestic currency)	Leftward: Decrease in AD	Lower exports and higher imports
Global growth	Rightward: Increase in AD	Higher exports

[1]Exhibit 17, Volume 2, CFA Program Curriculum 2022

Impact of Factors Shifting Aggregate Supply[2]

An Increase in	Shifts SRAS	Shifts LRAS	Reason
Supply of labor	Rightward	Rightward	Increases resource base
Supply of natural resources	Rightward	Rightward	Increases resource base
Supply of human capital	Rightward	Rightward	Increases resource base
Supply of physical capital	Rightward	Rightward	Increases resource base
Productivity and technology	Rightward	Rightward	Improves efficiency of inputs
Nominal wages	Leftward	No impact	Increases labor cost
Input prices (e.g., energy)	Leftward	No impact	Increases cost of production
Expectation of future prices	Rightward	No impact	Anticipation of higher costs and/or perception of improved pricing power
Business taxes	Leftward	No impact	Increases cost of production
Subsidy	Rightward	No impact	Lowers cost of production
Exchange rate	Rightward	No impact	Lowers cost of production

[2]Exhibit 19, Volume 2, CFA Program Curriculum 2022

Business Cycles

Fluctuations in aggregate demand and aggregate supply in the short-run explain why short run real GDP deviates from potential GDP. These deviations of actual GDP from full-employment GDP form phases of the business cycle.

Investment Applications of an Increase in AD Resulting in an Inflationary Gap

If economic data suggest that the economy is undergoing an expansion caused by an increase in AD, going forward:

- Corporate profits will be expected to rise.
- Commodity prices will be expected to increase.
- Interest rates will be expected to rise.
- Inflationary pressures will build in the economy.

Therefore, investors should:

- Increase investments in cyclical companies as their earnings would rise significantly in this scenario.
- Increase investments in commodities and/or commodity oriented companies. Reduce investments in defensive companies as their profits would not rise as significantly as those of cyclical companies.
- Reduce investments in fixed-income securities (especially those with longer maturities) as their values would fall when interest rates go up.
- Increase investments in junk bonds as default risk (already factored into their prices) should fall in an expansion (and result in an increase in their prices).

Investment Applications of a Decrease in AD Resulting in a Deflationary Gap

If economic data suggest that the economy is undergoing a recession caused by a decrease in AD, going forward:

- Corporate profits will be expected to fall.
- Commodity prices will be expected to decline.
- Interest rates will be expected to fall.
- Demand for credit will decrease.

Therefore, investors should:

- Reduce investments in cyclical companies.
- Reduce investments in commodities and/or commodity oriented companies.
- Increase investments in defensive companies as their profits would decline modestly compared to cyclical companies.
- Increase investments in investment-grade or government-issued fixed-income securities as their values (particularly of those with longer maturities) will rise if interest rates go down.
- Decrease investments in junk bonds as default risk should rise in a recession (and result in a decrease in their prices).

Stagflation

Shifts in the SRAS curve (due to any of the factors discussed earlier in the reading) cause structural fluctuations in real GDP. A decrease in SRAS causes stagflation (high unemployment and higher inflation), while an increase in SRAS brings about economic growth and low inflation.

Investment Applications of a Shift in SRAS

If the SRAS curve shifts to the left (SRAS declines), investors may want to:

- Reduce investments in fixed-income securities because increasing output prices (inflation) may put an upward pressure on nominal interest rates (which would decrease the value of fixed-income instruments).

- Reduce exposure to equities in anticipation of a decline in output and profit margins coming under pressure.
- Increase investments in commodities and/or commodity-oriented companies because their prices and profits are likely to rise (due to higher prices).

Conclusions on AD and AS

	Real GDP	Unemployment Rate	Aggregate Level of Prices
An increase in AD	Increases	Falls	Increases
A decrease in AD	Falls	Increases	Falls
An increase in AS	Increases	Falls	Falls
A decrease in AS	Falls	Increases	Increases

Effect of Combined Changes in AS and AD

Change in AS	Change in AD	Effect on Real GDP	Effect on Aggregate Price Level
Increase	Increase	Increase	Uncertain
Decrease	Decrease	Decrease	Uncertain
Increase	Decrease	Uncertain	Decrease
Decrease	Increase	Uncertain	Increase

Economic Growth

Economic growth may be calculated as:

- The **annual percentage change in real GDP**, which tells us how rapidly the economy is expanding as a whole; or
- The **annual change in real per capita GDP**. Real GDP per capita is calculated as total real GDP divided by total population. It is a useful indicator of the standard of living in a country.

The Production Function and Potential GDP

The production function asserts that an increase in an economy's potential GDP can be caused by:

- An increase in the quantity of inputs used in the production process (e.g., capital and labor).
- An increase in the productivity of these inputs with the application of better technology. Improving technology enables an economy to produce more output using the same quantity of inputs.

Because of diminishing marginal returns to labor and capital, the only way to "sustain" growth in potential GDP is growth in total factor productivity.

The Growth Accounting Equation

> Growth in potential GDP $=$ Growth in technology $+$ W_L(Growth in labor)
> $+$ W_K(Growth in capital)
>
> Growth in per capital potential GDP $=$ Growth in technology
> $+$ W_K(Growth in capital-labor ratio)

Takeaway: Advances in technology have a more significant impact on an economy's standard of living compared to capital.

Sources of Economic Growth

- Growth in labor supply
- Improvements in quality of human capital
- Growth in physical capital stock
- Improvements in technology
- Availability of natural resources

Measures of Sustainable Growth

Labor productivity refers to the quantity of goods and services (real GDP) that a worker can produce in one hour of work.

> Labor productivity $=$ Real GDP/ Aggregate hours

Labor productivity depends on:

- Physical capital per worker (K/L) or the mix of inputs (which is easily calculated based on input data)
- Total factor productivity or technology (A). This is a scale factor and can be estimated based on output and input data.

Labor productivity is much easier to measure directly than growth in potential GDP. Labor productivity can explain differences in living standards and long term sustainable growth rates across countries.

Measuring Sustainable Growth

Potential GDP is a combination of aggregate hours and productivity of labor:

> Potential GDP $=$ Aggregate hours $\times$ Labor productivity

> Potential GDP growth rate $=$ Long-term growth rate of labor force
> $+$ Long-term labor productivity growth rate

UNDERSTANDING BUSINESS CYCLES
Cross-Reference to CFA Institute Assigned Reading #11

Phases of the Business Cycle

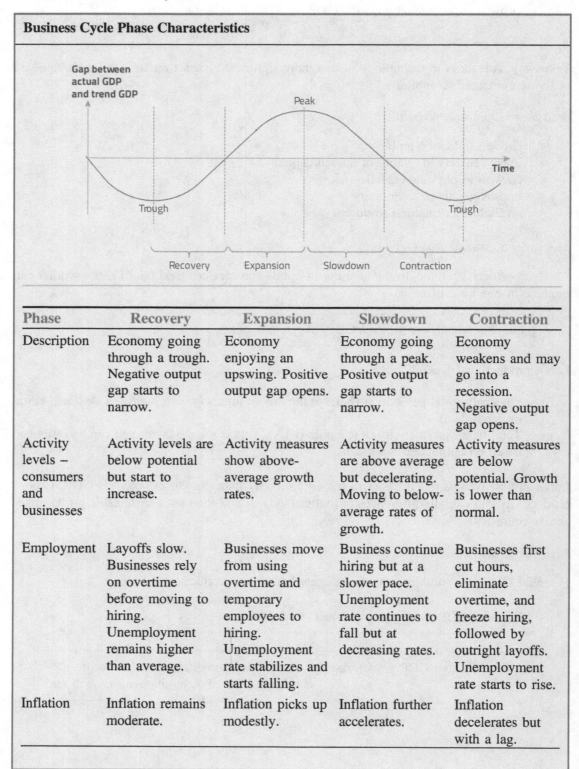

Business Cycle Phase Characteristics

Phase	Recovery	Expansion	Slowdown	Contraction
Description	Economy going through a trough. Negative output gap starts to narrow.	Economy enjoying an upswing. Positive output gap opens.	Economy going through a peak. Positive output gap starts to narrow.	Economy weakens and may go into a recession. Negative output gap opens.
Activity levels – consumers and businesses	Activity levels are below potential but start to increase.	Activity measures show above-average growth rates.	Activity measures are above average but decelerating. Moving to below-average rates of growth.	Activity measures are below potential. Growth is lower than normal.
Employment	Layoffs slow. Businesses rely on overtime before moving to hiring. Unemployment remains higher than average.	Businesses move from using overtime and temporary employees to hiring. Unemployment rate stabilizes and starts falling.	Business continue hiring but at a slower pace. Unemployment rate continues to fall but at decreasing rates.	Businesses first cut hours, eliminate overtime, and freeze hiring, followed by outright layoffs. Unemployment rate starts to rise.
Inflation	Inflation remains moderate.	Inflation picks up modestly.	Inflation further accelerates.	Inflation decelerates but with a lag.

Credit Cycles

Credit cycles describe the changing availability and pricing of credit.

- When the economy is strong/improving, the willingness of lenders to extend credit (and on favorable terms) is high.
- When the economy is weak/weakening, lenders pull back (and any credit offered is on stricter terms).

Investors must pay attention to the credit cycle because it can help them:

- Understand developments in the housing and construction markets.
- Assess the extent of business cycle expansions as well as contractions.
- Better anticipate policy makers' actions.

The Workforce and Company Costs

Business Cycle Phases—Levels of Employment				
Phase	**Recovery**	**Expansion**	**Slowdown**	**Contraction**
Description of activity levels	Economy starts at trough and output below potential. Activity picks up, and gap starts to close.	Economy enjoying an upswing, with activity measures showing above-average growth rates.	Economy at peak. Activity above average but decelerating. The economy may experience shortages of factors of production as demand may exceed supply.	Economy goes into a contraction, (recession, if severe). Activity measures are below potential. Growth is lower than normal.
Employment	Layoffs slow. Businesses rely on overtime before moving to hiring. Unemployment remains higher than average.	Businesses move from using overtime and temporary employees to hiring. Unemployment rate stabilizes and starts falling.	Businesses continue hiring but at a slower pace. Unemployment rate continues to fall but at slowly decreasing rates.	Businesses first cut hours, eliminate overtime, and freeze hiring, followed by outright layoffs. Unemployment rate starts to rise.
		Levels of employment lag the cycle		

Fluctuations in Capital Spending

Capital Spending during the Economic Cycle				
Phase of the Cycle	**Recovery**	**Expansion**	**Slowdown**	**Contraction**
Business conditions and expectations	Excess capacity during trough, low utilization, little need for capacity expansion. Interest rates tend to be low—supporting investment.	Companies enjoy favorable conditions. Capacity utilization increases from low levels. Over time, productive capacity may begin to limit ability to respond to demand. Growth in earnings and cash flow gives businesses the financial ability to increase investment spending.	Business conditions at peak, with healthy cash flow. Interest rates tend to be higher—aimed at reducing overheating and encouraging investment slowdown.	Companies experience fall in demand, profits, and cash flows.
Capital spending	Low but increasing as companies start to enjoy better conditions. Capex focus on efficiency rather than capacity. Upturn most pronounced in orders for light producer equipment. Typically, the orders initially reinstated are for equipment with a high rate of obsolescence, such as software, systems, and technological hardware.	Customer orders and capacity utilization increase. Companies start to focus on capacity expansion. The composition of the economy's capacity may not be optimal for the current structure of demand, necessitating spending on new types of equipment. Orders precede actual shipments, so orders for capital equipment are a widely watched indicator of the future direction of capital spending.	New orders intended to increase capacity may be an early indicator of the late stage of the expansion phase. Companies continue to place new orders as they operate at or near capacity.	New orders halted, and some existing orders canceled (no need to expand). Initial cutbacks may be sharp and exaggerate the economy's downturn. As the general cyclical bust matures, cutbacks in spending on heavy equipment further intensify the contraction. Maintenance scaled back.
Examples	Software, systems, and hardware (high rates of obsolescence) orders placed or re-instated first.	Heavy and complex equipment, warehouses, and factories. A company may need warehouse space in locations different from where existing facilities are.	Fiber-optic overinvestment in late 1990s that peaked with the "technology, media, telecoms bubble."	Technology and light equipment with short lead times get cut first. Cuts in construction and heavy equipment follow.

Fluctuations in Inventory Levels

Inventories throughout the Cycle				
Phase of the Cycle	**Recovery**	**Expansion**	**Slowdown**	**Contraction**
Sales and production	Sales decline slows. Sales subsequently recover. Production upturn follows but lags behind sales growth. Over time, production approaches normal levels as excess inventories from the downturn are cleared.	Sales increase. Production rises fast to keep up with sales growth and to replenish inventories of finished products. This increases the demand for intermediate products. "Inventory rebuilding or restocking stage."	Sales slow faster than production; inventories increase. Economic slowdown leads to production cutbacks and order cancellations.	Businesses produce at rates below the sales volumes necessary to dispose of unwanted inventories.
Inventory–sales ratio	Begins to fall as sales recovery outpaces production.	Ratio stable.	Ratio increases. Signals weakening economy.	Ratio begins to fall back to normal.

Consumer Behavior

Consumer Behavior				
Phase of the Cycle	**Recovery**	**Expansion**	**Slowdown**	**Contraction**
Incomes, employment, and confidence	Unemployment remains above average. Layoffs slow. Businesses rely on overtime before moving to hiring. Consumer confidence starts improving.	Hiring restarts. Unemployment rate stabilizes and starts falling. Consumers experience rising incomes, healthy employment prospects, and greater confidence.	Businesses continue hiring but at a slower pace. Unemployment rate continues to fall. Incomes are still growing. Consumers remain confident.	Businesses first cut hours of overtime prior to freezing hiring and starting layoffs. Employment levels decline, and consumer confidence weakens.

(Table continued on next page...)

Phase of the Cycle	Recovery	Expansion	Slowdown	Contraction
Spending on consumer durables (autos, motorcycles, appliances, furniture)	Spending limited as households postpone spending.	Spending increases.	Spending above average.	Purchases postponed; spending decreasing.
Consumer non-durables (i.e., medicines, food, household products)	Spending shows little change through the cycle.			
Services (entertainment, outdoor eating, communications, personal services)	Spending below average.	Spending increases.	Spending above average.	Spending declines.

Housing Sector Behavior and the Business Cycle

Although the housing sector forms a relatively small part of the economy, fluctuations in the sector occur so rapidly that it makes a significant contribution to overall economic movements.

- Since most home sales are usually financed by mortgage loans, housing sector activity is particularly sensitive to the level of interest rates. A rise (fall) in interest rates leads to a decline (an increase) in home purchasing and construction.
- Home sales are also affected by income levels relative to housing prices. Low housing prices relative to income, coupled with low costs of supporting an average house (when mortgage rates are low), increase demand for housing units.

External Trade Sector Behavior and the Business Cycle

- An increase in **domestic GDP** leads to an increase in demand for imports. Domestic exports usually tend to rise with an increase in **GDP of major trading partners** even if the domestic economy is weak. Therefore, patterns of external trade balances are not directly linked to domestic economic cycles.
- An appreciation of the domestic **currency** makes imports cheaper and, at the same time, makes domestic goods more expensive for trading partners, reducing net exports.
- GDP growth differentials have a more immediate and straightforward impact on the external trade balance.
- Currency movements have a more complex and gradual impact on the trade balance.

Business Cycle Theories

Neoclassical Economics

- **Neoclassical economists** (especially advocates of **real business cycle [RBC] theory**), place particular emphasis on movements in the supply curve.

- They believe a shift in the supply curve may be caused by technological progress, natural disasters, changes in relative prices of key inputs, or other supply-side constraints.
- They assert that the government should not intervene in the economy (through fiscal or monetary policy), primarily because of lags in recognition, implementation, and impact.
- They stress the importance of expectations and information management in mitigating economic volatility.
- They are believers in Schumpeterian "creative destruction." Innovations can generate movements in the aggregate supply curve that policy makers should not try to correct.

The Austrian School

- The Austrian school shares many views of the neoclassical economists (including advocating for no government intervention).
- However, it places greater important on the role of money. The Austrian school argues that when governments try to increase employment and GDP through expansionary monetary policies, interest rates fall below their natural rate, which leads to overinvestment (an inflationary gap). Once companies realize that they have gone overboard, they cut back spending drastically, which reduces aggregate demand and causes a recession.
- Basically, the Austrian school asserts that only the government causes a "boom-and-bust" cycle. To restore equilibrium, the economy must be left alone, and all prices (including wages) must decrease.

These classical views assert that markets are generally flexible, and prices will easily adjust to changing situations. This makes the aggregate supply curve very steep, even in the short run.

Monetarism

- Monetarists believe the government's role in the economy should be limited to maintaining steady growth of the money supply.
- Fiscal and monetary policy should be clear and consistent over time so all economic agents can forecast government actions.
- Business cycles may occur both because of exogenous shocks and because of government intervention.
- In contrast to Keynesian economists, they reject active management of aggregate demand.
- In contrast to neoclassical economists, a key part of monetarist thought is that the money supply needs to continue to grow at a moderate rate.
  - If it falls (as was the case in the 1930s) the economic downturn could be severe.
  - On the other hand, if money grows too fast, inflation will follow.

Keynesianism

- Keynesians see an active role for the government in managing aggregate demand.
- They give limited importance to the supply curve, as they believe it is relatively flat in the short run (resulting in "sticky" prices).
- They believe that the general price and wage reduction (required under the Austrian and neoclassical schools to bring the economy out of a recession) are hard to attain.
- Even if nominal wages were reduced, lower salary expectations would only result in a further decline in aggregate demand and actually exacerbate a recession (the domino effect).

- Lower interest rates will not necessarily reignite growth due to weak business confidence.
- The economy's self-correcting mechanism may work in the long run, but definitely should not be relied upon in the short run. It is the short run that really matters.
- Therefore, the government should step in during a recession and stimulate aggregate demand (via larger fiscal deficits) to keep labor and capital employed.

Criticisms of Keynesian Fiscal Policy

- Fiscal deficits imply higher government debt, which must be serviced and repaid. The government may lose control over its finances trying to stimulate aggregate demand.
- While the government can try to fix the economy in the short run by stimulating demand, its actions may result in the economy overheating in the long run.
- There is a time lag until fiscal actions take effect in the economy. It is possible that the government's actions may only kick in once the economy is already recovering.
- Unlike the monetarist model, the Keynesian model does not recognize the supreme importance of the money supply.

Today's mainstream economists in practice use an analytical framework that encompasses neoclassical economics, Keynesian economics, and monetarism.

Economic Indicators

An **economic indicator** is a variable that provides information on the state of the broader economy.

- **Leading economic indicators** have turning points that **usually** precede the turning points of the broader economy. Economists use them to predict the economy's **future state**.
- **Coincident economic indicators** have turning points that usually occur **close to** the turning points of the broader economy. Economists use them to identify the **current state** of the economy.
- **Lagging economic indicators** have turning points that usually occur **after** the turning points of the broader economy. Economists use them to identify the economy's **past condition**.

More About Economic Indicators

- Practitioners take an aggregate perspective when interpreting various economic indicators. Typically aggregate measures are combined into composites known to lead the cycle, coincide with the cycle or lag the cycle.
- Composites for different countries are usually composed of different indicators based on their own historical experiences.
- The timing record of various composite indices has varied considerably.
- The relationship between an indicator and the business cycle can be quite uncertain.
  - This is why analysts combine different indicators with common factors among them when constructing indicator indices, and why diffusion indices are used.

U.S. Economic Indicators[3]

Indicator and Description	
Leading	*Reason*
1. Average weekly hours, manufacturing	Because businesses will cut overtime before laying off workers in a downturn and increase it before rehiring in a cyclical upturn, these measures move up and down before the general economy.
2. Average weekly initial claims for unemployment insurance	This measure offers a very sensitive test of initial layoffs and rehiring.
3. Manufacturers' new orders for consumer goods and materials	Because businesses cannot wait too long to meet demands for consumer goods or materials without ordering, these gauges tend to lead at upturns and downturns. Indirectly, they capture changes in business sentiment as well, which also often leads the cycle.
4. ISM new order index[a]	This index is a diffusion index that refects the month-to-month change in new orders for final sales. The weakening of demand, which can lead to a recession, is usually first refected in the decline of new orders.
5. Manufacturers' new orders for non-defense capital goods excluding aircraft	In addition to offering a first signal of movement, up or down, in an important economic sector, movement in this area also indirectly captures business expectations.
6. Building permits for new private housing units	Because most localities require permits before new building can begin, this gauge foretells new construction activity.
7. S&P 500 Index	Because stock prices anticipate economic turning points, both up and down, their movements offer a useful early signal on economic cycles.
8. Leading Credit Index	This index aggregates the information from six leading fnancial indicators, which refect the strength of the fnancial system to endure stress. A vulnerable fnancial system can amplify and propagate the effects of negative shocks, resulting in a widespread recession for the whole economy.
9. Interest-rate spread between 10-year Treasury yields and overnight borrowing rates (federal funds rate)	Because long-term yields express market expectations about the direction of short-term interest rates, and rates ultimately follow the economic cycle up and down, a wider spread, by anticipating short rate increases, also anticipates an economic upswing. Conversely, a narrower spread, by anticipating short rate decreases, also anticipates an economic downturn.
10. Average consumer expectations for business and economic conditions	If consumers are optimistic about future business and economic conditions, they tend to increase spending. Because consumption is economic conditions about two-thirds of the U.S. economy, its future movements offer early insight into the direction ahead for the whole economy.

	Coincident	Reason
1.	Employees on non-agricultural payrolls	Once recession or recovery is clear, businesses adjust their full-time payrolls.
2.	Aggregate real personal income (less transfer payments)	By measuring the income fow from non-corporate profts and wages, this measure captures the current state of the economy.
3.	Industrial Production Index	Measures industrial output, thus capturing the behavior of the most volatile part of the economy. The service sector tends to be more stable.
4.	Manufacturing and trade sales	In the same way as aggregate personal income and the industrial production index, this aggregate offers a measure of the current state of business activity.

	Lagging	Reason
1.	Average duration of unemployment	Because businesses wait until downturns look genuine to lay off, and wait until recoveries look secure to rehire, this measure is important because it lags the cycle on both the way down and the way up.
2.	Inventory-to-sales ratio	Because inventories accumulate as sales initially decline and then, once a business adjusts its ordering, become depleted as sales pick up, this ratio tends to lag the cycle.
3.	Change in unit labor costs	Because businesses are slow to fire workers, these costs tend to rise into the early stages of recession as the existing labor force is used less intensely. Late in the recovery when the labor market gets tight, upward pressure on wages can also raise such costs. In both cases, there is a clear lag at cyclical turns.
4.	Average bank prime lending rate	Because this is a bank-administered rate, it tends to lag other rates that move either before cyclical turns or with them.
5.	Commercial and industrial loans outstanding	Because these loans frequently support inventory building, they lag the cycle for much the same reason that the inventory-sales ratio does.
6.	Ratio of consumer installment debt to income	Because consumers only borrow heavily when confident, this measure lags the cyclical upturn, but debt also overstays cyclical downturns because households have trouble adjusting to income losses, causing it to lag in the downturn.
7.	Change in consumer price index for services	Inflation generally adjusts to the cycle late, especially in the more stable services area.

[3] Exhibit 5, Volume 2, CFA Program Curriculum 2022

[a] A diffusion index usually measures the percentage of components in a series that are rising in the same period. It indicates how widespread a particular movement in the trend is among the individual components.

Measuring Unemployment

- **Employed**: Number of people with a job. This excludes those working in the informal sector (e.g., unlicensed cab drivers, illegal workers, etc.).
- **Labor force**: Number of people who either have a job, or are actively looking for one. This excludes people who are not employed and are not actively seeking employment (e.g., retirees, children, stay-at-home parents, fulltime students, etc.).
- **Unemployed**: People who are currently without a job, but are actively looking for one.
  - **Long-term unemployed**: People who have been out of work for a long time (more than 3-4 months) and are still looking for a job.
  - **Frictionally unemployed**: People who have just left a job and are about to start another one i.e., they already have a job waiting for them, which they have not started yet.
- **Activity (or participation) ratio**: Ratio of the labor force to total working age population (usually those between 16 and 64 years of age).
- **Underemployed**: People who currently have jobs, but have the qualifications to do significantly higher-paying jobs. They are not considered unemployed.
- **Discouraged worker**: A person who has stopped looking for a job. These people are excluded from the labor force and therefore, not accounted for in the official unemployment rate.
- **Voluntarily unemployed**: These are people who choose to remain outside the labor force (e.g., workers who retire early, or those who are unwilling to take up a vacancy because the wage offered is lower than their threshold).

The Unemployment Rate

The unemployment rate equals the ratio of the number of people who are unemployed to the total labor force. Although unemployment measures provide useful insights into the current state of an economy, they are not very useful in predicting an economy's cyclical direction as they are lagging economic indicators. This is because:

- The size of the labor force responds to changes in economic conditions.
- Businesses are reluctant to lay off workers at the first sign of economic weakness and are slow to rehire previously laid-off workers in the early stages of a recovery.

Overall Payroll Employment and Productivity Indicators

- **Size of payrolls:** This measure is not biased by the number of discouraged workers. Generally speaking, payrolls tend to shrink when the economy slides into a recession, and rise when a recovery is underway.
- The **number of hours worked** (especially overtime), and the use of **temporary workers**, tend to increase at the first signs of a recovery, and decrease at the first signs of economic weakness.
- An economy's **productivity** is measured by dividing total output by the number of hours worked. It measures the intensity of workflow of existing employees. Productivity measures (if available promptly) can identify an economy's cyclical direction even before a change in the number of hours worked is noticed. Productivity increases during an expansion (as output rises) and decreases during a recession (as output falls).

Inflation, Disinflation, and Deflation

Inflation: Generally speaking, inflation is procyclical (i.e., it goes up and down with the business cycle), but with a lag of around one year. **Inflation** is defined as a persistent increase in the overall level of prices (aggregate price level) in an economy over a period of time. The **inflation rate** measures the speed of overall price movements by calculating the rate of change in a price index. Both investors and policy-makers watch the inflation rate very closely.

Deflation: Deflation is defined as a persistent decrease in the aggregate level of prices in an economy over a period of time. The value of money actually rises in a deflationary environment. Since most debt contracts are written in fixed monetary amounts, the liability (in real terms) of the borrower rises during deflation.

Hyperinflation: Hyperinflation refers to a situation when the inflation rate is extremely high. It typically occurs when, instead of being backed by real tax revenue, large-scale government spending is supported by an increase in money supply.

Disinflation: Disinflation is defined as a fall in the inflation rate (e.g., from 15% to 5%). Disinflation is very different from deflation in the sense that deflation refers to a situation when the inflation rate is negative (aggregate price level is decreasing), while disinflation refers to a situation when the inflation rate falls, but remains positive (the aggregate price level continues to increase, but at a slower rate).

Price Indices

A price index that holds quantities of goods in the consumption basket constant is called a **Laspeyres index**. Most price indices around the world are Laspeyres indices, and consumption baskets are only updated after a certain number of years (typically 5). Using a fixed basket of goods and services to measure the cost of living gives rise to three biases:

- **Substitution bias**: Changes in the relative prices of goods motivate consumers to replace expensive goods with cheaper substitutes. Use of a fixed basket results in an upward bias in the computed inflation rate. Use of **chained price index formulas** (e.g., the Fisher index) can mitigate this bias.
- **Quality bias**: Improvements in product quality sometimes come at the cost of higher prices. If price indices are not adjusted for quality improvements, there will be an upward bias in the measured inflation rate. Prices can be adjusted for quality improvements through a practice known as **hedonic pricing**.
- **New product bias**: Recently introduced products are not included in the price index if the consumption basket is fixed. This usually creates an upward bias in the measured inflation rate. In order to mitigate this bias, new products can be introduced into the basket more regularly.

A **Paasche Index** is based on the current composition of the basket.

A **Fisher Index** is calculated as the geometric mean of the Laspeyres index and the Paasche index.

Cost-Push Inflation

Cost-push inflation occurs when rising costs compel businesses to raise prices. Costs of production may rise because of an increase in money wage rates, or an increase in the price of raw materials.

The effect of labor market constraints on wage rates is usually observed relative to the **natural rate of unemployment (NARU)**. It is at the natural rate of unemployment (not at 0% unemployment) that the economy begins to experience bottlenecks in the labor market and feel wage-push inflationary pressures. It is preferred to combine trends in labor costs with productivity measures to evaluate the state of the labor market.

Labor productivity (output per hour) is important because it determines the number of units across which businesses can spread their labor costs. **Unit labor cost (ULC)** is calculated as:

$$ULC = W/O$$

- If wage rates grow at a faster rate than labor productivity, business's costs per unit of output (ULC) increase. Businesses then look to increase output prices to protect profit margins so the end result is cost-push inflation.
- If wage rates increase at a slower rate than labor productivity, ULC falls. This eases inflationary pressures.

Demand-Pull Inflation

Demand-pull inflation is caused by increasing demand, which causes higher prices and eventually results in higher wages to compensate for the rise in cost of living. Demand-pull inflation may be analysed based on the economy's capacity utilization levels:

- As the economy's actual GDP approaches its potential GDP (capacity utilization increases), there is an increase in the probability of shortages and bottlenecks occurring, so prices tend to rise.
- The further the economy operates below its potential output, the greater the probability of a slowdown in inflation (or even outright deflation).

Monetarists' Views on Inflation

Monetarists believe that inflation occurs when the growth rate of money supply in the economy outpaces growth in GDP. They explicitly place the blame for demand-pull inflation on excess money growth.

- If money growth exceeds nominal GDP growth, there is a possibility of inflation.
- If money growth is slower than nominal GDP growth, there could be disinflationary or deflationary pressures in the economy.

Inflation Expectations

Inflation expectations also play an important role in policy-making. Once economic agents start expecting prices to continue to rise going forward, they change their actions in line with those expectations. This can lead to higher inflation and cause it to persist in the economy even after its real underlying cause is no longer present.

MONETARY AND FISCAL POLICY
Cross-Reference to CFA Institute Assigned Reading #12

Monetary Policy

- **Monetary policy** refers to the government's or central bank's manipulation of money supply to influence the quantity of money and credit in the economy.

The Functions of Money

- Medium of exchange
- Store of value
- Unit of account

Paper Money and the Money Creation Process

> Required reserve ratio = Required reserves / Total deposits

> Money multiplier = 1/(Reserve requirement) = 1/(0.2) = 5

The banking system as a whole that goes through the following cycle and increases the quantity of money:

1. Banks have excess reserves.
2. They lend the excess reserves.
3. Bank deposits increase.
4. Quantity of money increases.
5. Deposits in the banking system increase.
6. These deposits in turn create excess reserves which are loaned out.

Definitions of Money

- **Narrow money** refers to notes and coins in circulation plus other highly liquid deposits.
- **Broad money** includes narrow money plus the entire range of liquid assets that can be used to make purchases.

Checking account balances are included in measures of money. Checks make this transfer possible but this does not make the check itself money. Credit cards are not money either.

The Quantity Theory of Money

The **quantity theory of money** expresses the relationship between money and the price level. The **quantity equation of exchange** states that:

$$M \times V = P \times Y$$

Money neutrality says that an increase in money supply will not result in an increase in real output (Y). Therefore, an increase in money supply will cause the aggregate price level (P) to rise. The assertions of the quantity theory of money are in line with the consequences of money neutrality (as velocity is assumed constant).

Monetarists use the quantity theory of money to support their belief that inflation can be controlled by manipulating the money supply growth rate.

The Demand for Money

Transactions-related demand for money arises from the need to use money to finance transactions. Generally speaking, transactions-related demand for money is positively related to average transaction size and overall GDP.

Precautionary money balances are held for use in unforeseen circumstances. Precautionary balances are positively related to average transactions size, total volume of transactions, and therefore to overall GDP as well.

Speculative or portfolio demand for money is related to perceived opportunities and risks of holding other financial instruments (such as bonds). Speculative demand for money is inversely related to the returns available on other financial assets. At the same time, it is positively related to the perceived risk in these financial assets.

Supply and Demand for Money

Money supply is assumed fixed so it is represented by a vertical line. Money demand is inversely related to interest rates (speculative money demand increases as interest rates fall). Therefore, money demand is represented by a downward-sloping line. The point of intersection between the money demand and supply curves determines short run equilibrium nominal interest rates.

The Fisher Effect

The Fisher effect is directly related to the concept of money neutrality. It states that the nominal interest rate (R_N) reflects the real interest rate (R_R) and the expected rate of inflation (Π^e).

$$R_N = R_R + \Pi^e$$

The Fisher effect does not consider uncertainty. The greater the uncertainty, the higher the required risk premium.

The Roles of the Central Bank

- Monopoly supplier of currency.
- Banker to the government (and to other banks) and lender of last resort.
- Supervise the banking system.
- Oversee, regulate, and set the standards for a country's payments system.
- Manage the country's foreign currency and gold reserves.
- Conducting monetary policy.

Objectives of Monetary Policy

- Maximum employment.
- Stable prices (this is the overarching objective of most central banks).
- Moderate long-term interest rates.

Costs of Inflation

Expected inflation is the inflation rate that economic agents expect to see in the economy in the future. Expected inflation gives rise to **menu costs** and **shoe leather costs**. Expected or anticipated inflation is reflected in all long-term contracts. People accept this level of inflation, and budget for it.

Unexpected inflation is the level of inflation that comes as a surprise to economic agents. It is arguably more costly than expected inflation. In addition to the costs of expected inflation, unexpected inflation also leads to:

- **Inequitable transfers of wealth** between borrowers and lenders.
  - If actual inflation is less than expected inflation (which is built into nominal interest rates) lenders benefit and borrowers lose out as the real value of payments on debts rises.
  - If actual inflation is greater than expected inflation, borrowers benefit and lenders lose out as the real value of payments on debts falls.
- **Higher risk premia in borrowing rates**: Higher uncertainty associated with future inflation leads to lenders demanding a higher risk premium, which inflates the nominal interest rate and hurts economic activity.
- **A reduction in the information content of market prices**: Businesses may attribute an increase in prices of their products to an increase in demand (or decrease in supply) when in fact, the price increase may be in line with the overall level of inflation in the economy. Businesses would increase production only to find that they are struggling to sell their output, and involuntarily build up inventories. As a result, they would cut back production drastically, which would hurt the economy.

Monetary Policy Tools

Required reserve ratio: An increase in the required reserve ratio results in a decrease in money supply.

The central bank's policy rate: Generally speaking, the higher the policy rate, the higher the penalty that banks will have to pay the central bank if they run short of liquidity. This would make them more conservative in lending, reducing broad money supply.

Open market operations: An open-market sale (purchase) directly reduces (increases) banks' reserves.

The Transmission Mechanism

If the central bank increases its official policy rate:

- Banks respond to the increase in the official interest rate by increasing their **base rates** (the reference rates on which they base lending rates to customers). As a result, individuals and businesses borrow less.
- Asset prices and values of capital projects tend to fall as present values of expected future cash flows decline.
- Economic agents' expectations regarding the economy are dampened as they associate higher interest rates with slower future economic growth and reduced profits.
- The domestic currency appreciates in value (as hot money flows in). This makes domestic goods and services more pricey (less competitive) in the international market, leading to a decline in exports.
- If the increase in interest rates is widely expected to be followed by further rate hikes, economic agents will change their behavior to reflect these revised expectations.
- Overall, the decline in consumption, borrowing, and asset prices will reduce aggregate demand.
- Weaker demand will reduce domestic prices. This, along with lower import prices, (due to appreciation of the domestic currency) will put a downward pressure on actual inflation.

Monetary Policy Strategies

Inflation targeting: Under this strategy, the central bank makes a public commitment to achieving an explicit inflation target, and to explaining how its actions will achieve that target. The argument here is that inflationary expectations must be managed, and, when everyone is aware (and believes) that the central bank will move to contain inflation within an acceptable range, spending and investing decisions will be made wisely.

Exchange rate targeting: The central bank supports a target exchange rate by buying and selling the domestic currency in the foreign exchange market. Basically, the aim here is to "import" the inflation experience of an economy with a good track record on inflation, by tying the domestic currency to the currency of that economy.

Qualities of Effective Central Banks

The central bank should be **independent** and not come under political pressures when formulating policy. There are two aspects of central bank independence:

- **Operational independence** is when the central bank decides the level of interest rates.
- **Target independence** is when the central bank determines the inflation rate that is targeted and the horizon over which this target is to be achieved.

The public should have confidence in the central bank i.e., it must have **credibility**. If economic agents believe that the central bank will hit its inflation target, the belief itself could become self-fulfilling.

There should be **transparency** in the central bank's decision-making. Transparency comes from the central bank clearly explaining its views on the economy and communicating its views on various economic indicators to economic agents on a regular basis.

Finally (if the central bank follows an inflation targeting strategy), the central bank must have a **realistic, forward-looking inflation target**.

Contractionary and Expansionary Monetary Policies

- When the central bank believes that the current growth rate of economic activity will lead to inflation, it will look to reduce money supply and increase interest rates. Such actions are known as **contractionary** measures as they are meant to rein in an overheating economy.
- When the central bank believes that the current level of economic growth is too slow and inflation is weakening, it will look to increase money supply and reduce interest rates. Such actions are known as **expansionary** measures as they are meant to stimulate a receding economy.

The Neutral Rate of Interest

The **neutral rate** is the rate of interest that neither slows down, nor spurs growth in the underlying economy. When the policy rate is below (above) the neutral rate, monetary policy is expansionary (contractionary). However, economists' estimates of the neutral rate for a given economy typically vary. What they do agree on, is that the neutral rate has two components:

1. **Real trend of growth in the underlying economy**: This corresponds to the rate of economic growth that gives rise to stable inflation in the long run.
2. **Long run expected inflation**.

Limitations of Monetary Policy

- Central banks cannot control the amount of money that households and businesses choose to save.
- While central banks can influence the ability of banks to extend loans and create credit, they cannot easily control the willingness of banks to do so.
- If the central bank lacks credibility, there is a lower chance of its "policy message" being successfully transmitted through the economy.

Fiscal Policy

Roles and Objectives of Fiscal Policy

The main aim of fiscal policy is to regulate the economy's real GDP by influencing aggregate demand.

Fiscal policy is an important tool for economic stabilization through its impact on output.

- In a recession, governments can increase spending and/or reduce taxes (expansionary fiscal policy) to try to raise employment and output.
- In an expansion, governments can reduce spending and/or increase taxes (contractionary fiscal policy) to try to control inflation.

The **budget surplus/deficit** equals the difference between the government's revenue and expenditure over a period of time. Analysts look at the change in the budgetary position to determine whether fiscal policy is getting tighter or looser:

- An increase (decrease) in a budget surplus is contractionary (expansionary).
- An increase (decrease) in a budget deficit is expansionary (contractionary).

Automatic stabilizers work in the absence of explicit action by the government to bring the economy towards full employment. There are two automatic stabilizers embedded in fiscal policy.

- Induced taxes
- Needs-tested spending

Discretionary fiscal actions are enacted by the government, and involve changing tax rates or the level of government spending. Basically, these actions are up to the government's discretion as opposed to automatic stabilizers, which act on their own to bring the economy towards full employment.

Deficits and National Debt

Reasons to be concerned about national debt relative to GDP:

- High debt levels may lead to high tax rates (to service the debt) going forward. Higher expected future tax rates may serve as a disincentive for labor and entrepreneurial activity.
- If markets lose confidence in the government, the central bank may have to print money to finance the deficit. This would lead to high inflation (e.g., Zimbabwe in 2008–2009).
- Government spending may **crowd out** private investment. Higher demand for borrowing (to finance the deficit) by the government would raise interest rates, reducing private sector investment.

Reasons not to be concerned about national debt relative to GDP:

- The problem is not really a major issue if debt is owed to the country's own citizens. In this case the government can just print money to retire the debt. However, note that this strategy comes with the risk of high inflation.
- Some of the borrowed funds may have been used for capital investment projects, which would raise the economy's productive capacity (and tax revenues) going forward.
- The private sector may adjust to offset fiscal deficits by increasing savings in anticipation of future tax increases (to finance the deficit). This is known as **Ricardian equivalence**: The increase in government spending (or reduction in taxes) meant to stimulate aggregate demand will have no impact on economic activity as economic agents will save more because they expect the government to finance the deficit by increasing taxes in the future.
- If there is widespread unemployment in the economy, fiscal deficits will not be diverting any resources away from productive uses so total output will increase.
- Large fiscal deficits require tax changes, which may correct the distortions created by the current tax structure.

Fiscal Policy Tools and the Macroeconomy

Government spending takes the following forms:

- Transfer payments
- Current government spending
- Capital expenditure

Justifications for Government Spending

- The government provides services such as defense that benefit all citizens equally.
- Infrastructure spending helps the country's economic growth.
- Helps redistribute wealth in society.
- Can be used as a tool to control inflation unemployment, and growth.
- Can be used to subsidize the development of innovative and high-risk new products (e.g., alternative energy).

Types of Taxes

- Direct taxes
- Indirect taxes

Taxes can be justified in terms of raising revenue to finance government expenditure and in terms of income and wealth redistribution.

Desirable Properties of Tax Policy

- Simplicity
- Efficiency
- Fairness
- Revenue sufficiency

Advantages and Disadvantages of Different Fiscal Policy Tools

Advantages:

- Indirect taxes can be adjusted very quickly. They are very effective in influencing spending behavior and in generating revenue at little cost to the government.
- Social objectives (e.g., reducing alcohol or cigarette consumption) can easily be met by raising indirect taxes.

Disadvantages:

- Direct taxes, and welfare and other social transfers are difficult to change without significant notice. However, they begin to have an impact on behavior soon after their announcement.
- Capital spending decisions are slow to plan, implement and execute.

In addition to their direct effects on the economy, the above-mentioned fiscal policy tools also have strong expectational effects on the economy.

- Direct government spending has a much bigger impact on aggregate spending and output than income tax cuts or transfer increases.
- However, if transfer increases target the poorest in society (whose marginal propensity to consume is highest), they can have a relatively strong impact on spending.

The Fiscal Multiplier

$$\frac{1}{[1 - \text{MPC}(1 - t)]}$$

The Balanced Budget Multiplier

The balanced budget multiplier is positive. An increase in government spending combined with an equivalent dollar increase in taxes leads to a higher real GDP.

Issues in Fiscal Policy Implementation

Deficits and the Fiscal Stance

The size of a fiscal deficit cannot be used to determine whether fiscal policy is expansionary or contractionary.

- Automatic stabilizers for example lead to changes in the budgetary status that are unrelated to fiscal policy changes. Therefore, economists look at the **structural** or **cyclically adjusted** budget deficit as an indicator of the government's fiscal stance. The structural deficit is the deficit that would exist were the economy working at full-employment.
- Government expenditure includes the cash amount of payments on debt, which inflates the actual deficit. This is because the real value of outstanding debt falls with inflation.

Difficulties in Executing Fiscal Policy

Recognition lag: This refers to the time that it takes the government to figure out that the economy is not functioning at its potential output.

EC

Action lag: The government might have recognized the need for action, but its implementation may be delayed in obtaining the necessary approvals.

Impact lag: This refers to the time it takes for a fiscal stimulus to flow through the economy and generate the changes in spending patterns that are desired.

The Relationships between Monetary and Fiscal Policy

Easy fiscal policy/tight monetary policy: Results in higher output, higher interest rates and government expenditure would form a larger component of national income.

Tight fiscal policy/easy monetary policy: The private sector's share of overall GDP would rise (as a result of low interest rates), while the public sector's share would fall.

Easy fiscal policy/easy monetary policy: This would lead to a sharp increase in aggregate demand, lowering interest rates and growing private and public sectors.

Tight fiscal policy/tight monetary policy: This would lead to a sharp decrease in aggregate demand, higher interest rates and a decrease in demand from both private and public sectors.

Factors Influencing the Mix of Fiscal and Monetary Policy

- If the government is primarily concerned with growing the economy's potential output, it should aim to keep interest rates low and keep fiscal policy relatively tight to ensure that free resources are available in the growing economy.
- If the government's main concern is to build infrastructure and develop high quality human capital, it should focus on spending in those areas. If monetary policy is kept loose during this time, inflation may result.

INTERNATIONAL TRADE AND CAPITAL FLOWS
Cross-Reference to CFA Institute Assigned Reading #13

Gross Domestic Product (GDP) measures the market value of all **final** goods and services produced by factors of production (e.g., labor, capital, etc.) located **within** a country/economy during a period of time.

- GDP *includes* goods and services produced by foreigners within the country.
- GDP *excludes* goods and services produced by citizens outside the country.

Gross National Product (GNP) measures the market value of all final goods and services produced by factors of production (e.g., labor, capital, etc.) supplied by the citizens of the country, regardless of whether production takes place within or outside of the country.

- GNP *includes* goods and services produced by citizens outside the country.
- GNP *excludes* goods and services produced by foreigners within the country.

Terms of trade refer to the ratio of the price of exports to the price of imports.

FDI versus FPI

When a firm in the source country makes an investment in the productive assets of the host country, it is referred to as **Foreign Direct Investment (FDI)**.

Foreign Portfolio Investment (FPI) refers to shorter-term investments in foreign financial instruments (e.g., foreign stocks, foreign government bonds, etc.).

Benefits of International Trade

- Countries gain from exchange and specialization.
- Efficient resource allocation.
- Domestic companies gain access to global markets and customers, which leads to increased exchange of ideas and greater awareness of changing consumer tastes and preferences.
- Capital intensive industries gain access to much larger markets, enabling them to reap the benefits of economies of scale.
- Domestic households are able to choose from a wider variety of goods and services.
- Increased foreign competition reduces monopoly power of domestic firms and forces them to continuously strive to become more efficient.
- Trade liberalization can lead to higher inflation-adjusted GDP as a result of a more efficient allocation of resources, learning by doing, knowledge spillovers and improved productivity.

Costs of International Trade

- Companies that are less efficient than international firms may go out of business if foreign firms are allowed to enter the market. This will lead to **higher (structural) unemployment.**
- The counter argument is that despite the short and medium term costs and unemployment, these resources will eventually be reemployed in more efficient industries.

Comparative versus Absolute Advantage

Absolute advantage refers to a country's ability to produce a good at a lower cost or using fewer resources than its trading partners.

Comparative advantage refers to a country's ability to produce a particular good at a lower opportunity cost than its trading partners.

Even if a country does not have an absolute advantage in the production of a good or service, it (and its trading partners) can still gain from trade if it produces and exports goods in which it has a comparative advantage.

Trade Models and Sources of Comparative Advantage

Ricardian Model

- Assumes that labor is the only variable factor of production.
- A country gains a comparative advantage in the production of a good based on differences in labor productivity, which reflect underlying differences in technology.
- Differences in technology are the key source of comparative advantage.
- Even if the country is very small compared to the size of its trading partner, it will continue to produce the good that it holds a comparative advantage in, and trade some of it to obtain other goods.
- Technological gaps between countries can decrease over time, leading to shifts in comparative advantage.

Heckscher-Ohlin Model (also referred to as the factor-proportions theory)

- Assumes that both capital and labor are variable factors of production, so a good can be produced with varying combinations of the two.
- Technology is the same in each industry across countries, but it varies across different industries.
- Differences in factor endowments are the primary source of comparative advantage.
- A country has a comparative advantage in a good whose production requires intensive use of a factor with which it is relatively abundantly endowed.
- Allows for redistribution of income through trade as it assumes that more than one factor of production is variable.
- Theoretically, free trade should eventually result in equal prices of goods and services and equal prices of factors of production across countries.
  - However, in the real world trade only results in a tendency for factor prices to converge in the long run.

Arguments for Trade Restrictions

- Protection of established domestic industries from foreign competition.
- Protection of new (infant) industries from foreign competition until they mature.
- Protection of employment in the country.
- Generation of revenue from tariffs.
- Retaliation against trade restrictions imposed by trading partners.

Tariffs

When the government imposes a tariff on imports, the price effectively rises, domestic demand falls, domestic supply rises and the volume of imports falls.

- The government manages to lower the trade deficit (by decreasing imports) and also manages to earn some revenue for itself (Region C).
- There is an increase in producer surplus (Region A).
- Consumer surplus falls (Regions B, C, and D).
- The overall effect is a net decrease in welfare (Regions B and D).

Quotas

Quotas are restrictions on the quantity of a good that can be imported into a country for a specified period. When a quota is in place, each importing firm receives an **import license**, which specifies the quantity that it can import.

The main difference between tariffs and quotas is that the government earns direct revenue through tariffs, but this is not the case with quotas. With a quota, foreign producers may raise their prices to earn higher profits than they would in the absence of the quota. These profits are known as **quota rents**.

- Region C (previously government revenue from the tariff) is now more likely to be captured by foreign producers (quota rents), increasing the welfare loss for the importing country to Regions B+C+D (relative to just Regions B+D under a tariff).
- If the importing country can generate an amount equal to Area C by auctioning import licenses for a fee, then its welfare loss can be limited to just Regions B+D (as is the case with tariffs).
- Quota rents arising from a quota can be captured by the exporting country or the importing country.

Voluntary Export Restraints

Voluntary Export Restraints (VERs) are restrictions on the quantity of a good that can be exported. While quotas are imposed by the importing country, VERs are imposed by the exporting country. Under VERs, the exporting country captures the quota rent (Region C) but the welfare loss to the importing country equals Regions B, C and D.

Export Subsidies

Export subsidies refer to payments made by the government to domestic exporters of certain goods. While they aim to stimulate exports, export subsidies interfere with the free market mechanism and may result in trade patterns that diverge from those dictated by comparative advantage. Further, domestic producers would be more inclined to export their output rather than selling it in the domestic market.

Effects of Alternative Trade Policies

Panel A: Effects of Alternative Trade Policies

	Tariff	Import Quota	Export Subsidy	VER
Impact on	Importing country	Importing country	Exporting country	Importing country
Producer surplus	Increases	Increases	Increases	Increases
Consumer surplus	Decreases	Decreases	Decreases	Decreases
Government revenue	Increases	Mixed (depends on whether the quota rents are captured by the importing country through sale of licenses or by the exporters)	Falls (government spending rises)	No change (rent to foreigners)
National welfare	Decreases in small country Could increase in large country	Decreases in small country Could increase in large country	Decreases	Decreases

Panel B: Effects of Alternative Trade Policies on Price, Production, Consumption, and Trade

	Tariff	Import Quota	Export Subsidy	VER
Impact on	Importing country	Importing country	Exporting country	Importing country
Price	Increases	Increases	Increases	Increases
Domestic consumption	Decreases	Decreases	Decreases	Decreases
Domestic production	Increases	Increases	Increases	Increases
Trade	Imports decrease	Imports decrease	Exports increase	Imports decrease

Capital Restrictions

Capital restrictions are defined as controls placed on foreigners' ability to own domestic assets and/or domestic citizens' ability to own foreign assets.

Common Objectives

- The government may place restrictions on inward investment by foreigners relating to how much can be invested, and in which industries.
    - The government may impose ownership restrictions on strategic industries such as defense and telecommunications.
    - The government may forbid foreign investment into certain industries to protect domestic companies from foreign competition, and to protect jobs.

- The government may place restrictions on outflow of capital from repatriation of capital, interest, profits, royalty payments, and license fees, and on foreign investments by its citizens in order to conserve scarce foreign exchange reserves.
- Capital restrictions are often used in conjunction with other policy instruments, such as fixed exchange rate targets to achieve policy objectives in times of macroeconomic crises.
  - Capital controls are used to control the economy's external balance, while other, more traditional policy tools are used to pursue other objectives.

Forms of Capital Controls

- Taxes
- Price controls
- Quantity controls
- Outright prohibitions on international trade in assets

Benefits of Free Movement of Financial Capital

- Allows capital to be invested wherever it will earn the highest return.
- The economy's productive capacity can grow at a higher rate than possible based on domestic savings alone.
- Foreign firms may enter domestic industries, bringing competition to local firms, which may:
  - Encourage local firms to improve the quality of their goods and services.
  - Lead to better prices.
  - Bring new technologies into the country.

Effectiveness of Capital Controls

An IMF study found that:

- Effective controls on capital inflows entail significant administrative costs.
- Imposition of controls on capital outflows during times of financial crisis have produced mixed results:
  - They have only provided temporary relief to some countries, but offered others (e.g., Malaysia in 1997) enough time to restructure their economies.
  - If the government is wary of capital leaving the country, capital controls (when combined with fixed exchange rates) afford the central bank a degree of monetary policy independence that would not be possible without capital controls.

Costs of Capital Controls

- Administrative costs.
- Controls may give rise to negative market perceptions and make it more costly for the country to raise foreign funds.
- Protection of domestic financial markets may delay necessary policy adjustments or impede private-sector adaptation to changing international circumstances.

Trade Blocs

Members of a regional trading agreement (RTA) agree to eliminate barriers to trade and movement of factors of production among the members of the bloc.

Members of a **free trade area (FTA)**, for example NAFTA, eliminate almost all barriers to free trade with each other. However, each member still maintains its own policies regarding trade with non-member countries.

A **customs union** (e.g., Benelux) is very similar to an FTA, but all member countries have similar policies regarding trade with non-member countries.

A **common market** (e.g., MERCOSUR) incorporates all the provisions of a customs union, and also allows free movement of factors of production among the member countries.

An **economic union** (e.g., EU) incorporates all the aspects of a common market and also requires common economic institutions and coordination of economic policies among member countries. If the members of the economic union decide to adopt a common currency, it is also referred to as a **monetary union**.

Trade Creation versus Trade Diversion

Only if trade creation is larger than trade diversion, is there a positive net effect on welfare from forming the trade bloc.

- **Trade creation** occurs when higher-cost domestic production is replaced with lower-cost imports from fellow members of a trade bloc.
- **Trade diversion** occurs when lower-cost imports from non-member countries are replaced with higher-cost imports from member countries (because tariffs are imposed on imports from non-member countries but not on imports from member countries).

Advantages of Trade Blocs

All the benefits of free trade (greater specialization, reduction in monopoly power due to competition, economies of scale, learning by doing, knowledge spillovers, technology transfers, better quality intermediate inputs, etc.) apply to trade blocs as well. Further, trade blocs:

- Reduce the potential for conflict among members.
- Give members greater bargaining power in the global economy as they form a united front.
- Offer new opportunities for trade and investment.
- Typically, growth in a member country tends to spill over into other members as well.

Challenges in the Formation of an RTA

- Cultural differences and historical conflicts may complicate the process of integration.
- Free trade and mobility of labor limit the extent to which member countries can pursue independent economic and social policies.

The Balance of Payments

The **balance of payments (BOP)** is a double entry bookkeeping system that summarizes a country's economic transactions with the rest of the world over a period of time.

Balance of Payment Components

The **current account** can be decomposed into the following sub-accounts:

- **Merchandise trade** consists of all commodities and manufactured goods bought, sold or given away.
- **Services** include tourism, transportation, engineering and business services.

- **Income receipts** include income from ownership of foreign assets (e.g., interest and dividends).
- **Unilateral transfers** represent one-way transfers of assets (e.g., worker remittances, foreign aid and gifts).

The **capital account** can be decomposed into the following sub-accounts:

- **Capital transfers** include debt forgiveness and migrants' transfers. They also include:
    - Transfer of ownership of fixed assets
    - Transfer of funds received for the sale or acquisition of fixed assets
    - Gift and inheritance taxes
    - Death duties
    - Uninsured damage to fixed assets
- **Sales and purchases of non-produced, non-financial assets** such as rights to natural resources, intangible assets (e.g., patents, copyrights, etc.)

The **financial account** can be decomposed into the following sub-accounts:

- **Financial assets abroad** are composed of:
    - Official reserve assets
    - Government assets
    - Private assets
- **Foreign owned financial assets** in the reporting country are composed of:
    - Official assets
    - Other foreign assets

National Economic Accounts and the Balance of Payments

$$Y = C + I + G + X - M$$

- A current account deficit must be financed by foreign direct investment, loans by foreign banks, or the sale of domestic debt and equity securities to foreign investors.
- A current account surplus is used to finance the current account deficit of trading partners (through loans and investments in real and financial assets).

$$CA = X - M = Y - (C + I + G)$$

- A country can have a current account deficit and consume more than it produces ($C + I + G$ greater than Y) if it borrows the shortfall from foreigners.
- A country can have a current account surplus and consume less than it produces ($C + I + G$ less than Y) if it lends the shortfall to foreigners.

$$S_P + S_G = I + CA$$

- In a closed economy, savings can only be used for domestic investment.
- In an open economy, savings can be used for domestic and foreign investment.

$$S_P = I + CA - S_G$$

This equation clearly shows that an economy's private savings can be used for:

- Domestic investment.
- Foreign investment (purchasing assets from foreigners).
- Purchasing government debt.

$$CA = S_P + S_G - I$$

A current account deficit results from:

- Low private savings
- A government deficit
- High private investment

If a country running a trade deficit mainly borrows to finance consumption, then eventually it must reduce consumption to repay its debts. If the borrowings are mainly used to finance investment, then future economic growth is likely to provide the means to repay its liabilities.

World Bank Group

The World Bank's main objective is to fight poverty and enhance environmentally sound economic growth. The World Bank and its affiliated entities:

- Provide cheap loans and grants to countries that have limited or no access to international financial markets.
- Provide analysis, advice and information to countries to encourage social and economic development.
- Share knowledge and promote dialogue to increase the capabilities of their partners and members.
- Help members create the basic economic infrastructure that is essential for the development of domestic financial markets.

World Trade Organization (WTO)

The WTO's primary objective is to enhance and liberalize international trade.

- The WTO's important functions include the implementation, administration, and operation of individual agreements, providing a platform for negotiations and settling trade disputes.
- It also provides technical cooperation and training to developing, under developed and poor countries to bring them in compliance with WTO rules.
- It reviews members' trade policies on a regular basis and ensures coherence and transparency of trade policies through surveillance.
- It is a major source of economic research and analysis.
- Its framework of global trade rules provides a major institutional and regulatory base, without which large multinationals would not be able to operate on such a large scale.

International Monetary Fund

The main objective of the IMF is to ensure the stability of the international monetary system, the system of exchange rates and international payments that enables countries to participate in international trade. More specifically, the IMF:

- Provides a forum for cooperation on international monetary problems.
- Facilitates the growth of international trade, thereby promoting job creation, economic growth, and poverty reduction.
- Promotes exchange rate stability and an open system of international payments.
- Lends foreign exchange to member countries when needed, on a temporary basis and under adequate safeguards, to help them address balance of payments problems.

In the aftermath of the global financial crisis of 2007–2009, the IMF has redefined its operations by:

- Enhancing its lending facilities.
- Strengthening the monitoring of global, regional, and country economies.
- Helping resolve global economic imbalances.
- Analysing capital market developments.
- Assessing financial sector vulnerabilities.
- Working to cut poverty.

From an investment perspective the IMF helps to keep country-specific market risk and global systematic risk under control.

EC

CURRENCY EXCHANGE RATES
Cross-Reference to CFA Institute Assigned Reading #14

An exchange rate represents the price of one currency in terms of another currency. It is stated in terms of the number of units of a particular currency (**price currency**) required to purchase a unit of another currency (**base currency**). Stated differently, it is the cost of one unit of the base currency in terms of the price currency.

In this reading, we will refer to exchange rates using the convention "A/B," i.e. the number of units of Currency A (price currency) required to purchase one unit of Currency B (base currency). For example, suppose that the USD/GBP exchange rate is currently 1.5125. From this exchange rate quote we can infer that:

- The GBP is the base currency and USD is the price currency.
- It will take 1.5125 USD to purchase 1 GBP.
- 1 GBP will buy 1.5125 USD or 1 GBP costs 1.5125 USD.
- A decrease in this exchange rate (e.g., to 1.5120) means that 1 GBP will be able to purchase fewer USD.
- Alternatively, less USD will now be required to purchase 1 GBP (the cost of a GBP has fallen).
- This decrease in the exchange rate means that the GBP has **depreciated** (lost value) against the USD, or equivalently, the USD has **appreciated** (gained value) against the GBP.
- It would help you to think of exchange rates in the following manner: An increase in the quoted exchange rate (price/base) means an increase (appreciation) in the value of the currency in the denominator (base currency) and a decrease (depreciation) in the value of the currency in the numerator (price currency).
- The numerical value of the exchange rate and the value of the base currency are positively related.
- The numerical value of the exchange rate and the value of the price currency are negatively related.

Nominal versus Real Exchange Rates

- When the value of a currency is stated in terms of units of another currency (as in the example above), it is referred to as a **nominal exchange rate**.
- On the other hand, **real exchange rates** measure changes in the relative purchasing power of one currency compared with another.

Purchasing power parity (PPP) asserts that nominal exchange rates adjust to ensure that identical goods (or baskets of goods) have the same price in different countries.

- The nominal exchange rate and relative purchasing power are **inversely** related.
- The price level in the foreign country (or foreign inflation) and relative purchasing power are **inversely** related.
- The price level in the home country (or domestic inflation) and relative purchasing power are **positively** related.

Determining the Real Exchange Rate

An increase in purchasing power implies a decrease in the real exchange rate (in terms of DC/FC), i.e. purchasing power and the real exchange rate are **inversely** related. Therefore, we can say that the real exchange rate is:

- An increasing function of the nominal exchange rate (in terms of DC/FC).
- An increasing function of the foreign price level.
- A decreasing function of the domestic price level.

The real exchange rate may be calculated as:

$$\text{Real exchange rate}_{DC/FC} = S_{DC/FC} \times (P_{FC}/P_{DC})$$

Spot versus Forward Exchange Rates

Spot exchange rates (S) are quotes for transactions that call for immediate delivery. For most currencies, immediate delivery means "T + 2" delivery i.e., the transaction is actually settled 2 days after the trade is agreed upon by the parties.

Forward exchange rates (F) are quotes for transactions that are contracted (agreed upon) today, but settled at a pre-specified date in the future (settlement occurs after a longer period than the two days for spot transactions).

Types of Contracts Used for Trading Currencies

- Futures contracts
- FX swaps
- FX options

Functions of the Foreign Exchange Market

- Facilitate international trade
- Allow investors to convert between currencies in order to move funds into (or out of) foreign assets.
- Enable market participants who face exchange rate risk to hedge their risks.
- Allow investors to speculate on currency values.

Market Participants

Sell Side

- The very largest dealing banks
- All other regional and local banks

Buy Side

- Corporate accounts
- Real money accounts
- Leveraged accounts
- Retail accounts
- Governments
- Central banks
- Sovereign wealth funds (SWFs)

Market Size and Composition

- Investment pools and professional traders account for a large (and growing) proportion of FX market volumes. Portfolio flows and speculative activities dominate FX market volumes.
- High frequency algorithmic traders are accounting for a growing proportion of FX market volumes.
- Purchases and sales of foreign goods and services by individuals and corporations form a relatively small proportion of FX market volumes.
- London, New York, and Tokyo account for the highest FX market volumes.
- The majority of FX market transactions occur in the FX swap market.

Direct versus Indirect Quotes

- In a **direct currency quote (DC/FC)**, the *domestic* currency is stated as the *price* currency and *foreign* currency is stated as the *base* currency.
- In an **indirect currency quote (FC/DC)**, the *foreign* currency is stated as the *price* currency and *domestic* currency is stated as the *base* currency.

Direct and indirect quotes are just the inverse (reciprocal) of each other.

Exchange Rate Quote Conventions

FX Rate Quote Convention	Name Convention	Actual Ratio (Price currency/Base currency)
EUR	Euro	USD/EUR
JPY	Dollar–yen	JPY/USD
GBP	Sterling	USD/GBP
CAD	Dollar–Canada	CAD/USD
AUD	Aussie	USD/AUD
NZD	Kiwi	USD/NZD
CHF	Swiss franc	CHF/USD
EURJPY	Euro–yen	JPY/EUR
EURGBP	Euro–sterling	GBP/EUR
EURCHF	Euro–Swiss	CHF/EUR
GBPJPY	Sterling–yen	JPY/GBP
EURCAD	Euro–Canada	CAD/EUR
CADJPY	Canada–yen	JPY/CAD

Understanding Exchange Rate Quotes

When both currencies are mentioned in the code or the name convention, the first currency is the base currency and the second currency is the price currency. For example, dollar-yen refers to the exchange rate of JPY/USD i.e., USD is the base currency and JPY is the price currency. Note that dollar-yen (quote: JPY) may also be written as USDJPY, USD:JPY or USD-JPY. They all mean the same thing i.e., JPY/USD.

In professional FX markets, an exchange rate is usually quoted as a **two-sided price**. Dealers usually quote a **bid-price** (the price at which they are willing to buy), and an **ask-price** or **offer price** (the price at which they are willing to sell). Bid-ask prices are always quoted in terms of buying and selling the *base* currency. For example, a EUR:USD (or USD/EUR) quote of 1.3802–1.3806 means that the dealer is willing to buy EUR for 1.3802 USD and is willing to sell EUR for 1.3806 USD. From the client's perspective, she will receive 1.3802 USD for selling 1 EUR, but will have to pay 1.3806 USD to purchase 1 EUR.

Suppose that the JPY/USD exchange rate increases from 77.58 to 78.45. An increase in the JPY/USD exchange rate means that USD has now become more costly in terms of JPY (it now takes more units of JPY to purchase 1 unit of USD). Stated differently, USD has appreciated against JPY, and JPY has depreciated against USD. The unannualized percentage increase in the value of the USD against JPY can be calculated as:

$$(78.45/77.58) - 1 = 1.12\%$$

The percentage increase in the value of the USD against JPY does not equal the percentage decrease in the value of JPY against USD. In order to determine the percentage decrease in the value of JPY against USD, we must make JPY the *base* currency in the exchange rates that we use in the calculation.

Cross Rates

A **cross rate** is an exchange rate between two currencies that is derived from each currency's relationship with a third currency. For example, using the EUR (which represents USD/EUR) and JPY (which represents JPY/USD) exchange rates, we can calculate the cross rate between the euro and the yen (EURJPY or JPY/EUR) as follows:

$$\frac{JPY}{EUR} = \frac{\cancel{USD}}{EUR} \times \frac{JPY}{\cancel{USD}}$$

The given exchange rates should be multiplied such that the third currency (common currency) disappears (or mathematically cancels out as it forms the numerator of one quote and the denominator of the other).

In order to cancel out the third currency, you might sometimes need to invert one of the exchange rate quotes. For example, consider the EUR (which represents USD/EUR) and GBP (which represents USD/GBP) exchange rates. A trader who wants to calculate the cross rate between the Euro and the British pound cannot do so by simply multiplying these two exchange rates in their presented forms (because the USD will not cancel out). One of the exchange rates must be inverted. The Euro-sterling exchange rate (which represents GBP/EUR) can be calculated as:

$$\frac{GBP}{EUR} = \frac{USD}{EUR} \times \left(\frac{USD}{GBP}\right)^{-1} = \frac{USD}{EUR} \times \frac{GBP}{USD}$$

Forward Rate Quotes

In professional FX markets, forward exchange rates are quoted in terms of points (pips), which simply represent the difference between the forward rate and the spot rate. Note that these points (pips) are scaled so that they can be related to the last digit in the spot quote (usually the fourth decimal place).

- If the forward rate is higher than the spot rate, the points are positive and the base currency is said to be trading at a **forward premium** because it is expected to appreciate in the future. At the same time, the price currency would be trading at a **forward discount**, which means it is expected to depreciate.
- If the forward rate is lower than the spot rate, the points are negative and the base currency is trading at a forward discount as it is expected to depreciate. At the same time, the price currency would be trading at a forward premium and is expected to appreciate.

For example, assume that a trader is quoted a spot CAD/USD exchange rate of 1.0155 and a one-year forward CAD/USD exchange rate of 1.0183. The forward rate is higher than the spot rate which means that the USD (base currency) is trading at a forward premium and is expected to appreciate. The one-year forward points will be quoted as 28, calculated as follows:

$$\text{Forward points:} (1.0183 - 1.0155) \times 10{,}000 = 28 \text{ points}$$

Dealers typically quote forward rates in terms of the number of forward points. Forward point quotes may be converted into forward rates by dividing the number of points by 10,000 and adding the result to the spot rate quote (assuming that the quote has 4 decimal places). Continuing with our CAD/USD example, the one-year forward rate may be computed based on forward points as:

$$1.0155 + (28/10{,}000) = 1.0155 + 0.0028 = 1.0183$$

Sometimes forward rates or points may be quoted as a percentage of the spot rate rather than in terms of an absolute number of points. Continuing with our CAD/USD example, the one year forward rate for the USD can be quoted as:

$$[(1.0155 + 0.0028)/1.0155] - 1 = (1.0183/1.0155) - 1 = 0.2757\%$$

The base currency (USD) is said to be trading at a forward premium of 0.2757%.

When the forward premium is presented in terms of a percentage, the forward rate may be calculated by multiplying the spot rate by one plus (minus) the percentage premium (discount). Continuing with the CAD/USD example, the forward premium of 0.2757% can be used to calculate the forward rate as:

$$1.0155 \times (1 + 0.002757) = 1.0183$$

If the number of points were −28 (if the base currency were trading at a forward discount), the forward rate would be expressed in terms of a percentage as:

$$[(1.0155 - 0.0028)/1.0155] - 1 = -0.2757\%$$

In this case, the forward exchange rate would be calculated as:

$$1.0155 \times (1 - 0.002757) = 1.0127; \text{ or}$$
$$1.0155 - 0.0028 = 1.0127$$

Forward Rates, Spot Rates, and Interest Rates

Forward exchange rates are calculated in a manner that ensures that traders are not able to earn arbitrage profits. This means that a trader with a specific amount of domestic currency should be able to earn the exact same amount from both the following investment options:

- **Option 1:** She invests the funds at the domestic risk-free rate (r_{DC}) for a particular period of time.
- **Option 2:** She converts the funds into a foreign currency (at the current spot rate, $S_{FC/DC}$), invests them at the foreign risk-free rate (r_{FC}) for the same period of time (as in Option 1), and then converts them back to the domestic currency at the forward exchange rate ($F_{DC/FC}$) which she locks in today.

Both these investment options are risk-free because they require the money to be invested at risk-free interest rates. Further, the exchange rate risk in the second option is eliminated (hedged) by locking in the forward rate at the time of investment. Since these two investments have identical risk characteristics, it follows that they must have the same return (to preclude arbitrage profits), leading to the following equality:

> The CFA Program curriculum presents this equation in the following form:
>
> $$(1 + i_d) = S_{f/d}(1 + i_f)\frac{1}{F_{f/d}}$$
>
> We believe that our approach is easier and more intuitive. Both the formulas will of course give you the same answer.

$$(1 + r_{DC}) = S_{FC/DC}(1 + r_{FC})\,F_{DC/FC}$$

The above equality can be used to derive the formula for the forward rate:

$$F_{DC/FC} = \frac{1}{S_{FC/DC}} \times \frac{(1 + r_{DC})}{(1 + r_{FC})} \text{ or } F_{DC/FC} = S_{DC/FC} \times \frac{(1 + r_{DC})}{(1 + r_{FC})}$$

> This version of the formula is perhaps easiest to remember because it contains the DC term in numerator for all three components: $F_{DC/FC}$, $S_{DC/FC}$ and $(1 + r_{DC})$

Forward rates are sometimes interpreted as expected future spot rates.

$$F_t = S_{t+1}$$

$$\frac{(S_{t+1})}{S} - 1 = \Delta\%S(DC/FC)_{t+1} = \frac{(r_{DC} - r_{FC})}{(1 + r_{FC})}$$

Under this interpretation, the expected percentage change in the spot rate is proportional to the interest rate differential ($r_{DC} - r_{FC}$). However, such an interpretation should be used cautiously. Forward rates are unbiased predictors of future spot rates, but this does not make them accurate predictors of future spot rates:

- The direction of the predicted change in spot rates is counterintuitive.
- Historical data show that forward rates are poor predictors of future spot rates. Aside from interest rate differentials, exchange rates are influenced by several other factors.

Important Takeaways

- Given the same interest rate differential, the longer the term to maturity, the higher the absolute number of forward points.
  - However, note that the number of forward points is not exactly proportional to the horizon of the forward contract.

- Given the same term to maturity, the higher the interest rate differential, the higher the absolute number of forward points.
  - The number of forward points is exactly proportional to the interest rate differential.

Exchange Rate Regimes

Desirable Properties

- The exchange rate between any two currencies should be **credibly fixed**.
- All currencies should be **fully convertible** to ensure unrestricted flow of capital.
- Each country should be able to undertake **fully independent monetary policy**.

Generally speaking, the more freely the currency is allowed to float and the more tightly convertibility is controlled, the greater the effectiveness of monetary policy.

Types of Exchange Rate Regimes

Arrangements with No Separate Legal Tender

- **Dollarization:** A country uses the currency of another nation (usually the U.S. dollar) as its medium of exchange and unit of account.
- **Monetary union:** Member countries share the same legal tender (e.g., the European Economic and Monetary Union (EMU) whose members use the Euro as their currency).

Currency Board System

- The central bank holds foreign currency reserves to cover, at the fixed parity, the entire monetary base of a country (e.g., Hong Kong).
- Expansion and contraction of the monetary base are directly linked to trade and capital flows.
- The exchange rate is essentially fixed, but it is allowed to fluctuate within a narrow band.
- The central bank cannot act as the lender of last resort, but can provide short term liquidity.
- The monetary authority can earn a profit by paying little or no interest on its liabilities (the monetary base), and earning a market rate on its assets (foreign currency reserves). This profit is referred to as **seigniorage**. Under dollarization, seigniorage goes to the country whose currency is used.

Fixed Parity

- The exchange rate is either pegged to a single currency or to a basket of currencies of major trading partners. The monetary authority stands ready to buy or sell foreign currency reserves to maintain the exchange rate within a narrow band.
- Although monetary independence is limited, the central bank can act as a lender of last resort.
- The success of this system depends on both the country's willingness as well as its ability to maintain the fixed exchange rate.

Target Zone

- Similar to a fixed-rate system.
- The only difference is that the monetary authority aims to maintain the exchange rate within a slightly broader range.
  - This gives the central bank greater ability to conduct discretionary policy.

Active and Passive Crawling Pegs

- Under a passive crawling peg system, the exchange rate is adjusted frequently in line with the rate of inflation.
- Under an active crawling peg system, the exchange rate is pre-announced for the coming weeks and changes are made in small steps.

Fixed Parity with Crawling Bands

- The country initially fixes its exchange rate to a foreign currency, but gradually moves towards a more flexible system by pre-announcing the widening of bands around the central parity. This allows the country greater flexibility in determining its monetary policy.

Managed Float

- The country does not explicitly state its exchange rate target, but intervenes in the FX markets to meet its policy objectives (regarding balance of trade, price stability or unemployment).
- Such intervention (also called dirty floating) typically also causes the country's trading partners to retaliate in a similar fashion and leads to instability in FX markets as a whole.

Independently Floating Rates

- The central bank rarely intervenes in the determination of its exchange rate, which is left to be determined by market supply and demand factors.
- Enables the central bank to engage in independent monetary policy aimed at achieving price stability and full employment.
- Also allows it to act as a lender of last resort to troubled institutions.

Relating the Trade Balance to Savings

$$(X - M) = (S - I) + (T - G)$$

$$\text{Trade surplus} = \text{Government saving} + \text{Private saving} - \text{Investment}$$

- A trade surplus means that the economy as whole (government saving and private saving combined) saves enough to fund its investment needs. The excess saving is used to accumulate financial claims against the rest of the world.
- A trade deficit means that the country must borrow from the rest of the word to meet its investment needs.

Exchange Rates and the Trade Balance

The Elasticities Approach

A devaluation or depreciation of the domestic currency makes domestic goods relatively cheaper for foreigners (reduces the price of domestic goods). At the same time it implies an appreciation of foreign currencies, which makes foreign goods relatively more expensive for domestic citizens (increases the price of foreign goods).

The ideal combination for a country that wants to reduce its trade deficit and expects its currency to depreciate is that its imports and exports both be relatively elastic. This is the basic idea behind the Marshall-Lerner condition. Demand for imports and exports must be sufficiently price sensitive such that increasing the price of imports increases the difference between export revenue and import expenditures.

> Marshall-Lerner condition: $\omega_X \epsilon_X + \omega_M(\epsilon_M - 1) > 0$
>
> Where :
> ω_X = Share of exports in total trade
> ω_M = Share of imports in total trade
> ϵ_X = Price elasticity of demand for exports
> ϵ_M = Price elasticity of demand for imports

If this condition is satisfied, devaluation/depreciation in the domestic currency will lead the trade balance towards a surplus.

Note that the elasticity of demand for imports becomes more important (and export elasticity less important) as the trade deficit gets larger.

Generally speaking, exchange rates will be more effective in adjusting trade imbalances if the countries' imports and exports are composed of items that have relatively elastic demand.

Finally, note that the impact of exchange rates on the trade balance may not always be immediate due to the fact that there is a time lag between the initial depreciation and the eventual impact on quantities of imports and exports. The increase in import prices will lead to an increase in total expenditure on imports over the short run (leading to a deepening of the deficit). However, as the currency stabilizes at the new (lower) levels, economic agents adapt and eventually the trade balance improves (towards a surplus). Overall, the trade deficits makes a "*J*-like" formation.

The Absorption Approach

Devaluation of the exchange rate can direct the trade balance towards a surplus if it increases:

- National income relative to expenditure; or equivalently
- National saving relative to investment in physical capital

If an economy is operating below full employment, then, by diverting demand towards domestically produced goods, devaluation can increase income/output.

If the economy is operating at full employment, output/income cannot be increased further. As a result, expenditure must decline for there to be an improvement in the trade balance.

Study Session 5: Financial Statement Analysis (1)

INTRODUCTION TO FINANCIAL STATEMENT ANALYSIS
Cross-Reference to CFA Institute Assigned Reading #15

The **role of financial statement reporting** is to provide information about a company's financial performance, financial position and changes in financial position.

The **role of financial statement analysis** is to assess a company's past performance and evaluate its future prospects using financial reports along with other relevant company information.

- *Liquidity* refers to a company's ability to meet its short term obligations.
- *Solvency* refers to a company's ability to meet its long term obligations.

Footnotes contain important details about accounting methods, estimates and assumptions that have been used by the company in preparing its financial statements. For example, information about the choice of revenue recognition method and assumptions made to calculate depreciation expense are found in the footnotes. The availability of such information allows comparisons between companies that prepare their financial statements in accordance with different accounting standards (IFRS versus U.S. GAAP).

The management discussion and analysis section (required under **U.S. GAAP**) highlights important trends and events that affect a company's liquidity, capital resources and operations. Management also discusses prospects for the upcoming year with respect to inflation, future goals, material events and uncertainties. The section must also discuss critical accounting policies that require management to make subjective judgments and have a material impact on the financial statements. Although it contains important information, analysts should bear in mind that the MD&A section is not audited.

IFRS provides a framework that offers guidance rather than requirements in a standard. According to the framework, "decision-useful" management commentary includes:

- The nature of the business
- Management objectives and strategies
- The company's significant resources, risks and relationships
- Results of operations
- Critical performance measures

Auditor's Reports

Under International Standards for Auditing, objectives of an auditor are:

1. To obtain reasonable assurance about whether the financial statements as a whole are free from material misstatement, whether due to fraud or error, thereby enabling the auditor to express an opinion on whether the financial statements are prepared, in all material respects, in accordance with an applicable financial reporting framework; and
2. To report on the financial statements, and communicate as required by the ISAs, in accordance with the auditor's findings.

Types of Audit Opinions

- An **unqualified opinion** states that the financial statements have been fairly presented in accordance with applicable accounting standards.

- A **qualified opinion** states that the financial statements have been prepared fairly, but do contain exception(s) to the accounting standards. The audit report provides further details and explanations relating to the exception(s).
- An **adverse opinion** states that the financial statements have not been presented fairly, and significantly deviate from acceptable accounting standards.
- A **disclaimer of opinion** is issued when the auditor, for whatever reason, is not able to issue an opinion on the financial statements.

Other Sources of Company-Related Information

- **Interim reports** are prepared either semiannually or quarterly. They contain the four financial statements and footnotes but are *not audited*.
- **Proxy statements** are distributed to shareholders to decide on matters that require a shareholder vote. They provide information about management and director compensation, company stock performance and potential conflicts of interest between management, the board of directors and shareholders.
- **Press releases**, in addition to company websites and conference calls, provide current information about companies.
- **External sources** provide information about the economy, the industry that the company operates in, and the company's competitors. Examples of external sources include trade journals and government agencies.

Steps in the Financial Statement Analysis Framework

- Define the context and purpose of analysis.
- Collect data.
- Process data.
- Analyze/interpret the processed data.
- Develop and communicate conclusions.
- Follow up.

FSA

FINANCIAL REPORTING STANDARDS
Cross-Reference to CFA Institute Assigned Reading #16

Financial statements are not designed only to facilitate asset valuation; they provide information to a host of users (e.g., creditors, employees and customers). At the same time, they do provide important inputs for the asset valuation process. For analysts, it is extremely important to understand how, and when judgments and subjective estimates affect the financial statements. Such an understanding is important to evaluate the wisdom of business decisions, and to make comparisons between companies.

Standard-Setting Bodies versus Regulatory Bodies

- **Standard-setting bodies**, such as the International Accounting Standards Board (IASB) and U.S. Financial Accounting Standards Board (FASB), are private sector organizations, of accountants and auditors, who *develop* financial reporting rules, regulations and accounting standards.
- **Regulatory authorities** like the Securities and Exchange Commission (SEC) in the United States, and FSA in the United Kingdom, have legal authority to *enforce* financial reporting requirements, and can overrule private-sector standard-setting bodies.

Standard-Setting Bodies

The **IASB** is the independent standard-setting body of the **IFRS Foundation**, which is an independent, not-for-profit private sector organization.

The FASB standards are contained in the **FASB Accounting Standard Codification**™ **(Codification)**. The Codification is the source of all authoritative U.S. generally accepted accounting principles (U.S. GAAP) for non-governmental entities.

Regulatory Authorities

Regulatory authorities are governmental entities that have the legal authority to enforce the financial reporting requirements set forth by the standard-setting bodies, and to exert control over entities that participate in capital markets within their jurisdiction.

IOSCO (International Organization of Securities Commission) is not a regulatory authority, but its members regulate a large portion of the world's financial capital markets.

Any company issuing securities in the U.S., or otherwise involved in U.S. capital markets is subject to the rules of the **Securities and Exchange Commission (SEC)**. The SEC requires companies to submit numerous forms periodically. These filings, which are available on the SEC website (www.sec.gov), are a key source of information for analysis of listed firms.

Objective of Financial Statements

Under the Conceptual Framework, the objective of general purpose financial reporting is to provide financial information that is useful in making decisions about providing resources to the entity to existing and potential providers of resources (e.g., investors, lenders and creditors) to the entity.

Qualitative Characteristics

Fundamental qualitative characteristics that make financial information useful:

- Relevance
- Faithful representation

Faithful representation requires that the information presented is:

- Complete
- Neutral
- Free from error

Supplementary qualitative characteristics that increase the usefulness of relevant and faithfully represented financial information.

- Comparability
- Verifiability
- Timeliness
- Understandability

Constraints on Financial Statements

While it would be ideal for financial statements to exhibit all the desirable characteristics listed earlier, there are several constraints to achieving this goal:

- There may be a **trade-off** between certain desirable characteristics.
- There is a **cost** of providing useful financial information. The benefits from information should exceed the costs of providing it.
- **Intangible aspects** (e.g., company reputation, brand name, customer loyalty and corporate culture) cannot be quantified and reflected in financial statements.

Reporting Elements

The elements of financial statements that are related to the **measurement of financial position** are:

- Assets
- Liabilities
- Equity

Elements related to the **measurement of financial performance** are:

- Income
- Expenses

Underlying Assumptions in Financial Statements

- **Accrual basis** accounting requires that transactions should be recorded on the financial statements (other than on the cash flow statement) when they actually occur, irrespective of when the related exchange of cash occurs.
- **Going concern** refers to the assumption that the company will continue operating for the foreseeable future. If this is not the case, fair representation would require all assets to be written down to their liquidation values.

Recognition and Measurement of Financial Statement Elements

An element should be recognized on the financial statements if the future benefit from the item (flowing into or out of the firm) is **probable**, and if its value/cost can be **estimated with reliability**.

Measurement Bases

- **Historical cost:** For an asset historical cost refers to the amount that it was originally purchased for. For liabilities, it refers to the amount of proceeds that were received initially in exchange for the obligation.
- **Amortised cost:** Historical cost adjusted for amortisation, depreciation, or depletion and/or impairment.
- **Current cost:** For an asset, current cost refers to the amount that the asset can be purchased for today. For liabilities, it refers to the total undiscounted amount of cash that would be required to settle the obligation today.
- **Realizable (settlement) value:** In reference to assets, realizable value refers to the amount that the asset can be sold for in an ordinary disposal today. For liabilities, it refers to the undiscounted amount of cash expected to be paid to settle the liability in the normal course of business.
- **Present value:** For assets, present value refers to the discounted value of future net cash flows expected from the asset. For liabilities, it refers to the present discounted value of future net cash outflows that are expected to be required to settle the liability.
- **Fair value:** Fair value is defined as an exit price, the price that would be received to sell an asset, or paid to transfer a liability, in an orderly transaction between market participants at the measurement date. This may involve either market measures or present value measures, depending on the availability of information.

Required Financial Statements

- Statement of financial position (balance sheet).
- Statement of comprehensive income (in a single statement or in two separate statements i.e., the income statement + statement of comprehensive income).
- Statement of changes in equity.
- Statement of cash flows.
- Significant accounting policies and explanatory notes to facilitate the understanding of financial statements.
- In certain cases, a statement of financial position from earliest comparative period.

General Features of Financial Statements

- **Fair presentation:** This requires faithful representation of transactions, in compliance with the definitions and recognition criteria for reporting elements (assets, liabilities, equity, income and expenses) set out in the Conceptual Framework.
- **Going concern:** Financial statements should be prepared on a going concern basis unless management has plans to liquidate the company.
- **Accrual basis:** All financial statements, except the cash flow statement, should be prepared on an accrual basis.
- **Materiality and aggregation:** Financial statements should be free from omissions and misrepresentations that could influence decisions taken by users. Similar items should be grouped and presented as a material class. Dissimilar items, unless immaterial, should be presented separately.
- **No offsetting:** Assets and liabilities, and income and expenses should not be used to offset each other, unless a standard requires or allows it.

- **Frequency of reporting:** Financial statements must be prepared at least annually.
- **Comparative information:** Comparative amounts should be presented for prior periods unless a specific standard permits otherwise.
- **Consistency:** Items should be presented and classified in the same manner every period.

Structure and Content Requirements

- **Classified statement of financial position:** Current and noncurrent assets and current and noncurrent liabilities should be shown separately on the balance sheet.
- **Minimum information on the face of financial statements:** Certain items must be explicitly disclosed on the face of the financial statements.
- **Minimum information in the notes (or on the face of financial statements):** Disclosures relating to certain items must be in the notes to the financial statements (e.g., measurement bases used).
- **Comparative information:** Comparative amounts should be presented for prior periods unless a specific standard permits otherwise.

Monitoring Developments in Financial Reporting Standards

It is important for analysts to keep track of developments in financial reporting standards and assess their implications for security analysis and valuation. Analysts must pay careful attention to:

- New products and transactions in capital markets.
- Actions of standard-setting bodies.
- Company disclosures including the footnotes and the MD&A section.

Current Important Differences between IFRS and U.S. GAAP

Basis for Comparison	U.S. GAAP	IFRS
Developed by	Financial Accounting Standard Board (FASB)	International Accounting Standard Board (IASB)
Based on	Rules	Principles
Inventory valuation	FIFO, LIFO, and weighted average method	FIFO and weighted average method
Extraordinary items	Shown below (at the bottom of the income statement)	Not segregated in the income statement
Development cost	Treated as an expense	Capitalized, only if certain conditions are satisfied
Reversal of inventory	Prohibited	Permissible, if specified conditions are met

STUDY SESSION 6:
FINANCIAL STATEMENT ANALYSIS (2)

UNDERSTANDING INCOME STATEMENTS
Cross-Reference to CFA Institute Assigned Reading #17

Under **IFRS**, the income statement may be presented as:

- A section of a single statement of comprehensive income; or
- A separate statement (showing all revenues and expenses) followed by a statement of comprehensive income that begins with net income.

Under **U.S. GAAP**, the income statement may be presented as:

- A section of a single statement of comprehensive income.
- A separate statement followed by a statement of comprehensive income that begins with net income.
- A separate statement with the components of other comprehensive income presented in the statement of changes in shareholders' equity.

Revenues versus Gains

Income includes revenues and gains. Revenues arise from ordinary, core business activities, whereas gains arise from non-core or peripheral activities. For example, for a software development company, the sale of software to customers will be classified as revenue, but profit on the sale of some old office furniture will be classified as a gain.

Income Statement Formats

A company may prepare its income statement using a single-step or multi-step format. When an income statement explicitly calculates gross profit, it uses a multi-step format.

For nonfinancial firms, operating profit refers to earnings *before* financing costs (interest expense) and income taxes. For financial firms, interest expense is usually considered an operating expense. Their operating profit is calculated *after* accounting for interest expense.

If a company has a subsidiary in which it enjoys majority ownership, the subsidiary's accounts are consolidated with its own. Consolidation requires the parent company to combine all the revenues and expenses of the subsidiary with its own and present the combined results on its income statement. If the subsidiary is not wholly-owned, minority interest is deducted from total income as it represents the proportionate share of the subsidiary's minority share holders in the subsidiary's net income.

The IASB framework defines income as "an increase in economic benefits during the accounting period in the form of inflows or enhancements of assets, or reduction in values of liabilities that result in increases in equity, other than those relating to contributions from equity participants."

Under U.S. GAAP, only if the following conditions are met can the company recognize revenue based on gross reporting:

- The company is the primary obligor under the contract.
- The company bears inventory and credit risk.
- The company can choose its suppliers.
- The company has reasonable latitude to establish price.

Revenue Recognition

In May 2014, the IASB and FASB each issued nearly identical new standards for revenue recognition aimed at achieving convergence, consistency, and transparency in revenue recognition globally.

The IASB Conceptual Framework defines income as "increases in economic benefits during the accounting period in the form of inflows or enhancements of assets or decreases in liabilities that result in increases in equity, other than those relating to contributions from equity participants." Income includes revenues and gains.

The most important principle of revenue recognition is accrual accounting, which requires that revenues and costs are recognized independently of the timing of related cash flows. For example, if a company receives cash in advance and delivers the product later, the company would record a liability for **unearned revenue** when the cash is initially received, and revenue would be recognized as being earned over time as products and services are delivered.

Accounting Standards for Revenue Recognition

The converged accounting standards issued by the IASB and FASB in May 2014 introduced some changes to the basic principles of revenue recognition and enhanced comparability. The converged standard aims to provide a principles-based approach to revenue recognition that can be applied to many types of revenue-generating activities.

Core Principle

The **core principle** is that revenue should be recognized in order to "depict the transfer of promised goods or services to customers in an amount that reflects the consideration to which the entity expects to be entitled in an exchange for those goods or services." In order to attain this core principle, the standards describe five steps in recognizing revenue:

1. Identify the contract(s) with a customer.
2. Identify the separate or distinct performance obligations in the contract.
3. Determine the transaction price.
4. Allocate the transaction price to the performance obligations in the contract.
5. Recognize revenue when (or as) the entity satisfies a performance obligation.

A **contract** is an agreement and commitment, with commercial substance, between the contacting parties. It establishes each party's obligations and rights, including payment terms. In addition, a contract exists only if collectability is **probable**. While IFRS and U.S. GAAP use the same word (probable), they apply a different threshold for probable collectability. Under **IFRS**, probable means more likely than not, while under **U.S. GAAP**, it means likely to occur. This subtle difference can result in economically similar contracts being treated differently under the two standards.

Performance obligations represent promises to transfer **distinct** good(s) or service(s). A good or service is distinct if (1) the customer can benefit from it on its own or in combination with readily available resources and (2) the promise to transfer it can be separated from other promises in the contract. Each identified performance obligation is accounted for separately.

The **transaction price** is the amount that the seller estimates it will receive in exchange for transferring the good(s) or service(s) identified in the contract to the buyer. The transaction price is then allocated to each identified performance obligation. The amount recognized reflects expectations about collectability and (if applicable) an allocation to multiple obligations within the same contract. Revenue is recognized when the obligation-satisfying transfer is made.

Accounting Treatment

- When revenue is recognized, a **contract asset** is presented on the balance sheet.
- If all performance obligations have been satisfied, but payment has not been received, a **receivable** appears on the seller's balance sheet.
- If payment is received in advance of transferring good(s) or service(s), the seller presents a **contract liability**.

For complex contracts, **variable consideration** may only be recognized as revenue if the company can conclude that it will not have to reverse the cumulative revenue in the future. The converged standards also provide guidance on whether a change in a contract is a **new contract or just a modification** of an existing contract.

- In order to be considered a new contract, the change would need to involve goods and services that are distinct from the goods and services already transferred.
- If the changes do not meet the criteria for a new contract then they are treated as contract modifications. The company must reflect the impact on a **cumulative catch-up basis**, by updating the transaction price and measure of progress.

The converged standards also lay down specific accounting treatments for certain related costs and also require extensive disclosures. The impact of converged standards will be felt more by industries where bundled sales are common, such as telecommunications and software.

Expense Recognition

The IASB framework defines expenses as "decreases in economic benefits during the accounting period in the form of outflows or depletions of assets or incurrence of liabilities that result in decreases in equity, other than those relating to distributions to equity participants."

Expenses also include losses, which result from non-operating activities of the business. The most important principle of expense recognition is the **matching principle**, which requires that expenses be matched with associated revenues when recognizing them in the income statement. If goods bought in the current year remain unsold at the end of the year, their cost is not included in the cost of goods sold for the current year. Instead, the cost of these goods will be deducted from next period's revenues once they are sold.

Certain expenses, such as administrative costs, cannot be directly linked to the generation of revenues. These expenses are called **period costs** and are expensed in the period in which they are incurred.

Issues in Expense Recognition

- Doubtful accounts.
- Warranties.
- Depreciation and amortization

Operating versus Nonoperating Components of the Income Statement

IFRS does not define operating activities. Therefore, companies that choose to report operating income or the results of operating activities need to ensure that such activities would normally be regarded as operating.

FSA

On the other hand, U.S. GAAP defines operating activities as those that generally involve producing and delivering goods and providing services, and include all transactions and other events that are not defined as investing or financing activities.

Discontinued Operations

Under both IFRS and U.S. GAAP, the income statement must report an operation separately as a "discontinued operation" when the company disposes of, or is expected to dispose of a component that is operationally and physically separable from the rest of the firm.

- Discontinued operations are reported *net of tax* as a *separate* line item *after* income from continuing operations (this treatment is permitted under IFRS and U.S. GAAP).
- As the disposed operation will not earn revenue for the company going forward, it will not be taken into account in forecasting the company's future profits.

Unusual or Infrequent Items

These items are **either** unusual in nature **or** infrequent in occurrence. Examples of such items include restructuring charges and gains and losses arising from selling an asset for a price other than its carrying value.

- These items are listed as separate line items on the income statement but are *included* in income from continuing operations and hence, reported *before-tax*.
- Analysts should not ignore all unusual or infrequent items. They should assess whether these items are likely to reoccur when forecasting future operations.

Accounting Changes

- A change in accounting policy could be required by standard setters or be decided on by management to provide a better reflection of the company's performance.
  - If required by standard setters, companies may be permitted to adopt the standards prospectively (in the future) or retrospectively (restate financial statements as though the standard existed in the past).
  - If the company chooses to change an accounting policy (e.g., in order to provide a better reflection of the company's performance), the change must be applied retrospectively—financial data for all periods shown in the financial report must be presented as if the new principle were in use through the entire period. This retrospective change facilitates comparisons across reporting periods. Further, a description of and justification for the change are provided in the footnotes to the financial statements.
- A change in an accounting estimate (e.g., a change in the residual value of an asset) is applied prospectively and only affects financial statements for current and future periods. Significant changes in accounting estimates must be disclosed in the footnotes.
- A correction of prior-period errors is made by restating all prior-period financial statements presented in the financial report. In addition, disclosure about the error is required in the footnotes. Analysts should carefully assess these disclosures as they may point to weaknesses in a company's accounting system or financial controls.

Earnings Per Share

A firm may have a simple capital structure or a complex capital structure. A company has a simple capital structure when it does not have any securities outstanding that can be converted into common stock. Firms with simple capital structures are required to report basic earnings per share (EPS) only.

$$\text{Basic EPS} = \frac{\text{Net income} - \text{Preferred dividends}}{\text{Weighted average number of shares outstanding}}$$

If a company declares a stock split or a stock dividend during the year, the calculation of the weighted average number of issued shares outstanding is based on the assumption that the additional (newly issued) shares have been outstanding since the date that the original shares were outstanding from.

A **complex capital structure** includes securities that can be converted into common stock (e.g., convertible bonds, convertible preferred stock, warrants and options). These securities are *potentially dilutive* so companies with complex capital structures are required to report basic and diluted EPS. A dilutive security is one whose conversion into shares of common stock would result in a reduction in EPS. EPS calculated after taking into account all dilutive securities in the capital structure is known as **diluted EPS**.

In determining which potentially dilutive securities should be included in the calculation of diluted EPS, each of the securities must be evaluated individually and independently to determine whether they are dilutive. Any anti-dilutive securities must be ignored from the diluted EPS calculation.

$$\text{Diluted EPS} = \frac{\left[\text{Net income} - \dfrac{\text{Preferred}}{\text{dividends}}\right] + \dfrac{\text{Convertible}}{\text{preferred}} + \left[\dfrac{\text{Convertible}}{\text{debt}} \times (1-t)\right]}{\dfrac{\text{Weighted}}{\text{average}} + \dfrac{\text{Shares from}}{\text{conversion of}} + \dfrac{\text{Shares from}}{\text{conversion of}} + \dfrac{\text{Shares}}{\text{issuable from}}}$$

Both U.S. GAAP and IFRS require the presentation of EPS (basic EPS and their diluted EPS) on the face of the income statement.

Treasury Stock Method

In the calculation of diluted EPS, stock options and warrants are accounted for by using the **treasury stock method** (required under U.S. GAAP). The treasury stock method assumes that all the funds received by the company from the exercise of options and warrants are used by the company to repurchase shares at the average market price. The resulting net increase in the number of shares equals the increase in shares from exercise of options and warrants minus the decrease in the number of outstanding shares from repurchases.

Common-size income statements present each item on the income statement as a percentage of *sales*. They facilitate financial statement analysis as the data can be used to conduct time-series (across time periods) and cross-sectional (across companies) analysis.

Comprehensive Income

IFRS defines total comprehensive income as "the change in equity during a period resulting from transactions and other events, other than those changes resulting from transactions with owners in their capacity as owners."

IFRS requires the use of a similar method, but does not refer to it as the Treasury stock method. The proceeds of option exercise are assumed to be used to repurchase shares at the average market price and these shares are known as inferred shares. The excess of new issued shares over inferred shares is added to the weighted average number of shares outstanding.

FSA

Under U.S. GAAP, comprehensive income is defined as "the change in equity (net assets) of a business enterprise during a period from transactions and other events and circumstances from nonowner sources. It includes all changes in equity during a period except those resulting from investments by owners and distributions to owners."

Four types of items are classified as other comprehensive income under both IFRS and U.S. GAAP:

- Foreign currency translation adjustments.
- Unrealized gains or losses on derivatives contracts accounted for as hedges.
- Unrealized holding gains and losses on a certain category of investment securities, namely, available-for-sale debt securities under U.S. GAAP and securities designated as "fair value through other comprehensive income" under IFRS. (Note: IFRS, but not U.S. GAAP, also includes a category of equity investments designated at fair value through other comprehensive income.)
- Certain costs of a company's defined benefit post-retirement plans that are not recognized in the current period.

Under IFRS, certain changes in the value of long-lived assets that are measured using the revaluation model (as opposed to the cost model) at fair value are also included in other comprehensive income. Further, under IFRS, companies are not permitted to reclassify certain items of other comprehensive income to profit or loss, and companies must present separately the items of other comprehensive income that will and will not be reclassified subsequently to profit or loss.

It is important to reemphasize that even when certain income/expense items are excluded from a company's net income (profit and loss), they are included in other comprehensive income and thus form a part of a company's comprehensive income.

UNDERSTANDING BALANCE SHEETS
Cross-Reference to CFA Institute Assigned Reading #18

Limitations of the Balance Sheet

- Under current accounting standards, measurement bases of different assets and liabilities may vary considerably, which can have a significant impact on reported figures.
- The value of items reported on the balance sheet reflects their value at the end of the reporting period, which may not necessarily remain "current" at a later date.
- The balance sheet does not include qualitative factors (e.g., reputation, management skills, etc.) that have an important impact on the company's future cash-generating ability and therefore, its overall value.

Alternative Formats of Balance Sheet Presentation

- **Report format:** Assets, liabilities and equity are presented in a single column. This format is the most commonly-used balance sheet presentation format.
- **Account format:** Assets are presented on the left hand side of the balance sheet, with liabilities and equity on the right hand side.
- **Classified balance sheet:** Different types of assets and liabilities are grouped into subcategories to give a more effective overview of the company's financial position. Classifications typically group assets and liabilities into their current and non-current portions.
- **Liquidity-based presentation: IFRS** allows the preparation of a balance sheet using a liquidity-based presentation format (rather than a current/non-current format), if such a format provides more reliable and relevant information. In a liquidity-based presentation, all assets and liabilities are broadly presented in order of liquidity. This format is typically used by banks.

IFRS and U.S. GAAP Balance Sheet Presentation

Both **IFRS** and **U.S. GAAP** require that assets and liabilities be grouped separately into their current and non-current portions, which makes it easier for analysts to examine the company's liquidity position as of the balance sheet date. However, it is not required that current assets be presented before noncurrent assets, or that current liabilities be presented before noncurrent liabilities. Further, under **IFRS**, the current/non-current classifications are not required if a liquidity-based presentation provides more relevant and reliable information.

Measurement Bases of Various Financial Assets

Measured at Fair Value	Measured at Cost or Amortized Cost
Financial Assets	**Financial Assets**
Financial assets held for trading (stocks and bonds).	Unlisted instruments.
Available-for-sale-financial assets (stocks and bonds).	Held-to-maturity investments.
Derivatives.	Loans and receivables.
Non-derivative instruments with face value exposures hedged by derivatives.	

FSA

Measurement of Financial Assets[1]

Measured at Cost or Amortized Cost	Measured at Fair Value through Other Comprehensive Income	Measured at Fair Value through Profit and Loss
• Debt securities that are to be held to maturity • Loans and notes receivable • Unquoted equity instruments (in limited circumstances where the fair value is not reliably measurable, cost may serve as a proxy (estimate) for fair value)	• "Available-for-sale" debt securities (U.S. GAAP); debt securities where the business model involves both collecting interest and principal and selling the security (IFRS) • Equity investments for which the company irrevocably elects this measurement at acquisition (IFRS only)	• All equity securities unless the investment gives the investor significant influence (U.S. GAAP only) • "Trading" debt securities (U.S. GAAP) • Securities not assigned to either of the other two categories, or investments for which the company irrevocably elects this measurement at acquisition (IFRS only)

[1]Exhibit 10, Volume 3, CFA Program Curriculum 2022

The Components of Shareholders' Equity

- Capital contributed by owners (common stock or issued capital).
  - **Authorized shares** are the maximum number of shares that can be sold under the company's Articles of Incorporation.
  - **Issued shares** are the total number of shares that have been sold to shareholders.
  - **Outstanding shares** equal the number of shares that were issued less the number of **shares repurchased** (**treasury stock**).
- Preferred shares
- Treasury shares
- Retained earnings
- Accumulated other comprehensive income
- Noncontrolling interest (minority interest)

Statement of Changes in Owners' Equity

This statement presents the effects of all transactions that increase or decrease company's equity over the period. Under **IFRS**, the following information should be included in the statement of changes in equity:

- Total comprehensive income for the period.
- The effects of any accounting changes that have been retrospectively applied to previous periods.
- Capital transactions with owners and distributions to owners; and
- Reconciliation of the carrying amounts of each component of equity at the beginning and end of the year.

Under U.S. GAAP, companies are required to provide an analysis of changes in each component of stockholders' equity that is shown in the balance sheet.

Uses and Analysis of Balance Sheets

Analysts can gain information regarding a company's liquidity, solvency, and the economic resources controlled by the company by examining its balance sheet.

- Liquidity refers to a company's ability to meet its short-term financial obligations.
- Solvency refers to a company's ability to meet its long-term financial obligations.

Two of the techniques that may be used to analyze a company's balance sheet are common-size analysis and ratio analysis.

Common-Size Balance Sheets

A **vertical common-size balance sheet** expresses each balance sheet item as a percentage of total assets. This allows an analyst to perform historical analysis (time-series analysis) and cross-sectional analysis across firms within the same industry.

Balance Sheet Ratios

These are ratios that have balance sheet items in the numerator and the denominator. The two main categories of balance sheet ratios are **liquidity ratios**, which measure a company's ability to settle short-term obligations and **solvency ratios**, which evaluate a company's ability to settle long-term obligations.

The *higher* a company's liquidity ratios, the *greater* the likelihood that the company will be able to meet its short-term obligations.

Liquidity Ratios

	Numerator	Denominator
Current ratio	Current assets	Current liabilities
Quick ratio (acid test ratio)	Cash + marketable securities + receivables	Current liabilities
Cash ratio	Cash + marketable securities	Current liabilities

Higher solvency ratios, on the other hand, are *undesirable* and indicate that the company is highly leveraged and risky.

Solvency Ratios

	Numerator	Denominator
Long-term debt-to-equity ratio	Total long-term debt	Total equity
Debt-to-equity ratio	Total debt	Total equity
Total debt ratio	Total debt	Total assets
Financial leverage ratio	Total assets	Total equity

UNDERSTANDING CASH FLOW STATEMENTS
Cross-Reference to CFA Institute Assigned Reading #19

Under both IFRS and U.S. GAAP, cash flows are classified into the following categories:

Cash Flows from Operating Activities (CFO) are inflows and outflows of cash generated from a firm's day-to-day business activities.

Cash Flows from Investing Activities (CFI) are inflows and outflows of cash generated from purchase and disposal of long-term investments. Long-term investments include plant, machinery, equipment, intangible assets, and non-trading debt and equity securities.

All securities that are considered highly liquid (cash equivalents) are not included in investing activities and neither are securities held for trading. Cash flows associated with the purchase and sale of highly liquid cash equivalents, and of securities for trading purposes are classified as cash flows from operating activities.

Cash Flows from Financing Activities (CFF) are cash inflows and outflows generated from issuance and repayment of capital (long-term debt and equity).

Indirect short term borrowings from suppliers that are classified as accounts payable and receivables from customers are not financing activities; they are classified as operating activities.

Cash Flow Classification

CFO

Inflows	Outflows
Cash collected from customers.	Cash paid to employees.
Interest and dividends received.	Cash paid to suppliers.
Proceeds from sale of securities held for trading.	Cash paid for other expenses.
	Cash used to purchase trading securities.
	Interest paid.
	Taxes paid.

CFI

Inflows	Outflows
Sale proceeds from fixed assets.	Purchase of fixed assets.
Sale proceeds from long-term investments.	Cash used to acquire LT investment securities.

CFF

Inflows	Outflows
Proceeds from debt issuance.	Repayment of LT debt.
Proceeds from issuance of equity instruments.	Payments made to repurchase stock.
	Dividends payments.

Cash Flow Presentation Formats

Under both IFRS and U.S. GAAP, there are two acceptable formats for presenting the cash flow statement—the direct method and the indirect method. These methods differ only in the *presentation* of the *CFO* section of the cash flow statement; calculated values for CFO are the same under both. Further, the presentation of financing and investing activities is exactly the same.

Direct Method versus Indirect Method

- The direct method explicitly lists the actual sources of operating cash inflows and outflows, whereas indirect method only provides net results for these inflows and outflows. The information provided under the direct method is very useful in evaluating past performance and making projections of future cash flows.
- The indirect method provides a list of items that are responsible for the difference between net income and operating cash flows. The differences can then be used to estimate future operating cash flows. The indirect method facilitates forecasting of future cash flows since forecasts of future net income simply have to be adjusted for changes in working capital accounts.

Sources and Uses of Cash

- *Increases* in current assets are *uses* of cash, and *decreases* in current assets are *sources* of cash. Changes in asset balances and cash are *negatively* related.
- *Increases* in current liabilities are *sources* of cash, while *decreases* in current liabilities are *uses* of cash. Changes in liability balances and cash are *positively* related.

FSA

The Direct Method

- **Step 1:** Start with sales on the income statement.
- **Step 2:** Go through each income statement account and adjust it for changes in all relevant working capital accounts on the balance sheet. This serves to remove the effects of the timing difference between the recognition of revenues or expenses, and the actual receipt or payment of cash.
- **Step 3:** Check whether changes in these working capital accounts indicate a source or use of cash. Make sure you put the right sign in front of the income statement item. Sales are an inflow item so they have a positive effect on cash flow, while COGS, wages, taxes, and interest expense are all outflow items that have negative effects on cash flow.
- **Step 4:** Ignore all nonoperating items (e.g., gain/loss on sale of plant and equipment) and noncash charges (e.g., depreciation and amortization).

The Indirect Method

- **Step 1:** Start with net income.
- **Step 2:** Go up the income statement and remove the effect of all noncash expenses and gains from net income. For example, the negative effect of depreciation is removed from net income by adding depreciation back to net income. Cash net income will be higher than accrual-based net income by the amount of noncash expenses.
- **Step 3:** Remove the effects of all nonoperating activities from net income. For example the positive effect of a gain on sale of fixed assets on net income is removed by subtracting the gain from net income.
- **Step 4:** Make adjustments for changes in all working capital accounts. Add all sources of cash (increases in current liabilities and decreases in current assets) and subtract all uses of cash (decreases in current liabilities and increases in current assets).

Cash Flow Statements under IFRS and U.S. GAAP

	IFRS	U.S. GAAP
Classification of Cash Flows		
Interest and dividends received	CFO or CFI	CFO
Interest paid	CFO or CFF	CFO
Dividend paid	CFO or CFF	CFF
Dividends received	CFO or CFI	CFO
Taxes paid	CFO, but part of the tax can be categorized as CFI or CFF if it is clear that the tax arose from investing or financing activities.	CFO
Bank overdrafts	Included as a part of cash equivalents.	Not considered a part of cash equivalents and included in CFF.
Presentation Format		
CFO (No difference in CFI and CFF presentation)	Direct or indirect method. The former is preferred.	Direct or indirect method. The former is preferred. However, if the direct method is used, a reconciliation of net income and CFO must be included.
Disclosures		
	Taxes paid should be presented separately on the cash flow statement.	If taxes and interest paid are not explicitly stated on the cash flow statement, details can be provided in footnotes.

Cash Flow Analysis

Major sources and uses of cash	Sources and uses of cash depend on the company's stage of growth. • Companies in the early stages of growth may have negative operating cash flows as cash is used to finance inventory and receivables. These negative operating cash flows are supported by financing inflows from issuance of debt or equity. • Inflows of cash from financing activities are not sustainable. Over the long-term, a company must generate positive cash flows from operating activities that exceed capital expenditures and payments to providers of debt and equity capital. • Companies in the mature stage of growth usually have positive cash flows from operating activities. These inflows can be used for debt repayment and stock repurchases. They can also be used by the company to expand its scale of operations (investing activities).

Operating cash flows	Changes in relevant asset and liability accounts should be used to determine whether business operations are a source or use of cash. • Operating cash flow should be compared to net income. If high net income is not being translated into high operating cash flows, the company might be using aggressive revenue recognition policies. • Companies should ideally have operating cash flows that are greater than net income. • The variability of operating cash flows and net income is an important determinant of the overall risk inherent in the company.
Investing cash flows	Changes in long-term asset and investment accounts are used to determine sources and uses of investing cash flows. • Increasing outflows may imply capital expenditures. Analysts should then evaluate how the company plans to finance these investments (i.e., with excess operating cash flows or by undertaking financing activities).
Financing cash flows	Changes in long-term debt and equity are used to determine sources and uses of financing cash flows. • If debt issuance contributes significantly to financing cash flows, the repayment schedule must be considered. • Increasing use of cash to repay debt, repurchase stock and make dividend payments might indicate a lack of lucrative investment opportunities for the company.

Free Cash Flow

Free cash flow is the excess of a company's operating cash flows over capital expenditure undertaken during the year. Free cash flow to the *firm* and free cash flow to *equity* are more precise measures of free cash flow as they identify specifically whom the cash is available to.

Free cash flow to the firm (FCFF) is cash available to equity and debt holders after the company has met all its operating expenses, and satisfied its capital expenditure and working capital requirements.

$$\text{FCFF} = \text{NI} + \text{NCC} + [\text{Int} \times (1 - \text{tax rate})] - \text{FCInv} - \text{WCInv}$$
$$\text{FCFF} = \text{CFO} + [\text{Int} \times (1 - \text{tax rate})] - \text{FCInv}$$

Free cash flow to equity (FCFE) is the cash that is available only to common shareholders.

$$\text{FCFE} = \text{CFO} - \text{FCInv} + \text{Net borrowing} - \text{Net debt repayment}$$

FINANCIAL ANALYSIS TECHNIQUES
Cross-Reference to CFA Institute Assigned Reading #20

Limitations of Ratio Analysis

- Companies may have divisions that operate in different industries. This can make it difficult to find relevant industry ratios for comparison purposes.
- There are no set ranges within which particular ratios for a company must lie. An analyst must use her own judgment to evaluate the implications of a given value for a ratio. This usually involves examining the entire operations of a company, the external industry and economic scenario.
- Firms enjoy significant latitude in the choice of accounting methods that are acceptable given the jurisdiction that they operate in. For example, under U.S. GAAP, companies can:
  - Choose from a variety of inventory cost flow assumptions (e.g., FIFO, AVCO or LIFO).
  - Choose from a variety of depreciation methods (e.g., MACRS and straight-line).
- Comparing ratios of firms across international borders is even more difficult, in that several countries use IFRS. Despite the growing convergence between IFRS and U.S. GAAP, significant differences remain.

Common Ratios Used in Financial Analysis

Activity ratios measure how productive a company is in using its assets and how efficiently it performs its everyday operations.

$$\text{Inventory turnover} = \frac{\text{Cost of goods sold}}{\text{Average inventory}}$$

$$\text{Days of inventory on hand (DOH)} = \frac{365}{\text{Inventory turnover}}$$

$$\text{Receivables turnover} = \frac{\text{Revenue}}{\text{Average receivables}}$$

$$\text{Days of sales outstanding (DSO)} = \frac{365}{\text{Receivables turnover}}$$

$$\text{Payables turnover} = \frac{\text{Purchases}}{\text{Average trade payables}}$$

$$\text{Number of days of payables} = \frac{365}{\text{Payables turnover}}$$

$$\text{Working capital turnover} = \frac{\text{Revenue}}{\text{Average working capital}}$$

FSA

$$\text{Fixed asset turnover} = \frac{\text{Revenue}}{\text{Average fixed assets}}$$

$$\text{Total Asset Turnover} = \frac{\text{Revenue}}{\text{Average total assets}}$$

Liquidity ratios measure the company's ability to meet its short-term cash requirements.

$$\text{Current ratio} = \frac{\text{Current assets}}{\text{Current liabilities}}$$

$$\text{Quick ratio} = \frac{\text{Cash} + \text{Short-term marketable investments} + \text{Receivables}}{\text{Current liabilities}}$$

$$\text{Cash ratio} = \frac{\text{Cash} + \text{Short-term marketable investments}}{\text{Current liabilities}}$$

$$\text{Defensive interval ratio} = \frac{\text{Cash} + \text{Short-term marketable investments} + \text{Receivables}}{\text{Daily cash expenditures}}$$

$$\text{Cash conversion cycle} = \text{DSO} + \text{DOH} - \text{Number of days of payables}$$

Solvency ratios measure a company's ability to meet its long-term obligations.

$$\text{Debt-to-assets ratio} = \frac{\text{Total debt}}{\text{Total assets}}$$

$$\text{Debt-to-capital ratio} = \frac{\text{Total debt}}{\text{Total debt} + \text{Shareholders' equity}}$$

$$\text{Debt-to-equity ratio} = \frac{\text{Total debt}}{\text{Shareholders' equity}}$$

$$\text{Financial leverage ratio} = \frac{\text{Average total assets}}{\text{Average total equity}}$$

$$\text{Debt-to-EBITDA ratio} = \frac{\text{Total debt}}{\text{EBITDA}}$$

$$\text{Interest coverage ratio} = \frac{\text{EBIT}}{\text{Interest payments}}$$

FSA

$$\text{Fixed charge coverage ratio} = \frac{\text{EBIT} + \text{Lease payments}}{\text{Interest payments} + \text{Lease payments}}$$

Profitability ratios measure a company's ability to generate an adequate return on invested capital.

$$\text{Gross profit margin} = \frac{\text{Gross profit}}{\text{Revenue}}$$

$$\text{Operating profit margin} = \frac{\text{Operating profit}}{\text{Revenue}}$$

$$\text{Pretax margin} = \frac{\text{EBT (earnings before tax, but after interest)}}{\text{Revenue}}$$

$$\text{Net profit margin} = \frac{\text{Net profit}}{\text{Revenue}}$$

$$\text{ROA} = \frac{\text{Net income}}{\text{Average total assets}}$$

$$\text{Adjusted ROA} = \frac{\text{Net income} + \text{Interest expense} (1 - \text{Tax rate})}{\text{Average total assets}}$$

$$\text{Operating ROA} = \frac{\text{Operating income or EBIT}}{\text{Average total assets}}$$

$$\text{Return on total capital} = \frac{\text{EBIT}}{\text{Average short-term debt} + \text{Average long-term debt} + \text{Average equity}}$$

$$\text{Return on equity} = \frac{\text{Net income}}{\text{Average total equity}}$$

$$\text{Return on common equity} = \frac{\text{Net income} - \text{Preferred dividends}}{\text{Average common equity}}$$

Interpretation and Context

- Actual ratios should be compared to the company's stated objectives. This helps in determining whether the company's operations are moving in line with its strategy.
- A company's ratios should be compared with those of others in the industry. When comparing ratios across firms from the same industry, analysts must be careful because:

- ○ Not all ratios are important to every industry.
- ○ Companies can have several lines of business, which can cause aggregate financial ratios to be distorted. In such a situation, analysts should evaluate ratios for each segment of the business in relation to the relevant industry average.
- ○ Companies might be using different accounting methods.
- ○ Companies could be at different stages of growth, or may have different strategies. This can result in different values for various ratios for firms in the same industry.
- Ratios should be studied in light of the current phase of the business cycle.

DuPont Analysis: The Decomposition of ROE

ROE measures the return a company generates on its equity capital. Decomposing ROE into its components through DuPont analysis has the following uses:

- It facilitates a meaningful evaluation of the different aspects of the company's performance that affect reported ROE.
- It helps in determining the reasons for changes in ROE over time for a given company. It also helps us understand the reasons for differences in ROE for different companies over a given time period.
- It can direct management to areas that it should focus on to improve ROE.
- It shows the relationship between the various categories of ratios and how they all influence the return that owners realize on their investment.

$$\text{ROE} = \frac{\text{Net income}}{\text{Average shareholders' equity}}$$

$$\text{ROE} = \frac{\text{Net income}}{\text{Average total assets}} \times \frac{\text{Average total assets}}{\text{Average shareholder's equity}}$$

$$\text{ROE} = \frac{\text{Net income}}{\text{Revenue}} \times \frac{\text{Revenue}}{\text{Average total assets}} \times \frac{\text{Average total assets}}{\text{Average shareholders' equity}}$$

$$\text{ROE} = \frac{\text{Net income}}{\text{EBT}} \times \frac{\text{EBT}}{\text{EBIT}} \times \frac{\text{EBIT}}{\text{Revenue}} \times \frac{\text{Revenue}}{\text{Average total assets}} \times \frac{\text{Average total assets}}{\text{Avg. shareholders' equity}}$$

Valuation ratios measure the quantity of an asset or flow (for e.g., earnings) associated with ownership of a specific claim (for e.g., common stock).

$$\text{P/E} = \frac{\text{Price per share}}{\text{Earnings per share}}$$

$$\text{P/CF} = \frac{\text{Price per share}}{\text{Cash flow per share}}$$

$$\text{P/S} = \frac{\text{Price per share}}{\text{Sales per share}}$$

$$P/BV = \frac{\text{Price per share}}{\text{Book value per share}}$$

$$\text{Cash flow per share} = \frac{\text{Cash flow from operations}}{\text{Average number of shares outstanding}}$$

$$\text{EBITDA per share} = \frac{\text{EBITDA}}{\text{Average number of shares outstanding}}$$

$$\text{Dividends per share} = \frac{\text{Common dividends declared}}{\text{Weighted average number of ordinary shares}}$$

$$\text{Dividend payout ratio} = \frac{\text{Common share dividends}}{\text{Net income attributable to common shares}}$$

$$\text{Retention Rate} = \frac{\text{Net income attributable to common shares} - \text{Common share dividends}}{\text{Net income attributable to common shares}}$$

$$\text{Sustainable growth rate} = \text{Retention rate} \times \text{ROE}$$

Selected Credit Ratios[2]

Credit Ratio	Numerator[a]	Denominator
EBITDA interest coverage	EBITDA[b]	Interest expense, including noncash interest on conventional debt instruments
FFO[c] (funds from operations) to debt	FFO	Total debt
Free operating cash flow to debt	CFO[d] (adjusted) minus capital expenditures	Total debt
EBIT margin	EBIT[e]	Total revenues
EBITDA margin	EBITDA	Total revenues
Debt to EBITDA	Total debt	EBITDA
Return on capital	EBIT	Average beginning-of-year and end-of-year capital[f]

[a] Note that both the numerator and the denominator definitions are adjusted from ratio to ratio and may not correspond to the definitions used elsewhere in this reading.

[b] EBITDA = earnings before interest, taxes, depreciation, and amortization.

[c] FFO = funds from operations, defined as EBITDA minus net interest expense minus current tax expense (plus or minus all applicable adjustments).

[d] CFO = cash flow from operations.

[e] EBIT = earnings before interest and taxes.

[f] Capital = debt plus noncurrent deferred taxes plus equity (plus or minus all applicable adjustments).

Source: Based on data from Standard & Poor's *Corporate Methodology: Ratios And Adjustments* (2013). This represents the last updated version at the time of publication.

[2]Exhibit 20, Volume 3, CFA Program Curriculum 2022

FSA

Industry Specific Ratios

Ratios	Numerator	Denominator
Business Risk		
Coefficient of variation of operating income	Standard deviation of operating income	Average operating income
Coefficient of variation of net income	Standard deviation of net income	Average net income
Coefficient of variation of revenues	Standard deviation of revenues	Average revenue
Financial Sector Ratios		
Capital adequacy—banks	Various components of capital	Risk weighted assets, market risk exposure, and level of operational risk assumed
Monetary reserve requirement	Reserves held at central bank	Specified deposit liabilities
Liquid asset requirement	Approved "readily marketable securities"	Specified deposit liabilities
Net interest margin	Net interest income	Total interest-earning assets
Retail Ratios		
Same store sales	Average revenue growth year on year for stores open in both periods	Not applicable
Sales per square foot (meter)	Revenue	Total retail space in feet or meters
Service Companies		
Revenue per employee	Revenue	Total number of employees
Net income per employee	Net income	Total number of employees
Hotels		
Average daily rate	Room revenue	Number of rooms sold
Occupancy rate	Number of rooms sold	Number of rooms available

Segment Analysis

Segment Ratios	Numerator	Denominator	Measures
Segment margin	Segment profit (loss)	Segment revenue	Operating profitability relative to sales.
Segment turnover	Segment revenue	Segment assets	Overall efficiency-how much revenue is generated per dollar of assets.
Segment ROA	Segment profit (loss)	Segment assets	Operating profitability relative to assets.
Segment debt ratio	Segment liabilities	Segment assets	Solvency of the segment.

FSA

Model Building and Forecasting

Sensitivity analysis shows the range of possible outcomes as underlying assumptions are altered.

Scenario analysis shows the changes in key financial quantities that result from events such as a loss of supply of raw materials or a reduction in demand for the firm's products.

Simulations are computer generated sensitivity or scenario analyses that are based on probability models for the factors that drive outcomes.

STUDY SESSION 7:
FINANCIAL STATEMENT ANALYSIS (3)

INVENTORIES
Cross-Reference to CFA Institute Assigned Reading #21

Cost of Inventories

IFRS and U.S. GAAP suggest a similar treatment of various expenses in the determination of inventory cost. The following items are capitalized inventory costs, which are included in the cost of inventories.

- Costs of purchase.
- Costs of conversion.

Capitalization of these costs results in a build-up of asset balances, and delays recognition of costs until inventory is sold.

The following items are not capitalized as inventory costs; they are expensed on the income statement as incurred:

- Abnormal costs from material wastage.
- Storage costs that are not a part of normal production processes.
- Administrative expenses.
- Selling and marketing costs.

Capitalization of costs that should be expensed results in overstatement of net income due to the delay in recognition of costs, and an overstatement of inventory value on the balance sheet.

Inventory Valuation Methods

FIFO
- Older units are the first ones sold.
- Units that are purchased recently are included in EI.
- COGS is composed of units valued at older prices.
- EI is composed of units valued at recent prices.

LIFO
- Recently acquired units are the first ones to be sold.
- Oldest units are included in EI.
- COGS is composed of units valued at recent prices.
- Ending inventory is composed of units valued at older prices.

AVCO (weighted-average cost)
- COGS is composed of units valued at average prices.
- Ending inventory is also composed of units that are valued at average prices.

FIFO will always give a better reflection of the current economic value of inventory because the units currently in stock are valued at the most *recent* prices.
- If prices are *rising* LIFO and AVCO will *understate* ending inventory value.
- If prices are *falling*, LIFO and AVCO will *overstate* ending inventory value.
- When prices are stable, the three methods will value inventory at the same level.

FSA

LIFO will always offer a closer reflection of replacement costs in COGS because it allocates *recent* costs to COGS. LIFO is the most economically accurate method for income statement purposes because it provides a better measure of current income and future profitability.

- If prices are *rising*, FIFO and AVCO will *understate* replacement costs in COGS and *overstate* profits.
- If prices are *falling*, FIFO and AVCO will *overstate* replacements costs in COGS and *understate* profits.
- When prices are stable, the three methods will value COGS at same level.

When prices are *rising* during the year and inventory levels are stable or rising:

- $COGS_{LIFO} > COGS_{AVCO} > COGS_{FIFO}$
- $EI_{FIFO} > EI_{AVCO} > EI_{LIFO}$

When prices are *falling* during the year and inventory levels are stable or rising:

- $COGS_{FIFO} > COGS_{AVCO} > COGS_{LIFO}$
- $EI_{LIFO} > EI_{AVCO} > EI_{FIFO}$

LIFO versus FIFO when Prices Are Rising

	LIFO	FIFO
COGS	Higher	Lower
Income before taxes	Lower	Higher
Income taxes	Lower	Higher
Net income	Lower	Higher
Cash flow	Higher	Lower
EI	Lower	Higher
Working capital	Lower	Higher

Periodic versus Perpetual Inventory Systems

Periodic inventory system: Under this system, the quantity of inventory on hand is calculated periodically. The cost of goods available for sale during the period is calculated as beginning inventory plus purchases over the period. The ending inventory amount is then deducted from cost of goods available for sale to determine COGS.
Perpetual inventory system: Under this system, changes in the inventory account are updated continuously. Purchases and sales are recorded directly in the inventory account as they occur.

Under the **LIFO** cost flow assumption, in a period of rising prices, use of the periodic system for inventory results in a:

- *Lower* value of ending inventory.
- *Higher* value for COGS.

Therefore, gross profit would be *lower* under the periodic system.

Other important takeaways:

- The value of sales and cost of goods available for sale are the same under the two systems in the first year of operations.

- In subsequent years, the amounts of cost of goods available for sale can be different under the two systems due to different values of opening inventory (previous periods' ending inventory).
- If a company uses FIFO, COGS and EI is the same under the periodic and perpetual inventory systems.
- If a company uses separate identification, COGS and EI is the same under the periodic and perpetual inventory systems.
- If a company uses AVCO:
    - COGS and EI are the same as under FIFO and AVCO under the perpetual inventory system.
    - COGS and EI are different from their value under FIFO under the periodic inventory system.

Generally speaking, analysts do not make adjustments when comparing financial statements of a company that uses AVCO to one that uses FIFO. This is because:

- The perpetual inventory system is more common (the values of COGS and EI are similar under FIFO and AVCO if the perpetual system is used).
- There is a general dearth of relevant disclosures in this area.

Assuming rising prices and stable or increasing inventory quantities, use of the LIFO method generally results in higher COGS, lower EI, lower GP, and lower NP than with the FIFO method, under both periodic and perpetual inventory systems.

LIFO to FIFO Conversion

$$EI_{FIFO} = EI_{LIFO} + LIFO \text{ reserve}$$

$$COGS_{FIFO} = COGS - (LR_{Ending} - LR_{Beginning})$$

During a period of rising prices and stable or rising inventory quantities:

- Net income after tax under FIFO will be greater than LIFO net income after tax by:
    - Change in LIFO reserve $\times$ (1 − tax rate)
- Equity (retained earnings) under FIFO will be greater by:
    - LIFO reserve $\times$ (1− tax rate)
- Liabilities (deferred taxes) under FIFO will be greater by:
    - LIFO reserve $\times$ (tax rate)
- Current assets (inventory) under FIFO will be greater by:
    - LIFO reserve

Increase in LIFO Reserve

In every period during which prices are rising and inventory quantities are stable or rising, the LIFO reserve will increase as the excess of FIFO ending inventory over LIFO ending inventory increases.

Decline in LIFO Reserve

There can be two reasons for a decline in LIFO reserve:

1. LIFO liquidation.
2. Declining prices.

LIFO Liquidation

LIFO liquidation occurs when, during an inflationary period, a firm that uses LIFO sells more units during a given period than it purchases over the period. This causes year-end inventory levels to be lower than beginning-of-year inventory levels.

When a LIFO firm sells more units than it purchases, some of the goods sold are units that were included in beginning inventory. LIFO allocates the oldest prices to inventory, and in some cases these older prices could be outdated by many years. When a company includes older, cheaper stock in its COGS, it severely understates its COGS, and LIFO COGS no longer reflect recent, current prices. Consequently a firm with LIFO liquidation overstates net income. The higher profits are unsustainable because eventually, the firm will run out of cheaper, older stock to liquidate. The higher net income also comes at the cost of higher taxes that reduce operating cash flow. To postpone these taxes on holding gains on old units of inventory, a LIFO firm must always purchase as many as, if not more units, than it sells.

LIFO liquidation can result from strikes, recessions, or a decline in demand for the firm's product. The irony is that when there is LIFO liquidation, the firm reports surprisingly high profits (due to the realization of holding gains) in hard times when production cuts result in the liquidation of lower cost LIFO inventory.

Analysts should be aware that management can inflate their company's reported gross profits and net income by intentionally reducing inventory quantities and liquidating older (cheaper) units of stock. Therefore, it is important to analyse the LIFO reserve footnote disclosures to determine if LIFO liquidation has occurred. If it is found that LIFO liquidation has occurred, analysts must exclude the increase in earnings due to LIFO liquidation from their analysis. COGS must be adjusted upwards for the decline in LIFO reserve, and net income must be lowered.

LIFO liquidations are more likely to occur with firms that break inventory down into numerous categories. When the different types of inventory are pooled into only a few broad categories, decreases in quantities of certain items are usually offset by increases in quantities of others.

Declining Prices

When prices of the firm's products fall over a given period, the firm will see a decline in its LIFO reserve. If the change in LIFO reserve is negative, $COGS_{FIFO}$ will be greater than $COGS_{LIFO}$. FIFO would continue to reflect the latest (and in this case lower) prices in inventory, and will provide the most economically accurate measure of inventory value, while LIFO would continue to reflect current replacement costs in COGS. When the reduction in LIFO reserve is caused by declining prices, no analytical adjustments are necessary.

Inventory Method Changes

Consistency in the inventory costing method used is required under U.S. GAAP and IFRS.

Under **IFRS**, a change in policy is acceptable only if the change results in the provision of more reliable and relevant information in the financial statements.

- Changes in inventory accounting policy are applied retrospectively.
- Information for all periods presented in the financial report is restated.
- Adjustments for periods prior to the earliest year presented in the financial report are reflected in the beginning balance of retained earnings for the earliest year presented in the report.

U.S. GAAP has a similar requirement for changes in inventory accounting policies.

- However, a company must thoroughly explain how the newly-adopted inventory accounting method is superior and preferable to the old one.
- The company may be required to seek permission from the Internal Revenue Service (IRS) before making any changes.
- If inventory-related accounting policies are modified, changes to the financial statements must be made retrospectively, unless the LIFO method is being adopted (which is applied prospectively).

Inventory Adjustments

Under **IFRS**, inventory must be stated at the **lower of cost or net realizable value (NRV)**. **NRV** is the estimated selling price in the ordinary course of business less the estimated costs necessary to make the sale and estimated costs to get the inventory in condition for sale. If the NRV of inventory falls below the cost recorded on the balance sheet, inventory must be written down, and a loss must be recognized (as a part of COGS or separately) on the income statement. A subsequent increase in NRV would require a reversal of the previous write-down, which would reduce COGS in the period that the increase in value occurs. However, the increase in value that can be recognized is limited to the total write-down that had previously been recorded. Effectively, inventory value can never exceed the amount originally recognized.

U.S. GAAP used to require the application of the lower of cost or market (LCM) principle to value inventory. For fiscal years beginning after December 15, 2016, inventories measured using other than LIFO and retail inventory methods are measured at the lower of cost or net realizable value. This is broadly consistent with IFRS, with one major difference: that U.S. GAAP prohibits the reversal of write-downs.

When the LCM principle must be applied under U.S. GAAP (for inventories measured using LIFO and retail inventory methods), market value is defined as replacement cost, where replacement cost must lie within a range of values from NRV minus normal profit margin to NRV. If replacement cost is higher than NRV, it must be brought down to NRV, and if replacement cost is lower than NRV minus normal profit margin, it must be brought up to NRV minus normal profit margin. This adjusted replacement cost is then compared to carrying value (cost), and the lower of the two is used to value inventory. Any write-down of inventory reduces the value of inventory and increases COGS.

An inventory write-down reduces both profit and the carrying amount of inventory on the balance sheet and thus has a negative effect on profitability, liquidity, and solvency ratios. However, activity ratios such as inventory turnover will be positively affected. Due to overall negative financial impact, some companies may be reluctant to record inventory write-downs unless the decline in value is believed to be permanent. This is especially true under U.S. GAAP where reversal of a write-down is prohibited.

Companies that use separate identification, AVCO, or FIFO inventory methods are more likely to incur inventory write-downs than companies that use LIFO. This is because LIFO values units of inventory at the oldest prices, which, given that prices are generally on the rise, results in lower carrying values for inventory. Since LIFO inventory is based on oldest and lowest costs, there is a lower chance of an inventory write-down, and if there is a write-down, it will likely be of a lesser magnitude.

In certain industries like agriculture, forest products, and mining, both U.S. GAAP and IFRS allow companies to value inventory at NRV even when it exceeds historical cost. If an active market exists for the product, quoted market prices are used as NRV; otherwise the price of the most recent market transaction is used. Unrealized gains and losses on inventory resulting from fluctuating market prices are recognized on the income statement.

The impact of an inventory write-down on a company's reported financial position can be substantial. Therefore, analysts should careful evaluate the potential for any inventory write-downs and gauge their impact on financial ratios, especially if debt covenants entail financial ratio requirements. The potential for inventory write-downs tends to be higher in industries where technological obsolescence of inventories is a significant risk.

Inventory write-downs raise concerns regarding management's ability to anticipate how much and what type of inventory is required. Further, they affect a company's future reported earnings.

Impact of an Inventory Write-Down on Various Financial Ratios

Type of Ratio	Effect on Numerator	Effect on Denominator	Effect on Ratio
Profitability ratios			
NP and GP margins	COGS increases so profits fall	Sales remain the same	Lower (worsens)
Solvency ratios			
Debt-to-equity and debt ratio	Debt levels remain the same	Equity decreases (due to lower profits) and current assets decrease (due to lower inventory)	Higher (worsens)
Liquidity ratios			
Current ratio	Current assets decrease (due to lower inventory)	Current liabilities remain the same	Lower (worsens)
Activity ratios			
Inventory turnover	COGS increases	Average inventory decreases	Higher (improves)
Total asset turnover	Sales remain the same	Total assets decrease	Higher (improves)

Presentation and Disclosure

IFRS requires companies to make the following disclosures relating to inventory:

1. The accounting policies used to value inventory.
2. The cost formula used for inventory valuation.
3. The total carrying value of inventories, and the carrying value of different classifications (e.g., merchandise, raw materials, work-in-progress, finished goods).
4. The value of inventories carried at fair value less selling costs.
5. Amount of inventory-related expenses for the period (cost of sales).
6. The amount of any write-downs recognized during the period.
7. The amount of reversal recognized on any previous write-down.
8. Description of the circumstances that led to the reversal.
9. The carrying amount of inventories pledged as collateral for liabilities. **U.S. GAAP** does not permit the reversal of prior-year inventory write-downs. U.S. GAAP also requires disclosure of significant estimates applicable to inventories and of any material amount of income resulting from the liquidation of LIFO inventory.

Inventory Ratios

$$\text{Inventory turnover} = \frac{\text{COGS}}{\text{Average inventory}}$$

$$\text{No. of days of inventory} = \frac{365}{\text{Inventory turnover}}$$

$$\text{Gross profit margin} = \frac{\text{Gross profit}}{\text{Sales revenue}}$$

If a company has a *higher* inventory turnover ratio and a *lower* number of days of inventory than the industry average, it could mean one of two things:

- It could indicate that the company is more efficient in inventory management as less resources are tied up in inventory at any given point in time.
- It could also suggest that the company does not carry enough inventory at any point in time, which might be hurting sales.

To determine which explanation holds true, analysts should compare the firm's revenue growth with that of the industry. A low sales growth compared to the industry would imply that the company is losing out on sales by holding low inventory quantities. A sales growth rate similar to, or higher than industry sales growth would suggest that the company manages inventory more efficiently than its peers.

A firm whose inventory turnover is *lower* and number of days of inventory is *higher* than industry average could have a problem with slow moving or obsolete inventory.

The gross profit margin indicates the percentage of sales that is contributing to net income as opposed to covering the cost of sales.

- Firms in relatively competitive industries have lower gross profit margins.
- Firms selling luxury products tend to have lower volumes and higher gross profit margins.
- Firms selling luxury products are likely to have lower inventory turnover ratios.

Remember that inventory ratios are directly affected by the cost flow assumption used by the firm. When making comparisons across firms, analysts must understand the differences that arise from the use of different cost flow assumptions.

Financial Statement Analysis Issues

- A significant increase in unit volumes of raw materials and/or WIP inventory may suggest that the company expects an increase in demand for its products.
- An increase in finished goods inventory with declining raw materials and WIP inventory may signal decrease in demand for the company's products.
- If growth in inventories is greater than the growth in sales, it could indicate a decrease in demand.
- To obtain additional information about a company's inventory and its future sales, analysts should examine the MD&A section, industry-related news and publications, and industry data.

LIFO versus FIFO Ratio Comparisons when Prices are Rising

Type of Ratio	Effect on Numerator	Effect on Denominator	Effect on Ratio
NP and GP margins	Income is lower under LIFO because COGS is higher	Sales are the same under both	Lower under LIFO
Debt to equity	Same debt levels	Lower equity under LIFO	Higher under LIFO
Current ratio	Current assets are lower under LIFO because EI is lower.	Current liabilities are the same	Lower under LIFO
Quick ratio	Assets are higher as a result of lower taxes paid	Current liabilities are the same	Higher under LIFO
Inventory turnover	COGS is higher under LIFO	Average inventory is lower under LIFO	Higher under LIFO
Total asset turnover	Sales are the same	Lower total assets under LIFO	Higher under LIFO

Example

- A superficial comparison between inventory-related ratios of two companies (let's say ABC and XYZ) may show that ABC has a lower percentage of assets ties up in inventory, suggesting that ABC is using its working capital more efficiently. However, if ABC were using LIFO and XYZ were using FIFO in an inflationary environment with stable or rising inventory quantities, ABC's lower ratio could be explained by its use of the LIFO cost flow assumption (inventory is carried at a lower value under LIFO in an inflationary environment), not by relative efficiency in inventory management.
- Further, growth in inventory may exceed growth in sales for both ABC and XYZ, suggesting that both companies may be accumulating excess inventory. A superficial comparison of the ratio of inventory growth to sales growth for the companies may indicate that ABC's growth rate in finished goods compared to growth rate in sales is lower than XYZ's (indicating that XYZ in more danger of being left with too much inventory). However, if ABC were using LIFO and XYZ were using FIFO in an inflationary environment with stable or rising inventory quantities, the analyst would be able to conclude that ABC's growth rate in finished goods to growth rate in sales is relatively lower (at least partially) due to its use of LIFO (which carries ending inventory at a lower value than FIFO in an inflationary environment).

LONG-LIVED ASSETS
Cross-Reference to CFA Institute Assigned Reading #22

Long-Lived Tangible Assets: Property Plant & Equipment (PP&E)

Long-lived assets are expected to provide economic benefits to a company over an extended period of time, typically longer than one year. There are three types of long-lived assets:

- **Tangible assets** have physical substance, (e.g., land, plant, and equipment).
- **Intangible assets** do not have physical substance (e.g., patents and trademarks).
- **Financial assets** include securities issued by other companies.

The cost of most long-lived assets is allocated over the period of time that they are expected to provide economic benefits. The two types of long-lived assets whose costs are not expensed over time are **land** and **intangible assets with indefinite useful lives**.

Capitalization versus Expensing

Effects of Capitalization

	Effects on Financial Statements
Initially when the cost is capitalized	<ul><li>Noncurrent assets *increase*.</li><li>Cash flow from investing activities *decreases*.</li></ul>
In future periods when the asset is depreciated or amortized	<ul><li>Noncurrent assets *decrease*.</li><li>Net income *decreases*.</li><li>Retained earnings *decrease*.</li><li>Equity *decreases*.</li></ul>

Effects of Expensing

	Effects on Financial Statements
When the item is expensed	<ul><li>Net income *decreases* by the entire after-tax amount of the cost.</li><li>No related asset is recorded on the balance sheet and therefore no depreciation or amortization expense is charged in future periods.</li><li>Operating cash flow *decreases*.</li><li>Expensed costs have no financial statement impact in future years.</li></ul>

Impact on Financial Statements and Ratios

Financial Statement Effects of Capitalizing versus Expensing

	Capitalizing	Expensing
Net income (first year)	Higher	Lower
Net income (future years)	Lower	Higher
Total assets	Higher	Lower
Shareholders' equity	Higher	Lower
Cash flow from operations activities	Higher	Lower
Cash flow from investing activities	Lower	Higher
Income variability	Lower	Higher
Debt-to-equity ratio	Lower	Higher

All other factors remaining the same, the decision to expense an item as opposed to capitalizing it would give the impression of *greater earnings growth*. Further, expensing allows companies to report lower taxable income in the current period and pay out *lower taxes* (conserving cash).

On the other hand, the decision to capitalize an item as opposed to expensing may make it easier for a company to *achieve earnings targets* for a particular period. Further, capitalization allows companies to report *higher operating cash flow*, which is an important valuation metric.

Therefore, when making comparisons across companies, it is important to account for differences in the companies' expenditure capitalizing policies. Analysts should be wary of companies that:

- Inflate reported cash flow from operations by capitalizing expenditures that should be expensed.
- Inflate profits to meet earnings targets by capitalizing costs that should be expensed.
- Depress current period income by expensing costs that should be capitalized, in order to be able to exhibit impressive profitability growth going forward without any real improvement in operating performance.

If a company continues to purchase comparable or increasing amounts of fixed assets every year, capitalization will result in higher profits over an extended period. This would continue to be the case until the value of fixed assets purchased in a given year (amount expensed by the expensing firm) is lower than depreciation charged on capitalized assets by the capitalizing firm.

Acquisition of Long-Lived Tangible Assets Acquired through an Exchange

- If an asset is acquired in a nonmonetary exchange, the amount recognized on the balance sheet typically equals the fair value of the asset acquired.
- In accounting for such exchanges the carrying amount of the asset given up is removed from noncurrent assets on the balance sheet, the fair value of the asset acquired is added, and any difference between the two values is recognized on the income statement as a gain or a loss.
- If the fair value of the asset acquired is greater (lower) than the value of the asset given up, a gain (loss) is recorded on the income statement.
- In rare cases, if the fair value of the acquired asset cannot be determined, the amount recognized on the balance sheet equals the carrying amount of the asset given up. In this case, no gain or loss is recognized.

Acquisition of Long-Lived Tangible Assets Acquired through a Purchase

When a long-lived asset is purchased, expenses other than the purchase price may be incurred.

- These costs are also capitalized and included in the value of the asset on the balance sheet.
- Subsequent expenses related to the long-lived asset may be capitalized if they are expected to provide economic benefits beyond one year, or expensed if they are not expected to provide economic benefits beyond one year.
- Expenditures that extend an asset's useful life are usually capitalized.

Capitalization of Interest Costs

Companies must capitalize interest costs associated with financing the acquisition or construction of an asset that requires a long period of time to ready for its intended use. For example, if a company constructs a building for its own use, interest expense incurred to finance construction must be capitalized along with the costs of constructing the building. The interest rate used to determine the amount of interest capitalized depends on the company's existing borrowings or, if applicable, on borrowings specifically incurred to finance the cost of the asset.

- Under **IFRS**, but not **U.S. GAAP**, income earned from temporarily investing borrowed funds that were acquired to finance the cost of the asset must be subtracted from interest expense on the borrowed funds to determine the amount that can be capitalized.
- If a company is constructing the asset for its own use, capitalized interest is included in the cost of the asset and appears on the balance sheet as a part of property, plant, and equipment. Once the asset is brought into use, the entire cost of the asset, inclusive of capitalized interest, is depreciated over time, so capitalized interest is then a part of depreciation expense, not interest expense. As a result of this accounting treatment, a company's interest costs can appear on the balance sheet (when capitalized) or on the income statement (when expensed).
- If construction and sale of buildings is the core business activity of the firm, and a building is constructed with the intention of selling it, capitalized interest costs are included along with costs of construction in inventory as a part of current assets. The capitalized interest is expenses as a part of COGS in the period that the building is sold.
- Interest payments made prior to completion of construction that are **capitalized** are classified under cash flow from *investing activities*.
- Interest payments that are **expensed** may be classified as *operating* or *financing* cash outflows under **IFRS**, and are classified as *operating* cash outflows under **U.S. GAAP**.

Analytical Issues Relating to Capitalization of Interest Costs

- Capitalized interest costs reduce investing cash flow, while expensed interest costs reduce operating cash flow. Therefore, analysts may want to examine the impact of classification on reported cash flows.
- To provide a true picture of a company's interest coverage ratio, the entire amount of interest expense for the period, whether capitalized or expensed, should be used in the denominator. If the company is depreciating interest that was capitalized in previous years, net income should be adjusted to remove the effect of depreciation of capitalized interest.

$$\text{Interest coverage ratio} = (\text{EBIT}/\text{Interest expense})$$

The interest coverage ratio measures the number of times that a company's operating profits (EBIT) cover its interest expense. A higher ratio indicates that the company can comfortably service its debt through operating earnings.

- Any interest costs capitalized in the current period should be treated as interest expense. Net income should be reduced by the amount of interest capitalized in the current period.

Intangible Assets

Intangible assets lack physical substance and include items that involve exclusive rights such as patents, copyrights, and trademarks. Some intangible assets have finite lives, while others have indefinite lives.

- The cost of an intangible asset with a **finite life** (e.g., patent) is **amortized** over its useful life.
- The cost of an intangible asset with an **indefinite life** (e.g., goodwill) is not amortized; instead, the asset is tested (at least annually) for **impairment**. If deemed impaired, the asset's balance sheet value is reduced and a loss is recognized on the income statement.

Intangible assets can also be classified as **identifiable** or **unidentifiable** intangible assets.

Under **IFRS**, **identifiable intangible assets** must meet three definitional criteria and two recognition criteria.

Definitional criteria:

- They must be identifiable. This means that they should either be separable from the entity or must arise from legal rights.
- They must be under the company's control.
- They must be expected to earn future economic benefits.

Recognition criteria:

- It is probable that their expected future economic benefits will flow to the entity.
- The cost of the asset can be reliably measured.

An **unidentifiable intangible asset** is one that cannot be purchased separately and may have an indefinite life. The best example of such an asset is goodwill, which arises when one company purchases another and the acquisition price exceeds the fair value of the identifiable (tangible and intangible) assets acquired.

Accounting for an intangible asset depends on the manner of its acquisition.

Intangible Assets Acquired in Situations Other than Business Combinations (e.g., Buying a Patent)

These assets are recorded at their **fair value** when acquired, where the fair value is assumed to equal the purchase price. They are recognized on the balance sheet, and costs of acquisition are classified as *investing* activities on the cash flow statement. If several intangible assets are acquired as a group, the purchase price is allocated to each individual asset based on its fair value.

Companies use a significant degree of judgment to determine fair values of individual intangible assets purchased. Therefore, analysts focus more on the types of intangible assets purchased as opposed to the value assigned to each individual asset. Understanding the types of intangible assets the company is acquiring can offer valuable insight into the company's overall strategy and future potential.

Intangible Assets Developed Internally

These are generally expensed when incurred, but may be capitalized in certain situations. Due to the differences in requirements regarding expensing/capitalizing when it comes to intangible assets developed internally versus those acquired, a company's strategy (developing versus acquiring intangible assets) can significantly impact reported financial ratios.

- A company that develops intangible assets internally will expense costs of development and recognize no related assets, while a firm that acquires intangible assets will recognize them as assets.
- A company that develops intangible assets internally will classify development-related cash outflows under *operating* activities on the cash flow statement, while an acquiring firm will classify these costs under *investing* activities.

Research and Development Costs (R&D)

IFRS requires that expenditures on *research* or during the *research phase* of an internal project be **expensed** rather than capitalized as an intangible asset.

IFRS allows companies to recognize an intangible asset arising from *development* or the *development phase* of an internal project if certain criteria are met, including a demonstration of the technical feasibility of completing the intangible asset and the intent to use or sell the asset.

Generally speaking, **U.S. GAAP** requires that R&D costs be **expensed** when incurred. However, it does require that certain costs related to *software development* be **capitalized**.

- Costs incurred to develop software for sale are expensed until the product's technological feasibility has been established. Once feasibility has been established, associated development costs are capitalized.
- Costs related directly to the development of software for internal use are also expensed until it is probable that the project will be completed and that the software will be used as intended. After that, related development costs are capitalized.

Note the following:

- The probability of "the project being completed" is easier to establish than "technological feasibility."
- The involvement of subjective judgment in determining technological feasibility means that capitalization practices vary to a significant extent across companies.
- Capitalized costs related directly to developing software for sale of internal use include the cost of employees who help build and test the software.
- The treatment of software development costs under **U.S. GAAP** is similar to the treatment of all costs of internally developed intangible assets under **IFRS**.

Expensing rather than capitalizing development costs results in:

- *Lower* net income in the current period.
- *Lower* operating cash flow and higher investing cash flow in the current period.

Note that if current period software development costs exceed amortization of prior periods' capitalized development costs, net income would be *lower* under expensing. If, however, software development expenditures were to slow down such that current year expenses are lower than amortization of prior periods' capitalized costs, net income would be *higher* under expensing.

Intangible Assets Acquired in a Business Combination

When a company acquires another company, the transaction is accounted for using the acquisition method (under both **IFRS** and **U.S. GAAP**). Under this method, if the purchase price paid by the acquirer to buy a company exceeds the fair value of its net assets, the excess is recorded as **goodwill**.

Goodwill is an intangible asset that cannot be identified separately from the business as a whole.

- Only goodwill created in a business acquisition can be recognized on the balance sheet; internally generated goodwill cannot be capitalized.

Under **IFRS**, acquired intangible assets are classified as identifiable intangible assets if they meet the definitional and recognition criteria that we listed earlier. If an item acquired does not meet these criteria and cannot be recognized as a tangible asset, it is recognized as a part of goodwill.

Under **U.S. GAAP**, an intangible asset acquired in a business combination should be recognized separately from goodwill if:

- The asset arises from legal or contractual rights; or
- The item can be separated from the acquired company.

Examples of intangible assets treated separately from goodwill include intangible assets like patents, copyrights, franchises, licenses and internet domain names.

Analyst Adjustments for Variation in Capitalization Practices Across Companies

Adjustments must be made to compare the financial performance of a company that expenses software development costs with that of a peer company that capitalizes these costs. For the company that capitalizes software development costs, an analyst should make the following adjustments:

- The income statement for the current period should include related software development costs as an expense and exclude amortization of development costs capitalized in prior periods.
- The capitalized asset should be removed from the balance sheet (decrease assets and equity).
- Operating cash flow should be reduced and investing cash flow should be increased by the amount of development costs that have been capitalized in the current period.
- Ratios that include income, long-lived assets, or cash flow from operations should be recalculated using adjusted values.

Depreciation Methods and Calculation of Depreciation Expense

The Cost Model

The cost model is required under **U.S. GAAP** and permitted under **IFRS**. Under this model, the cost of long-lived tangible assets (except land) and intangible assets with finite useful lives is allocated over their useful lives as depreciation and amortization expense. Under the cost model, an asset's carrying value equals its historical cost minus accumulated depreciation/amortization (as long as the asset has not been impaired).

Straight line depreciation expense:

$$\text{Depreciation expense} = \frac{\text{Original cost} - \text{Salvage value}}{\text{Depreciable life}}$$

Double declining balance depreciation:

$$\text{DDB depreciation in Year X} = \frac{2}{\text{Depreciable life}} \times \text{BV at the beginning of Year X}$$

Straight Line versus Accelerated Depreciation

All other factors remaining the same, a company that uses the straight-line method to depreciate its assets will report:

- A lower asset turnover ratio during the early years of the asset's use because a lower depreciation charge results in higher net assets.
- Higher operating profit margin in the early years of the asset's use because lower depreciation expense results in higher operating income.
- Higher operating return on assets (ROA) in the early years of the asset's use (due to lower depreciation expense) and lower ROA in later years.

Further, a company that uses an accelerated depreciation method will report an improving asset turnover ratio, operating profit margin, and ROA over time.

Estimates Used for Calculating Depreciation

Assumptions of a *longer* useful life and a *higher* expected residual value result in *lower* annual depreciation expense compared to assumptions of a shorter useful life and a lower salvage value. The subjective nature of these assumptions allows management to manipulate earnings.

Management could significantly write-down the value of long-lived assets and recognize a hefty charge against net income in the current period. While this would depress earnings in the current year, it would allow management to recognize lower annual depreciation expense going forward, inflate profits, and report impressive growth in profitability.

Management could also overstate the useful life and the salvage value of an asset to show impressive profits over the near term, and recognize a significant loss at a later point in time when the asset is eventually retired.

Additional assumptions are required to allocate depreciation expense between cost of goods sold (COGS) and selling, general, and administrative expenses (SG&A). Including a higher proportion of total depreciation expense in COGS lowers the gross profit margin and lowers operation expenses. However, it does not affect the net profit margin.

There are no significant differences between IFRS and U.S. GAAP regarding the definition of depreciation and acceptable depreciation methods. However, **IFRS** requires companies to use the **component method of depreciation**. Under this method, companies depreciate different components of assets separately (using estimates for each component). Under **U.S. GAAP**, this method is allowed but not widely used.

The Revaluation Model

IFRS allows companies to use the **revaluation model** or the cost model to report the carrying amounts of noncurrent assets on the balance sheet. Revaluation results in the carrying amount of an asset reflecting its fair value (as long as it can be measured reliably). Under **U.S. GAAP**, only use of the cost model is permitted.

A key difference between the revaluation and the cost model is that revaluation allows for the reported value of the asset to be higher than its historical cost. Under the cost model on the other hand, the reported value of an asset can never exceed its historical cost.

IFRS allows the revaluation model to be used for certain classes of assets and for the cost model to be used for others as long as:

1. The company applies the same model to assets in a particular class (e.g., land and buildings, machinery, factory equipment etc.)
2. Whenever a revaluation is performed, all assets in the particular class must be revalued (to avoid selective revaluation).

The revaluation model may also be used to value intangible assets, but only if an active market for the asset exists where its fair value can be determined.

Under the revaluation model, whether a revaluation affects earnings (net income) depends on whether the revaluation initially increases or decreases the carrying amount of the asset class.

- If a revaluation initially *decreases* the carrying amount of an asset:
  - The decrease in value is recognized as a loss on the income statement.
  - Later, if the value of the asset class increases:
    - The increase is recognized as a gain on the income statement to the extent that it reverses a revaluation loss previously recognized on the income statement against the same asset class.
    - Any increase in value beyond the reversal amount will not be recognized on the income statement, but adjusted directly to equity through the revaluation surplus account.
- If a revaluation initially *increases* the carrying amount of an asset:
  - The increase in value bypasses the income statement and goes directly to equity through the revaluation surplus account.
  - Later, if the value of the asset class decreases:
    - The decrease reduces the revaluation surplus to the extent of the gain previously recognized in the revaluation surplus against the same asset class.
    - Any decrease in value beyond the reversal amount will be recognized as a loss on the income statement.

If an asset is sold or disposed of, any associated revaluation surplus recognized in other comprehensive income is transferred directly to retained earnings.

Considerations for Financial Analysis

Asset revaluations require many considerations for financial statement analysis.

- An increase in the carrying value of depreciable long-lived assets increases total assets and shareholders' equity. Hence, revaluation of assets can be used to reduce reported leverage

- Asset revaluations that decrease the value of an asset also decrease net income in the year of revaluation. In the year of revaluation, return on assets and return on equity decline. In future years however, the lower values of assets and equity may result in higher ROA and ROE. Further, reversals of downward revaluations also go through income. Managers can then opportunistically time the reversals to manage earnings and increase income.
- If the carrying value of the asset is increased in a revaluation, assets and equity increase, and annual depreciation expense also increases. As a result, performance measures such as ROA and ROE may decline in the future. This is ironic given that an upward revaluation is usually associated with an improvement in the operating capacity of the asset and is beneficial for the company.
- Analysts should also look into who performs asset value appraisals and how often revaluations are recognized.

Amortization Methods and Calculation of Amortization Expense

Intangible Assets with Finite Lives

Intangible assets with finite useful lives are amortized over their useful lives. This results in the cost of these assets being "matched" with the benefits that accrue from them. Acceptable amortization methods are the same as acceptable depreciation methods. The estimates required to calculate yearly amortization expense for an intangible fixed asset with a finite life are:

- The original value of the intangible asset.
- The residual value at the end of its useful life.
- The length of its useful life.

Impairment of Assets

An **impairment** charge is made to reflect the unexpected decline in the fair value of an asset. Impairment recognition has the following effects on a company's financial statements:

- The carrying value of the asset decreases.
- The impairment charge reduces net income.
- Impairment does not affect cash flows because it is a noncash charge.

Impairment of Property, Plant, and Equipment

Companies are required to assess whether there are indications of impairment of property, plant, and equipment at the end of each reporting period. If there are no suggestions of impairment, the asset is not tested for impairment. However, if there are indications of impairment, the recoverable amount of the asset must be measured in order to test the asset for impairment. Indications of impairment include evidence of obsolescence, decrease in demand for the asset's output, and technological advancements.

Under **IFRS**, an asset is considered impaired when its carrying amount exceeds its recoverable amount. The recoverable amount equals the higher of "fair value less costs to sell" and "value in use," where value in use refers to the discounted value of future cash flows expected from the asset. The impairment loss that must be recognized equals the carrying amount minus the recoverable amount.

Under **U.S. GAAP**, determining whether an asset is impaired is different from measuring the impairment loss. An asset is considered impaired when its carrying value exceeds the total value of its undiscounted expected future cash flows (recoverable amount). Once the carrying value is determined to be unrecoverable, the impairment loss is measured as the difference between the asset's carrying amount and its fair value (or the discounted value of future cash flows, if fair value is not known).

Impairment of Intangible Assets with a Finite Life

Intangible assets with finite lives are amortized. These assets are not tested for impairment annually (unlike intangible assets with indefinite lives); they are only tested for impairment upon the occurrence of significant adverse events (e.g., a significant decrease in market price or adverse changes in legal and economic factors). Accounting for impairment of these assets is essentially the same as accounting for impairment of property, plant, and equipment.

Impairment of Intangibles with Indefinite Lives

Goodwill and other intangible assets with indefinite lives are not amortized. They are carried on the balance sheet at historical cost and tested at least annually for impairment. Impairment must be recognized when carrying value exceeds fair value.

Impairment of Long-Lived Assets Held for Sale

A long-lived asset is reclassified (from being an asset "held-for-use") to an asset "held-for-sale" when it is no longer in use and management intends to sell it. These assets are tested for impairment when they are categorized as held-for-sale. If it is found that the carrying value exceeds their fair value less selling costs, an impairment loss is recorded and their carrying value is brought down to fair value less selling costs. Once classified as held-for-sale, these assets are no longer depreciated or amortized by the company.

Reversals of Impairments of Long-Lived Assets

Under **U.S. GAAP**, once an impairment loss is recorded for assets held-for-use, it cannot be reversed. However, for assets held-for-sale, if the fair value of the asset increases subsequent to impairment recognition, the loss can be reversed and the asset's value can be revised upward.

IFRS allows reversal of impairment losses if the value of the asset increases regardless of classification of the asset. Reversal of a previously recognized impairment charge increases reported profits. Note that IFRS only allows reversals of impairment losses. It does not allow the value of the asset to be written up to a value greater than the previous carrying amount even if the new recoverable amount is greater than the previous carrying value.

Derecognition

A company **derecognizes** or removes an asset from its financial statements when the asset is disposed of or is not expected to provide any future economic benefits from use or disposal.

Sale of Long-Lived Assets

> Gain (loss) on asset disposal = Selling price − Carrying/book value of asset

> Carrying/book value = Historical cost − Accumulated depreciation

A gain or loss on the sale of a fixed asset is disclosed on the income statement either as a component of other gains and losses (if the amount is insignificant) or as a separate line item (if the amount is significant). Gains and losses on disposal of fixed assets can also be found on the cash flow statement if prepared using the indirect method. A company may disclose further details about the sale of long-lived assets in the management discussion and analysis (MD&A) section and/or financial statement footnotes.

Long-Lived Assets Disposed of Other than by a Sale

Long-lived assets intended to be disposed of other than by a sale (e.g., abandoned, exchanged for another asset, or distributed to owners in a spin-off) are classified as held for use until disposal. Just like other noncurrent assets held by the company, they continue to be depreciated and tested for impairment until actual disposal.

When an asset is **retired or abandoned**, the company does not receive any cash for it. Assets are reduced by the carrying value of the asset at the time of retirement or abandonment, and a loss equal to the asset's carrying amount is recorded on the income statement.

When an asset is **exchanged** for another asset, the carrying amount of the asset given up is removed from the company's balance sheet, and replaced by the fair value for the asset acquired. Any difference between the carrying amount and the fair value is recognized as a gain or loss on the income statement. Note that the fair value used is the fair value of the asset given up unless the fair value of the asset acquired is more clearly evident. If no reliable measure of fair value exists, the acquired asset is measured at the carrying amount of the asset given up.

In a **spin-off** an entire cash-generating unit of a company is separated into a new entity, with shareholders of the parent company receiving a proportional number of shares in the new company. All the assets of the new entity are removed from the balance sheet of the parent at the time of the spin-off.

FSA

Presentation and Disclosures

Disclosures: Tangible Assets

IFRS	U.S. GAAP
<ul><li>The measurement bases used.</li><li>The depreciation method used.</li><li>Useful lives (or depreciation rate).</li><li>Accumulated depreciation at the beginning and end of the period.</li><li>Restrictions on title.</li><li>Pledges of property as security.</li><li>Contractual agreements to acquire PP&E.</li><li>If the revaluation model is used, the company must disclose:<ul><li>The date of revaluation.</li><li>Details of fair value determination.</li><li>The carrying amount under the cost model.</li><li>Amount of revaluation surplus.</li></ul></li></ul>	<ul><li>Depreciation expense for the period.</li><li>The balances of major classes of depreciable assets.</li><li>Accumulated depreciation by major classes or in total.</li><li>General description of depreciation methods used for major classes of depreciable assets.</li></ul>

Disclosures: Intangible Assets

IFRS	U.S. GAAP

• For each class of intangible assets whether they have a finite or indefinite life.
   ○ If finite, for each class disclose:
     ■ The useful life (or amortization rate).
     ■ The amortization methods used.
     ■ The gross carrying amount.
     ■ Accumulated amortization at the beginning and end of the period.
     ■ Where amortization is included on the income statement.
     ■ Reconciliation of carrying amounts at the beginning and end of the period.
   ○ If indefinite:
     ■ Carrying amount of the asset.
     ■ Why it is considered to have an indefinite life.
• Restrictions on title.
• Pledges as security.
• Contractual agreement to purchase any intangible assets.
• If the revaluation model is used, the company must disclose:
   ○ The date of revaluation.
   ○ Details of fair value determination.
   ○ The carrying amount under the cost model.
   ○ Amount of revaluation surplus.
	• Gross carrying amounts in total and by major classes of intangible assets.
	• Accumulated amortization in total and by major classes of intangible assets.
	• Aggregate amortization expense for the period.
	• Estimated amortization expense for the next 5 fiscal years.

Disclosures: Impairment

IFRS	U.S. GAAP
• The amounts of impairment losses and reversal of impairment losses recognized in the period. • Where these impairment losses and reversals are recognized on the financial statements. • Main classes of assets affected by impairment losses and reversals. • Events and circumstances that led to these impairment losses and reversals.	• Description of the impaired asset. • Circumstances that led to impairment. • The method of fair value determination. • The amount of impairment loss. • Where the loss is recognized on the financial statements.

Disclosures about long-lived assets appear throughout the financial statements:

- The balance sheet reports the carrying value of the asset.
- On the income statement, depreciation expense may or may not appear as a separate line item.
- On the cash flow statement:
  - Acquisitions and disposals of fixed assets are found in the investing section.
  - Further, if prepared using the indirect method, depreciation and amortization are shown as separate line item adjustments to net income in the computation of cash flow from operating activities.
- The notes to the financial statements describe the company's accounting methods, estimated useful lives, historical cost by categories of fixed asset, accumulated depreciation, and annual depreciation expense.

Evaluating a Company's Fixed Assets

The higher the fixed asset turnover ratio, the higher the amount of sales a company is able to generate with a given amount of investment in fixed assets, suggesting that the company is operating more efficiently.

> Estimated useful life = Gross investment in fixed assets/Annual depreciation expense

> Average age of asset = Accumulated depreciation/Annual depreciation expense

> Remaining useful life = Net investment in fixed assets/Annual depreciation expense

Asset age ratios help identify older, obsolete assets that might make the firm's operations less efficient. Further, they help forecast future cash flows from investing activities and identify major capital expenditures that the company might need to raise cash for in the future. If the calculated average depreciable life of a company's assets is in line with that of other firms in the industry that use similar equipment, we can conclude that management is not tweaking useful life and salvage value assumptions to manipulate reported profits.

Another popular method for making comparisons across companies is calculating annual capital expenditure as a percentage of depreciation expense.

- A company for whom this ratio is significantly lower than 100% is currently replacing its fixed assets at a rate that is slower than the rate at which they are being depreciated.

FSA

This might indicate the need for hefty capital expenditure in the future and that further examination of the company's capital expenditure policies is required.

- A company for whom this ratio is close to 100% is replacing its fixed assets at a rate similar to that of their use.

Investment Property

IFRS defines **investment property** as property that is owned (or leased under a finance lease) for the purpose of earning rentals or capital appreciation or both. Investment property differs from long-lived tangible assets (e.g., PP&E) in that investment property is not owner occupied, nor is used for producing the company's products and services.

Under IFRS, investment property may be valued using either the cost model or the fair value model.

Cost model: This is identical to the cost model used for property, plant, and equipment.

Fair value model: This differs from the revaluation model used for PP&E in the way net income is affected.

- Under the revaluation model, the impact of the revaluation on net income depends on a previously recognized increase or decrease in the carrying amount of the asset.
- Under the fair value model, all changes in the fair value of an asset have an impact on net income.

Further, note that:

- A company is required to use one model (either cost or fair value) for all its investment properties.
- The fair value model may be used only if the company is able to reliably estimate the property's fair value on a continuing basis.
- If a company chooses the fair value model, it must continue to do so until it disposes of the property or changes its use such that it is no longer classified as investment property.

Valuation Issues

- If investment property is valued using the cost model, a move to owner-occupied property or inventory will not lead to a change in the carrying amount of the property.
- If investment property is valued using the fair value model, a move to owner- occupied property or inventory will be made at fair value. The property's fair value will become its new cost for the purpose of ongoing accounting for the property.
- If owner-occupied property is reclassified as investment property (and the owner prefers to use the fair value model), the change in the value from depreciated cost to fair value at the time of transfer is treated like a revaluation.
- If inventory is reclassified as investment property (and the owner prefers to use the fair value model), the difference between the carrying amount and fair value at the time of transfer is recognized as a profit or loss.

Investment property is reported as a separate line item on the balance sheet. Further, companies must disclose which model they have used (cost or fair value) to value the property.

U.S. GAAP does not specifically define investment property. U.S. companies that hold investment property use the historical cost model.

INCOME TAXES
Cross-Reference to CFA Institute Assigned Reading #23

The tax return is prepared to calculate **taxes payable** to the authorities. Taxes payable result in an outflow of cash from the firm, so firms try to minimize taxes payable and retain cash. This objective is achieved by recognizing *higher* expenses on the tax return, which leads to *lower* **taxable income** and consequently, *lower* taxes payable.

Financial statements are prepared to report the company's operating performance over the year to shareholders, financial institutions and other stakeholders. For financial reporting purposes, companies try to show healthy performance and profitability. This objective is achieved by recognizing *lower* expenses on the income statement, which leads to *higher* **pretax income**, and (despite *higher* **income tax expense**) *higher* net income than on the tax return.

- The **tax base** of an asset or liability is the amount that is recognized on the balance sheet for tax purposes.
- The **carrying value** is the amount recognized on the balance sheet for financial reporting.

Determining the Tax Base of an Asset

An **asset's tax base** is the amount that will be expensed on the income statement in the future as the economic benefits are realized from the asset. For example, if the historical cost of the asset is $10,000, and $4,000 worth of accumulated depreciation has already been charged against it on *tax returns* over previous years, the asset's tax base equals $6,000. This amount will be depreciated in future periods (expensed on the tax return) as the asset is utilized over its remaining life (economic benefits of the asset are realized).

The **carrying value** of the asset is simply the historical cost of the asset minus the accumulated depreciation charged against over previous years on the company's *financial statements*.

Determining the Tax Base of a Liability

Two types of liabilities can result from accrual accounting; unearned revenues and accrued expenses. The *carrying value* of these liabilities is the amount recognized on the balance sheet in the financial statements. The rules for calculating the *tax base* of liabilities are given below:

1. Tax base of accrued *expense* liability = Carrying amount of the liability on the balance sheet (financial reporting) minus amounts that have **not** been expensed for tax purposes yet; but can be expensed (are tax-deductible) in the future.
2. The tax base of unearned *revenue* liability = Carrying value of the liability minus the amount of revenue that **has already been taxed**, and therefore, will not be taxed in the future.

Deferred Tax Liabilities

A deferred tax liability usually arises when:

- *Higher* expenses are charged on the tax return as compared to the financial statements.
- Taxable income is *lower* than pretax or accounting profit.
- Taxes payable are *lower* than income tax expense.
- An asset's tax base is *lower* than its carrying value.

FSA

Accounting Entries for an Increase in Deferred Tax Liabilities

- Any *increase* in deferred tax liabilities **increases total liabilities** on the balance sheet.
- The increase in deferred tax liabilities is added to taxes payable in the calculation of income tax expense, so it decreases net income, retained earnings and **reduces owners' equity**.

Deferred Tax Assets

A deferred tax asset usually arises when:

- *Higher* expenses are charged on the financial statements than on the tax return.
- Taxable income is *higher* than pretax or accounting profit.
- Taxes payable are *higher* than income tax expense.
- A liability's tax base is *lower* than its carrying value.

Accounting Entries for an Increase in Deferred Tax Assets

- Any *increase* in deferred tax assets **increases total assets** on the balance sheet.
- The increase in deferred tax assets is subtracted from taxes payable in the calculation of income tax expense, so it **increases net income, retained earnings and equity**

Effects of Changes in Tax Rates

When tax rates *rise*, the balances of both deferred tax assets and liabilities *rise*. When tax rates *fall*, the balances of both deferred tax assets and liabilities fall.

$$\text{Income tax expense} = \text{Taxes payable} + \text{Change in DTL} - \text{Change in DTA}$$

- If a company has a net DTL (excess of DTL over DTA), a reduction in tax rates would *reduce* liabilities, *reduce* income tax expense, and *increase* equity.
- If the company has a net DTA (excess of DTA over DTL), a reduction in tax rates will *reduce* assets, *increase* income tax expense, and *decrease* equity.
- If a company has a net DTL, an increase in tax rates would *increase* liabilities, *increase* income tax expense, and *reduce* equity.
- If the company has a net DTA, an increase in tax rates will *increase* assets, *decrease* income tax expense, and *increase* equity.

Temporary versus Permanent Differences

- **Temporary differences** arise because of differences between the tax base and carrying amounts of assets and liabilities.
- **Permanent differences** are differences between tax and financial reporting of revenues and expenses that *will not* reverse at any point in the future. Examples of the items that give rise to permanent differences include:

1. Revenue items that are not taxable.
2. Expense items that are not tax deductible.
3. Tax credits for some expenses that directly reduce taxes.

The important thing to remember is that permanent differences do not result in deferred taxes. They result in a difference between effective and statutory tax rates and should be considered in the analysis of effective tax rates. A firm's reported effective tax rate is given by:

$$\text{Effective tax rate} = \frac{\text{Income tax expense}}{\text{Pretax income}}$$

Temporary differences can be divided into two categories:

Taxable Temporary Differences

Taxable temporary differences result in deferred tax liabilities. They are expected to result in future taxable income. Deferred tax liabilities arise when:

- The carrying amount of an asset *exceeds* its tax base; or
- The carrying amount of a liability is *less* than its tax base.

Deductible Temporary Differences

Deductible temporary differences result in deferred tax assets. They are expected to provide tax deductions in the future. Deferred tax assets arise when:

- The tax base of an asset *exceeds* its carrying amount; or
- The tax base of a liability is *less* than its carrying amount.

Treatment of Temporary Differences

Balance Sheet Item	Carrying Value vs. Tax Base	Results in...
Asset	Carrying amount is greater.	DTL
Asset	Tax base is greater.	DTA
Liability	Carrying amount is greater.	DTA
Liability	Tax base is greater.	DTL

Temporary Differences at Initial Recognition of Assets and Liabilities

In some situations, the carrying value and tax base of certain assets and liabilities may not be equal at initial recognition. In such circumstances (even though the tax base and the carrying amount of the item are different) a company cannot recognize deferred tax assets or liabilities.

In a business combination, if the fair value of acquired intangible assets (including goodwill) is different from their carrying amounts, deferred taxes can be recognized.

With regards to investments in subsidiaries, branches, associates and interests in joint ventures, deferred tax liabilities can be recognized unless:

- The parent is in a position to control the timing of the future reversal of the temporary difference, and
- It is probable that the temporary difference will not reverse in the future.

While deferred tax assets will only be recognized if:

- The temporary difference will reverse in the future, and
- Sufficient taxable profits exist against which the temporary difference can be used.

FSA

Unused Losses and Tax Credits

Under IFRS, unused tax losses and credits may only be recognized to the extent of probable future taxable income against which these can be applied. On the other hand, under U.S. GAAP, deferred tax assets are recognized in full and then reduced through a valuation allowance if they are unlikely to be realized. A company that has a history of tax losses may be unlikely to earn taxable profits in the future against which it can apply deferred tax assets.

Recognition and Measurement of Current and Deferred Tax

Current taxes are based on the tax rates applicable at the balance sheet date. Deferred taxes on the other hand, are measured at the rate that is expected to apply when they are realized (when the temporary differences that gave rise to them reverse).

Even though deferred tax assets and liabilities arise from temporary differences that are expected to reverse at some point in the future, present values are not used in determining the amounts to be recognized. Deferred taxes should always be recognized unless they pertain to:

- Taxes or deferred taxes charged directly to equity.
- A possible provision for deferred taxes relates to a business combination.

Even if there has been no change in temporary differences during the current period, the carrying amount of DTA and DTL may change due to:

- Changes in tax rates.
- Reassessments of recoverability of DTA.
- Change in expectations as to how the DTA or DTL will be realized.

Valuation Allowance

Deferred tax assets must be evaluated at each balance sheet date to ensure that they will be recovered. If there are any doubts regarding their realization, their carrying value should be reduced to the expected recoverable amount. Doubts regarding realization of deferred tax assets may stem from the expectation of insufficient future taxable income to recover the tax assets (prepaid taxes).

DTA are reduced by creating a contra-asset account known as the valuation allowance. An increase in the valuation allowance reduces deferred tax assets. The negative change in deferred tax assets causes an increase in income tax expense. Higher income tax expense translates into lower net income, retained earnings and equity. Subsequently, if the likelihood of realizing deferred tax assets increases, the previous reduction in DTA is reversed by reducing the valuation allowance.

Recognition of Current and Deferred Tax Charged Directly to Equity

Under both IFRS and U.S. GAAP, deferred tax assets and liabilities should generally have the same accounting treatment as the assets and liabilities that give rise to them. If the item that gave rise to the deferred tax asset/liability be taken directly to equity, the resulting deferred tax item should also be taken directly to equity.

A deferred tax liability should be reduced if it is not expected to reverse. The amount by which it is reduced should be taken directly to equity.

NON-CURRENT (LONG-TERM) LIABILITIES
Cross-Reference to CFA Institute Assigned Reading #24

A bond is a contract between a borrower and a lender that obligates the borrower to make payments to the lender over the term of the bond. Two types of payments are usually involved-periodic interest payments and principal repayments.

Accounting for Financing Liabilities

The **effective interest method** results in a constant rate of interest over the life of the bond. It is required under IFRS and preferred under U.S. GAAP. Under this method, the market interest rate at issuance is applied to the carrying amount of the bonds to determine periodic interest expense. Further, the difference between interest expense and the actual coupon payment equals the amount of discount/premium amortized over the period.

The **straight-line method**, which is also permitted under U.S. GAAP, evenly amortizes the premium or discount over the life of the bond (similar to straight-line depreciation).

The **par or face value** is the amount that the borrower has to pay back at the maturity of the bond. It does not necessarily equal the amount that the issuer receives upon issuing debt.

The **coupon rate** is multiplied by the par value of the bond to compute the periodic coupon payment.

Market interest rates are used to value bonds. These rates incorporate various types of risks inherent in the bond, and must not be confused with coupon rates. Market interest rates change frequently.

- To value a company's debt obligations at a particular point in time, we discount the remaining payments at current market interest rates.
- For accounting purposes, under the effective interest method, the book value of the liability recognized on a firm's balance sheet upon debt issuance equals the present value of its obligations discounted at *market interest rates at issuance*.
- Market interest rates at issuance determine how much the company receives in bond proceeds.
    - If market interest rates equal the bond's coupon rate, the bond will be issued at par.
    - If the market interest rate is *greater* than the coupon rate, the bond will be issued at a *discount*.
    - If the market interest rate is *lower* than the coupon rate, the bond will be issued at *a premium*.

Interest Expense versus Coupon Payment

- **Interest expense** (under the effective interest method) for a given period is calculated as the book value of the liability at the beginning of the period multiplied by market interest rates at issuance. Interest expense is charged every year on the *income statement*.
- **Coupon payments** are calculated as the coupon rate times the par value of the bonds. Coupon payments are classified as outflows from operating activities on the *cash flow statement*.

Effects of Issuing a Par Bond on Financial Statements

Balance sheet: The year end value of the liability is listed on the balance sheet. For bonds issued at par, the liability balance remains at par throughout the life of the bond.

Income statement: Interest expense is deducted from operating profits. For bonds issued at par, interest expense equals the coupon payment, and is constant over the life of the bond.

Statement of cash flows:

- At issuance, the bond proceeds are reported as inflows from financing activities.
- During the term of the bond, coupon payments (not interest expense) are deducted from CFO.
- At maturity, cash used to repay the principal amount (par value) is deducted from CFF.

For bonds issued at par the inflows recorded at issuance under CFF equal the outflows at maturity from CFF. Coupon payments are deducted from CFO every year.

Effects of Issuing a Discount Bond on Financial Statements

Balance sheet: The liability increases over the life of the bond as the discount is amortized over the term of the bond. The value of the liability at bond maturity equals par.

Income statement: Interest expense rises each year in line with the increasing balance of the liability.

FSA

Statement of cash flows: Inflows recorded at issuance under CFF are lower than outflows at maturity from CFF. Coupon payments are deducted from CFO every year.

Effect of Issuing a Premium Bond on Financial Statements

Balance sheet: The liability decreases over the life of the bond as the premium is amortized over the term of the bond. The value of the liability at maturity equals par.

Income statement: Interest expense declines every year in line with the decreasing balance of the liability.

Statement of cash flows: Inflows recorded at issuance under CFF are greater than the outflows at maturity from CFF. Coupon payments are deducted from CFO every year.

Important Shortcuts

- Interest expense over the term of the bond can also be calculated as all the issuer's outflows over the life of the bond (coupon payments plus principal repayment) minus the inflows received at issuance (bond proceeds).
- To determine the book value of the liability at any point in time simply compute the present value of the bond's remaining cash flows discounting them at market interest rates at issuance.

IFRS versus U.S. GAAP

- The **effective interest** method is *required* under IFRS and *preferred* under U.S. GAAP because it accurately reflects the economics of the transaction. U.S. GAAP also permits use of the **straight-line method** of amortization, which evenly amortizes the premium or discount over the life of the bond.

- Printing costs, legal fees and other charges are incurred when debt is issued. Under IFRS, these costs are included in the measurement of the liability. Under U.S. GAAP, companies used to capitalize these costs and write them off over the bond's term on a straight-line basis. However, U.S. GAAP now requires that debt issuance costs be deducted from the related debt liability. Debt issuance costs for lines of credit may still be treated as an asset.
- U.S. GAAP requires interest payments on bonds to be classified under cash flows from operations. IFRS allows more flexibility in that classification of interest payments as CFO or CFF is permitted.
- Amortization of the bond discount/premium is a non-cash item so it has no effect on cash flows (aside from the effect on taxable income). In the reconciliation of net income to operating cash flow, amortization of a discount (premium) is added back to (deducted from) net income.

Fair Value Reporting Option

When a company uses the effective interest method to amortize bond discounts and premiums, the book value of debt is based on market interest rates at issuance. Over the life of the bonds, as market interest rates fluctuate, the actual value of the firm's debt deviates from its reported book value. For example, if interest rates rise, the current market value of debt would fall. The reported book value of debt (based on the market interest rates at issuance) would be *higher* than the true economic value of the firm's obligations. In this case, using the book value will *overstate* leverage levels as the firm is actually better off than its financial statements indicate.

Companies have the option to report financial liabilities at fair value. Financial liabilities reported at fair value are designated as **financial liabilities at fair value through profit or loss** under IFRS, or as **liabilities under the fair value option** under U.S. GAAP.

- If the company chooses to not report fair values, IFRS and U.S. GAAP require fair value disclosures in the financial statements unless the carrying amount approximates fair value or fair value cannot be reliably measured.
- A company electing to measure a liability at fair value will report decreases in the liability's fair value as income and increases in the liability's fair value as losses.
- Changes in a liability's fair value can result from changes in market rates and/or changes in the credit quality of the issuing company.
  - Companies must report the portion of the change in value attributable to changes in their credit risk in other comprehensive income.
  - Only the portion of the change in value not attributable to changes in their credit risk will be recognized in profit or loss.

Derecognition of Debt

A company may leave the bonds that it issues outstanding until maturity or retire them prior to maturity by either purchasing them from the open market or calling them (if a call provision exists). If the company leaves the bonds outstanding until maturity, it pays investors the par value of the bonds at maturity.

However, if the company decides to retire the bonds prior to maturity, the book value of the liability is reduced to zero and a **gain or loss on extinguishment** is computed by subtracting the amount paid to retire the bonds from their book value.

- Under **U.S. GAAP**, because issuance costs are capitalized, any unamortized issuance costs must also be subtracted from gains on extinguishment.

- Under **IFRS**, issuance costs are included in the book value of the liability so there is no need to adjust the gain on extinguishment for these expenses.

Financial Statement Presentation of and Disclosures Relating to Debt

On the balance sheet, long-term liabilities are listed as one aggregate figure for all liabilities due after one year. Liabilities due within one year are included in short-term liabilities (current liabilities). Financial statement footnotes usually include:

- Stated and effective interest rates.
- Maturity dates.
- Restrictions imposed by creditors (covenants).
- Pledged collateral.
- Scheduled repayments over the next five years.

More information regarding a firm's debt and off balance-sheet financing sources can be found in the MD&A section.

Leases

Advantages of Leasing an Asset

- Leases require little or no upfront payment.
- Leases typically carry an effective interest rate that is lower than an otherwise identical unsecured loan or bond.
- There are lower risks of asset ownership (e.g., obsolescence).

From the perspective of a lessor, compared to selling outright, leasing allows it to earn interest income, and increase sales by allowing customers to pay smaller amounts over time.

Classification as Finance or Operating Leases

A lease is a finance lease if any of the following five criteria are met. Note that these criteria are the same under IFRS and USGAAP. If none of the criteria are met, the lease is an operating lease.

1. The lease transfers ownership of the underlying asset to the lessee.
2. The lessee has an option to purchase the underlying asset and is reasonably certain it will do so.
3. The lease term is for a major part of the asset's useful life.
4. The present value of the sum of the lease payments equals or exceeds substantially all of the fair value of the asset.
5. The underlying asset has no alternative use to the lessor.

Note that the same criteria are used for both lessees and lessors in classifying the lease.

Lessee Accounting

Lessee Accounting — IFRS

Under IFRS, for lessees, the accounting treatment for finance and operating leases is the same.

- The lessee reports a "right-of-use" (ROU) asset and a lease liability (calculated as the present value of fixed lease payments), on its balance sheet.

  ○ Note that there is an exception for short-term leases if they are short term (less than 12 months) or low in value (less than $5,000 in sales price).

- The discount rate used in the lease liability computation is either the rate implicit in the lease or an estimated secured borrowing rate.

Accounting Entries During the Term of the Lease

Balance sheet:

- The value of the ROU asset falls every year as it is depreciated.
- Interest is charged on the liability as the appropriate discount rate times the beginning-of-year value of the liability.
  - The excess of the lease payment over the year's interest expense reduces the liability.

Income statement:

- Depreciation expense is charged against the asset.
- Interest expense is charged against the liability.

Cash flow statement:

- The portion of the lease payment equal to the interest expense is subtracted from CFO or CFF (depending on the lessee's reporting policies), while the remainder that serves to reduce the liability is subtracted from CFF.

Lease Accounting—US GAAP

Under US GAAP, accounting treatments for finance leases and operating leases are different.

- The finance lease accounting model is identical to the lessee accounting model for IFRS.
- The operating lease accounting model is different.

Under an operating lease, accounting at inception is also the same as under IFRS.

- The lessee records a lease payable liability and a corresponding right-of-use asset on its balance sheet.

The key difference under US GAAP is how the ROU asset is amortized over the lease term.

- Asset amortization expense is calculated as the lease payment minus interest expense.
  - This implies that total expense shown on the income statement will equal the lease payment (amortization plus interest expense).
  - Every year, the lease liability and the ROU asset will equal each other.
  - Amortization expense will equal the excess of the lease payment over interest expense (repayment of principle).

Accounting Entries

- On the balance sheet, the lessor reports (1) the lease liability (net of principal repayments) and (2) an ROU asset (net of accumulated amortization).
- Interest expense on the lease liability and the amortization expense related to the ROU asset are reported as a single line titled "lease expense" as an operating expense on the income statement. The total equals the annual lease payment.
- The entire lease payment is reported as cash flow from operating activities (CFO) on the cash flow statement.

Comparison of Finance and Operating Leases for Lessees Under US GAAP

- The ROU asset is lower under a finance lease in each period because amortization expense is higher.
- Total expenses are higher for finance leases initially (sum of amortization and interest expense) but lower for financial leases in the latter years. It is important to note however, that operating expenses are higher under an operating lease due to the single line item classification of both interest and amortization expenses.
- Total cash flow is the same, but the classification is different.
    - Operating cash flow is higher under a finance lease.
    - Financing cash flow is higher under an operating lease.

Impact on Ratios

- The EBITDA margin is lower under an operating lease.
    - Lease expense is classified as an operating expense rather than interest and amortization
- Asset turnover is lower under an operating lease.
    - Total assets are higher under an operating lease because the ROU asset is amortized at a slower pace in the initial years.
- CFO per share is lower under an operating lease.
    - Cash flow from operations is lower because the entire lease payment is included in operating activities whereas only interest expense is an operating cash out flow for a finance lease.

Lessor Accounting

The accounting for lessors is substantially identical under IFRS and US GAAP. Leases may be classified as finance or operating leases, which impacts financial reporting.

Accounting for Finance Leases

At inception:

- The lessor recognizes a lease receivable asset equal to the present value of future lease payments and removes the leased asset from its balance sheet.
    - The discount rate used in the present value calculation is the rate implicit in the lease.
- The difference between the two is immediately recognized as a gain or loss.

During the lease term:

The lease receivable asset is reduced by each lease payment using the effective interest method.

- Each lease payment is composed of interest income and repayment of principal.
    - Interest expense is calculated as the product of the lease receivable and the discount rate
    - The principal repayment equals the difference between the lease payment received and interest income.

Impact on Financial Statements

- Lease receivable (net of repayments) is reported on the balance sheet.
- Interest income is reported on the income statement.

○ If leasing is a primary business activity for the entity, as it commonly is for financial institutions and independent leasing companies, it is reported as revenue.

- The lease payment received is an operating cash inflow. It is reported under operating activities on the statement of cash flows.

Accounting for Operating Leases

Operating leases are more like rental agreements. As a result, the lessor keeps the leased asset on its books and recognizes lease revenue on a straight-line basis. No interest revenue is recognized.

Impact on Financial Statements

- No effect on the balance sheet. The lessor continues to recognize the leased asset at cost net of accumulated depreciation.
- Lease revenue (like rental income) is recognized on a straight-line basis on the income statement. Depreciation expense continues to be charged on the asset.
- The entire cash receipt is reported under operating activities on the statement of cash flows (same as a finance lease).

Financing versus Operating Leases

- If the present value of the lease payments is well above the carrying value of the asset, the finance lease classification results in a significant increase in assets.
- A finance lease only results in interest revenue, whereas the operating lease lessor recognizes (higher) straight-line lease revenue (which is mitigated by depreciation).
- The cash flow statement is the same for the lessor regardless of least classification.

Pensions

Defined contribution plans are pension plans in which the company contributes a certain amount of funds into the plan. Accounting for defined contribution plans is quite straightforward.

- On the income statement, the company recognizes the amount it is required to contribute into the plan as pension expense for the period.
- On the balance sheet, the company records a decrease in cash. If the agreed upon amount is not deposited into the plan during a particular period, the outstanding amount is recognized as a liability.
- On the cash flow statement, the outflow is treated as an operating cash flow.

Under a **defined benefit plan**, the company promises to make future payments to the employee during retirement. For example, a company could promise an employee annual pension payments equal to 60% of her final salary at retirement until death. A number of assumptions are made to determine the total amount that must be paid to the employee during retirement, including:

- Expected salary at date of retirement
- Number of years of retirement

The company estimates the amount of benefits it will pay out to an employee during retirement and then allocates the present value of these payments (known as pension obligation) over the employment term of the employee as a part of pension expense.

1. The service cost for an employee over a period refers to the present value of the increase in pension benefits earned by the employee over the year (as a result of her service to the company).

2. Interest costs are added to pension expense because the company does not pay out service costs earned by the employee over the year until her retirement. The company owes these benefits to the employee so interest accrues on the amount of benefits outstanding.

3. Companies make pension payments into a pension trust fund. The assets in this fund are invested until funds are required to make payments. The expected return on these investments is subtracted from other pension costs to determine pension expense for a particular period. In order to reduce the volatility in reported pension expense, companies are allowed to use the expected return on plan assets instead of the actual return on plan assets in the calculation of pension expense for the period. However, if the difference between expected return and actual return is significant, companies are required to amortize a portion of the difference into pension expense.

4. Actuarial gains and losses arise due to changes in the assumptions used for calculating pension expense (e.g., employee turnover, mortality rates, and compensation increases).

5. Prior service costs arise due to changes in promised benefits.

Evaluating Solvency Ratios

Solvency refers to the ability of a company to satisfy its long term debt obligation (both principal and interest payments). Ratio analysis is frequently used to evaluate a company's solvency levels relative to its competitors. The two main types of solvency ratios used are leverage ratios and coverage ratios.

Leverage ratios are derived from balance sheet numbers and measure the extent to which a company uses debt rather than equity to finance its assets. Higher leverage ratios indicate weaker solvency.

Coverage ratios focus more on income statement and cash flow numbers to measure the company's ability to service its debt. Higher coverage ratios indicate stronger solvency.

Solvency Ratios	Description	Numerator	Denominator
Leverage Ratios			
Debt-to-assets ratio	Expresses the percentage of total assets financed by debt	Total debt	Total assets
Debt-to-capital ratio	Measures the percentage of a company's total capital (debt + equity) financed by debt	Total debt	Total debt + Total shareholders' equity
Debt-to-equity ratio	Measures the amount of debt financing relative to equity financing	Total debt	Total shareholders' equity
Financial leverage ratio	Measures the amount of total assets supported by one money unit of equity	Average total assets	Average shareholders' equity

Solvency Ratios	Description	Numerator	Denominator
Coverage Ratios			
Interest coverage ratio	Measures the number of times a company's EBIT could cover its interest payments	EBIT	Interest payments
Fixed charge coverage ratio	Measures the number of times a company's earnings (before interest, taxes and lease payments) can cover the company's interest and lease payments	EBIT + Lease payments	Interest payments + Lease payments

STUDY SESSION 8:
FINANCIAL STATEMENT ANALYSIS (4)

FSA

FINANCIAL REPORTING QUALITY
Cross-Reference to CFA Institute Assigned Reading #25

Financial reporting quality refers to the usefulness of information contained in the financial reports, including disclosures in notes.

- High-quality reporting provides information that is useful in investment decision-making in that it is relevant and faithfully represents the company's performance and position.

Earnings quality (or **quality of reported results**) pertains to the earnings and cash generated by the company's core economic activities and its resulting financial condition.

- High-quality earnings (1) come from activities that the company will be able to sustain in the future and (2) provide an adequate return on the company's investment.
- Note that the term **earnings quality** encompasses quality of earnings, cash flow, and balance sheet items.

Relationship between Financial Reporting Quality and Earnings Quality

		Financial Reporting Quality	
		Low	**High**
Earnings (Results) Quality	High	LOW financial reporting quality impedes assessment of earnings quality and impedes valuation.	HIGH financial reporting quality enables assessment. HIGH earnings quality increases company value.
	Low		HIGH financial reporting quality enables assessment. LOW earnings quality decreases company value.

Quality Spectrum of Financial Reports

GAAP, decision-useful, sustainable, and adequate returns: These are high-quality reports that provide useful information about high-quality earnings.

GAAP, decision-useful, but sustainable? This level refers to a situation where reporting is of high quality, but earnings are either inadequate or unsustainable.

Within GAAP, but biased accounting choices: Biased choices result in financial reports that do not faithfully represent the company's true economic situation.

- Management can make aggressive or conservative accounting choices, both of which go against the concept of neutrality as **unbiased** financial reporting is the ideal.
- **Earnings smoothing** results from employing conservative assumptions to understate performance when the company is actually doing well and then using aggressive assumptions when the company is not doing as well.
- Biases can also creep into the way information is presented. A company may choose to present information in a manner that obscures unfavorable information and/or highlights favorable information.

Within GAAP, but "earnings management": Earnings can be managed by taking **real actions** or through **accounting choices**. Note that it is typically very difficult to determine intent so there is a very fine line between earnings management and biased accounting choices.

Departures from GAAP Non-Compliant Accounting: Financial information that deviates from GAAP is obviously of low quality. Further, such financial information cannot be used to assess earnings quality as comparisons with other entities or earlier periods cannot be made.

Departures from GAAP Fictitious Transactions: Companies may use fictitious transactions to (1) fraudulently obtain investments by inflating company performance, or (2) to obscure fraudulent misappropriation of company assets.

Conservative versus Aggressive Accounting

When it comes to financial reporting, the ideal situation would be if financial reporting were **unbiased**, i.e., neither conservative nor aggressive.

- **Aggressive choices** can (1) increase reported revenues, (2) increase reported earnings, (3) increase reported operating cash flow, (4) decrease reported expenses, and/or (5) decrease reported debt in the current period.
  - Aggressive accounting choices in the current period may create a sustainability issue.
- **Conservative choices** can (1) decrease reported revenues, (2) decrease reported earnings, (3) decrease reported operating cash flow, (4) increase reported expenses, and/or (5) increase reported debt in the current period.
  - Conservative accounting choices do not give rise to a sustainability issue.

Conservatism in Accounting Standards

Despite efforts to encourage neutrality in financial reporting, some conservatively biased standards remain. Further, different sets of accounting standards may have different degrees of conservatism embedded in them.

Bias in the Application of Accounting Standards

In order to characterize the application of an accounting standard as conservative or aggressive, we must look at *intent* (rather than at a definition). Intent can be inferred from a careful analysis of disclosures, facts, and circumstances. Examples of biased accounting disguised as conservatism include:

- **Big bath behavior:** This refers to the strategy of manipulating a company's income statement to make poor results look even worse. The big bath is often implemented in a bad year with a view to inflating subsequent period earnings. New management teams sometime use the big bath so that poor current performance can be blamed on previous management, while they take credit for the impressive growth that follows in subsequent periods.
- **Cookie jar reserve accounting:** This refers to the practice of creating a liability when a company incurs an expense that cannot be directly linked to a specific accounting period. Companies may recognize such expenses in periods during which profits are high as they can afford to take the hit to income, with a view to reducing the liability (the reserve) in future periods during which the company may struggle. The practice results in smoothing of income over time.

FSA

Context for Assessing Financial Reporting Quality

In assessing financial reporting quality, it is important to consider (1) whether a company's management may be motivated to issue financial reports that are not of high quality, and (2) whether the reporting environment is conducive to misreporting.

Motivations for Issuing Low-Quality Financial Reports

- To mask poor performance.
- To meet or beat analyst's forecasts or management's own forecasts.
  - **Equity market effects** refer to management trying to build credibility with market participants and to positively impact the company's stock price.
  - **Trade effects** refer to management trying to improve the company's reputation with customers and suppliers.
- To address managers' concerns regarding their careers.
- To avoid debt covenant violations.

Conditions Conducive to Issuing Low-Quality Financial Reports

- **Opportunity:** Poor internal controls, an ineffective board of directors, or accounting standards that allow divergent choices and/or provide minimal consequences for inappropriate choices can give rise to opportunities for management to issue low-quality financial reports.
- **Motivation:** Motivation to issue low-quality financial reports can come from personal reasons (e.g., increasing bonus payments) or corporate reasons (e.g., alleviating concerns about being able to raise funds in the future).
- **Rationalization:** This is important because individuals need to justify their choices to themselves.

Mechanisms that Discipline Financial Reporting Quality

- Markets
- Regulatory authorities
- Registration requirements
  - Disclosure requirements
  - Auditing requirements
  - Management commentaries
  - Responsibility statements
  - Regulatory review of filings
  - Enforcement mechanisms
- Auditors
- Private contracting

Detection of Financial Reporting Quality Issues

Presentation Choices

- Under the pretext of assisting investors in evaluating operating performance, struggling companies may (conveniently) **exclude restructuring charges** in pro forma measures of financial performance.
- Due to investors' focus on EBITDA, companies may come up with their own **definitions of EBITDA** (sometimes referring to it as adjusted EBITDA) which may exclude certain expenses.
- Companies may use **non-GAAP measures** to distract users from GAAP measures. US GAAP and IFRS have both moved to pacify these concerns.

FSA

Accounting Choices and Estimates

Revenue Recognition

- Sometimes management may be pushing shipments out the door (channel stuffing) under FOB shipping point arrangements in order to maximize revenue recognized in the current accounting period.
  - ○ If the ratio of accounts receivable to revenues is abnormally high relative to the company's history or its peers, there is a chance that channel stuffing has occurred.
- At other times, for shipments towards the end of the reporting period, management may set shipping terms as FOB destination. Management may engage in this practice if there was an overabundance of orders during the current period, and it does not want investors/analysts to get too optimistic.
- A company can reduce its allowance for sales returns as a proportion of sales to reduce expenses and increase profits.
  - ○ Analysts should examine whether the company's actual collection experience has tended to be different from historical provisioning in order to assess the accuracy of the company's provisioning policies.
- If a company participates in "bill-and-hold" transactions, it is possible that it is recognizing fictitious sales by reclassifying end-of-period inventory as "sold but held" through minimal effort and fake documentation.
- If the company uses rebates as part of its marketing approach, changes in estimates of rebate fulfillment can be used to manipulate reported revenues and profitability (similar to allowance for sales returns).
- Companies can use changes in depreciation estimates (useful life and salvage value) and depreciation methods to manipulate reported earnings and profits.
  - ○ If the company has recorded significant asset write-downs in the recent past, it may suggest that the company's policies relating to asset lives need to be examined.
- Management may try to capitalize costs that ought to be recorded as expenses to increase reported income.
  - ○ Management may use low fair value estimates for assets acquired in an acquisition in order to depress future depreciation expense and inflate future profitability.
  - ○ In order to determine the fair value of goodwill, forecasts of future financial performance must be made, and these projections may be biased upward to avoid a goodwill write-down.
  - ○ Analysts should also examine how the company's capitalization policies compare with the competition, and determine whether its amortization policies are reasonable.
- Analysts should determine how a company's inventory methods compare with others in its industry.
  - ○ If the company uses reserves for obsolescence in its inventory valuation, unusual fluctuations in this reserve might suggest that the company is manipulating them to attain a desired level of earnings.
  - ○ If a company uses LIFO in an inflationary environment, it can temporarily increase reported profits through LIFO liquidation.
- Analysts must evaluate whether the company's estimate of the valuation allowance (against deferred tax assets) is reasonable given its current operating environment and future prospects. Specifically they should:
  - ○ Determine whether there are contradictions between the management commentary and the allowance level, or the tax note and the allowance level.
  - ○ Look for changes in the tax asset valuation account.

FSA

- Analysts should examine whether warranty reserves have been manipulated to meet earnings targets. Further, the trend in actual costs relative to amounts allocated to reserves should be assessed as it can offer insight into the quality of products sold.
- If the company engages in extensive dealings with related parties, those entities could be used to absorb losses (e.g., through supply arrangements that are unfavorable to the non-public company) in order to improve the public company's reported performance.

Choices that Affect the Cash Flow Statement

- Management may try to delay payments to creditors (stretch out payables) until after the balance sheet date, so that the increase in accounts payable over the period (source of cash) results in an increase in cash generated from operations. In order to detect this issue, analysts could:
  - Examine changes in working capital to look for unusual patterns that may indicate manipulation of cash provided from operations.
  - Compare the company's cash generation with the cash operating performance of its competitors.
  - Compare the relationship between cash generated from operations and net income. Analysts should be concerned if cash generated from operations is less than net income, as it may suggest that accounting estimates are being used to inflate net income.
- A company may **misclassify uses of operating cash flow** into the investing or financing section of the cash flow statement to inflate cash generated from operating activities.
- In certain areas where investors may not even be aware that choices exist (e.g., amortization of discount/premium on capitalized interest), accounting standards offer companies the **flexibility** to manage cash generated from operations to a certain extent.

Accounting Warning Signs

Warning Signs Related to Revenue

Analysts should:

- Determine whether company policies make it easy to prematurely recognize revenue by allowing use of FOB shipping point shipping terms and bill-and-hold arrangements.
- Determine whether a significant portion of revenues come from barter transactions (which are difficult to value properly).
- Evaluate the impact of estimates relating to the company's rebate programs on revenue recognition.
- Look for sufficient clarity regarding revenue recognition practices relating to each item or service delivered under multiple-deliverable arrangements of goods and services.
- Determine whether the company's revenue growth is in line with its competitors, the industry, and the overall economy.
- Determine whether receivables are increasing as a percentage of sales. This may suggest channel-stuffing activities or even recognition of fictitious sales.
- Determine whether there are any unusual changes in the trend in receivables turnover and seek an explanation for any changes.
- Compare the company's receivables turnover (or DSO) with competitors and look out for suggestions that revenues have been recognized prematurely, or that the provision for doubtful accounts is insufficient.

FSA

- Examine asset turnover.
  - If post-acquisition revenue generation is weak, management may try to play with estimates to increase reported revenue in order to be able to justify their strategic choices.
  - If asset turnover is trending lower, or if it lags the asset turnover of competitors, it may signal future asset write-downs by the company.

Warning Signs Related to Inventories

Analysts should:

- Compare growth in inventories with competitors and industry benchmarks. If inventory levels are increasing with no accompanying increase in sales, it could suggest (1) poor inventory management or (2) inventory obsolescence. In case of the latter, current profitability and inventory value would be overstated.
- Compute the inventory turnover ratio. Declining inventory turnover could also suggest inventory obsolescence.
- Check for inflated profits through LIFO liquidations (only applicable for firms using LIFO).

Warning Signs Related to Capitalization Policies and Deferred Costs

- Analysts should examine the company's accounting policy notes for its capitalization policy for long-term assets (including interest costs) and for its handling of other deferred costs and compare those policies with industry practice.

Warning Signs Related to the Relationship between Cash Flow and Income

If a company's net income is persistently higher than cash provided by operations, it raises the possibility that aggressive accrual accounting policies have been used to shift current expenses to later periods.

- Analysts may consider constructing a time series of cash generated by operations divided by net income. If the ratio is consistently below 1.0, or has declined consistently, there may be problems in the company's accrual accounts.

Other Potential Warning Signs

- Depreciation methods and useful life estimates that are inconsistent with peer companies.
- Fourth-quarter surprises.
- Presence of related-party transactions.
- Non-operating income and one-time sales included in revenue.
- Classification of an expense as non-recurring.
- Gross/operating margins out of line with competitors or industry.
- Younger companies with an unblemished record of meeting growth projections.
- Management has adopted a minimalist approach to disclosure.
- Management fixation on earnings reports.
- Significant restructuring and/or impairment charges.
- Management has a merger and acquisition orientation.

FSA

APPLICATIONS OF FINANCIAL STATEMENT ANALYSIS
Cross-Reference to CFA Institute Assigned Reading #26

Evaluating Past Financial Performance

Analysts should focus on:

- Important changes that have occurred in corporate measures of profitability, efficiency, liquidity and solvency and the reasons behind these changes.
- Comparisons of ratios with firms from the same industry, and the reasons behind any differences.
- Examination of performance aspects that are critical for a company to successfully compete in the industry, and a comparison of the company's performance on these fronts with that of competitors.
- The company's business model and strategy, and how it influences operating performance.

Projecting Performance

The **top-down approach** that is typically used to forecast sales involves the following steps:

- Attain forecasts for the economy's expected GDP growth rate.
- Use regression models to determine the historical relationship between the economy's growth rate and the industry's growth rate.
- Undertake market share analysis to evaluate whether the firm being analyzed is expected to gain, lose or retain its market share over the forecasting horizon.

Once a forecast for sales has been established, earnings and cash flows can be estimated.

- Estimate gross profit margins over the forecasting horizon. Net profit margins are affected by leverage ratios and tax rates, so historical data provides a more reliable measure for gross profit margins. This model tends to be simpler and works well for mature companies that operate in non-volatile markets.
- Make separate forecasts for individual expense items, aggregate them, and subtract the total from sales to calculate net income. This is a very subjective exercise as each expense item must be projected based on a relationship with sales or some other relevant variable.

The most important things that an analyst needs to consider when forecasting cash flows are:

- Required increases in working capital.
- Capital expenditures on new fixed assets.
- Repayment and issuance of debt.
- Repurchase and issuance of stock (equity).

Assessing Credit Risk

Credit analysis involves evaluation of the 4 "C's" of a company.

- Character refers to the quality of management.
- Capacity deals with the ability of the issuer to fulfill its obligations.
- Collateral refers to the assets pledged to secure a loan.
- Covenants are limitations and restrictions on the activities of issuers.

FSA

The four general categories of items considered in credit analysis are:

- Scale and diversification of the business.
- Operational efficiency.
- Stability and sustainability of profit margins.
- Degree of financial leverage.

Screening is the process of filtering a set of potential investments into a smaller set by applying a set of criteria. Ratios computed from the information in financial statements and market data are used to screen potential equity investments.

Growth versus Value Investors

Growth investors invest in those companies that are expected to see higher earnings growth in the future. A growth investor would set screens like high price-to-cash flow ratios, and sales growth exceeding 20% over the last three years.

Value investors try to pay a low price relative to a company's net asset value or earning prowess. A value investor might set screens like a higher-than-average ROE, and a lower-than-average P/E ratio to shortlist equity investments that suit her style.

Back-Testing

Analysts evaluate how a portfolio based on particular screens would have performed historically through the process of **back-testing**. This method applies the portfolio selection rules to historical data and calculates returns that would have been realized had particular screens been used. Back-testing has its limitations in that it suffers from:

- Survivorship bias.
- Look-ahead bias.
- Data-snooping bias.

Analyst Adjustments to Reported Financials

Adjustments related to investments: Investments in securities issued by other companies can be classified under different categories. Unrealized gains and losses on securities classified as "available-for-sale" are not recorded on the income statement. Changes in their values are reflected in "other comprehensive income" as a part of equity on the balance sheet. Changes in the value of "trading" securities are recorded on the income statement and have an impact on reported profits. If an analyst is comparing two firms with significant differences in the classification of investments, adjustments for the different financial statement impact of the classifications will be necessary.

Adjustments related to inventory: A LIFO company's financial statements need to be adjusted before comparisons with FIFO firms can be undertaken. Important accounts affected by conversion from LIFO to FIFO are net income, retained earnings, inventory, COGS and deferred taxes.

FIFO to LIFO Conversions

- $EI_{FIFO} = EI_{LIFO} + \text{LIFO reserve}$
- $COGS_{FIFO} = COGS_{LIFO} - (LR_{ending} - LR_{beginning})$

During a period of rising prices:

- Net income after tax under FIFO will be greater than LIFO net income after tax by: Change in LIFO reserve × (1 − tax rate)
- Equity (retained earnings) under FIFO will greater by: LIFO reserve × (1 − tax rate)
- Liabilities (deferred taxes) under FIFO will be greater by: LIFO reserve × (tax rate)
- Current assets (inventory) under FIFO will be greater by: LIFO reserve

The calculations of estimated useful life, average age, and remaining useful life are important because:

- They help identify older, obsolete assets that might make the firm's operations less efficient.
- They help forecast future cash flows from investing activities and identify major capital expenditures that the company might need to raise cash for in the future.

Adjustments related to property, plant and equipment: A company that uses accelerated depreciation methods and shorter estimated life assumptions for long-lived assets will report lower net income than a firm that employs longer useful life assumptions and uses straight-line depreciation. Depreciation and net fixed asset values must be assessed and necessary adjustments must be made to bring sets of financial statements on the same footing before making comparisons.

$$\text{Estimated useful life} = \frac{\text{Gross investment in fixed assets}}{\text{Annual depreciation expense}}$$

$$\text{Average age of asset} = \frac{\text{Accumulated depreciation}}{\text{Annual depreciation expense}}$$

$$\text{Remaining useful life} = \frac{\text{Net investment in fixed assets}}{\text{Annual depreciation expense}}$$

Adjustments related to goodwill: Goodwill is recognized when the price paid for an acquisition exceeds the fair value of its net assets. A company that grows via acquisitions will have higher reported assets and a greater book value than a company that grows internally. Analysts must remove the inflating effect of goodwill on book values and rely on the price-to-tangible book value ratio to make comparisons.

FSA

STUDY SESSION 9: CORPORATE ISSUERS (1)

CI

INTRODUCTION TO CORPORATE GOVERNANCE AND OTHER ESG CONSIDERATIONS
Cross-Reference to CFA Institute Assigned Reading #27

Corporate governance is defined as the system of internal controls and procedures through which individual companies are managed. It aims to minimize and manage conflicts of interest between those within the company and stakeholders. A **stakeholder** is any person or group that has an interest in the company. Not all stakeholders' interests are aligned in the same manner, and they often conflict with each other.

Key Stakeholders

- **Shareholders** own shares of stock in a corporation and are entitled to certain rights, such as the right to receive dividends and the right to vote on certain corporate issues. They are typically focused on those efforts that support growing the profitability of the company and maximizing its value.
- **Creditors** have little influence on the company, other than covenants and restrictions they can put in place as its banks or bondholders.
- **Employees** have a significant stake in the company's operation, as they are paid salaries and wages as well as other incentives and perquisites for their work.
- The **board of directors** acts in the best interests of the shareholders who elect them.
- **Customers** would like a product that is a good value for the price and is safe to operate.
- Company **suppliers** have a goal of being paid for their services and materials.
- The **government and regulators** wish to protect the economy and the interests of the general public.

Key Relationships in Corporate Governance

- **Shareholder and manager/director relationships.** Although they are agents of shareholders, managers and directors may take advantage of information asymmetries to take more risk than warranted to maximize personal benefit.
- **Controlling and minority shareholders.** Controlling groups may behave in a manner that does not maximize value for minority shareholders (e.g., during voting on takeover offers, during related-party transactions, etc.).
- **Manager and board relationships.** If management provides only limited information to the directors, the board's ability to effectively monitor the business is reduced.
- **Shareholder versus creditor interests.** Shareholders may look for additional risk for greater return, while creditors look for stability and lower risk.
- **Other stakeholder conflicts.** Conflicts may arise between customers and shareholders (e.g., product safety), between customers and suppliers (e.g., when the company extends lenient terms of credit to customers), and between the government and shareholders (e.g., if the government raises company taxes).

Stakeholder Management

The foundations of stakeholder management frameworks are constructed from the various legal, contractual, organizational, and governmental components that define the rights, responsibilities, and powers of each group.

- The **legal** infrastructure lays out the framework of rights established by law as well as the ease or availability of legal recourse.

- The **contractual** infrastructure is the means used to secure the rights of both parties through contractual agreements between the company and its stakeholders.
- The way the company manages its stakeholder relationships through its governance procedures, internal systems, and practices is the **organizational** infrastructure.
- The regulations imposed on the company are considered the **governmental** infrastructure.

Mechanisms to Manage Stakeholder Relationships and Mitigate Associated Risks

- General meetings
- Board of directors
- Audit function
- Reporting and transparency
- Remuneration policies
- Say on pay
- Contractual agreements with creditors
- Employee laws and contracts
- Contractual agreements with customers and suppliers
- Laws and regulations

The Board of Directors

The board of directors monitors management and the strategic direction of the company while reporting to shareholders.

The board plays an active role in managing the company through managers, who are given the responsibility for day-to-day operations of the company. The board establishes milestones for the company based on the strategic direction it oversees. In monitoring progress, the board selects, appoints, and terminates the employment of senior management.

The board also establishes committees to aid in the oversight of key functions. Common committees are the following:

- Audit committee
- Governance committee
- Remuneration committee
- Nomination committee
- Risk committee
- Investment committee

Factors That Affect the Stakeholder Relationship and Corporate Governance

Market Factors

- **Shareholder engagement.** The transparency and information sharing from frequent engagement with shareholders tend to increase support for management and to reduce the potential for efforts by shareholders to more actively pursue other means to influence outcomes.
- **Shareholder activism.** Activism by shareholders involves more forceful paths to increase shareholder value. Examples include lawsuits, raising public awareness, and proxy battles.
- **Competition and takeovers.** Corporate takeovers can take the form of proxy contests, tender offers, or hostile takeovers.

Non-Market Factors

- **The legal environment.** Generally speaking, around the world, creditors enjoy better-protected positions compared to shareholders.
- **Media.** Increasingly, the media (especially social media) can influence stakeholder relationships.
- **The corporate governance industry.** External corporate governance services increasingly exert significant influence. Thus, corporations pay attention to their ratings and change their behavior if necessary.

Risks of Poor Corporate Governance and Stakeholder Management

- Weak control systems
- Ineffective decision-making
- Legal, regulatory, and reputational risks
- Default and bankruptcy risks

Benefits of Effective Governance

- Operational efficiency
- Improved control
- Better operating and financial performance
- Lower default risk and cost of debt

Analysis of Corporate Governance and Stakeholder Management

Key areas of interest are:

- **Economic ownership and voting control.** Dual-class companies tend to trade at a discount to their peers.
- **Board of directors representation.** Generally speaking, well-diversified, diverse, and skilled boards are desirable.
- **Remuneration and company performance.** It is important that compensation programs align with shareholders.
- **Investors in the company.** Concentrated holdings can dictate how the company is run. Further, a significant number of activist investors may force the company to focus on the short term.
- **Strength of shareholders' rights.** Ideally, shareholders would like the power to remove board members and convene special stockholder meetings.
- **Managing long-term risks.** It is desirable for the company to have healthy stakeholder relations and for management to be able to deal effectively with long-term risks.

ESG Investment Strategies

Responsible investing is an umbrella term used to describe investment strategies that incorporate environmental, social, and governance (ESG) factors into their approaches. It includes the following:

- **ESG integration (or ESG investing)** refers to the careful consideration of material ESG factors in the investment analysis and portfolio construction processes.
- **Socially responsible investing (SRI)** has traditionally referred to the practice of excluding investments in certain industries, such tobacco. The term has evolved to include investment objectives that promote positive environmental or social attributes.
- **Thematic investing** refers to investment in themes or assets specifically related to ESG factors. This approach is often based on needs arising from economic or social trends.

- **Impact investing** refers to investments made with the intention to generate positive, measurable social and environmental impact alongside a financial return.
- **Sustainable investing** is a term used in a similar context to responsible investing, but its key focus is on factoring in sustainability issues while investing.
- **Green finance** is a responsible investing approach that utilizes financial instruments that support a green economy.

ESG Investment Approaches

ESG Investment Approaches			
		Mapping to Other Classifications	
ESG Investment Approach	**Description**	*Financial Analysts Journal*	*Global Sustainable Investment Review*
Negative screening	Excluding companies or sectors based on business activities or environmental or social concerns	Negative screening	Negative/ exclusionary screening
			Norms-based screening
Positive screening	Including sectors or companies based on specific ESG criteria, typically ESG performance relative to industry peers	Positive screening	Positive/Best-in-class screening
		Relative/best-in-class screening	
ESG integration	Systematic consideration of material ESG factors in asset allocation, security selection, and portfolio construction decisions for the purpose of achieving or exceeding the product's stated investment objectives	Full integration	ESG integration
		Overlay/ Portfolio tilt	
		Risk factor/ Risk premium	
Thematic investing	Investing in themes or assets related to ESG factors	Thematic investing	Sustainability-themed investing
Engagement/ active ownership	Using shareholder power to influence corporate behavior to achieve targeted ESG objectives along with financial returns	Engagement/ Active ownership	Corporate engagement/ Shareholder action
Impact investing	Investments made with the intention to generate positive, measurable social and environmental impact alongside a financial return	N/A	Impact/ Community investing

Notes: For information on the *Financial Analysts Journal* column under "Mapping to Other Classifications," see www.tandfonline.com/doi/full/10.2469/faj.v74.n3.2. For the *Global Sustainable Investment Review* column, see http://www.gsi-alliance.org/wp-content/uploads/2019/06/GSIR_Review2018F.pdf.

USES OF CAPITAL
Cross-Reference to CFA Institute Assigned Reading #28

Steps in the Capital Allocation Process

1. Generating ideas
2. Analyzing individual proposals
3. Capital allocation planning
4. Monitoring and post-auditing

Types of Capital Projects

1. Replacement projects: These projects help in maintaining the normal course of business and do not usually require very thorough analysis.
2. Expansion projects: These are projects that increase the size of the business.
3. New products and services: Venturing into new products and services brings added uncertainties to the firm's overall operations.
4. Regulatory, safety, and environmental projects: These projects are sometimes made mandatory by a governmental agency or some external party.
5. Other projects: Some projects cannot be analyzed through capital budgeting techniques.

Capital Allocation Assumptions

1. Decisions are based on actual cash flows.
2. Timing of cash flows is crucial.
3. Cash flows are based on opportunity costs.
4. Cash flows are analyzed on an after-tax basis.
5. Financing costs are excluded from calculations of operating cash flows.
6. Accounting net income is not used as cash flows for capital budgeting.

Important Capital Allocation Concepts

- **Sunk costs** are those costs that cannot be recovered once they have been incurred. Capital budgeting ignores sunk costs because it is based only on current and future cash flows.
- **Opportunity cost** is the value of the next best alternative that is foregone in making the decision to pursue a particular project. Opportunity costs should be included in project costs.
- An **incremental cash flow** is the additional cash flow realized as a result of a decision.
- An **externality** is the effect of an investment decision on things other than the investment itself. Externalities can be positive or negative and, if possible, externalities should be considered in investment decision-making.
- A **conventional cash flow stream** is a cash flow stream that consists of an initial outflow followed by a series of inflows. The sign of the cash flows changes only once. For a nonconventional cash flow stream, however, the initial outflow is not followed by inflows only, but the direction of the flows changes from positive to negative again. There is more than one sign change in a nonconventional cash flow stream.

Interactions between Investment Opportunities

1. **Independent versus mutually exclusive projects.** Independent projects are those whose cash flows are unrelated. Mutually exclusive projects compete directly with each other for acceptance. If Project A and B are mutually exclusive, the firm may only accept one of them, not both.
2. **Project sequencing.** Many projects can only be undertaken in a certain order, so investing in one project creates the opportunity to invest in other projects in the future.
3. **Unlimited funds versus capital rationing.** When the company has no constraints on the amount of capital it can raise, it will invest in all profitable projects to maximize shareholder wealth. The need for capital rationing arises when the company has limited funds to invest. If the capital required to invest in all profitable projects exceeds the resources available to the company, it must allocate funds to only the most lucrative projects to ensure that shareholder wealth is maximized.

Investment Decision Criteria

Net Present Value (NPV)

A project's NPV equals the present value of all expected inflows minus the present value of all expected outflows. The rate used to discount each cash flow is the project's cost of capital.

- A project should be undertaken if its NPV is greater than zero. Positive NPV projects increase shareholder wealth.
- Projects with a negative NPV decrease shareholder wealth and should not be undertaken.
- A project with an NPV of zero has no impact on shareholder wealth.

Internal Rate of Return (IRR)

For an investment project that requires only one investment outlay that is made at inception, IRR is the discount rate that equates the sum of the present values of future after-tax cash flows to the initial investment outlay. Alternatively, IRR is the discount rate that equates the sum of present values of all after-tax cash flows for (inflows and outflows) to zero. Therefore, IRR is the discount rate at which NPV equals zero.

- A company should invest in a project if its IRR is greater than the required rate of return. When the IRR is greater than the required return, NPV is positive.
- A company should not invest in a project if its IRR is less than the required rate of return. When the IRR is lower than the required return, NPV is negative.

Corporate Usage of Capital Allocation Methods

The **return on invested capital (ROIC)** is a measure of the profitability of a company relative to the amount of capital invested by the equity- and debt-holders.

ROIC = After-tax net profit / Average book value of invested capital (common, preferred, and debt).

Impact of Inflation on Capital Allocation

- The cash flows and discount rate used by the company should both be nominal or both be real.
- Generally speaking, inflation reduces the value of depreciation tax savings to the company effectively increasing its real taxes.
- If inflation is higher than expected, the profitability of the investment is correspondingly lower than expected.
- Inflation does not affect all revenues and costs uniformly.

NPV, Company Value, and Stock Price

If a company invests in a positive NPV project, the expected addition to shareholder wealth should lead to an increase in the company's stock price. However, the effect of a project's NPV on share prices is not so simple. The value of a company is determined by valuing its existing investments and adding the expected NPV of its future investments. The impact of the decision to undertake a particular project on a company's stock price depends on how the actual profitability of the investment differs from its expected profitability. Expected profitability is usually already factored into current market prices.

If the profitability of a positive NPV project that the company is about to undertake is below expectations, stock prices may fall. On the other hand, certain capital projects undertaken by the company may signal that there are other potentially lucrative projects to follow. Taking on a project that brings with it the expectation of even greater future profits from subsequent opportunities may increase stock prices beyond the actual addition to the company value from the said project alone. Capital budgeting processes tell us two things about company management:

- The extent to which management pursues the goal of shareholder wealth maximization
- Management's effectiveness in pursuit of this goal

Real Options

Real options are just like financial options and give their holders the right, but not the obligation, to make a capital budgeting decision in the future. Real options are contingent upon future events and provide managers with greater flexibility, which enhances the NPV of projects. There are several types of real options:

- **Timing options** give the company an option to delay investment.
- **Sizing options** give the company an option to either abandon a project if market conditions deteriorate, or to expand it if market conditions improve.
- **Flexibility options** give the company an option to either set a different price or change the number of units produced depending on market conditions.
- **Fundamental options** are projects that behave as options as their payoffs are contingent on the price of an underlying asset.

Evaluating Capital Budgeting Projects with Real Options

- Use DCF analysis without considering real options.
- Use DCF analysis and add an estimated value of the real option.
- Use decision trees.
- Use option pricing models.

Common Capital Budgeting Pitfalls

- Not incorporating economic responses into the investment analysis.
- Misusing capital budgeting templates.
- Undertaking pet projects of senior managers.
- Basing investment decisions on EPS, net income, or return on equity instead of incremental cash flows.
- Using IRR instead of NPV to make investment decisions.
- Accounting for cash flows inaccurately.
- Over- or under-estimating overhead costs.
- Not using the appropriate risk-adjusted discount rate.
- Spending the entire investment budget just because it is available.
- Failing to consider investment alternatives.
- Handling sunk costs and opportunity costs incorrectly.

SOURCES OF CAPITAL
Cross-Reference to CFA Institute Assigned Reading #29

The weighted average cost of capital (WACC) is the expected rate of return that investors demand for financing an average risk investment of a company.

$$\text{WACC} = (w_d)(r_d)(1-t) + (w_p)(r_p) + (w_e)(r_e)$$

- Interest payments result in tax savings for the company. Therefore, the after-tax cost of debt is used in the WACC formula.
- Payments to holders of preferred and common stock do not result in tax savings.

Estimating Cost of Debt

Yield-to-Maturity Approach

The bond's yield to maturity (YTM) is the IRR of an investment in the bond, assuming that it is purchased at the current market price and held till maturity. It is the yield that equates the present value of a bond's expected future cash flows to its current market price.

Debt Rating Approach

When a reliable current market price for the company's debt is not available, the before-tax cost of debt can be estimated by using the yield on similarly-rated bonds that have terms to maturity that are similar to the company's existing debt.

Issues in Estimating Cost of Debt

- **Fixed-rate versus floating-rate debt:** The cost of floating-rate debt is reset periodically based on a reference rate (usually LIBOR) and is therefore, more difficult to estimate than the cost of fixed-rate debt.
- **Debt with option-like features:** If option-like features are expected to be removed from future debt issues, an analyst must adjust the yield to maturity on existing bonds for their option features, and use the adjusted rate as the company's cost of debt.
- **Nonrated debt:** If a company does not have any debt outstanding (to be rated) or yields on existing debt are not available (due to lack of current price information), an analyst may not be able to use the yield on similarly-rated bonds or the yield to maturity approach to estimate the company's cost of debt.
- **Leases:** If a company uses leases as a source of finance, the cost of these leases should be included in its cost of capital.

Estimating Cost of Preferred Stock

$$r_p = {D_p}\big/{V_p}$$

Estimating Cost of Equity

1. Capital Asset Pricing Model (CAPM)

The capital asset pricing model (CAPM) states that the expected rate of return from a stock equals the risk-free interest rate plus a premium for bearing risk.

$$r_e = R_F + B_i[E(R_M) - R_F]$$

2. Bond Yield plus Risk Premium Approach

The bond yield plus risk premium approach is based on the basic assumption that the cost of capital for riskier cash flows is higher than that of less risky cash flows. Therefore, we calculate the return on equity by adding a risk premium to the before-tax cost of debt.

$$r_e = r_d + \text{Risk premium}$$

Estimating Betas

- Beta can be calculated by regressing the company's stock returns against market returns over a given period of time.
- Analysts use the **pure-play method** to estimate the beta of a particular project or of a company that is not publicly traded. This method involves the adjustment of a comparable publicly-listed company's beta for differences in financial leverage.
    - First find a comparable company that faces similar business risks as the company or project under study and estimate the equity beta of that company.
    - To remove all elements of financial risk from the comparable's beta "unlever" the beta. The unlevered beta reflects only the business risk of the comparable and is known as **asset beta**.
    - Finally, adjust the unlevered beta of the comparable for the level of financial risk (leverage) in the project or company under study.

Flotation Costs

Flotation costs refer to the fee charged by investment bankers to assist a company in raising new capital. In the case of debt and preferred stock, we do not usually incorporate flotation costs in the estimated cost of capital because the amount of these costs is quite small. However, for equity issues, flotation costs are usually quite significant.

Accounting for Flotation Costs in Capital Budgeting

- Incorporate flotation costs into the cost of capital. This approach is theoretically incorrect.
- Adjust the cash flows used in the valuation by adding the estimated dollar amount of flotation costs to the initial cost of the project.

STUDY SESSION 10: CORPORATE ISSUERS (2)

CI

COST OF CAPITAL – FOUNDATIONAL TOPICS
Cross-Reference to CFA Institute Assigned Reading #30

Types of Financing Methods

- Internal Financing
  - Operating cash flows are after-tax operating cash flows less interest and dividend payments (adjusted for taxes) that can be used to invest in assets.
  - Accounts payable are amounts due suppliers of goods and services that have not been paid.
  - Accounts receivable are amounts owed by customers.
  - Inventory, which refers to good waiting to be sold, is a current asset on the balance sheet.
  - Marketable securities are financial instruments, such as stocks and bonds, that can be quickly sold and converted to cash.
- Financial Intermediaries
  - Uncommitted lines of credit.
  - Committed lines of credit (regular lines of credit).
  - Revolving credit agreements.
  - Asset-based loans.
- Capital Markets

Considerations Affecting Financing Choices

- Firm-Specific Considerations
  - Smaller companies tend to rely more on equity financing because debt financing is either not available or too expensive.
  - Companies with higher volatility of operating cash flows rely primarily on equity financing and tend to use little if any debt financing.
  - Companies that own assets that can be put up as collateral have greater access to debt financing and at a lower cost.
  - Large, publicly traded companies have an easier time raising funds.
  - Commercial banks carefully manage the maturity structure of their asset portfolios with the maturity structure of their financing.
  - Non-financial businesses such as utilities, manufacturing firms, real estate firms, and others that have long-term assets can safely use more long-term financing than firms with short-term assets.
  - Large, well-rated multinational companies will finance themselves in different currencies to match the currency exposure of their local operations.
  - If a company faces a risk of financial distress or bankruptcy, it may have limited options to raise funds.
  - Flotation costs can significantly affect the cost of capita. They are generally lower for debt offerings than for equity offerings.
- General Economic Considerations
  - The cost of debt financing is typically lower than the cost of equity financing because interest expense is tax deductible.
  - If inflation is expected to rise, companies would prefer to borrow at a fixed rate, while investors would prefer to lend at a variable rate.
  - Fiscal and monetary policy. Loose, stimulative policies encourage companies to raise cash reserves at low rates.

Sources of Liquidity

- **Primary sources** are readily available resources such as cash balances and short-term funds.
- **Secondary sources** provide liquidity at a higher cost than primary sources. They include negotiating debt contracts, liquidating assets or filing, for bankruptcy protection.

Drags versus Pulls on Liquidity

A **drag on liquidity** occurs when there is a delay in cash coming into the company. Major drags on liquidity include:

- Uncollected receivables.
- Obsolete inventory.
- Tight credit.

Drags on liquidity can be dealt with by enforcing strict credit and collection policies.

A **pull on liquidity** occurs when cash leaves the company too quickly. Major pulls on payments include:

- Making payments early.
- Reduced credit limits.
- Limits on short-term lines of credit.
- Low existing levels of liquidity.

Evaluation of Liquidity Management

Current ratio

- A higher current ratio means that a company is better positioned to meet its short term obligations.
- A current ratio of less than one indicates negative working capital, which might imply that the company faces a liquidity crisis.

In order to gauge whether a given quick or current ratio is good or bad, we must look at the trend in ratios, how they compare with ratios of competitors, and available opportunities to invest in more profitable, longer-term investments.

Accounts receivable turnover ratio

- It is desirable to have an accounts receivable turnover ratio close to the industry average.

Number of days of receivables

- A collection period that is too high might imply that customers are too slow in making payments and too much of the company's capital is tied up in accounts receivable.
- A collection period that is too low might suggest that the company's credit policy is too strict, which might hurt sales.

The number of days of receivables must be evaluated in light of the credit terms offered to customers, and the relation between sales and extension of credit.

Inventory turnover ratio

- An inventory TO ratio that is too high might indicate that the company has too little stock on hand at any given point in time, which might hurt sales.
- A low inventory TO ratio might suggest that the company has too much liquidity tied up in inventory, perhaps because the units held are obsolete.

Payables' turnover

- A high payables' turnover ratio might indicate that the company is not making full use of available credit facilities.
- A low ratio could suggest that the company has trouble making payments on time.

The **operating cycle** is a measure of the time needed to convert raw materials into cash from sales.

> **Operating cycle** = Number of days of inventory + Number of days of receivables

The **cash conversion cycle** or the **net operating cycle** equals the time period between paying suppliers for materials and collecting cash from sales to customers.

> **Net operating cycle** = Number of days of inventory + Number of days of receivables − Number of days of payables

Factors Influencing Short-Term Borrowing Strategy

- Size and creditworthiness
- Legal and regulatory considerations
- Sufficient access
- Flexibility of borrowing options

Passive versus Active Borrowing Strategies

- Passive borrowing strategies usually involve minimal activity, with one source or type of borrowing and with little planning.
- Active strategies are usually more flexible and reflect planning, reliable forecasting, and comparison pricing.

CI

CAPITAL STRUCTURE
Cross-Reference to CFA Institute Assigned Reading #31

Capital structure refers to the specific mix of debt and equity used to finance a company's assets and operations.

Capital Structure and Company Life Cycle

Capital Structure and Company Life Cycle

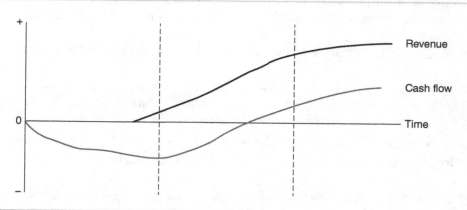

Stage in life cycle	Start-up	Growth	Mature
Financial management			
Revenue growth	Beginning	Rising	Slowing
Cash flow	Negative	Improving	Positive/Predictable
Business risk	High	Medium	Low
Debt capital/leverage			
Availability	Very limited	Limited/improving	High
Cost	High	Medium	Low
Typical cases	N/A	Secured (by receivables, fixed assets)	Unsecured (bank and public debt)
Typical % of capital structure[1]	Close to 0%	0%-20%	20% +

[1]Note: These ratios are calculated based on the market values of equity and debt.

Modigliani-Miller Propositions

The Capital Structure Decision

A company's capital structure refers to the combination of debt and equity capital it uses to finance its business. The goal is to determine the capital structure that results in the minimum weighted average cost of capital and consequently, in the maximum value of the company.

$$r_{WACC} = \left(\frac{D}{V}\right) r_D (1 - t) + \left(\frac{E}{V}\right) r_E$$

MM Assumptions

- Investors have homogeneous expectations.
- Capital markets are perfect.
- Investors can borrow and lend at the risk-free rate.
- There are no agency costs.
- The financing decision and the investment decision are independent of each other.

MM Proposition I without Taxes: Capital Structure Irrelevance

Given the assumptions listed above and no taxes, changes in capital structure do not affect company value.

$$V_L = V_U$$

MM Proposition II without Taxes: Higher Financial Leverage Raises the Cost of Equity

Debt finance is cheaper than equity finance. However, increased use of debt leads to an increase in the required rate of return on equity. The higher required return on equity is exactly offset by the cheaper cost of debt and therefore, there is no change in the company's weighted average cost of capital. Basically, the company's cost of capital is not determined by its capital structure but by business risk.

$$r_E = r_0 + (r_0 - r_D)\frac{D}{E}$$

$$V = \frac{Interest}{r_D} + \frac{EBIT - Interest}{r_E}$$

MM Propositions with Taxes

MM Proposition I with Taxes

Use of debt would actually increase the value of a company. Interest paid is tax deductible in most countries, so the use of debt results in tax savings for the company. Therefore, the value of a levered company is greater than that of an unlevered company by an amount equal to the marginal tax rate multiplied by the value of debt:

$$V_L = V_U + tD$$

In this scenario (with no costs of financial distress), the value of a company would be maximized if its capital structure comprised of 100% debt.

MM Proposition II with Taxes

The cost of equity would still increase with increased debt financing, but not fast enough to exactly offset the use of (cheaper) debt, thereby decreasing the company's weighted average cost of capital. Under this scenario, a company's weighted average cost of capital is minimized at 100% debt.

$$r_{WACC} = \left(\frac{D}{V}\right)r_D(1-t) + \left(\frac{E}{V}\right)r_E$$

$$r_E = r_0 + (r_0 - r_D)(1-t)\left(\frac{D}{E}\right)$$

$$V_L = \frac{Interest}{r_D} + \frac{EBIT - Interest}{r_E}$$

Cost of Capital with No Taxes. MM Proposition II (without taxes) states that the use of cheaper debt increases the cost of equity. The increase in the cost of equity exactly offsets the benefit of adding cheaper debt to the capital structure, resulting in a constant WACC (cost of capital).

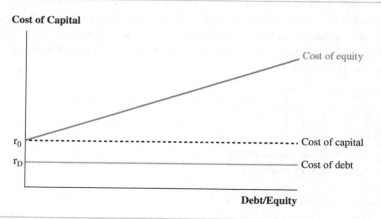

Cost of Capital with Taxes. Under MM Proposition II (with taxes) the cost of equity still increases, but not fast enough to completely undo the benefit of using cheaper debt (since debt also results in an interest tax shield), resulting in a decrease in the company's weighted average cost of capital.

Costs of Financial Distress

The expected cost of financial distress equals the actual cost of financial distress times the probability that the company will face financial distress. Leverage increases the costs of financial distress and the probability of financial distress.

The Optimal Capital Structure—Static Trade-Off Theory

Managers must balance the use of debt in a way that its tax shield benefits are exactly offset by its associated costs of financial distress.

$$V_L = V_U + tD - PV \text{ (Costs of financial distress)}$$

The capital structure at which company value is maximized is the same as the capital structure at which the cost of capital (WACC) is minimized. Further, note that the WACC curve is U-shaped:

- Initially as more debt is added to the capital structure, the WACC falls due to the lower cost of debt (compared to equity).
- Eventually, WACC increases as the cost of equity and the cost of debt both rise to compensate for the higher risk associated with high debt levels.

Trade-Off Theory with Taxes and Costs of Financial Distress

Value of Company and the D/E Ratio

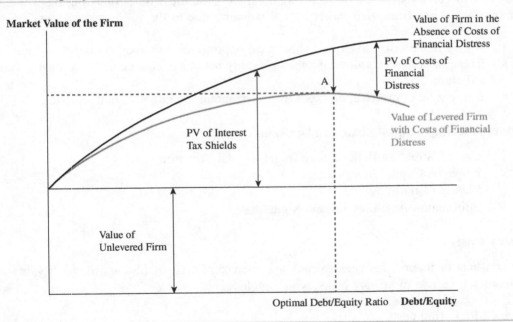

Cost of Capital and the D/E Ratio

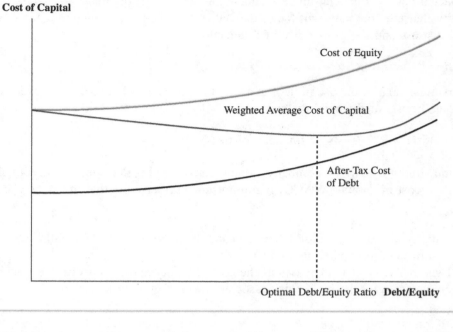

The weight of debt in an optimal capital structure is less than 100%. Companies usually adopt their optimal capital structure as their target capital structure with periods during which they temporarily deviate from their target capital structure due to the following reasons:

- It may make sense to exploit short-term opportunities in another source of financing.
- Changes in market values of debt and equity result in a change in the company's capital structure.
- It might be impractical or expensive to maintain the target capital structure.

Factors Affecting Capital Structure Decisions

1. Capital Structure Policies and Target Capital Structure
2. Financial Capital Investments
3. Market Conditions
4. Information Asymmetries and Signaling

Agency Costs

The conflicts of interest between owners and managers in all public and large private companies give rise to agency costs, which include:

- Monitoring costs
- Bonding costs
- Residual loss

Using more debt in the capital structure reduces net agency costs of equity.

MEASURES OF LEVERAGE
Cross-Reference to CFA Institute Assigned Reading #32

Leverage refers to a company's use of fixed costs in conducting business. Fixed costs include:

- Operating costs (e.g., rent and depreciation)
- Financial costs (e.g., interest expense)

Importance of Leverage

- Leverage increases the volatility of a company's earnings and cash flows, thereby increasing the risk borne by investors in the company.
- The more significant the use of leverage by the company, the more risky it is and therefore, the higher the discount rate that must be used to value the company.
- A company that is highly leveraged risks significant losses during economic downturns.

Leverage is affected by a company's cost structure. Generally companies incur two types of costs.

- **Variable costs** vary with the level of production and sales (e.g., raw materials costs and sales commissions).
- **Fixed costs** remain the same irrespective of the level of production and sales (e.g., depreciation and interest expense).

The higher the proportion of fixed costs (both operating and financial) in a company's cost structure (higher leverage) the greater the company's earnings volatility.

The greater the degree of leverage for a company, the steeper the slope of the line representing net income.

Business Risk

Business risk refers to the risk associated with a company's operating earnings. Operating earnings are risky because total revenues and costs of sales are both uncertain. Therefore, business risk can be broken down into sales risk and operating risk.

Sales risk: The uncertainty associated with total revenue is referred to as sales risk. Revenue is affected by economic conditions, industry dynamics, government regulation, and demographics.

The higher the standard deviation of price and units sold, the wider the distribution of operating profit.

Operating risk: The risk associated with a company's operating cost structure is referred to as operating risk. A company that has a greater proportion of fixed costs in its cost structure has greater operating risk.

In order to examine a company's sensitivity of operating income to changes in unit sales, we use the **degree of operating leverage (DOL)**. DOL is the ratio of the percentage change in operating income to the percentage change in units sold.

$$DOL = \frac{\text{Percentage change in operating income}}{\text{Percentage change in units sold}}$$

$$DOL = \frac{Q \times (P - V)}{Q \times (P - V) - F}$$

DOL is different at different levels of sales. If the company is making operating profits, the sensitivity of operating income to changes in units sold decreases at higher sales volumes (in units).

- DOL is negative when operating income (the denominator in the DOL equation) is negative, and is positive when the company earns operating profits.
- Operating income is most sensitive to changes in sales around the point where the company makes zero operating income.
- DOL is undefined when operating income is zero.
- The lower the proportion of fixed costs in a company's cost structure, the less sensitive its operating income is to changes in units sold and therefore, lower is the company's operating risk.

Business risk is composed of operating and sales risk, both of which are largely determined by the industry in which the company operates.

A company has more control over operating risk than sales risk.

Financial Risk

Financial risk refers to the risk associated with how a company chooses to finance its operations. The higher the amount of fixed financial costs taken on by a company, the greater is its financial risk.

Financial risk can be measured as the sensitivity of cash flows available to owners to changes in operating income. This measure is known as the **degree of financial leverage (DFL)**.

$$DFL = \frac{\text{Percentage change in net income}}{\text{Percentage change in operating income}}$$

$$DFL = \frac{[Q(P - V) - F](1 - t)}{[Q(P - V) - F - C](1 - t)} = \frac{[Q(P - V) - F]}{[Q(P - V) - F - C]}$$

The higher the use of fixed financing sources by a company, the greater the sensitivity of net income to changes in operating income and therefore, the higher the financial risk of the company.

The degree of financial leverage is also different at different levels of operating income. The degree of financial leverage is usually determined by the company's management. Companies with relatively high ratios of tangible assets to total assets or those with revenues that have below-average business cycle sensitivity are able to use more financial leverage.

Total Leverage

The degree of total leverage (DTL) looks at the combined effect of operating and financial leverage i.e., it measures the sensitivity of net income to changes in units produced and sold.

$$DTL = \frac{\text{Percentage change in net income}}{\text{Percentage change in the number of units sold}}$$

$$DTL = DOL \times DFL$$

$$DTL = \frac{Q \times (P - V)}{[Q(P - V) - F - C]}$$

DTL is also different at different numbers of units produced and sold. This is because DOL is different at different levels of units produced and sold, while DFL is different at different levels of operating earnings. DTL combines the effects of DOL and DFL.

Breakeven Points and Operating Breakeven Points

A company's breakeven point occurs at the number of units produced and sold at which its net income equals zero. It is the point at which a company's revenues equal its total costs and the company goes from making losses to making profits.

The breakeven point for a company occurs when:

$$PQ = VQ + F + C$$

The breakeven number of units can be calculated as:

$$Q_{BE} = \frac{F + C}{P - V}$$

While greater leverage entails higher risk, it also raises the company's potential for profit.

A breakeven point can also be specified in terms of operating profit, in which case it is known as the **operating breakeven point**. At this point, revenues equal operating costs. The expression for operating breakeven point is given as:

$$PQ_{OBE} = VQ_{OBE} + F$$

$$Q_{OBE} = \frac{F}{P - V}$$

The farther unit sales are from the breakeven point for high-leverage companies, the greater the magnifying effect of leverage.

The Risks of Creditors and Owners

Creditor claims on the assets of the company are senior to those of equity holders. In return for lending money to the company, creditors demand timely interest and principal payments. Payments to creditors must be made irrespective of whether the company is profitable. Inability to make these payments may lead to the company having to declare bankruptcy. Returns for creditors are predefined; even if the company does very well, they do not see any of the upside.

Owners only have a claim on what is left over after all the financial obligations of the company have been met. In return for the lower priority in claims, equity holders enjoy decision-making power in the company, and participate in the upside if the company does well.

Legal codes in most countries are provided for companies to file for bankruptcy protection. There are two main types of bankruptcy protection.

- **Reorganization (Chapter 11)**, which provides the company temporary protection from creditors so that it can reorganize its capital structure and emerge from bankruptcy as a going concern.
- **Liquidation (Chapter 7)**, which allows for an orderly settlement of the creditors' claims. In this category of bankruptcy, the original business ceases to exist.

Companies with high operating leverage have less flexibility in making changes to their operating structures so bankruptcy protection does little to help reduce operating costs. On the other hand, companies with high financial leverage can use Chapter 11 protection to change their capital structure and, once the restructuring is complete, emerge as ongoing concerns.

Under both Chapter 7 and Chapter 11, providers of equity capital generally lose out. On the other hand, debt holders typically receive at least a portion of their capital, but only after the period of bankruptcy protection ends.

Study Session 11: Equity Investments (1)

EQ

215

MARKET ORGANIZATION AND STRUCTURE
Cross-Reference to CFA Institute Assigned Reading #33

Functions of a Financial System

1. Help people achieve their purposes in using the financial system.
2. To facilitate the discovery of the rate of return where aggregate savings equal aggregate borrowings.
3. Allocating capital to its most efficient uses.

Classifications of Assets and Markets

Assets may be classified as financial or physical assets:

- Financial assets include securities, currencies and contracts.
- Physical assets include commodities and real assets.

Markets may be classified on the basis of:

- The timing of delivery.
- Who the seller is.
- The maturity of instruments that are traded.
- The types of securities.

Securities

Securities include bonds, notes, commercial paper, mortgages, common stock, preferred stock, warrants, mutual fund shares, unit trusts and depository receipts. They may be classified as:

- **Public securities** that trade in public markets (e.g., exchanges). Issuers of public securities are usually required to comply with strict rules and regulatory standards.
- **Private securities** that can typically only be purchased by qualified investors. Private securities are relatively illiquid.

Fixed Income Securities

Fixed income instruments are promises to repay borrowed money. Payments (which include interest and principal amounts) may be pre-specified or may vary according to a fixed formula based on a reference rate. Fixed income instruments may be classified as:

- **Notes:** Fixed income securities with maturities of 10 years or less.
- **Bonds:** Fixed income securities with maturities greater than 10 years.
- **Bills:** These are issued by governments and have maturities of one year or less.
- **Certificates of deposit:** These are issued by banks and usually mature within a year.
- **Commercial paper:** These are issued by corporations and usually mature within a year.
- **Repurchase agreements:** These are short-term lending instruments.
- **Money market instruments:** These are traded in the money market and have maturities of one year or less.

Equities

Equity owners have ownership rights in a company. Equity securities include:

- **Common shares:** Holders of common shares can participate in the company's decision-making process. They are entitled to receive dividends declared by the company, and if the company goes bankrupt, they have a claim on the company's assets after all other claims have been satisfied.
- **Preferred shares:** Preferred shareholders have a higher priority in claims on dividends and on the company's assets in case of liquidation. They are entitled to receive fixed dividends on a regular basis.
- **Warrants:** Holders of warrants have the right to purchase an entity's common stock at a pre-specified price at, or before the warrants' expiration date.

Pooled Investments

Pooled investment vehicles (e.g., mutual funds, depositories, and hedge funds) issue securities that represent shared ownership in the assets held by them. People invest in these vehicles to benefit from their investment management expertise and to diversify their portfolios.

- **Asset-backed securities:** Companies often use pools of loans or receivables (e.g., auto loans and leases, consumer loans, credit cards, etc.) as underlying assets to issue securities known as asset-backed securities. These securities then transfer any interest and principal payments from the underlying assets to their holders on a monthly basis.

Currencies

These are monies issued by national monetary authorities and primarily trade in the foreign currency market. Retail currency trades occur through ATM machines, credit cards and debit cards when transactions are executed in currencies different from the currency held in customers' accounts.

Contracts

Contracts are agreements between two or more parties to do something in the future. A contract's value depends on the value of its underlying, which may be a commodity, a security, an index, an interest rate or even another contract. Contracts may be settled in cash or may require physical delivery, and may be classified on the basis of:

- The nature of the underlying asset
- The timing of delivery

Forward Contracts

A forward is a contract between two parties, where one (the long position) has the obligation to buy, and the other (the short position) has an obligation to sell an underlying asset at a fixed price (established at the inception of the contract) at a future date. Market participants usually enter a forward contract to hedge a pre-existing risk.

Futures Contracts

Futures contracts are similar to forward contracts in that they may also be deliverable or cash-settled, but there are also significant differences between the two. Unlike forward contracts:

- Futures contracts are standardized and trade on organized exchanges.
- A clearinghouse is the counterparty to all futures contracts.

Swap

A swap is an agreement between two parties to exchange a series of cash flows at periodic settlement dates over a certain period of time. A swap may also be looked upon as a series of forward contracts.

Option Contracts

Option contracts give their holders the right to buy or sell a security at a predetermined price (exercise price) some time in the future.

- **Call options** give their holders the right to purchase the underlying asset at some future date at the option's exercise price. Holders are likely to exercise their call options when the price of the underlying asset is greater than the exercise price.
- **Put options** give their holders the right to sell the underlying asset at some future date at the option's exercise price. Holders are likely to exercise their put options when the price of the underlying asset is lower than the exercise price.

Options that can only be exercised at their expiration dates are known as European options, while options that can be exercised anytime until, or at their expiration dates are known as American options.

Insurance Contracts

People often enter into insurance contracts to protect themselves from unexpected losses. Insurance contracts include credit default swaps (CDSs) that promise to pay their holders the amount of principal in case a company defaults on its bonds.

Commodities

Commodities include precious metals, energy products, industrial metals, agricultural products, and carbon credits. Commodities may trade in the spot market (for immediate delivery) or in the forward or futures market (for delivery in the future).

Real Assets

Real assets include tangible properties such as real estate, airplanes, machinery and lumber stands. Institutional investors are increasingly adding them to their portfolios either directly (through direct ownership of the asset), or indirectly (through investments in securities of companies that invest in these assets). Real assets are attractive because:

- They may have low correlations with other assets in the investor's portfolio, thus providing diversification benefits.
- They offer income and tax benefits to investors.

Real asset valuation is very difficult due to the heterogeneous nature of each investment. Further, real assets tend to be relatively illiquid and entail high management costs.

Financial Intermediaries

Brokers, Exchanges, and Alternative Trading Systems

Brokers are agents who fulfill orders for their clients. They reduce costs of trading for their clients by finding counterparties for their trades.

- **Block brokers** provide brokerage services to large traders.

- **Investment banks** provide a variety of services to companies, including:
  - Arranging initial and seasoned security offerings.
  - Issuing securities to finance their business.
  - Identifying and acquiring other companies.

Exchanges provide a platform where traders can carry out their trades.

Alternative Trading Systems (ATSs) (also known as electronic communications networks, ECNs, and multilateral trading facilities, MTFs) are trading venues just like exchanges. However, they differ from exchanges in that they do not exercise regulatory authority over their members except with respect to the conduct of their trading in their trading networks. Many ATSs are known as "dark pools" because they do not display orders sent to them.

Dealers

Unlike brokers, dealers fulfil orders for their clients by actually taking positions as counterparties for their trades. Essentially, they indirectly connect two traders who arrive in the market at different points in time. By acting as counterparties to trades, dealers create liquidity in the market.

Dealers may also often act as brokers and vice-versa, so practitioners often use the term **broker-dealer** to refer to brokers and dealers.

Securitizers

Securitization is the process of buying assets, placing them in a pool, and issuing securities that represent ownership of the assets in the pool. Entities that undertake this process are known as securitizers. They create and sell securitized instruments and act as financial intermediaries by connecting borrowers and lenders.

Depository Institutions and Other Financial Corporations

Depository institutions include commercial banks, savings and loan banks, credit unions, and other institutions that gather funds from depositors and lend them to borrowers. Brokers also act as financial intermediaries when they lend funds deposited by their clients to other clients who wish to buy securities on margin. Such brokers are known as **prime brokers.**

Insurance Companies

Insurance companies create and sell contracts that protect buyers of these contracts from risks that they seek protection from. Insurance companies are financial intermediaries as they connect the buyers of insurance contracts with investors, creditors and reinsurers who are willing to bear the insured risks. Insurance buyers benefit as they are able to transfer risks to entities that are willing to assume them, while owners, creditors and reinsurers of the insurance company (who assume these risks) benefit from being able to sell their tolerance to risk without having to manage the contracts. Managing insurance contracts requires the insurance company to manage fraud, moral hazard and adverse selection.

- Fraud occurs when people deliberately report fake losses.
- Moral hazard occurs when people are less careful about avoiding losses as they are covered by insurance.
- Adverse selection occurs as only those who are most at risk usually buy insurance.

EQ

220

Arbitrageurs

Arbitrageurs, who buy and sell the same security in two different markets (at different prices), act as financial intermediaries as they effectively connect sellers in one market with buyers in another market. They also bring liquidity to markets.

Settlement and Custodial Services

Clearinghouses arrange for the final settlement of trades. They also serve as guarantors of performance in futures markets and as escrow agents in other markets. Banks and broker-dealers may offer custodial services for holding securities on behalf of their clients. This helps prevent the loss of securities through fraud or oversight.

A **position** in an asset refers to the quantity of the asset that an entity owns or owes.

- A person with a **long position** owns an assets or a contract. She benefits when there is an increase in the price of the asset or contract.
- A person with a **short position** has sold an asset that she does not own, or has written or sold a contract. She benefits when there is a decrease in the price of the asset or contract.

Positions on Forwards and Futures

The long position in a forward or a futures contract is the side that is obligated to take physical delivery of the asset or its cash equivalent at contract expiration. She will benefit from an increase in the price of the underlying asset.

The short position in a forward or a futures contract is the side that is obligated to make physical delivery of the asset or its cash equivalent at contract expiration. She will benefit from a decrease in the price of the underlying asset.

Positions on Options

The long position on an options contract is the party that holds the right to exercise the option. The short side refers to the writer of the option, who must satisfy any obligations arising from the contract.

- The long position on a call option will benefit when the underlying rises in value.
- The short position on a call option will benefit when the underlying falls in value.
- The long position on a put option will benefit when the underlying falls in value.
- The short position on a put option will benefit when the underlying rises in value.

Swap Contracts

The two parties in a swap contract simply agree to exchange contractually determined cash flows. There is no real buyer or seller, which makes it difficult to determine the long and short side of the contract. Usually, the party that benefits from an increase in the quoted price is referred to as the long.

Currency Contracts

A party that purchases one currency simultaneously sells another currency (the other currency in the price quote or exchange rate). Therefore, whenever we mention a long or a short position in a currency contract, we must mention the other currency as well. For example, we may state that a party is long on the dollar against the yen.

EQ

Short Positions

Short positions in contracts are created by selling contracts that the short seller does not own. The short seller is basically the issuer of the contract.

Short positions in securities are created by selling securities that the short seller does not own. In order to sell the securities, the short seller borrows the securities from long holders to deliver them to buyers. To unwind the position, the short seller then repurchases the security (hopefully at a lower price) from the market and returns it to the long holder.

The maximum profit for the holder of a long position on an asset is unlimited, while her losses are limited to the price she purchased the asset for. In contrast, the maximum profit for a short seller of an asset is limited to her selling price, while her losses are unlimited.

Levered Positions

Many markets allow investors to borrow funds from brokers to purchase securities. The investor borrows a portion of the price of the stock, contributes the rest of the funds herself and puts up the stock as collateral. The borrowed money is known as the **margin loan** and the interest rate paid on it is the **call money rate**.

Traders who purchase securities on margin face minimum margin requirements. The initial margin requirement refers to the proportion of the total cost of the asset that an investor must invest with her own equity. This requirement may be determined by the government, the exchange or the clearinghouse.

When traders borrow money to purchase securities, they are said to be leveraging their positions. The **leverage ratio** is the ratio of the value of the position to the value of the equity investment in it. The maximum leverage ratio for a position financed by a margin loan equals one divided by the minimum margin requirement.

Leverage enhances a trader's returns, but also magnifies losses.

In addition to the initial margin requirement, traders who invest on margin must also adhere to maintenance margin requirements. If the proportion of the value of the security financed by the investor's own equity (after adjusting for the price change) falls below the maintenance margin, the investor will receive a margin call, and she would have to deposit enough funds into her account to at least meet the maintenance margin level. If she fails to do so, her broker can sell the stock to pay off the margin loan.

The price at which an investor who goes long on a stock receives a margin call is calculated as:

$$P_0 \times \frac{(1 - \text{Initial margin})}{(1 - \text{Maintenance margin})}$$

Traders who sell securities short are also subject to margin requirements as they have borrowed securities to take their positions.

Execution, Validity, and Clearing Instructions

The prices at which dealers and other proprietary traders are willing to buy securities are called **bid** prices and those at which they are willing to sell are called **ask** (or offer) prices.

EQ

222

The quantities that market participants are willing to trade at the bid and ask prices are called **bid sizes** and **ask sizes** respectively.

The highest bid in the market is the highest price that a dealer is willing to pay for the security and is known as the **best bid**. On the other hand, the lowest ask price is the **best offer**. The difference between the best bid and the best offer is the **market bid-ask spread**. Liquid markets with low transaction costs generally have small bid-ask spreads.

Execution Instructions

Execution instructions indicate how an order should be filled. They include:

- **Market orders**, which instruct brokers or the exchange to fill an order immediately at the best available price. Market orders generally execute immediately as long as there are traders willing to take the other side of the trade. However, they may be expensive to execute, especially when the order size is large relative to the normal trading activity in the market.
- **Limit orders**, which instruct the broker or the exchange to fill an order at a specified price or better. These specified prices (maximum price for a limit buy order and minimum price for a limit sell order) are referred to as limit prices. Limit orders prevent trades from executing at unacceptable prices. However, this also means that they may not execute at all if the limit price on a buy order is too low or the limit price on a sell order is too high.
  - A limit buy order is aggressively priced when the limit price is high relative to the market "bid" and "ask" prices.
  - A limit buy order placed above the best offer is likely to be at least partially executed immediately and is called a marketable limit order.
  - A limit buy order placed above the best bid but below the best offer is said to have created a new market by establishing the new best bid.
  - A limit buy order placed at the best bid is said to make market. This order will have to wait for all buy orders (that were placed earlier) at that price to execute first.
  - A limit buy order placed below the best bid is referred to as behind the market and will not execute unless market prices drop. These orders are known as standing limit orders.

Exposure Instructions

Exposure instructions specify whether, how and to whom orders may be exposed.

Hidden orders are exposed only to the brokers or exchanges that receive them. Other traders can discover hidden size only after submitting orders that will trade with that size. However, hidden orders may not execute at all as other traders do not know about them. Therefore, traders may sometimes indicate a specific display size (which is lower than the actual order size) with their orders to signal to other traders that someone is willing to trade at the displayed price. As most of the order size is hidden, these orders are also referred to as iceberg orders.

Validity Instructions

Validity instructions indicate when an order may be filled. They include:

- Day orders, which are only valid for the day on which they are submitted. These orders expire if not filled at the close of business.
- Good till-cancelled orders, which are valid until cancelled by the broker.

EQ

- Immediate or cancel orders, which may only be filled, completely or in part, immediately and are otherwise cancelled. These are also known as fill or kill orders.
- Good-on-close orders, which only execute at the close of trading and are also called market-on-close orders.
- Stop orders (often referred to as stop-loss orders), which are placed by investors to protect themselves from adverse price movements.

Clearing Instructions

Clearing instructions indicate how the final settlement of trades should be arranged. They include details of the entities responsible for clearing and settling the trade. Further, security sale orders must also indicate whether the sale is a long sale or a short sale.

Primary Markets

Primary markets are markets where issuers first sell their securities to investors. When a security is issued to the public for the first time, it is referred to as an initial public offering (IPO). On the other hand, when additional units of a previously issued security are sold, it is referred to as a seasoned offering (or a secondary offering) and the issue is called a seasoned issue.

Public Offerings

Companies generally issue securities to the public through an investment bank. The investment bank performs the following functions:

- Through a process called book building, it lines up subscribers who wish to purchase the security.
- It provides investment information about the issuer to its clients and to the public.

The issuer's arrangement with the investment bank may take one of the following forms:

- In an **underwriting offer**, the investment bank guarantees the sale of the issue at an offering price negotiated with the issuer. If the issue is not fully subscribed, the investment bank commits to purchasing the leftover securities at the offer price.
- In a **best efforts offering**, the investment bank merely acts as a broker. It tries its best to sell the securities at the negotiated price, but does not promise to purchase unsold securities.

Private Placements

In a **private placement** securities are not offered to the public. Companies sell securities directly to a group of qualified investors, usually through an investment bank. Qualified investors are generally those who understand associated risks and have sufficient wealth to withstand significant losses. Privately placements are typically cheaper than public offerings as they do not require as much public disclosure. However, since privately placed securities do not trade on organized secondary markets, investors require a higher rate of return from them.

Other Primary Market Transactions

- Companies that issue securities via a **shelf registration** make all the public disclosures that are required in a regular offering, but they do not need to issue all the shares at once. They can sell them directly in the secondary market over time, which offers them flexibility as they can raise capital when they need it.

EQ

224

- Companies that issue securities through **dividend reinvestment plans (DRPs)** allow shareholders to reinvest their dividends by purchasing shares of the company. These shares may be newly issued or purchased from the open market.
- Companies sometimes offer **rights** to existing shareholders to purchase additional shares of the company in proportion to their current holdings at a fixed price.

Secondary Markets

The **secondary market** is that part of the financial market where previously issued securities and financial instruments are traded. Secondary markets play a very important role in that they provide liquidity to investors who purchased their securities in the primary market. Investors will hesitate to participate in the primary market if they cannot subsequently sell their holdings in the secondary market.

Secondary markets are also important for seasoned security issuers as the prices of their new offerings are derived from the secondary market prices of currently outstanding securities that trade on the secondary market.

Trading Sessions

In a **call market**, all bid and ask prices for an asset are gathered to determine one price where the quantity offered for sale is close to the quantity demanded. All transactions take place at this single price. Call markets are popular in smaller markets. However, they are also used on larger exchanges to determine the opening price of a trading session.

In a **continuous market**, transactions can take place whenever the market is open. Prices are set either through an auction process or by dealer bid-ask quotes. Most global stock exchanges are continuous markets.

The advantage of a call market is that it makes it easier for buyers and sellers to find each other by gathering all traders at the same place at the same time. In a continuous market, if a buyer and seller (or their orders) are not present at the same time, they cannot trade. The advantage of a continuous market is that a willing buyer and seller can trade anytime the market is open. In a call market they would only be able to trade when the market is called.

Execution Mechanisms

A **pure auction market (order-driven)** is one where participants submit their bid and ask prices to a central location. Matching bids and offers are paired together and orders are executed. Order-driven matching mechanisms are characterized by two sets of rules:

- Order matching rules match buy orders to sell orders. They rank buy and sell orders based on:
  - Price precedence: Highest priced buy orders and lowest priced sell orders are ranked first.
  - Display precedence: Displayed quantities have precedence over undisplayed quantities at the same price.
  - Time precedence: Orders that arrived first have precedence over orders that arrived later with the same price and with the same display status.
- Trade pricing rules determine the prices at which matched trades take place. Prices may be determined based on any of the following:
  - Under a uniform pricing rule, the same price is used for all trades. This rule is used by call markets where the market chooses the price that maximizes total quantity traded.

EQ

- Under a discriminatory pricing rule, the limit price of the order or quote that arrived first (the standing order) determines the trade price. Continuous trading markets use this rule.
- A derivative pricing rule uses the mid-point of the best bid and ask quotes from another market. Crossing networks (which may themselves be organized as call or continuous trading markets) use this pricing rule.

A **dealer market (quote driven market or price-driven market)** consists of individual dealers who are assigned specific securities. These dealers create liquidity by purchasing and selling against their own inventory of securities. Competition between dealers ensures that competitive prices are available.

In a **brokered market**, brokers arrange trades among their clients. Brokers organize markets for unique items (e.g., real estate properties and fine art masterpieces) that only interest a limited number of people.

Market Information Systems

Markets may be structured based on the type and quantity of information they disseminate to the public.

- Pre-trade transparent markets publish real time data about quotes and orders.
- Post-trade transparent markets publish data about trade prices soon after trades occur.

Characteristics of a Well-Functioning Financial System

- **Timely and accurate information** on the price and volume of recent transactions. If timely information is not available, a seller may not get the best possible price, and a buyer may end up paying too high a price.
- **Liquidity**, which refers to the ability to buy or sell the asset quickly, at a price close to that of a recent market transaction, assuming no new information has been received. To achieve price continuity, the market must be significantly deep.
- **Internal efficiency** in that there are low transaction costs, which include the costs of reaching the market and brokerage costs.
- **External or informational efficiency**, which is achieved when market prices reflect all external available information about an asset. Prices should rapidly adjust to reflect any new information.

Objectives of Market Regulation

- Control fraud or deception of uninformed market participants.
- Control agency problems by setting minimum standards of competence for agents and by defining and enforcing minimum standards of practice.
- Promote fairness by creating a level playing field for market participants.
- Set mutually beneficial standards for financial reporting.
- Prevent undercapitalized financial firms from exploiting their investors by making excessively risky investments; and
- Ensure that long-term liabilities are funded.

EQ

226

SECURITY MARKET INDEXES
Cross-Reference to CFA Institute Assigned Reading #34

A **security market index** consists of individual securities (also called constituent securities) that represent a given security market, market segment, or asset class. Each security market index may have two versions depending on how returns are calculated:

- A **price return index** only reflects the prices of constituent securities.
- A **total return index** not only reflects prices, but also assumes reinvestment of all income received since inception.

The values of both versions of an index are the same at inception. However, as time passes, the total return index will be greater in value than the price return index by an increasing amount.

Index Construction

Constructing and managing a security market index involves:

- Target market selection
- Security selection
- Index weighting
- Rebalancing
- Reconstitution

Target Market and Security Selection

The **target market** may be based on:

- Asset class (e.g., equities, fixed income, or real estate)
- Geographic region (e.g., Japan, South Africa or Europe)
- The exchange on which the securities are traded (e.g., New York, London or Tokyo)
- Other characteristics (e.g., economic sector, company size and investment style)

An index may consist of all the securities in the target market or just a representative sample of the target market.

Index Weighting

Price Weighting

In a price-weighted index the weight of each constituent security is determined by dividing its price by the sum of the prices of all constituent securities:

$$w_i^P = \frac{P_i}{\sum_{i=1}^{N} P_i}$$

The value of a price-weighted index is computed by dividing the sum of the security prices by the divisor. At inception, the divisor is typically set to the number of securities in the index.

The advantage of a price-weighted index is its simplicity. One of the issues with a price-weighted index is that a stock split or stock dividend by one of the constituent securities changes the weights of all securities in the index. To prevent stock splits and stock dividends from changing the value of the index, the divisor of a price-weighted index must be adjusted.

Equal Weighting

In an equal-weighted index, each constituent security is given an identical weight in the index at inception. The weights are calculated as:

$$w_i^E = \frac{1}{N}$$

The number of shares of each security included in the index is calculated as the value allotted to each constituent security divided by the price of the security. Unlike a price-weighted index, where the weights are arbitrarily determined by market prices, the weights in an equal-weighted index are effectively determined by the index provider (in choosing the particular weighting mechanism).

Equal-weighted indexes are also preferred because of their simplicity. However, they have a few disadvantages:

- Assigning an equal weight to all securities under-represents (over-represents) those securities that constitute a relatively large (small) fraction of the target market.
- The index does not remain equally weighted once the prices of the constituent securities change. Frequent adjustments must be made to maintain equal weighting.

Market-Capitalization Weighting

A market-capitalization weighted (value weighted) index is based on the total market value (current stock price times the total number of shares outstanding) of all stocks in the index. The proportion of each constituent security is determined by dividing its market capitalization by the total market capitalization of all the securities in the index:

$$w_i^M = \frac{Q_i P_i}{\sum_{j=1}^{N} Q_j P_j}$$

The initial market value is assigned a base number (e.g., 100) and a new market value is computed periodically. The change in the index is measured by comparing the new market value to the base market value.

Value-weighted indexes automatically adjust for stock splits and stock dividends.

Float-Adjusted Market-Capitalization Weighting

In a float-adjusted market-capitalization weighted index, the proportion of each constituent security is determined by adjusting its market capitalization for its market float.

Market float generally refers to the number of shares of the constituent security that are available to the investing public. Shares held by controlling shareholders, other corporations and governments are subtracted from the total number of outstanding shares to determine the market float.

The float-adjusted market-capitalization weight of each constituent security is calculated as:

$$w_i^M = \frac{f_i Q_i P_i}{\sum_{j=1}^{N} f_j Q_j P_j}$$

The primary advantage of market capitalization weighting (and float-adjusted market capitalization weighting) is that securities are held in proportion to their value in the target market. A disadvantage is that stocks with larger market values have a larger impact on the index. Stocks that have seen their prices rise (fall) will see their relative weight in the index increase (decline). The effect of market value weighting is therefore similar to that of a momentum trading strategy.

Fundamental Weighting

Instead of using prices of constituent securities, a fundamental weighted index uses other measures of a company's size (that are independent of the stock price) such as book value, cash flow, revenues and earnings to determine weights of securities in the index. Some fundamental indexes use a single measure to weight the constituent securities, while others combine weights from several measures to form a composite value that is used for weighting.

The fundamental weight on security i can be calculated as:

$$w_i^F = \frac{F_i}{\sum_{j=1}^{N} F_j}$$

In contrast to market-capitalization weighted indexes, in which the weight of a stock in the index moves in the same direction as its price, fundamental weighted indexes have a "contrarian" effect in that the portfolio weights move away from securities whose prices have risen.

Rebalancing

In order to keep the weights of constituent securities consistent with the index's weighting method security weights must be adjusted or rebalanced.

- In equal-weighted indexes, the weights of securities that have witnessed price appreciation increase over time, and weights of securities that have underperformed decrease over time. Rebalancing an equal-weighted index would require reducing the weight of securities that have outperformed and increasing the weight of securities that have underperformed.
- Price-weighted indexes do not need to be rebalanced as the weight of each constituent security is determined by its price.
- Market-capitalization weighted indexes rebalance themselves to reflect changes in the market-capitalization of constituent securities. They only need to be rebalanced to reflect mergers, acquisitions, liquidations, etc.

Reconstitution

Constituent securities need to be examined on a regular basis to evaluate whether they still meet the criteria for inclusion in the index. If they no longer meet the criteria, they must be replaced with securities that do meet the criteria. Index reconstitution is performed in order to:

- Reflect changes in the target market as a result of bankruptcies, de-listings, mergers, etc.
- Reflect the judgement of the selection committee.

Uses of Security Market Indexes

- To gauge market sentiment.
- As proxies for measuring and modeling returns, systematic risk, and risk-adjusted performance.
- As proxies for asset classes in asset allocation models.
- As benchmarks for actively managed portfolios.
- As the basis for the creation of numerous investment products.

Types of Equity Indexes

Broad market indexes: A broad equity market index contains securities representing more than 90% of the selected market.

Multi-market indexes: Multi-market indexes consist of security market indexes from different countries and may represent multiple national markets, geographic regions, economic development groups or even the entire world.

Sector indexes: Sector indexes only include securities representing a particular economic sector (e.g., finance, health care, technology, etc.) where the economic sector may be classified on a national, regional or global basis.

Style indexes: Financial firms like Dow Jones and Standard & Poor's have developed different indexes based on specific investment strategies used by portfolio managers. These indexes include those based on size (e.g., small-cap versus large-cap equities) and others based on style (e.g., growth versus value stocks). Style indexes generally have much higher turnover than broad market indexes.

Fixed-Income Indexes

Creating bond-market indexes presents the following challenges:

- There is a broader universe of bonds than of stocks.
- The universe of bonds is constantly changing as a result of new issues, calls, and maturities.
- The price volatility of a bond (as measured by duration) is constantly changing. Duration changes with a bond's maturity and market yields.
- Current and continuous transaction prices are not available for bonds.

Types of Fixed-Income Indexes

Fixed-income securities can be classified along the following dimensions:

- Type of issuer (government, government agency, corporation).
- Type of financing (general obligation, collateralized).
- Currency of payments.

- Maturity.
- Credit quality (investment grade, high yield, credit agency ratings).
- Absence or presence of inflation protection.

Fixed-income indexes can be categorized as follows:

- Aggregate or broad market indexes.
- Market sector indexes.
- Style indexes.
- Economic sector indexes.
- Specialized indexes such as high-yield, inflation-linked, and emerging market indexes.

Indexes Representing Alternative Investments

Commodity indexes: Commodity indexes consist of futures contracts on one or more commodities and have the following characteristics:

- They do not have an obvious weighting method so index providers create their own weighting methods.
- Different weighting methods lead to different exposures to specific commodities, which result in very different risk and return profiles of commodity indexes.
- The performance of commodity indexes may differ from that of the underlying commodities because indexes consist of futures contracts on commodities rather than the actual commodities.

Real estate investment trust indexes: Real estate indexes represent the market for real estate and real estate securities. They can be categorized as:

- Appraisal indexes
- Repeat sales indexes
- Real estate investment trust (REIT) indexes

REIT indexes consist of shares of publicly traded REITs (public or private organizations that combine individual investors' funds and provide them access to real estate investments). Shares issued by REITs trade on various exchanges around the world and are priced continuously.

Hedge fund indexes: Hedge fund indexes are designed to represent the performance of hedge funds (private investment vehicles that typically use leverage and long and short investment strategies) on a very broad, global level or the strategy level. Hedge fund indexes have the following characteristics:

- They rely on voluntary disclosures from funds as it is not mandatory for hedge funds to disclose performance to any party other than investors.
- If they do decide to disclose performance, hedge funds have a choice regarding which index or indexes they report their performance to. Therefore, rather than index providers determining the constituents, the constituents determine the index. Further, different hedge fund indexes may reflect very different performance for the hedge fund industry over the same period of time based on the hedge funds represented in those indexes.
- Poorly performing hedge funds may stop reporting their performance to hedge fund indexes or may cease to exist altogether. This leads to survivorship bias and an upward bias in hedge fund performance as represented by these indexes.

EQ

MARKET EFFICIENCY
Cross-Reference to CFA Institute Assigned Reading #35

An **informationally efficient market** (an **efficient market**) is one where security prices adjust rapidly to reflect any new information. It is a market where asset prices reflect all past and present information.

Investment managers and analysts are interested in market efficiency because it dictates how many profitable trading opportunities may abound in the market.

- In an **efficient market**, it is difficult to find inaccurately priced securities. Therefore, superior risk-adjusted returns cannot be attained in an efficient market, and it would be wise to pursue a passive investment strategy which entails lower costs.
- In an **inefficient market**, securities may be mispriced and trading in these securities can offer positive risk-adjusted returns. In such a market, an active investment strategy may outperform a passive strategy on a risk-adjusted basis.

In an efficient market, the time frame required for security prices to reflect any new information is very short. Further, prices only adjust to new or unexpected information (surprises).

Market Value versus Intrinsic Value

The **market value or market price** of the asset is the price at which the asset can currently be bought or sold. It is determined by the interaction of demand and supply for the security in the market. **Intrinsic value** or **fundamental value** is the value of the asset that reflects all its investment characteristics accurately. Intrinsic values are estimated in light of all the available information regarding the asset; they are not known for certain.

In an efficient market, investors widely believe that the market price reflects a security's intrinsic value. On the other hand, in an inefficient market, investors may try to develop their own estimates of intrinsic value in order to profit from any mispricing (difference between the market price and intrinsic value).

Factors Contributing to and Impeding a Market's Efficiency

Market participants: Generally speaking, the greater the number of active market participants (investors and financial analysts) that analyze an asset or security, the greater the degree of efficiency in the market.

Information availability and financial disclosure: The availability of accurate and timely information regarding trading activities and traded companies contributes to market efficiency.

Limits to trading: The activities of arbitrageurs, who seek opportunities to trade on mispricings in the market to earn arbitrage (riskless) profits, contribute to market efficiency.

Transactions costs and information acquisition costs: Investors should consider transaction costs and information-acquisition costs in evaluating the efficiency of a market.

Two securities that should trade for the exact same price in an efficient market may trade at different prices if the costs of trading on the mispricing (to make a profit) for the lowest cost

EQ

232

traders are greater than the potential profit. In such cases, these prices are still "efficient" within the bounds of arbitrage. The bounds of arbitrage are relatively narrow in highly liquid markets (e.g., U.S. T-bills), but wider in relatively illiquid markets.

Further, there are always costs associated with gathering and analyzing information. Net of information acquisition costs, the return offered on a security should be commensurate with the security's level of risk. If superior returns can be earned after deducting information-acquisition costs, the market is relatively inefficient.

Efficient Market Hypotheses

Weak-Form Efficient Market Hypothesis

Weak-form EMH assumes that current stock prices reflect all security market information including historical trends in prices, returns, volumes and other market-generated information such as block trades and trading by specialists. Under this hypothesis, because current stock market prices have essentially factored in all historical data, future returns on a stock should be independent of past returns or patterns.

Proponents of weak-form EMH assert that abnormal risk-adjusted returns cannot be earned by using trading rules and technical analysis, which make investing decisions based on historical security market data.

On the whole, various tests for weak-form EMH have backed the theory that current market prices reflect all available security market information and lead to the conclusion that the markets tend to be weak-form efficient. However, there is evidence that in countries with developing markets (e.g., China, Bangladesh and Turkey) opportunities to profit from technical analysis do exist.

Semi-Strong Form Efficient Market Hypothesis

Semi-strong form EMH assumes that current security prices fully reflect all security market information and other public information. It encompasses weak-form EMH and also includes non-market public information such as dividend announcements, various financial ratios, and economic and political news in the set of information that is already factored into market values.

Proponents of the hypothesis assert that investors cannot earn abnormal risk-adjusted returns if their investment decisions are based on important material information after it has been made public. They stress that security prices rapidly adjust to reflect all public information.

Overall, semi-strong form EMH has received considerable support from studies in developed markets. In these markets, it has been found that abnormal risk-adjusted returns cannot be earned based on public information because security prices adjust for the information very quickly. However, there is some evidence that developing countries may not have semi-strong form efficient markets.

Strong-Form Efficient Market Hypothesis

Strong form EMH contends that stock prices reflect all public and private information. It implies that no group of investors has sole access to any information that is relevant in price formation. Basically, there is no information out there that has not already been accounted for in current market prices.

EQ

Strong-form EMH encompasses weak-form and semi-strong form EMH and assumes perfect markets where information is cost free and available to all. Under strong-form EMH, no one can consistently achieve abnormal risk-adjusted returns, not even company insiders.

Studies have found that securities markets are not strong form efficient. Abnormal risk-adjusted returns can be earned if material non-public information is used.

Implications of Efficient Market Hypothesis

- Securities markets are weak-form efficient. Therefore, past trends in prices cannot be used to earn superior risk-adjusted returns.
- Securities markets are also semi-strong form efficient. Therefore, investors who analyze information should consider what information is already factored into a security's price, and how any new information may affect its value.
- Securities markets are not strong-form efficient. This is because insider trading is illegal.

Efficient Markets and Technical Analysis

Technical analysts utilize charts to identify price patterns, which are used to make investment decisions. If the market is weak-form efficient, prices already reflect all available security market public information, and technical trading systems that depend only on past trading and price data cannot hold much value. Since tests have predominantly confirmed weak-form efficiency of markets, technical trading rules should not generate abnormal risk adjusted-profits after accounting for risks and transaction costs.

Efficient Markets and Fundamental Analysis

Fundamental analysts are concerned with the company that underlies the stock. They evaluate a company's past performance and examine its financial statements. They compute many performance ratios that aid them in assessing the validity of the stock's current price. They believe that a company's stock price can differ from its true intrinsic value, and investors who recognize the discrepancy can profit from it.

Fundamental analysis is necessary in a well-functioning securities market as it helps market participants understand the implications of any new information. Further, fundamental analysis can help generate abnormal risk-adjusted returns if an analyst is superior to her peers in valuing securities.

Efficient Markets and Portfolio Management

If markets and weak and semi-strong form efficient, active management is not likely to earn superior risk-adjusted returns on a consistent basis. Therefore, passive portfolio management would outperform active management. Studies have shown that on a risk-adjusted basis, mutual funds perform as well as the market before considering fees and expenses, but underperform the market after considering these costs.

The implication here is that the role of the portfolio manager is not necessarily to beat the market, but to manage the portfolio in light on the investor's risk and return objectives.

Pricing Anomalies

An anomaly occurs when a change in the price of an asset cannot be explained by the release of new information into the market.

EQ

- If markets are efficient, trading strategies designed to exploit market anomalies will not generate superior risk-adjusted returns on a consistent basis.
- An exception to the notion of market efficiency (an anomaly) would occur if a mispricing can be used to earn superior risk adjusted returns consistently.

Observed anomalies can be placed into three categories.

1. Time-Series Anomalies

Calendar Anomalies

January effect: Studies have shown that since the 1980s, investors have earned significantly higher returns in the equity market during January compared to other months of the year. Recent evidence has suggested that the January effect is not persistent and does not produce superior returns on a risk-adjusted basis. Therefore, it is not a pricing anomaly.

Momentum and Overreaction Anomalies

Investors tend to inflate (depress) stock prices of companies that have released good (bad) news. Studies have shown that "losers" (stocks that have witnessed a recent price decline due to the release of bad news) have outperformed the market in subsequent periods, while winners have underperformed in subsequent periods. Other studies have also shown that securities that have outperformed in the short term continue to generate high returns in subsequent periods (carrying on price momentum).

The overreaction and momentum anomalies go against the assertions of weak-form efficiency in markets.

2. Cross-Sectional Anomalies

Size Effect

Studies conducted in the past showed that shares of smaller companies outperformed shares of larger companies on a risk-adjusted basis. However, recent studies have failed to reach the same conclusion.

Value Effect

Studies have found that low P/E stocks have experienced higher risk-adjusted returns than high P/E stocks. These results go against semi-strong form market efficiency. However, when the Fama and French three-factor model is used instead of the CAPM to predict stock returns, the value stock anomaly disappears.

Other Anomalies

Closed-End Investment Fund Discounts

Several studies have shown that closed-end funds tend to trade at a discount (sometimes exceeding 50%) to their per share NAVs. Theoretically, investors could purchase all the shares in the fund, liquidate the fund, and make a profit by selling the constituent securities at their market prices. However, after accounting for management fees, unrealized capital gains taxes, liquidity and transaction costs, any profit potential is eliminated.

EQ

Earnings Surprises

Several studies have shown that although earnings surprises are quickly reflected in stock prices most of the time, this is not always the case. Investors may be able to earn abnormal returns using publicly available earnings information by purchasing stocks of companies that have announced positive earnings surprises. However, recent evidence has suggested that abnormal returns observed after earnings surprises do not control for transaction costs and risk.

Initial Public Offerings (IPOs)

Evidence suggests that investors who are able to acquire the shares of a company in an IPO at the offer price may be able to earn abnormal profits. However, this has not always proven to be the case. Further, over the long run, performance of IPOs has generally been below average.

Predictability of Returns Based on Prior Information

Considerable research has suggested that equity returns are based on factors such as interest rates, inflation rates, stock volatility, etc. However, the fact that equity returns are related to economic fundamentals is not evidence of market inefficiency.

Implications for Investment Strategies

Although there is some evidence to support the existence of valid anomalies, it is difficult to consistently earn abnormal returns by trading on them. On average, markets are efficient. Further, it is possible that identified anomalies may not be violations of market efficiency, but the result of the statistical methodologies used to detect them.

Behavioral Finance

Behavioral finance looks at investor behavior to explain why individuals make the decisions that they do, whether these decisions are rational or irrational. It is based on the premise that individuals do not always make 'efficient' investment decisions, nor do they always act "rationally" due to the presence of **behavioral biases**.

Behavioral Biases

Loss Aversion

> Most asset-pricing models assume that markets are rational and that the intrinsic value of a security reflects the rationality. But market efficiency and asset-pricing models do not require that each individual is rational–rather, only that the market is rational.

Behavioral finance asserts that investors exhibit **loss aversion** i.e., they dislike losses more than they like comparable gains, which results in a strong preference for avoiding losses as opposed to achieving gains. Advocates of this bias argue that loss aversion is more important to investors than risk aversion, which is why the "overreaction" anomaly is observed. While loss aversion can explain the overreaction anomaly, studies have shown that under reactions are just as common as overreactions, which counters the assertions of this bias.

Herding

Herding behavior is a behavioral bias that explains both under reactions and overreactions in financial markets. Herding occurs when investors ignore their own analysis, and instead make investment decisions in line with the direction of the market.

Overconfidence

Overconfidence bias asserts investors have an inflated view of their ability to process new information appropriately. Overconfident investors are inaccurate when it comes to valuing securities given new information, and therefore stocks will be mispriced if there is an adequate number of such investors in the market.

Evidence has suggested that overconfidence has led to mispricing in most major markets around the world, but the bias has been observed predominantly in higher-growth companies, whose prices are slow to factor in any new information.

Another aspect of this bias is that overconfident investors tend to maintain portfolios that are less-than-optimally diversified because they tend to overestimate their stock-picking abilities.

Information Cascades

An information cascade refers to the transfer of information from market participants who are the first to take investment action upon the release of new information, and whose decisions influence the decisions of others.

Information cascades can be rational. If informed traders act first and uninformed traders follow their lead, there will be an improvement in market efficiency as the cascade is helping the market correctly incorporate relevant information. Information cascades can also result in serial correlation in stock returns and to overreactions to information. Studies have shown that information cascades tend to be greater for stocks when reliable and relevant information about the underlying company is not easily available. They can actually improve the quality of information available to investors.

Other Behavioral Biases

- **Representativeness**, where investors assess probabilities of future outcomes based on how similar they are to the current state.
- **Mental accounting**, where investors keep track of gains and losses from different investments in separate mental accounts.
- **Conservatism**, where investors are slow to react to changes and continue to maintain their initial views.
- **Narrow framing**, where investors focus on issues in isolation.

Concluding Remarks

Whether investor behavior can explain market anomalies is a subject open to debate.

- If investors must be rational for the market to be efficient, then markets cannot be efficient.
- If markets are defined as being efficient, investors cannot earn superior risk-adjusted profits consistently, available evidence suggests that markets are efficient even though investors do exhibit irrational behavior, such as herding.

Study Session 12: Equity Investments (2)

EQ

OVERVIEW OF EQUITY SECURITIES
Cross-Reference to CFA Institute Assigned Reading #36

Importance of Equities in Global Financial Markets

- In 2008, on a global level, the equity market capitalization to GDP ratio was close to 100% (more than twice the long run average of 50%).
- Studies have shown that during 1900-2008, government bonds and bills earned annualized real returns of 1% to 2% on average, which is in line with the inflation rate. On the other hand, equity markets earned real returns in excess of 4% per year in most markets.
- In most developed countries, equity ownership as a percentage of the population was between 20% and 50%.

Types of Equity Securities

Common Shares

Investors in common shares have an ownership interest in the company. They share the operating performance of the company, participate in the governance process through voting rights, and have a residual claim on the company's net assets in case of liquidation.

Preference Shares

Preference shares (also known as preferred stock) have the following characteristics:

- They do not give holders the right to participate in the operating performance of the company and they do not carry voting rights unless explicitly allowed for at issuance.
- They receive dividends before ordinary shareholders. Further, preferred dividends are fixed and are usually higher than dividends on common shares. However, the company is still not contractually obligated to make regular payments to holders of preferred stock.
- In case of liquidation, they have a higher priority in claims on the company's net assets than common shares. However, they still have a lower priority than bondholders.
- They can be perpetual (i.e., have no fixed maturity date), can pay dividends indefinitely, and can be callable or putable.

Preference shares can be classified into the following categories:

- **Cumulative:** Unpaid dividends on cumulative preference shares accrue over time and must be paid in full before dividends on common shares can be paid.
- **Non-cumulative:** Unpaid dividends for one or more periods are forfeited permanently and are not accrued over time to be paid at a later date.
- **Participating:** These are entitled to preferred dividends plus additional dividends if the company's profits exceed a pre-specified level. Further, investors in participating preferred shares might be entitled to an additional distribution of the company's assets upon liquidation above the par value of the preference shares. Participating preference shares are more common in smaller, riskier companies in which investors are concerned about the company's possible future liquidation.
- **Non-participating:** These are only entitled to a fixed preferred dividend and the par value of shares in the event of liquidation.

EQ

- **Convertible:** These are convertible into a specified number of common shares based on a conversion ratio that is determined at issuance. They have the following advantages:
    - They allow investors to earn a higher dividend than if they had invested in the company's common shares.
    - They offer investors the opportunity to share the profits of the company.
    - They allow investors to benefit from a rise in the price of common shares through the conversion option.
    - Their price is less volatile than the underlying common shares because their dividend payments are known and more stable.

Convertible preference shares are becoming increasingly common in venture capital and private equity transactions.

Private Equity Securities

Private securities are issued primarily to institutional investors via non-public offerings, such as private placements, and have the following characteristics:

- There is no active secondary market for them as they are not listed on public exchanges. Therefore, they do not have market-determined quoted prices.
- They are highly illiquid, and require negotiations between investors in order to be traded.
- The issuing companies are not required by regulatory authorities to publish financial statements and other important information regarding the company, which makes it difficult to determine fair values.

Types of Private Equity Investments

- Venture capital
- Leveraged Buyout (LBO)
- Private Investment in Public Equity

Advantages of Private Companies

- The longer investment horizons allow investors to focus on long-term value creation and to address any underlying operational issues facing the company. Publicly-traded companies feel pressured to focus on short term performance (e.g., to meet market expectations regarding earnings, growth, etc.).
- Certain costs that public companies must bear, such as those incurred to meet regulatory and stock exchange filing requirements, are avoided by private companies.

Advantages of Public Companies

- Public equity markets are much larger than private equity networks. Therefore, they provide more opportunities to companies for raising capital cheaply.
- Publicly traded companies are encouraged to be open about their policies, which ensures that they act in shareholder interest.

Non-Domestic Equity Securities

- An increasing number of companies have issued shares in markets outside of their home country.
- The number of companies whose shares are traded in markets outside of their home country has increased.

- An increasing number of companies are dual-listed i.e., their shares are simultaneously issued and traded in two or more markets.

Listing a company on an international exchange has the following benefits:

- It improves awareness about the company's products and services.
- It enhances the liquidity of the company's shares.
- It increases corporate transparency due to the additional market exposure and the need to meet a greater number of filing requirements.

Methods for Investing in Non-Domestic Equity Securities

Direct Investing

The most obvious way to invest in equity securities of foreign companies is to buy and sell securities directly in foreign markets. However, direct investing has the following implications:

- All transactions are in the company's, not the investor's domestic currency. Therefore, investors are also exposed to exchange rate risk.
- Investors must be familiar with the trading, clearing, and settlement regulations and procedures of the foreign market.
- Investing directly may lead to less transparency (due to the unavailability of audited financial statements on a regular basis) and increased volatility (due to limited liquidity).

Depository Receipts

A depository receipt (DR) is a security that trades like an ordinary share on a local exchange and represents an economic interest in a foreign company. It is created when a foreign company deposits its shares with a bank (the depository) in the country on whose exchange the shares will trade. The bank then issues a specific number of receipts representing the deposited shares based on a pre-determined ratio. Hence, one DR might represent one share, a number of shares or a fractional share of the underlying stock.

A DR can be sponsored or unsponsored.

- A sponsored DR is when the foreign company that deposits its shares with the depository has a direct involvement in the issuance of receipts.
- In an unsponsored DR, the foreign company that deposits its shares with the depository has no involvement in the issuance of receipts.

There are two types of depository receipts:

- Global Depository Receipts (GDRs): GDRs are issued by the depository bank outside of the company's home country and outside of the U.S.
- American Depository Receipts (ADRs): ADRs are denominated in U.S. dollars and trade like a common share on U.S. exchanges. They are basically GDRs that can be publicly traded in the U.S.

Global Registered Shares (GRS)

A GRS is an ordinary share that is quoted and traded in different currencies on different stock exchanges around the world. GRSs offer more flexibility than DRs as the shares represent actual ownership in the issuing company, they can be traded anywhere and currency conversions are not required to trade them.

EQ

Basket of Listed Depository Receipts (BLDR)

This is an exchange-traded fund (ETF) that represents a portfolio of DRs. Like all other ETFs, it trades throughout the day and can be bought, sold, or sold short just like an individual share. Further, it can be purchased on margin and used in hedging and arbitrage strategies.

Return Characteristics of Equity Securities

The two main sources of an equity security's total return are:

- Capital gains from price appreciation.
- Dividend income.

The total return on non-dividend-paying stocks only consists of capital gains.

Investors in depository receipts and foreign shares also incur foreign exchange gains (or losses).

Another source of return arises from the compounding effects of reinvested dividends.

Risks of Equity Securities

- Preference shares are less risky than common shares.
- Putable common shares are less risky than callable or non-callable common shares.
- Callable common and preference shares are more risky than their non-callable counterparts.
- Cumulative preference shares are less risky than non-cumulative preference shares as they accrue unpaid dividends.

Equity Securities and Company Value

The primary aim of management is to increase the book value and market value of the company. Book value (shareholders' equity on the company's balance sheet) is calculated as total assets less total liabilities. It reflects the historical operating and financing decisions made by the company. Management can directly influence book value (e.g., by retaining net income).

However, management can only indirectly influence a company's market value as it is primarily determined by investors' expectations about the amount, timing and uncertainty of the company's future cash flows. A company may increase its book value by retaining net income, but it will only have a positive effect on the company's market value if investors expect the company to invest its retained earnings in profitable growth opportunities. If investors believe that the company has a significant number of cash flow generating investment opportunities coming through, the market value of the company's equity will exceed its book value.

A useful ratio to evaluate investor's expectations about a company is the price-to-book ratio (also known as the market-to-book) ratio.

- If a company has a price-to-book ratio that is greater than industry average, it suggests that investors believe that the company has more significant future growth opportunities than its industry peers.
- It may not be appropriate to compare price-to-book ratios of companies in different industries because the ratio also reflects investors' growth outlook for the industry itself.

EQ

244

An important measure used by investors to evaluate the effectiveness of management in increasing the company's book value is accounting return on equity.

Accounting Return on Equity

The accounting return on equity (ROE) measures the rate of return earned by a company on its equity capital. It indicates how efficient a firm is in generating profits from every dollar of net assets. The ROE is computed as net income available to ordinary shareholders (after preference dividends have been paid) divided by the average total book value of equity.

$$ROE_t = \frac{NI_t}{\text{Average BVE}_t} = \frac{NI_t}{(BVE_t + BVE_{t-1})/2}$$

An increase in ROE might not always be a positive sign for the company.

- The increase in ROE may be the result of net income decreasing at a slower rate than shareholders' equity. A declining net income is a source of concern for investors.
- The increase in ROE may be the result of debt issuance proceeds being used to repurchase shares. This would increase the company's financial leverage (risk).

Book values and ROE do help analysts evaluate companies, but they cannot be used as the primary means to determine a company's intrinsic value. Intrinsic value refers to the present value of the company's expected future cash flows, and can only be estimated as it is impossible to accurately predict the amount and timing of a company's future cash flows. Astute investors aim to profit from differences between market prices and intrinsic values.

The Cost of Equity and Investors' Required Rates of Return

A company may raise capital by issuing debt or equity, both of which have associated costs.

- A company's cost of debt is easy to estimate as it is reflected in the interest payments that the company is contractually obligated to make to debt holders.
- Estimating cost of equity is difficult because the company is not contractually obligated to make any payments to common shareholders.

Investors' minimum required rates of return refer to the return they require for providing funds to the company.

- For investors who provide debt capital to the company, their minimum required rate of return is the periodic interest rate they charge the company for using their funds. Further, all providers of debt capital receive the same interest rate. Therefore, the company's cost of debt and investors' minimum required rate of return on debt are the same.
- For investors who provide equity capital to the company, the future cash flows that they expect to receive are uncertain (in both timing and amount) so their minimum required rate of return must be estimated. Further, each investor may have different expectations regarding future cash flows. Therefore, the company's cost of equity may be different from investors' minimum required rate of return on equity.

You should think about the cost of equity as the minimum expected rate of return that a company must offer investors to purchase its shares in the primary market and to maintain its share price in the secondary market. If the required rate of return is not maintained, the price of

EQ

the security in the secondary market will adjust to reflect the minimum rate of return required by investors.

- If investors require a higher return than the company's cost of equity, they will sell the company's shares and invest elsewhere, which would bring down the company's stock price. This decline in the stock price will lead to an increase in the expected return on equity and bring it in line with the (higher) required rate of return.

Note:

- The company's cost of equity can be estimated using the dividend discount model (DDM) and capital asset pricing model (CAPM) which are discussed in other readings.
- The costs of debt and equity are used to estimate a company's weighted average cost of capital (WACC), which represents the minimum required rate of return that the company must earn on its average investment.

EQ

246

INTRODUCTION TO INDUSTRY AND COMPANY ANALYSIS
Cross-Reference to CFA Institute Assigned Reading #37

Industry analysis has the following uses:

- To understand a company's business and business environment.
- To identify active equity investment opportunities.
- To attribute portfolio performance.

APPROACHES TO INDUSTRY CLASSIFICATION

Products and/or Services Supplied

This classification scheme groups companies that make similar products and/or services. Companies are placed in industries based on their **principal business activity** i.e., the source from which the company derives most of its revenues and/or earnings. Industries that are related to each other are grouped together to form a **sector**.

Business-Cycle Sensitivities

This approach groups companies based on their relative sensitivity to business cycles.

A **cyclical** company is one whose performance is positively correlated with the performance of the overall economy. Cyclical companies perform very well when the economy is booming, but perform relatively poorly during recessions. Cyclical companies typically have high operating leverage, which may be accompanied by high financial risk. Examples of cyclical industries include autos, industrials and technology.

A **non-cyclical** company is one whose performance is relatively independent of the business cycle. Demand for products made by non-cyclical companies remains relatively stable. Examples of non-cyclical industries include healthcare and utilities.

Analysts also often classify industries as defensive or growth industries. **Defensive** or stable industries are those whose profits are least affected by fluctuations in overall economic activity. **Growth** industries are industries whose specific demand dynamics override economic factors in determining their performance. These industries generate growth irrespective of overall economic conditions, though their growth rates may decline in recessions.

Limitations of these Classifications:

- The classification of companies as cyclical or non-cyclical is somewhat arbitrary. Economic downturns affect all companies so cyclical and non-cyclical industries are better understood on a relative basis.
- At a given point in time different countries and regions may be undergoing different stages of the business cycle. Comparing companies in the same industry that are currently operating in very different economic conditions may help identify investment opportunities, but establishing industry benchmark values with the data would be misleading.

Statistical Similarities

Statistical approaches group companies on the basis of correlations of historical returns. This approach has the following limitations:

EQ

247

© 2022 Wiley

- The composition of industry groups may vary significantly over time and across geographical regions.
- There is no guarantee that past correlations will continue to hold going forward.
- A relationship may arise by chance.
- A relationship that is actually economically significant may be excluded.

Industry Classification Systems

Commercial Industry Classification Systems

- Global Industry Classification Standard (GICS)
- Industry Classification Benchmark (ICB)

Peer Groups

A **peer group** is a group of companies engaged in similar business activities whose economics and valuation are influenced by closely-related factors. Comparing a company to a well-defined peer group is very useful in evaluating company performance and in relative valuation.

Steps in constructing a preliminary list of peer companies:

- Examine commercial classification systems to identify companies operating in the same industry.
- Review the subject company's annual report to identify any mention of competitors.
- Review competitors' annual reports to identify other potential comparable companies.
- Review industry trade publications to identify comparable companies.
- Confirm that comparable companies have primary business activities that are similar to those of the subject company.

Strategic Analysis

Analysis of the industry with a view to examining the implications of the industrial environment on corporate strategy is known as **strategic analysis**.

Porter's Five Forces Framework

- Threat of substitute product
- Bargaining power of customers
- Bargaining power of suppliers
- Threat of new entrants
- Intensity of rivalry

Barriers to Entry

Generally speaking:

- Low barriers to entry mean that new competitors can easily enter the industry, which makes the industry highly competitive. Companies in relatively competitive industries typically have little pricing power.
- High barriers to entry mean that existing companies are able to enjoy economic profits for a long period of time. These companies have greater pricing power.

However, bear in mind that the above mentioned characteristics of high and low barrier industries are not always observed. Further, it is important to note that:

EQ

248

- Barriers to entry should not be confused with barriers to success.
- Barriers to entry can change over time.

Industry Concentration

Generally speaking:

- If an industry is relatively concentrated i.e., a few large firms dominate the industry, there is relatively less price competition. This is because:
  - It is relatively easy for a few firms to coordinate their activities.
  - Larger firms have more to lose from destructive price behavior.
  - The fortunes of large firms are more tied to those of the industry as a whole so they are more likely to be wary of the long run impact of a price war on industry economics.
- If an industry is relatively fragmented i.e., there is a large number of small firms in the industry, there is relatively high price competition. This is because of the following reasons:
  - Firms are unable to monitor their competitors' actions, which makes coordination difficult.
  - Each firm only has a small share of the market, so a small market share gain (through aggressive pricing) can make a large difference to each firm.
  - Each firm is small relative to the overall market so it tends to think of itself individualistically, rather than as a member of a larger group.

Bear in mind that there are important exceptions to the rules defined above. For example, Boeing and Airbus dominate the aircraft manufacturing industry, but competition between the two remains fierce.

Industry Capacity

Generally speaking:

- Limited capacity gives companies more pricing power as demand exceeds supply.
- Excess capacity results in weak pricing power as excess supply chases demand.

In evaluating the future competitive environment in an industry, analysts should examine current capacity levels as well as how capacity levels are expected to change in the future. Further, it is important to keep in mind that:

- If new capacity is physical (e.g., manufacturing facilities) it will take longer for the new capacity to come online so tight supply conditions may linger on for an extended period. Usually however, once physical capacity is added, supply may overshoot, outstrip demand, and result in weak pricing power for an extended period.
- If new capacity requires financial and human capital, companies can respond to tight supply conditions fairly quickly.

Market Share Stability

Generally speaking:

- Stable market shares indicate less competitive industries.
- Unstable market shares often indicate highly competitive industries with little pricing power.

EQ

Market shares are affected by the following factors:

- Barriers to entry
- New products
- Product differentiation

Industry Life-Cycle Analysis

Embryonic: Industries in this stage are just beginning to develop. They are characterized by:

- Slow growth as customers are still unfamiliar with the product.
- High prices as volumes are too low to achieve significant economies of scale.
- Significant initial investment.
- High risk of failure.

Companies focus on raising product awareness and developing distribution channels during this stage.

Growth: Once the new product starts gaining acceptance in the market, the industry experiences rapid growth. The growth stage is characterized by:

- New customers entering the market, which increases demand.
- Improved profitability as sales grow rapidly.
- Lower prices as economies of scale are achieved.
- Relatively low competition among companies in the industry as the overall market size is growing rapidly. Firms do not need to wrestle market share away from competitors to grow.
- High threat of new competitors entering the market due to low barriers to entry.

During this stage, companies focus on building customer loyalty and reinvest heavily in the business.

Shakeout: The period of rapid growth is followed by a period of slower growth. The shakeout stage is characterized by:

- Slower demand growth as fewer new customers are left to enter the industry.
- Intense competition as growth becomes dependent on market share growth.
- Excess industry capacity, which leads to price reductions and declining profitability.

During this stage, companies focus on reducing their costs and building brand loyalty. Some firms may fail or merge with others.

Mature: Eventually demand stops growing and the industry matures. Characteristics of this stage are:

- Little or no growth in demand as the market is completely saturated.
- Companies move towards consolidation. They recognize that they are interdependent so they stay away from price wars. However, price wars may occur during downturns.
- High barriers to entry in the form of brand loyalty and relatively efficient cost structures.

During this stage, companies are likely to be pursuing replacement demand rather than new buyers and should focus on extending successful product lines rather than introducing revolutionary new products. Companies have limited opportunities to reinvest and often have strong cash flows. As a result, they are more likely to pay dividends.

Decline: Technological substitution, social changes or global competition may eventually cause an industry to decline. The decline stage is characterized by:

- Negative growth.
- Excess capacity due to diminishing demand.
- Price competition due to excess capacity.
- Weaker firms leaving the industry.

Limitations of Industry Life-Cycle Analysis

- The following factors may change the shape of the industry life cycle, cause some stages to be longer or shorter than expected, or even result in certain stages being skipped altogether.
  - Technological changes
  - Regulatory changes
  - Social changes
  - Demographics
- Industry life-cycle analysis is most useful in analyzing industries during periods of relative stability. It is not as useful in analyzing industries experiencing rapid change.
- Not all companies in an industry display similar performance.

Price Competition

Generally speaking:

- Industries in which price is the most significant consideration in customers' purchase decisions tend to be highly competitive. A slight increase in price may cause customers to switch to substitute products if they are widely available.
- Price is not as important if companies in an industry are able to effectively differentiate their products in terms of quality and performance. Customers may not focus on price as much if product reliability is more important to them.

Factors Affecting Industry Growth, Profitability, and Risk

- Macroeconomic influences
- Technological influences
- Demographic influences
- Governmental influences
- Social influences

Competitive Strategies

Cost Leadership

Companies pursuing this strategy strive to cut down their costs to become the lowest cost producers in an industry so that they can gain market share by charging lower prices. Pricing may be defensive (to protect market positions when competition is low) or aggressive (to increase market share when competition is intense).

EQ

Product/Service Differentiation

Companies pursuing this strategy strive to differentiate their products from those of competitors in terms of quality, type, or means of distribution. These companies are then able to charge a premium price for their products. This strategy is successful only if the price premium is greater than the cost of differentiation and the source of differentiation appeals to customers and is sustainable over time.

Elements that should be Considered in a Company Analysis

A thorough company analysis should:

- Provide an overview of the company.
- Explain relevant industry characteristics.
- Analyze the demand for the company's products and services.
- Analyze the supply of products and services including an analysis of costs.
- Explain the company's pricing environment.
- Present and interpret relevant financial ratios, including comparisons over time and comparisons with competitors.

EQ

252

EQUITY VALUATION: CONCEPTS AND BASIC TOOLS
Cross-Reference to CFA Institute Assigned Reading #38

The aim of equity analysis is to identify mispriced securities. Securities are mispriced or incorrectly priced by the market when their market prices are different from their intrinsic values. Intrinsic or fundamental value refers to a security's true value and is estimated by analysts using a variety of models/techniques.

- If the estimate for a security's intrinsic value is lower than the market price, the security is overvalued by market.
- If the estimate for a security's intrinsic value is greater than the market price, the security is undervalued by the market.
- If the estimate for a security's intrinsic value equals the market price, the security is fairly valued.

EQUITY VALUATION MODELS

Present Value Models

Generally speaking, there are two sources of return from investing in a stock: (1) cash dividends received during the holding period and (2) the change in the stock price over the holding period.

- A **cash dividend** is a cash distribution made to a company's shareholders. Cash dividends are typically paid out regularly at known intervals, and these are known as **regular cash dividends**.
- An **extra dividend** or **special dividend** refers to a dividend payment by a company that does not usually pay dividends, or a dividend payment on top of the company's regular dividend.
- A **stock dividend** or a **bonus issue** occurs when a company issues additional common shares in the company (instead of cash) to shareholders.
  It basically divides the market value of shareholders' equity into smaller pieces without affecting (1) the total value of the pie, or (2) shareholders' proportional ownership in the company. Thus, stock dividends are not relevant for valuation.
- **Stock splits** and **reverse stock splits** also have no economic effect on the company or shareholders.
  - A stock split results in an increase in the number of shares outstanding and a consequent decrease in share price.
  - A reverse stock split increases the share price and reduces the number of shares outstanding.
- **Share repurchases** refer to a company buying back its own shares.
  - Shares that are repurchased by the company are known as treasury shares and, once repurchased, are not considered for dividends, voting, or calculating earnings per share.
  - All other things remaining the same, share repurchases can be viewed as equivalent to cash dividends in terms of their impact on shareholder wealth.

Arguments for Share Repurchases

- Share repurchases send out a signal to the market that management believes that the company's stock is undervalued, or that management will support the stock price.

EQ

253

© 2022 Wiley

- They offer the company flexibility in its cash distributions. A share repurchase does not set the expectation of continued distributions in the future as cash dividends might.
- There is a tax advantage to distributing cash through stock repurchases in markets where capital gains are taxed at a lower rate than dividends.
- They can be used to limit the increase in the number of shares outstanding when a significant number of employee stock options have been exercised.

Dividend Payment Chronology

- **Declaration date** is the date on which a company announces a particular dividend.
- The company also announces the holder-of-record date and the payment date on the declaration date.
- **Ex-dividend date** or **ex-date** is the first day that the share trades without the dividend.
- Any investor who holds the stock on the ex-dividend date or who purchased it the day before the ex-dividend date is entitled to receive the dividend.
- On the ex-dividend date, the share price is adjusted for the amount of the dividend.
- **Holder-of-record date**, also known as the **owner-of-record date**, **shareholder-of-record date**, **record date**, **date of record**, or **date of book closure**, is the date at which a shareholder listed in the company's records will be entitled to receive the upcoming dividend.
- **Payment date** or **payable date** is the date on which the company actually mails out or transfers the dividend payment to shareholders.

Dividend Discount Model

The **dividend discount model (DDM)** values a share of common stock as the present value of its expected future cash flows (dividends).

$$\text{Value} = \frac{D_1}{(1 + k_e)^1} + \frac{D_2}{(1 + k_e)^2} + \ldots + \frac{D_\infty}{(1 + k_e)^\infty}$$

$$\text{Value} = \sum_{t=1}^{n} \frac{D_t}{(1 + k_e)^t}$$

- When an investor sells a share of common stock, the value that the purchaser will pay equals the present value of the future stream of cash flows (i.e., the remaining dividend stream). Therefore, the value of the stock at any point in time is still determined by its expected future dividends. When this value is discounted to the present, we are back at the original dividend discount model.
- If a company pays no dividends currently, it does not mean that its stock will be worthless. There is an expectation that after a certain period of time the firm will start making dividend payments. Currently, the company is reinvesting all its earnings in its business with the expectation that its earnings and dividends will be larger and will grow faster in the future. If the company does not make positive earnings going forward, there will still be an expectation of a liquidating dividend. The amount of this dividend will be discounted at the required rate of return to compute the stock's current price.
- The required rate of return on equity (k_e) is usually estimated using the CAPM. Another approach for calculating the required return on equity simply adds a risk premium to the before-tax cost of debt of the company.

One Year Holding period: If our holding period is just one year, the value that we will place on the stock today is the present value of the dividends that we will receive over the year plus the present value of the price that we expect to sell the stock for at the end of the holding period.

$$\text{Value} = \frac{\text{dividend to be received}}{(1 + k_e)^1} + \frac{\text{year-end price}}{(1 + k_e)^1}$$

Multiple-Year Holding Period DDM: We apply the same discounting principles for valuing common stock over multiple holding periods. In order to estimate the intrinsic value of the stock, we first estimate the dividends that will be received every year that the stock is held and the price that the stock will sell for at the end of the holding period. Then we simply discount these expected cash flows at the cost of equity (required return).

$$V = \frac{D_1}{(1 + k_e)^1} + \frac{D_2}{(1 + k_e)^2} + \dots + \frac{P_n}{(1 + k_e)^n}$$

where :

P_n = Price at the end of n years.

Infinite Period DDM (Gordon Growth Model): The infinite period dividend discount model assumes that a company will continue to pay dividends for an infinite number of periods. It also assumes that the dividend stream will grow at a constant rate (g_c) over the infinite period. In this case, the intrinsic value of the stock isz calculated as:

$$PV_0 = \frac{D_0(1 + g_c)^1}{(1 + k_e)^1} + \frac{D_0(1 + g_c)^2}{(1 + k_e)^2} + \frac{D_0(1 + g_c)^3}{(1 + k_e)^3} + \dots + \frac{D_0(1 + g_c)^\infty}{(1 + k_e)^\infty}$$

This equation simplifies to:

$$PV = \frac{D_0(1 + g_c)^1}{(k_e - g_c)^1} = \frac{D_1}{k_e - g_c}$$

The relation between k_e and g_c is critical:

- As the difference between k_e and g_c *increases*, the intrinsic value of the stock *falls*.
- As the difference *narrows*, the intrinsic value of the stock *rises*.
- Small changes in either k_e or g_c can cause *large* changes in the value of the stock.

For the infinite-period DDM model to work, the following assumptions must hold:

- Dividends grow at a rate, g_c, which is not expected to change.
- k_e must be greater than g_c; otherwise, the model breaks down because of the denominator being negative.

Notice that the DDM formula on the previous page can be rearranged to make the required return, k_e, the subject:

EQ

255

© 2022 Wiley

$$k_e = \frac{D_1}{PV_0} + g_c$$

This expression for the cost of equity tells us that the return on an equity investment has two components:

- The dividend yield (D_1/P_0).
- Growth over time (g_c).

Applying Present Value Models: The Gordon growth model is highly appropriate for valuing dividend-paying stocks that are relatively immune to the business cycle and are relatively mature (e.g., utilities). It is also useful for valuing companies that have historically been raising their dividend at a stable rate.

Applying the DDM is relatively difficult if the company is not currently paying out a dividend. A company may not pay out a dividend because:

- It has a lot of lucrative investment opportunities available and it wants to retain profits to reinvest them in the business.
- It does not have sufficient excess cash flow to pay out a dividend.

Even though the Gordon growth model can be used for valuing such companies, the forecasts used are generally quite uncertain. Therefore, analysts use one of the other valuation models to value such companies and may use the DDM model as a supplement.The DDM can be extended to numerous stages. For example:

- A three-stage DDM is used to value fairly young companies that are just entering the growth phase. Their development falls into three stages—growth (with very high growth rates), transition (with decent growth rates) and maturity (with a lower growth into perpetuity).
- A two-stage DDM can be used to value a company currently undergoing moderate growth, but whose growth rate is expected to improve (rise) to its long term growth rate.

Valuation of Common Stock with Temporary Supernormal Growth: The correct valuation model to value such "supernormal growth" companies is the **multi-stage dividend discount model** that combines the multi-period and infinite-period dividend discount models.

$$\text{Value} = \frac{D_1}{(1+k_e)^1} + \frac{D_2}{(1+k_e)^2} + \ldots + \frac{D_n}{(1+k_e)^n} + \frac{P_n}{(1+k_e)^n}$$

where :

$$P_n = \frac{D_{n+1}}{k_e - g_c}$$

D_n = Last dividend of the supernormal growth period
$D_{n} + 1$ = First dividend of the constant growth period

EQ

256

The Free-Cash-Flow-to-Equity (FCFE) Model: Many analysts assert that a company's dividend-paying capacity should be reflected in its cash flow estimates instead of estimated future dividends. FCFE is a measure of dividend paying capacity and can also be used to value companies that currently do not make any dividend payments. FCFE can be calculated as:

$$FCFE = CFO - FC\ Inv + Net\ borrowing$$

Analysts may calculate the intrinsic value of the company's stock by discounting their projections of future FCFE at the required rate of return on equity.

$$V_0 = \sum_{t=1}^{\infty} \frac{FCFE_t}{(1 + k_e)^t}$$

Intrinsic Value of Preferred Stock

When preferred stock is non-callable, non-convertible, has no maturity date and pays dividends at a fixed rate, the value of the preferred stock can be calculated using the perpetuity formula:

$$V_0 = \frac{D_0}{r}$$

For a non-callable, non-convertible preferred stock with maturity at time, n, the value of the stock can be calculated using the following formula:

$$V_0 = \sum_{t=1}^{n} \frac{D_t}{(1 + r)^t} + \frac{F}{(1 + r)^n}$$

Price Multiples—Relative Valuation

Price multiples are ratios that compare the price of a stock to some sort of value. Price multiples allow an analyst to evaluate the relative worth of a company's stock. Popular multiples used in relative valuation include price-to-earnings, price-to-sales, price-to-book and price-to-cash flow.

Multiples Based on Fundamentals

A price multiple may be related to fundamentals through a dividend discount model such as the Gordon growth model. The expressions developed in such an exercise are interpreted as the justified (or based on fundamental) values for a multiple.

The Justified P/E Ratio:

$$\frac{P_0}{E_1} = \frac{D_1/E_1}{r - g}$$

- The P/E ratio is inversely related to the required rate of return.
- The P/E ratio is positively related to the growth rate.
- The P/E ratio appears to be positively related to the dividend payout ratio. However, this relationship may not always hold because a higher dividend payout ratio implies that the

EQ

company's earnings retention ratio is lower. A lower earnings retention ratio translates into a lower growth rate. This is known as the "dividend displacement" of earnings.

Multiples Based on Comparables

This method compares relative values estimated using multiples to determine whether an asset is undervalued, overvalued or fairly valued. The benchmark multiple can be any of:

- A multiple of a closely matched individual stock.
- The average or median multiple of a peer group or the firm's industry.
- The average multiple derived from trend or time-series analysis.

Analysts should be careful to select only those companies that have similar size, product lines, and growth prospects to the company being valued as comparables.

$$\text{Price to cash flow ratio} = \frac{\text{Market price of share}}{\text{Cash flow per share}}$$

$$\text{Price to sales ratio} = \frac{\text{Market price per share}}{\text{Net sales per share}}$$
$$\text{Price to sales ratio} = \frac{\text{Market value of equity}}{\text{Total net sales}}$$

$$P/BV = \frac{\text{Current market price of share}}{\text{Book value per share}}$$
$$P/BV = \frac{\text{Market value of common shareholders' equity}}{\text{Book value of common shareholders' equity}}$$
where:
Book value of common shareholders' equity = (Total assets − Total liabilities) − Preferred stock

Enterprise Value Multiples

Enterprise value (EV) is calculated as the market value of the company's common stock plus the market value of outstanding preferred stock if any, plus the market value of debt, less cash and short term investments (cash equivalents). It can be thought of as the cost of taking over a company.

The most widely used EV multiple is the EV/EBITDA multiple. EBITDA measures a company's income before payments to any providers of capital are made.

- The EV/EBITDA multiple is often used when comparing two companies with different capital structures.
- Loss-making companies usually have a positive EBITDA, which allows analysts to use the EV/EBITDA multiple to value them. The P/E ratio is meaningless (negative) for a loss-making company as its earnings are negative.

EQ

258

Asset-Based Valuation

Asset-based valuation uses market values of a company's assets and liabilities to determine the value of the company as a whole.

Asset based valuation works well for:

- Companies that do not have a significant number of intangible or "off-the-book" assets, and have a higher proportion of current assets and liabilities.
- Private companies, especially if applied together with multiplier models.
- Financial companies, natural resource companies and companies that are being liquidated.

Asset-based valuation may not be appropriate when:

- Market values of assets and liabilities cannot be easily determined.
- The company has a significant amount of intangible assets.
- Asset values are difficult to determine (e.g., in periods of very high inflation).
- Market values of assets and liabilities significantly differ from their carrying values.

FIXED-INCOME SECURITIES: DEFINING ELEMENTS
Cross-Reference to CFA Institute Assigned Reading #39

Important Relationships

- The higher (lower) the coupon rate on a bond, the higher (lower) its price.
- An increase (decrease) in interest rates or the required yield on a bond will lead to a decrease (increase) in price, i.e., bond prices and yields are inversely related.
- The more risky the bond, the higher the yield required by investors to purchase the bond, and the lower the bond's price.

Overview of a Fixed-Income Security

Issuers

- Supranational organizations.
- Sovereign (national) governments.
- Non-sovereign (local) governments.
- Quasi-government entities.

Bond issuers can also be classified based on their credit-worthiness as judged by credit rating agencies. Bonds can broadly be categorized as investment-grade or non-investment grade (or high-yield or speculative) bonds.

Maturity

- Fixed-income securities which, at the time of issuance, are expected to mature in one year or less are known as money market securities.
- Fixed-income securities which, at the time of issuance, are expected to mature in more than one year are referred to as capital market securities.
- Fixed-income securities which have no stated maturity are known as perpetual bonds.

Par Value

The par value (also known as face value, nominal value, redemption value and maturity value) of a bond refers to the principal amount that the issuer promises to repay bondholders on the maturity date. Bond prices are usually quoted as a percentage of the par value.

- When a bond's price is above 100% of par, it is said to be trading at a premium.
- When a bond's price is at 100% of par, it is said to be trading at par.
- When a bond's price is below 100% of par, it is said to be trading at a discount.

Coupon Rate and Frequency

The coupon rate (also known as the nominal rate) of a bond refers to the annual interest rate that the issuer promises to pay bondholders until the bond matures. The amount of interest paid each year by the issuer is known as the coupon, and is calculated by multiplying the coupon rate by the bond's par value.

Zero-coupon (or pure discount) bonds are issued at a discount to par value and redeemed at par (the issuer pays the entire par amount to investors at the maturity date). The difference between the (discounted) purchase price and the par value is effectively the interest on the loan.

Currency Denomination

- **Dual-currency bonds** make coupon payments in one currency and the principal payment at maturity in another currency.
- **Currency option bonds** give bondholders a choice regarding which of the two currencies they would like to receive interest and principal payments in.

Yield Measures

- The **current yield** or **running yield** equals the bond's annual coupon amount divided by its current price (not par value), expressed as a percentage.
- The **yield-to-maturity (YTM)** is also known as the **yield-to-redemption** or the **redemption yield**. It is calculated as the discount rate that equates the present value of a bond's expected future cash flows until maturity to its current price.
  - Given a set of expected future cash flows, the lower (higher) the YTM or discount rate, the higher (lower) the bond's current price.

The Bond Indenture

A bond is a contractual agreement between the issuer and the bondholder. The **trust deed** is the legal contract that describes the form of the bond, obligations of the issuer and the rights of bondholders, and it is commonly referred to as the **bond indenture**. The indenture captures the following information:

- The name of the issuer.
- The principal value of the bond.
- The coupon rate.
- Dates when the interest payments will be made.
- The maturity date.
- Funding sources for the interest payments and principal repayments.
- Collaterals (i.e., assets or financial guarantees underlying the debt obligation above and beyond the issuer's promise to pay).
- Covenants (i.e., actions that the issuer is obligated to perform or prohibited from performing).
- Credit enhancements (i.e., provisions designed to reduce the bond's credit risk).

Areas that Investors Should Review Before Purchasing a Bond

Legal Identity of the Bond Issuer and its Legal Form

- For sovereign bonds, the legal issuer is typically the institution responsible for managing the national budget.
- Corporate bonds are typically issued by the corporate legal entity.
  - Note that bonds may be issued by the parent company or a subsidiary.
    - If issued by a subsidiary, investors must focus on the creditworthiness of the subsidiary, unless the bond is guaranteed by the parent. Oftentimes, subsidiaries carry a lower credit rating than the parent.
    - If issued by the parent company, it becomes important to analyze the assets actually held by the parent, as investors may not have recourse to assets held by subsidiaries or operating companies.
- In case of securitized bonds, the relationship between the sponsor and the SPE must be evaluated. Investors must ensure that the SPE is structured as a **bankruptcy-remote vehicle**.

Sources of Repayment Proceeds

- Bonds issued by supranational organizations are usually repaid through (1) proceeds from repayments of previous loans made by the organization or (2) paid-in capital from its members.
- Sovereign bonds are backed by the "full faith and credit" of the national government.
    - Sovereign bonds issued in local currency are usually considered safer than those issued in a foreign currency.
- Non-sovereign government debt can usually be repaid through the following sources:
    - The general taxing authority of the issuer.
    - Cash flows from the project that the bonds were issued to finance.
    - Special taxes or fees specifically set up to make interest and principal payments.
- Corporate bond issuers typically rely on their cash flow-generating ability to repay bonds, which in turn depends on their financial strength and integrity.
- For securitized bonds, repayment depends on the cash flow generated by the underlying pool of financial assets.

Asset or Collateral Backing

- **Seniority ranking: Secured bonds** are backed by assets or financial guarantees to ensure debt repayment in case of default, while **unsecured bonds** are not protected by a pledge of any specific assets (i.e., they only have a general claim on the issuer's assets and cash flows).
    - In the event of default, unsecured bonds are repaid after secured bonds have been paid off.
        - **Senior secured debt** is paid off before **subordinated** or **junior** secured debt.
    - Investors should review the indenture to identify whether a particular **debenture** is actually secured or unsecured.
- **Types of collateral backing:**
    - **Collateral trust bonds** are secured by securities such as common stock, other bonds, or other financial assets.
    - **Equipment trust certificates** are secured by specific types of equipment or physical assets (e.g., aircraft, railroad cars, or oil rigs).
    - **Mortgage-backed securities (MBS)** are backed by a pool of mortgage loans. Cash flows generated by the pool are used to make payments on MBS.
    - **Covered bonds** are backed by a segregated pool of assets (known as the **cover pool**).

Credit Enhancements

Credit enhancements are provisions that serve to reduce the credit risk of a bond issue, resulting in a lower yield.

- **Internal credit enhancement** focuses on the structure of the issue regarding priority of payment or the value of collateral. It includes:
    - **Subordination:** This refers to the allocation of cash flows among the various bond classes or **tranches** based on their **seniority**.
    - **Overcollateralization:** This occurs when the value of the collateral posted to secure an issue exceeds the par value of the securities issued.
    - **Excess spread (or excess interest cash flow):** A transaction can be structured in a manner such that the cash flows generated from the collateral pool exceed

the amount of interest payable to bondholders so that there is a cushion for making interest payments.

- **External credit enhancement** refers to guarantees received from a third-party guarantor. Types of external credit enhancement include:
  - **Surety bonds (issued by an insurance company) and bank guarantees:** In the event of default, both these forms of enhancement reimburse investors for losses (up to a pre-specified maximum amount known as the **penal sum**).
  - **Letters of credit:** These are lines of credit provided by a financial institution to the issuer to reimburse any shortfalls in the cash flow generated from the collateral pool.

Note that surety bonds, bank guarantees, and letters of credit all expose investors to third party credit risk (i.e., the risk that the guarantor will not be able to fulfill its obligations). This risk can be mitigated by setting up a **cash collateral account**.

Covenants

Covenants are legally enforceable rules agreed upon by the borrower/issuer and lenders/investors at the time of bond issuance.

- **Affirmative covenants** are **requirements** placed on the issuer. They are typically administrative in nature so they do not lead to additional costs for the issuer, nor do they significantly restrict the issuer's ability to make business decisions.
- **Negative covenants** are **restrictions** placed on the issuer. While they entail more costs than affirmative covenants and can constrain the issuer in operating the business, they protect bondholders from dilution of their claims, asset withdrawals or substitutions, and inefficient investments by the issuer.

Legal and Regulatory Considerations

The differences between domestic bonds, foreign bonds, Eurobonds, and global bonds are important to investors as these different types of bonds are subject to different legal, regulatory, and tax requirements. There are also differences in terms of frequency of interest payments and how interest payments are calculated, both of which influence the bond's cash flows and price. Bear in mind however, that the currency denomination has a bigger influence on a bond's price than where it is issued or traded.

National Bond Markets versus Eurobond Market

A **national bond market** includes all the bonds that are issued and traded in a particular country, and denominated in that country's local currency.

- Bonds issued by entities that are incorporated in that country are known as **domestic bonds**.
- Bonds issued by entities that are incorporated in another country are known as **foreign bonds**.

Eurobonds refer to bonds that are denominated in a currency other than the local currency where they are issued. They may be issued in any country and in any currency (including the issuer's domestic currency), and are named based on the currency in which they are denominated.

- Generally speaking, Eurobonds are less regulated than domestic and foreign bonds as they do not fall under the jurisdiction of any single country.

Global bonds are bonds that are issued simultaneously (1) in the Eurobond market and (2) in at least one domestic bond market.

Tax Considerations

- Interest income is generally taxed at the ordinary income tax rate, which is the same rate that an individual pays tax on her wage or salary.
- Municipal bonds in the U.S. are often tax-exempt, in that interest income is often exempt from federal income tax and state income tax in the state of issue.
- In most jurisdictions, capital gains are taxed at a lower rate than interest income.
- In some countries, a prorated portion of any **original issue discount** must be included in interest income each year for tax purposes.
- In other jurisdictions, investors who have purchased bonds at a premium can either (1) deduct a prorated portion of the premium paid from taxable income each year until the bond matures, or (2) declare a capital loss when the bond is eventually redeemed at maturity.

Principal Repayment Structures

Credit risk is reduced if there are any provisions that call for periodic retirement of some of the principal amount outstanding during the term of the loan.

- A **bullet bond** is one that only makes periodic interest payments, with the entire principal amount paid back at maturity.
- An **amortizing bond** is one that makes periodic interest **and** principal payments over the term of the bond.
  - A **fully amortized bond** is one whose outstanding principal amount at maturity is reduced to zero through a fixed periodic payment schedule.
  - A **partially amortized bond** also makes fixed periodic principal repayments, but the principal is not fully repaid by the maturity date. Therefore, a **balloon payment** is required at maturity to repay the outstanding principal amount.

Sinking Fund Arrangements

A **sinking fund arrangement** requires the issuer to repay a specified portion of the principal amount every year throughout the bond's life or after a specified date.

Sometimes a call provision may also be added to the bond issue. This call provision usually gives the issuer the option to repurchase bonds before maturity at the lowest of (1) market price (2) par, and (3) a specified sinking fund price.

From the bondholders' perspective, the advantage of a sinking fund arrangement is that it reduces credit risk. However, it entails two disadvantages. First, it results in **reinvestment risk**, and second, if the issue has an embedded call option, the issuer may be able to repurchase bonds at a price lower than the current market price.

Coupon Payment Structures

Floating-Rate Notes (FRN)

- The coupon rate of an **FRN** has two components: a reference rate (such as LIBOR) plus a spread (also known as margin).
- FRNs have less interest rate risk (i.e., the risk of bond price volatility resulting from changes in market interest rates) than fixed-rate bonds, but still entail credit risk.

- FRNs may be structured to include a floor and/or a cap on the periodic coupon rate.
- **Reverse FRNs** or **inverse floaters** are structured such that the periodic coupon rate is inversely related to the reference rate.

Step-Up Coupon Bonds

A **step-up coupon bond** (which can be fixed or floating) is one where the periodic coupon rate increases by specified margins at specified dates. Typically, the step-up coupon structure is offered with callable bonds to protect bondholders in a rising interest rate environment. However, note that despite the step-up in coupons (and the consequent increase in interest expense), the issuer may not call the bond if refinancing is less advantageous.

Credit-Linked Coupon Bonds

The coupon rate on **credit-linked coupon bonds** changes when the bond's credit rating changes. Credit-linked coupon bonds protect investors against a decline in the credit quality, and are therefore attractive to investors who are concerned about the future creditworthiness of the issuer. They also provide some protection against poor economic conditions as credit ratings tend to decline during recessions. A problem with credit-linked coupon bonds is that since a rating downgrade results in higher interest payments for the issuer, it can contribute to further downgrades or even an eventual default.

Payment-in-Kind (PIK) Coupon Bonds

PIK coupon bonds allow the issuer to pay interest in the form of additional bonds instead of cash. They are preferred by issuers that are financially distressed and fear liquidity and solvency problems in the future. Investors usually demand a higher yield on these bonds to compensate them for the higher credit risk and high leverage of the issuer.

Deferred Coupon Bonds (or Split Coupon Bonds)

Deferred Coupon Bonds do not pay any coupon for the first few years after issuance, but then pay a higher coupon than they normally would for the remainder of their terms. Deferred coupon bonds are usually preferred by issuers who want to conserve cash in the short run, or for project financing where cash-generation will commence after an initial development phase.

Investors are attracted to deferred coupon bonds as they are usually priced significantly below par. Further, the deferred coupon structure may help investors manage their tax liability by delaying taxes due on interest income (in certain jurisdictions).

Index-Linked Bonds

These are bonds whose coupon payments and/or principal repayments are linked to a specified index (such as a commodity or equity index). An example of index-linked bonds are **inflation-linked bonds** (also known as **linkers**) whose coupon and/or principal payments are linked to an index of consumer prices (e.g., **Treasury Inflation Protection Securities** or **TIPS** issued by the U.S. Government are linked to the Consumer Price Index, CPI, in the U.S.). Investors are attracted to inflation-linked bonds because they offer a long-term asset with a fixed **real** return that is protected against inflation risk.

- **Zero-coupon-indexed bonds** do not pay any coupon so only the principal repayment is linked to a specified index.
- For **interest-indexed bonds,** only coupon payments are adjusted to changes in the specified index. They repay the fixed nominal principal at maturity.

- **Capital-indexed bonds** pay a fixed coupon rate, but this rate is applied to a principal amount that is adjusted to reflect changes in the specified index. As a result, both interest payments as well as the principal repayment are adjusted for inflation.
- **Indexed-annuity bonds** are fully amortized bonds. The annual payment on these bonds is linked to the specified index so effectively that both interest and principal payments reflect changes in the index.

An **equity-linked note (ELN)** is a fixed-income security whose final payment is linked to the return on an equity index.

- ELNs are generally principal-protected.
- If the underlying index increases in value, investors receive an amount greater than par upon maturity.
- Note that the principal payment is still subject to credit risk of the issuer.

Bonds with Contingency Provisions

Callable Bonds

Callable bonds give the **issuer** the right to redeem (or call) all or part of the bond before maturity. This embedded option offers the issuer the ability to take advantage of (1) a decline in market interest rates and/or (2) an improvement in its creditworthiness.

From the perspective of the bondholder, she would pay less for a callable bond than for an otherwise identical non-callable bond. The difference in the value of a non-callable bond and an otherwise identical callable bond is the value of the embedded call option.

> Value of callable bond = Value of non-callable bond − Value of embedded call option

> Value of embedded call option = Value of non-callable bond − Value of callable bond

From the perspective of the issuer, it would have to pay more (in the form of a higher coupon or higher yield) to get investors to purchase a callable bond than an otherwise identical non-callable bond. The difference between the yield on a callable bond and the yield on a non-callable bond is the cost of the embedded option to the issuer.

> Yield on callable bond = Yield on non-callable bond + Embedded call option cost in terms of yield

> Embedded call option cost in terms of yield = Yield on callable bond − Yield on non-callable bond

- The more heavily the embedded call option favors the issuer, the lower the value of the callable bond to the investor and the higher the yield that must be offered by the issuer.
- Some callable bonds are issued with an initial **call protection period** (also known as **lockout period**, **cushion** or **deferment period**), during which the issuer is prohibited from calling the bond. The bond can only be called at or after the specified call date.
- A **make-whole provision** in a callable bond usually requires the issuer to pay a relatively high lump-sum amount to call the bonds.

Putable Bonds

Putable bonds give **bondholders** the right to sell (or put) the bond back to the issuer at a pre-determined price on specified dates. The embedded put option offers bondholders protection against an increase in interest rates, i.e., if interest rates increase (decreasing the value of the bond), they can sell the bond back to the issuer at a pre-specified price and then reinvest the principal at (higher) newer interest rates.

From the perspective of the bondholder, she would pay more for a putable bond than for an otherwise identical non-putable bond. The difference in the value between a putable bond and an otherwise identical non-putable bond is the value of the embedded put option (which the bond holder has effectively purchased from the issuer):

$$\text{Value of putable bond} = \text{Value of non-putable bond} + \text{Value of embedded put option}$$

$$\text{Value of embedded put option} = \text{Value of putable bond} - \text{Value of non-putable bond}$$

From the perspective of the issuer, it would pay out less (in the form of a lower coupon or lower yield) on a putable bond than it would on an otherwise identical non-putable bond. The difference between the yield on a non-putable bond and the yield on a putable bond is the cost of the embedded option borne by the investor.

$$\text{Yield on putable bond} = \text{Yield on non-putable bond} - \text{Embedded put option cost in terms of yield}$$

$$\text{Embedded put option cost in terms of yield} = \text{Yield on non-putable bond} - \text{Yield on putable bond}$$

Note that the more heavily the embedded put option favors the investor, the higher the value of the putable bond to the investor and the lower the yield that must be offered by the issuer.

Convertible Bonds

A **convertible bond** gives the bondholder the right to convert the bond into a pre-specified number of common shares of the issuer.

Convertible bonds are attractive to investors as the conversion (to equity) option allows them to benefit from price appreciation of the issuer's stock. On the other hand, if there is a decline in the issuer's share price (which causes a decline in the value of the embedded equity conversion/call option), the price of the convertible bond cannot fall below the price of an otherwise identical straight bond. Because of these attractive features, convertible bonds offer a lower yield and sell at higher prices than similar bonds without the conversion option. Note however, that the coupon rate offered on convertible bonds is usually higher than the dividend yield on the underlying equity.

- The **conversion price** is the price per share at which the convertible bond can be converted into shares.
- The **conversion ratio** refers to the number of common shares that each bond can be converted into. It is calculated as the par value divided by the conversion price.

- The **conversion value** is calculated as current share price multiplied by the conversion ratio.
- The **conversion premium** equals the difference between the convertible bond's price and the conversion value.
- **Conversion parity** occurs if the conversion value equals the convertible bond's price.

Although it is common for convertible bonds to reach conversion parity before they mature, bondholders rarely exercise the conversion option, choosing to retain their bonds and receive (higher) coupon payments instead of (lower) dividend payments. As a result, issuers often embed a call option alongside the conversion option in the convertible bond, making them **callable convertible bonds**.

Warrants

A **warrant** is somewhat similar to a conversion option, but it is not embedded in the bond's structure. It offers the holder the right to purchase the issuer's stock at a fixed exercise price until the expiration date. Warrants are attached to bond issues as sweeteners, allowing investors to participate in the upside from an increase in share prices.

Contingent Convertible Bonds ("CoCos")

CoCos are bonds with contingent write-down provisions. They differ from traditional convertible bonds in two ways:

- Unlike traditional convertible bonds, which are convertible at the **option** of the bondholder, CoCos convert **automatically** upon the occurrence of a pre-specified event.
- Unlike traditional convertible bonds, in which conversion occurs if the issuer's share price **increases** (i.e., on the upside), contingent write-down provisions are convertible on the **downside**.

FIXED-INCOME MARKETS: ISSUANCE, TRADING, AND FUNDING
Cross-Reference to CFA Institute Assigned Reading #40

OVERVIEW OF GLOBAL FIXED-INCOME MARKETS

Classification of Fixed-Income Markets

Type of Issuer

1. Households.
2. Non-financial corporates.
3. Government.
4. Financial institutions.

Credit Quality

- Bonds with a credit rating of Baa3 or above by Moody's, or BBB– or above by S&P and Fitch are classified as **investment-grade bonds**.
- Bonds with ratings below these levels are classified as **non-investment grade** (or **high-yield**, **speculative** or **junk**) bonds.

Maturity

- **Money market securities** are fixed-income securities that have a maturity of one year or less at the time of issuance.
- **Capital market securities** are fixed-income securities that have a maturity of more than one year at the time of issuance.

Currency Denomination

- The currency in which a bond is issued determines which country's interest rates affect its price.

Geography

- Bonds that are issued in a specific country, denominated in the currency of that country and sold in that country are classified as:
  - **Domestic bonds,** if they are issued by entities incorporated in that country.
  - **Foreign bonds,** if the issuer is domiciled in another country.
- A **Eurobond** is issued internationally i.e., outside the jurisdiction of the country whose currency it is denominated in.

Other Classifications of Fixed-Income Markets

- **Inflation-linked bonds** offer investors protection against inflation by linking the coupon payment and/or the principal repayment to a consumer price index.
- **Tax-exempt bonds**, such as municipal bonds (or **munis**) in the U.S. are attractive for investors who are subject to income tax because interest income from these bonds is usually exempt from federal income tax and from state income tax (subject to some restrictions).

Type of Coupon

- The coupon rate for a bond may (1) be fixed throughout its term, or (2) may change periodically based on some reference rate.

Reference Rates

The reference rate used for a particular floating-rate bond issue depends on where the bonds are issued and the currency denomination. For example, a FRN denominated in GBP that pays coupon semi-annually, would typically calculate the coupon as 6-month Libor (or LIBOR-180) plus a spread.

Fixed-Income Indexes

Fixed-income indexes are generally used by investors (1) to describe a bond market or sector, and (2) to evaluate investment performance.

Investors in Fixed-Income Securities

- Central banks.
- Institutional investors.
- Retail investors.

Primary Markets

In a **public offering** (or **public offer**), any member of the public may purchase the bonds.

- In an **underwritten offerings** (or **firm commitment offering**), the investment bank guarantees the sale of the issue at that price. The risk associated with selling the bonds is therefore borne by the investment bank (also known as the **underwriter**).
- In a **best efforts offering**, the investment bank only acts as a broker and tries its best to sell the bond at the negotiated offering price for a commission.
- In an **auction**, bonds are sold to investors through a bidding process, which helps in price discovery and allocation of securities.

Shelf registration allows certain (authorized) issuers to offer additional bonds to the general public without having to prepare a new and separate prospectus for each bond issue. Since shelf issuances are subject to lower levels of scrutiny than standard public offerings, only well-established issuers with proven financial strength can make use of this facility. Further, in some jurisdictions, shelf registrations can only be purchased by **qualified investors**.

In a **private placement**, only a selected group of qualified investors (typically large institutional investors) are allowed to invest in the issue.

- The bonds are neither underwritten nor registered, and can be relatively illiquid as there is usually no secondary market to trade them.
- Investors are usually able to influence the terms of the issue, so privately placed bonds typically have more customized and restrictive covenants compared to publicly issued bonds.

Secondary Markets

Secondary markets (or **aftermarkets**) are those in which existing bonds are traded among investors.

- **Organized exchanges** are places where buyers and sellers can meet to arrange their trades. Buyers and sellers may come from anywhere, but transactions must be executed at the exchange in accordance with the rules and regulations of the exchange.

- In **over-the-counter (OTC) markets**, buyers and sellers submit their orders from various locations through electronic trading platforms. Orders are then matched and executed through a communications network.
- **Bond tender offer**: This involves an issuer making an offer to existing bondholders of the company to repurchase a specified number of bonds at a particular price and a specified time.

The vast majority of bond trading occurs in OTC markets.

Sovereign Bonds

Sovereign bonds are bonds that are issued by a country's central government (or their treasuries). They are issued primarily to cover expenditures when tax revenues are insufficient.

- Sovereign bonds are backed by the taxing authority of the national government.
- Sovereign bonds can be issued in the sovereign's local (domestic) currency or in a foreign currency.

Secondary market trading of sovereign bonds is primarily in securities that were most recently issued (known as **on-the-run securities** or **benchmark issues**). Generally speaking, as a sovereign issue ages (or becomes more seasoned), it tends to trade less frequently.

Non-Sovereign Government Bonds

Non-sovereign bonds are those issued by levels of government that lie below the national level (e.g., provinces, regions, states, and cities). These bonds can be serviced through the following sources of income:

- The taxing authority of the local government.
- The cash flows from the project that is being financed with bond proceeds.
- Special taxes and fees established specifically for making interest payments and principal repayments.

Generally speaking, non-sovereign bonds are of high credit quality, but they still trade at higher yields (lower prices) than sovereign bonds.

Quasi-Government Bonds

Quasi-government or **agency bonds** are issued by organizations that perform various functions for the national government, but are not actual governmental entities. These bonds are issued to fund specific financing needs.

- Quasi-government bonds guaranteed by the national government trade at lower yields than similar bonds not carrying the government guarantee.
- Generally speaking, quasi-government entities do not have direct taxing authority, so bonds are serviced with cash flows generated by the entity or from the project that is being financed by the issue.
- In some cases, quasi-government bonds may be backed by collateral.
- Historical default rates on quasi-government bonds have been extremely low.

Supranational Bonds

These bonds are issued by **supranational** (or **multilateral) agencies** such as the World Bank (WB) and the International Monetary Fund (IMF). Generally speaking, supranational bonds are issued as plain vanilla bonds. They are typically highly-rated and issued in large sizes (so they tend to be very liquid).

Corporate Debt

Bank Loans and Syndicated Loans

- Most bank loans are floating-rate loans, with Libor, a sovereign rate (e.g., the T-bill rate), or the **prime rate** serving as the reference rate.
- Bank loans can be customized (with respect to maturity and payment structure) to borrower requirements.
- Access to bank loans depends on (1) the company's financial position and (2) market conditions and capital availability.

Commercial Paper

- Commercial paper is an unsecured debt instrument that is popular among issuers because it is a source of flexible, readily-available, and relatively low-cost financing.
- It can be used to meet seasonal demands for cash and is also commonly used to provide **bridge financing**.
- Commercial paper is usually "rolled over" by issuers, which is why they tend to retain access to backup bank lines of credit.
- Terms to maturity can range from overnight to one year.
- Historically, defaults on commercial paper have been relatively rare because commercial paper has a short maturity and tends to be rolled over.
- Most investors hold on to commercial paper until maturity, which results in very little secondary market trading in these instruments.
- Yields on commercial paper are higher than yields on short-term sovereign bonds of the same maturity.

Corporate Notes and Bonds

- Corporate bonds can differ based on:
  - Coupon payment structures.
  - Principal payment structures.
    - Bonds with a **serial maturity structure** have maturity dates that are spread out over the bond's life.
    - Bonds with a **term maturity structure** are paid off in one lump sum payment at maturity.
  - Terms to maturity.
  - Asset or collateral backing.
  - Contingency provisions.
  - Issuance, trading and settlement.

Medium-Term Notes (MTNs)

- The MTN market can be broken down into three segments:
  - **Short-term securities** that may be fixed- or floating-rate.
  - **Medium- to long-term securities** that generally tend to be fixed-rate.
  - **Structured notes**, which are essentially notes combined with derivative instruments to create special features desired by certain institutional investors.

Structured Financial Instruments

Generally speaking, structured financial instruments have customized structures that often combine a bond and at least one derivative. The use of derivatives gives the holder of the instrument exposure to one or more underlying assets, such as equities, bonds, or commodities.

The redemption value and often the coupons of structured financial instruments are tied to the performance of the underlying asset(s), as opposed to being tied to the issuer's cash flows (as is the case with traditional bonds).

Capital-Protected Instruments

Capital-protected instruments may offer different levels of capital protection. A guarantee certificate offers full capital protection, but other structured financial instruments may offer only partial capital protection. It is important to note that the capital protection is only as good as the creditworthiness of the issuer of the instrument. Should the issuer of guarantee certificates go bankrupt, investors may lose their entire capital.

Yield Enhancement Instruments

Yield enhancement aims to improve the expected return on an investment by increasing risk exposure. An example of such an instrument is a credit-linked note (CLN), which is basically a bond that pays regular coupons but whose redemption value depends on the occurrence of a well-defined credit event (e.g., a rating downgrade or the default of a reference asset).

- If the specified credit event does not occur, the investor receives the par value of the CLN at maturity.
- However, if the specified credit event occurs, the investor receives the par value of the CLN minus the nominal value of the reference asset to which the CLN is linked.

A CLN allows the issuer to effectively transfer the effect of a particular credit event to investors. The issuer is the protection buyer (as it benefits from having to redeem a lower amount if the credit event occurs), whereas the investor is the protection seller. In return for taking on credit risk, investors are offered higher coupons on CLNs than on otherwise identical bonds. Additionally, CLNs are usually issued at a discount, which further improves the potential return for investors.

Participation Instruments

Participation instruments allow investors to participate in the return of an underlying asset. Floating-rate bonds (whose coupon rates are reset periodically and brought in line with market interest rates) are examples of such instruments, as they offer investors the opportunity to participate in movements of interest rates.

Most participation instruments are designed to give investors indirect exposure to a particular index or asset price that they are precluded from investing in directly. While both may offer equity exposure, it is important to note that participation instruments differ from capital-protected instruments in that they do not offer capital protection.

Leveraged Instruments

Leveraged instruments are structured financial instruments that aim to magnify returns. An inverse floater is an example of a leveraged instrument, where cash flows move in the opposite direction from changes in the reference rate.

An inverse floater's periodic coupon rate is determined as:

$$\text{Inverse floater coupon rate} = C - (L \times R)$$

- Inverse floaters with a coupon leverage greater than zero but lower than 1.0 are called **deleveraged inverse floaters**.
- Those with a coupon leverage greater than 1.0 are called **leveraged inverse floaters**.
- Inverse floaters often have a floor that specifies a minimum coupon rate (e.g., a floor may be set at zero to avoid the possibility of a negative coupon).

Short-Term Funding Alternatives Available to Banks

Retail deposits: These include funds deposited at the bank by individual and commercial depositors into their accounts.

Short-term wholesale funds: These include:

- Central bank funds.
- Interbank funds.
- Certificates of deposit (CDs).

Repurchase and Reverse Repurchase Agreements

A **repurchase agreement** is an arrangement between two parties, where one party sells a security to the other with a commitment to buy it back at a later date for a predetermined higher price. The difference between the (lower) selling price and the (higher) repurchase price is the interest cost of the loan. Effectively, what is happening is that the seller is borrowing funds from the buyer and putting up the security as collateral.

- The annualized interest cost of the loan is called the **repo rate**.
- A repurchase agreement for one day is known as an **overnight repo**, and an agreement for a longer period is known as a **term repo**.
- Repo rates are usually lower than the rates that a broker or bank would charge on a margin loan.
- The percentage difference between the market value of the security and the amount of the loan is known as the **repo margin** or **haircut**.
- Any coupon income received from the bond during the repo term belongs to the seller (borrower).
- Both parties in the repo face counterparty credit risk.
- When looking at things from the perspective of the seller or borrower, the transaction is referred to as a **repo**.
- When looking at things from the perspective of the buyer or lender, the transaction is referred to as a **reverse repo**.
  - Reverse repos are used to borrow securities to cover **short positions**.
- Standard practice is to define the transaction based on the perspective of the dealer.

Factors that Affect the Repo Rate

- Repo rates increase with the level of credit risk in the collateral.
- A longer term typically entails higher repo rates.
- Repo rates are lower when the collateral must be delivered to the lender.
- The more scarce a particular piece of collateral, the lower the repo rate.
- If rates for borrowing from other sources are higher, repo rates will also tend to be higher.

Factors that Affect the Repo Margin

- The longer the term, the higher the repo margin.
- The higher the quality of the collateral, the lower the repo margin.
- The higher the creditworthiness of the counterparty, the lower the repo margin.
- The higher the demand or the lower the supply of the collateral, the lower the repo margin.

INTRODUCTION TO FIXED-INCOME VALUATION
Cross-Reference to CFA Institute Assigned Reading #41

Bond Prices and the Time Value of Money

Bond Pricing with a Market Discount Rate

- If the coupon rate offered on the bond equals the rate of return required by investors to compensate them for the risk inherent in the instrument, the bond will sell for its par value.
- If the coupon rate offered on the bond is higher than the required yield, the bond will sell for a **premium**.
- If the coupon rate offered on the bond is lower than the required yield, the bond will sell for a **discount**.
- The higher the discount rate, the lower the present value of each individual cash flow, and the lower the value of the fixed income security.
- The lower the discount rate, the higher the present value of each individual cash flow, and the higher the value of the fixed income security.

Yield-to-Maturity

The **yield-to-maturity** is the (uniform) interest rate that equates the sum of the present values of the bond's expected future cash flows (when discount at that rate) to its current price. It also represents the internal rate of return on the bond's cash flows given that:

1. The investor holds on to the bond until maturity.
2. The issuer makes all promised payments on time in their full amount.
3. The investor is able to reinvest all coupon payments received during the term of the bond at the stated yield to maturity until the bond's maturity date.

Relationships between the Bond Price and Bond Characteristics

1. A bond's price is inversely related to the market discount rate (**the inverse effect**). When the discount rate increases (decreases), the price of the bond decreases (increases).
2. Given the same coupon rate and term to maturity, the percentage price change is greater in terms of absolute magnitude when the discount rate decreases than when it increases (**the convexity effect**).
3. For the same term to maturity, a lower coupon bond is more sensitive to changes in the market discount rate than a higher coupon bond (**the coupon effect**).
4. Generally speaking, for the same coupon rate, a longer term bond is more sensitive to changes in the market discount rate than a shorter term bond (**the maturity effect**). Note that while the maturity effect always holds for zero-coupon bonds and for bonds priced at par or premium to par, it does not always hold for long-term low coupon (but not zero-coupon) bonds that are trading at a discount.

Relationship between Price and Maturity

If the yield remains constant:

- A *premium* bond's value *decreases* towards par as it nears maturity.
- A *discount* bond's value *increases* towards par as it nears maturity.
- A *par* bond's value remains *unchanged* as it nears maturity.

Pricing Bonds with Spot Rates

The **arbitrage-free valuation approach** does not use the same rate to discount each cash flow, but uses the relevant spot rate to discount each cash flow that occurs at a different point in time. A **spot rate** (or **zero rate**) is the yield on a zero-coupon bond for a given maturity.

$$PV = \frac{PMT}{(1+Z_1)^1} + \frac{PMT}{(1+Z_2)^2} + \dots + \frac{PMT+FV}{(1+Z_N)^N}$$

Flat Price, Accrued Interest and the Full Price

When the price of the bond is determined by calculating the present value of future cash flows as of the settlement date, the computed value is known as the **full price** (also known as the **invoice** or **dirty price**). This price includes accrued interest and reflects the amount that the buyer pays the seller. From this full price, the accrued interest is deducted to determine the **flat price** (also known as the **clean price** or **quoted price**) of the bond.

$$PV^{Full} = PV^{Flat} + AI$$

Accrued interest is the seller's proportional share of the next coupon payment. It is calculated as:

$$AI = t/T \times PMT$$

- For government bonds, the actual/actual day count convention is usually applied. The actual number of days is used including weekends, holidays, and weekdays.
- For corporate bonds, the 30/360 day-count convention is often used.

$$PV^{Full} = PV \times (1+r)^{t/T}$$
PV_{Full} = Full price of the bond (value between coupon payments)
PV = Price of bond at last/previous coupon payment date
r = Discount rate per period
t = Number of last coupon payment date to the settlement date
T = Number of days in coupon period
t/T = Fraction of coupon period that has gone by since last payment

Matrix Pricing

Matrix pricing is used to estimate the market discount rate and price of bonds that are not actively traded. Essentially, prices of comparable (in terms of terms to maturity, coupon rates and credit quality) are used to interpolate the price of the subject bond. Matrix pricing can also be used when underwriting new bonds to estimate the required yield spread over the benchmark rate on the bonds to be issued.

Yield Measures for Fixed-Rate Bonds

The **effective annual rate** (or **effective annual yield**) on a fixed-rate bond depends on the assumed number of periods in the year, which is known as the **periodicity** of the **stated annual rate** or **stated annual yield**.

- An **annual-pay bond** would have a stated annual yield for periodicity of one. The stated annual yield would equal the discount rate per year.
- A **semiannual-pay bond** would have a stated annual yield for periodicity of two. The rate per semiannual period would be computed as the stated annual yield divided by two.
- A **quarterly-pay bond** would have a stated annual yield for periodicity of four. The rate per quarter would be computed as the stated annual yield divided by four.

Note that:

- Given the stated annual rate, as the number of compounding periods (periodicity) increases, the effective annual rate increases.
- Given the effective annual rate, as the number of compounding periods (periodicity) increases, the stated annual rate decreases.

The stated annual rate that has a periodicity of two is known as a semiannual bond basis yield or semiannual bond equivalent yield. The semiannual bond basis yield is calculated as the yield per semiannual period multiplied by two.

Converting Stated Annual Rates (SARs)

$$\left(1 + \frac{SAR_M}{M}\right)^M = \left(1 + \frac{SAR_N}{N}\right)^N$$

Bond Yield Quoting Conventions

> Important: What we refer to as stated annual rate (SAR) is referred to in the curriculum as APR or annual percentage rate. We stick to SAR to keep your focus on a stated annual rate versus the effective annual rate. Just remember that if you see an annual percentage rate on the exam, it refers to the stated annual rate.

- The street convention yield represents the internal rate of return on the bond's cash flows assuming all payments are made on scheduled dates regardless of whether any scheduled payment dates fall on weekends or holidays.
- The true yield uses these actual payment dates to compute the IRR.
- The government equivalent yield (usually quoted for corporate bonds) restates a yield-to-maturity based on a 30/360 day-count convention to one based on an actual/actual day-count convention.
- The current yield (also called the income yield or interest yield) is calculated as the sum of coupon payments received over the year divided by the flat price. The current yield is a relatively crude measure of the rate of return to an investor.
    - It neglects the frequency of coupon payments in the numerator.
    - It neglects any accrued interest in the denominator.
    - It neglects any gains (losses) from purchasing the bond at a discount (premium) and redeeming it for par.
- The simple yield is calculated as the sum of coupon payments received over the year plus (minus) straight line amortization of the gain (loss) from purchasing the bond at a discount (premium), divided by the flat price.

Yields for Callable Bonds

- The yield-to-call is computed for each call date (based on the call price and the number of periods until the call date), and then determine the yield-to-worst as the worst or lowest yield among the yield to maturity and the various yields to call for the bond.
- The option-adjusted yield is based on the option-adjusted price, which is calculated by adding the value of the embedded call option to the flat price of the callable bond. The option adjusted yield is lower than the yield to maturity on a callable bond because

callable bonds offer higher yields than otherwise identical non-callable bonds to compensate investors for effectively selling the embedded call option to the issuer.

Yield Measures for Floating-Rate Notes

The effective coupon rate for a specified period is determined at the beginning of the period but actually paid out at the end of the period (in arrears).

If the **quoted margin** equals the **required margin**, the FRN will trade at par at each reset date, but if the quoted margin is lower (greater) than the required margin, the FRN will trade at a discount (premium).

Changes in the required margin can be caused by changes in the issue's (1) credit risk, (2) liquidity and/or (3) tax status.

Risk Exposure of Fixed- versus Floating-Rate Bonds

- Fixed-rate and floating-rate bonds respond very similarly when it comes to credit risk. An increase (decrease) in credit risk leads to a decline (increase) in the value of both types of bonds.
- However, fixed-and floating-rate bonds respond very differently when it comes to changes in benchmark interest rates.

Yield Measures for Money Market Instruments

Money-market instruments are short-term debt securities with maturities ranging from one day (e.g., repos) to one year (e.g., bank certificates of deposit). Money market yields differ from yields in the bond market in the following respects:

1. Bond yields-to-maturity are annualized and compounded. Money market yields are annualized but not compounded (they are stated on simple interest basis).
2. Bond yields-to-maturity can usually be calculated by applying standard time value of money analysis and using a financial calculator. Money market yields are often quoted in terms of nonstandard interest rates so users need to work with various pricing equations.
3. Bond yields-to-maturity are typically stated for a common periodicity for all terms-to-maturity. Money market instruments that have different times-to-maturity have different periodicities for the stated annual rate.

Pricing formula for money market instruments quoted on a discount rate basis

$$PV = FV \times \left(1 - \frac{Days}{Year} \times DR \right)$$

$$DR = \left(\frac{Year}{Days} \right) \times \left(\frac{FV - PV}{FV} \right)$$

A money market discount rate understates the rate of return to the investor and understates the cost of borrowing for the issuer (because PV is generally less than FV).

Pricing formula for money market instruments quoted on an add-on rate basis

$$PV = \frac{FV}{\left(1 + \dfrac{Days}{Year} \times AOR\right)}$$

$$AOR = \left(\frac{Year}{Days}\right) \times \left(\frac{FV - PV}{PV}\right)$$

The add-on rate a reasonable measure for the yield on a money market investment.

Typically money-market yields are converted to a rate known as the **bond-equivalent yield** or **investment yield** for comparisons. The bond equivalent yield is a money-market rate stated on a **365-day year** on an **add-on rate basis.**

Generally speaking, the lower the level of interest rates, the smaller the difference between the stated annual rates for any two periodicities.

The Maturity Structure of Interest Rates

The **spot rate curve** reflects **spot rates** for a range of maturities. The distinguishing feature of spot rates is that they are yields that have no element of reinvestment risk. Using spot rates provides a more accurate relationship between yields and terms to maturity relative to using yields to maturity on coupon-bearing Treasuries.

A **yield curve for coupon bonds** shows the yields-to-maturity for coupon-paying bonds of different maturities. To build the Treasury yield curve, analysts use only the most recently-issued and actively-traded government bonds as they have similar liquidity and tax status. YTMs for maturities where there are gaps can be estimated through a variety of interpolation methods.

A **par curve** represents a series of yields-to-maturity such that each bond trades at par. The par curve is derived from the spot rate curve.

Forward Curve

A **forward rate** represents the interest rate on a loan that will be originated at some point in the future. Forward rates are used to construct the **forward curve**, which represents a series of forward rates, each having the same horizon. Typically the forward curve shows one-year forward rates stated on a semiannual bond basis

Implied forward rates (also known as **forward yields**) can be computed from spot rates.

If the yields presented are semiannual bond basis:

$$\left(1 + \frac{\text{6-mth spot rate}}{2}\right)\left(1 + \frac{\text{6-mth forward rate 6 mths from now}}{2}\right) = \left(1 + \frac{\text{12-mth spot rate}}{2}\right)^2$$

To calculate the x-period forward rate y periods from today, simply remember the following formula: Note that x and y here respresent the periodic spot rate.

$$(1 + {_y}s_0)^y(1 + {_x}f_y)^x = (1 + {_{x+y}}s_0)^{x+y}$$

Example: Calculating Forward Rates

Calculate the 1-year forward rate 6 years from today if the 6-year spot rate is 6.25% and the 7-year spot rate is 6%.

Solution:

$$(1 + {_6}s_0)^6(1 + {_1}f_6) = (1 + {_7}s_0)^7$$

$$(1 + {_1}f_6) = \frac{(1.06)^7}{(1.0625)^6} \Rightarrow {_1}f_6 = 4.51\%$$

A forward rate can be looked upon as the marginal or incremental return from expanding the time to maturity by one more year or as a **breakeven reinvestment rate**. Forward rates are useful to investors in making maturity choice decisions.

Important: Please note that finance authors use different notation when it comes to forward rates. We use $_xf_y$, which refers to the x-period forward rate y years from today, or the interest rate on a loan that has a term of x years, where the loan will be originated y years from today. The CFA Program curriculum uses different notation. In the curriculum, the forward rate 2y5y refers to the 5-year rate 2 years into the future and 3y2y refers to the 2-year rate 3 years from now. We have stuck with our (different) notation because we feel it is easier to work with. You can work with either notation, as it won't affect your answers.

Yield Spreads

Yield Spreads over Benchmark Rates

- The **benchmark yield** (or **risk-free rate**) captures **macroeconomic factors**. The benchmark can be broken down into (1) the expected inflation rate and (2) the expected real rate.
- The **spread** (or **risk premium**) refers to the difference between the yield-to-maturity on a bond and on the benchmark. It captures all **microeconomic factors** specific to the issuer.

Types of Yield Spreads

- The yield spread in basis points over an actual or interpolated government bond yield is known as the **G-spread**.
- The yield spread over the standard swap rate in the same currency and with the same tenor as the subject bond is known as the **I-spread** or **interpolated spread** to the swap curve.

- Note that the government bond yield or the swap rate used as the benchmark for a specific bond will change over time as the remaining term to maturity of the bond changes.
- For floating-rate bonds, Libor is often used as a benchmark. Note that Libor is an interbank rate, not a risk-free rate.

Yield Spreads over the Benchmark Yield Curve

Given the term to maturity of a security, the appropriate benchmark yield-to-maturity applies the same discount rate for each cash flow. Theoretically, this method is unappealing because each cash flow received from the bond carries a different amount of risk (typically, cash flows expected to be received further out into the future entail more risk). It makes more sense to use individual spot rate rates to discount each of the bond's expected cash flows as spot rates accurately capture the risk entailed by each corresponding cash flow (i.e., for each time horizon, there is a specific spot rate unless the yield curve is flat). Therefore, practitioners tend to favor use of the z-spread over the G- and I-spreads.

The z-spread (or zero-volatility spread or static spread) of a bond is a constant spread over the government (or interest rate swap) spot rate curve.

The z-spread is also used to calculate the option-adjusted spread (OAS) on a callable bond. The OAS is calculated by subtracting the value of the embedded call option (stated in terms of bps per year) from the z-spread.

$$\text{OAS} = \text{z-spread} - \text{Option value (bps per year)}$$

Stated simply, the OAS removes the cost of the option from the z-spread, so the OAS is the spread on top of the spot rate curve that the bond would offer if it were option-free. Since the embedded call option in a callable bond favors the issuer, the OAS (the spread that an otherwise identical option-free bond would offer) is less than the z-spread. An issuer would pay out more (in terms of yield) on a callable bond than on an option-free bond.

INTRODUCTION TO ASSET-BACKED SECURITIES
Cross-Reference to CFA Institute Assigned Reading #42

Benefits of Securitization

- It removes the layer between borrowers and investors.
- It allows investors to have a stronger legal claim on the collateral pool of assets.
- Investors can pick and choose the types of securities they want to invest in (in terms of interest rate and credit risk).
- Financial intermediaries are able to originate more loans (by using financing provided by outside investors to originate loans) than they would be able to if they were only able to issue loans that they could finance themselves.
- The increase in the total supply of loanable funds benefits organizations (governments and companies) that need to borrow.
- Since securitized bonds are sold in the public market, they enjoy much better liquidity (lower liquidity risk) than the original loans on bank balance sheets.
- Financial markets are made more efficient.
- Securitization encourages innovation in investment products, which can offer investors access to (otherwise directly unavailable) assets that match their risk, return, and maturity profiles.
- Even large investors, who may be able to purchase real estate loans, automobile loans, or credit card loans directly, would prefer to invest in asset-backed bonds since they would not be required to originate, monitor, and collect payments from the underlying loans themselves.
- ABS offer companies an alternative means of raising finance that can be considered alongside bond and equity issuance.

Parties to a Securitization

Party	Description	Party in Illustration
Seller	Originates the loans and sells loans to the SPV	ABC Company
Issuer/ Trust	The SPV that buys the loans from the seller and issues the asset-backed securities	SPV
Servicer	Services the loans	Servicer

In order for a securitization to serve its purpose, the SPV must be a **bankruptcy remote entity**, i.e., its obligations remain secure even if the parent company goes bankrupt.

Residential Mortgage Loans

- A **mortgage loan** is a borrowing that is secured by some form of real estate.
- Upon initiation of the mortgage loan, the borrower's equity equals the down payment, but over time, the borrower's equity changes as a result of (1) changes in the market value of the property and (2) payment of periodic mortgage payments (that include a principal component).
- The lower (higher) the LTV ratio, the higher (lower) the borrower's equity, the less (more) likely the borrower is to default, and the more (less) protection the lender has for recovering the amount loaned in case the borrower defaults.
- Most mortgages around the world are structured as amortizing loans.

- A mortgage loan may allow the borrower to prepay (make a principal repayment that exceeds the scheduled repayment for the month) a portion, or the entire amount, of the outstanding mortgage principal at any point during the term of the mortgage.

Residential Mortgage-Backed Securities

- **Agency RMBSs** are issued by (1) federal agencies (e.g., Ginnie Mae, which is a federally related institution), and (2) quasi-government entities (e.g., Freddie Mac and Fannie Mae, which are government sponsored enterprises or GSEs).
  - There is no credit risk for agency RMBSs issued by Ginnie Mae as they are backed by the full faith and credit of the U.S. Government.
  - There is minimal credit risk for agency RMBSs issued by GSEs as they are guaranteed by the GSEs themselves.
    - Mortgage loans issued by GSEs must satisfy specific underwriting standards established by various government agencies to qualify for the collateral pool backing agency RMBSs issued by GSEs.
- **Non-agency RMBSs** are issued by private entities.
  - They typically come with **credit enhancements** to reduce credit risk.
    - There are no restrictions on the types of non-agency mortgage loans that can be used to back non-agency RMBSs.

Mortgage Pass-Through Securities

- A **mortgage pass-through security** is created when shares or participation certificates in a pool of mortgage loans are sold to investors.
- The cash flow collected from the collateral pool includes scheduled principal and interest payments, and prepayments.
- The amount and timing of cash flows paid to investors in the pass-through securities are different from those of the cash flows collected from the collateral pool of mortgages.
- Payments made by borrowers pass through the government agency (and on to investors) net of servicing and guaranteeing fees. Therefore, the **pass-through rate** (coupon rate on the pass-through security, which is net interest/net coupon) is lower than the mortgage rate on the underlying pool of mortgages.
- Mortgage loans that are securitized to create pass-through securities do not all carry the same mortgage rate and maturity. Therefore, a **weighted average coupon rate (WAC)** and **weighted average maturity (WAM)** are calculated to describe the pool of mortgages that serves as collateral for the pass-through securities.
- Market participants use **average life** (the weighted average time it will take for all the principal payments, i.e., scheduled repayments and projected prepayments, to be received) as a measure of the interest rate risk of a mortgage-backed security.
  - The average life of an RMBS depends on the assumed prepayment speed—the higher the prepayment speed assumed, the shorter the average life of the mortgage backed security.
- The prepayment rate is measured in terms of the **single monthly mortality rate (SMM)**. It is calculated as the amount of prepayment for a month as a percentage of the mortgage balance that was available to be prepaid that month.

Contraction Risk versus Extension Risk

Prepayment risk encompasses **contraction risk** and **extension risk**.

Contraction risk occurs when interest rates fall.

- Option-free bond prices increase when interest rates fall. However, for mortgage loans, the issuer (homeowner) has the right to prepay and can easily do so by refinancing her mortgage. This option to prepay is similar to the call option granted to the issuer of a callable bond. When interest rates fall, it becomes feasible for the mortgage issuer/borrower to prepay (just like it becomes feasible for an issuer to call a callable bond), so the upside potential of the pass-through security is limited. It experiences price compression at low interest rates and exhibits negative convexity.
- To make things worse, when interest rates fall, refinancing activity typically increases and leads to an increase in prepayments, reducing or shortening the average life of the pass-through. The (higher-than-expected) cash flows from the pass-through must then be reinvested at current (lower) rates.

Extension risk occurs when interest rates rise.

- The price of a pass-through (just like the price of any bond) will decline when interest rates increase.
- To make things worse, refinancing activity and prepayment rates slow down when interest rates rise, increasing or lengthening the average expected life of the pass-through. Consequently, a greater-than-anticipated amount remains invested in the pass-through at the coupon rate of the instrument, which is lower than current interest rates.

Collateralized Mortgage Obligations

Collateralized mortgage obligations (CMOs) redistribute the cash flows from mortgage pass-through securities into packages/classes/tranches with different risk exposures to prepayment risk.

- For CMOs, the mortgage-related products from which cash flows are obtained are considered the collateral, i.e., a pool of mortgage pass-through security serves as the collateral. For mortgage pass-through securities, a pool of mortgage loans serves as collateral.

Sequential-Pay Tranches

- Each class of bond is retired sequentially.
- Interest payments are periodically made to each tranche based on its coupon rate and principal amount outstanding at the beginning of the period.
- Principal payments are first forwarded to Tranche A, then to Tranche B (after Tranche A has been fully paid off) and so on.
- The principal payment pattern for each of the tranches is not known. However, the shorter-term tranches receive protection from extension risk, while the longer term tranches receive protection from contraction risk.

Planned Amortization Class (PAC) Tranches

- PAC bonds bring increased predictability of cash flows, as they specify a repayment schedule that will be satisfied as long as actual prepayments realized from the collateral fall within a pre-defined band.
- The greater certainty in payments for the PAC tranche comes at the expense of greater uncertainty for the **support** or **companion tranche**, which absorbs the prepayment risk.
- The average life of the support tranche fluctuates more wildly than that of the PAC tranche.

- The support tranche provides **two-sided protection** (i.e., protection against extension **and** contraction risk) to the PAC tranche.
- The greater the par value of the support tranche relative to that of the PAC tranche, the greater the prepayment protection for the PAC, the lower the PAC's average life variability, and the greater the support tranche's average life variability.

Floating-Rate Tranches

- Even though the collateral for CMOs carries a fixed rate, it is possible to create a floating-rate tranche (along with an inverse-floater tranche) from any of the fixed-rate tranches in a CMO structure.
- Since the floater varies positively with interest rates, and the inverse floater varies negatively with interest rates, they offset each other.

Non-Agency Residential Mortgage-Backed Securities

Non-agency RMBSs are not guaranteed by the government or a GSE, which make the evaluation of credit risk an important consideration when investing in them.

- Cash flows are distributed according to a set of rules that determines the distribution of interest and principal payments to tranches with varying levels of priority/seniority.
- There are also rules for allocating realized losses, with senior tranches having a priority claim over payments and subordinated tranches absorbing losses.
- When it comes to forecasting cash flows on non-agency RMBSs, investors must make assumptions regarding (1) the default rate for the collateral and (2) the recovery rate.

Internal Credit Enhancements

- **Reserve funds:**
  - **Cash reserve funds:** The entity seeking to raise the funds deposits some of the proceeds of sale of the loan pool with the SPV. This cash can be used to pay for potential future losses.
  - **Excess spread accounts:** The excess spread or cash that remains after the payment of net coupon, servicing fees, and all other expenses is kept in reserve to pay for future credit losses on the collateral.
- **Overcollateralization:** This refers to a situation where the value of the collateral exceeds the par value of the securities issued by the SPV.
  - The amount of overcollateralization for an issue changes over time due to (1) defaults, (2) amortization, and (3) prepayments.
- **Senior/subordinate structure:** This type of structure has **senior bond classes** and **subordinate bond classes** (also known as **non-senior/junior bond classes**).
  - The structure basically provides **credit tranches** as the subordinate bond classes provide credit protection to the senior classes.
  - To provide credit protection to investors in the senior bond classes, a **shifting interest mechanism** is added to the structure. This mechanism locks out subordinated classes from receiving payments for a period of time if the collateral performs poorly.

External Credit Enhancements

External credit enhancements are third-party guarantees for payments to security holders should the issuer not be able to meet payment requirements.

- **Monoline insurers** are the most common third-party financial guarantors.

Time Tranching versus Credit Tranching

- Time tranching occurs when prepayment risk (or the timing of distribution of cash flows) is redistributed among the various classes of ABS as in a sequential-pay CMO structure.
- Credit tranching occurs when credit risk (or risk of loss from default) is redistributed among the various classes of ABS as in a senior/subordinate structure

Commercial Mortgage–Backed Securities (CMBS)

CMBSs are backed by a pool of commercial mortgage loans on income-generating properties (e.g., apartments, warehouses, shopping centres, etc.). In the U.S. (and many other countries), commercial mortgage loans are non-recourse loans. Therefore, evaluation of credit risk for commercial mortgage loans requires examining the income-generating capacity and value of each property on a stand-alone basis.

Two measures are commonly used to evaluate the potential credit performance of a commercial property:

- The **debt-service coverage (DSC) ratio** is used to evaluate the adequacy of income generated from the property to service the loan. It is calculated as net operating income (NOI) divided by debt service. NOI is calculated as rental income minus cash operating expenses and a non-cash replacement reserve that reflects depreciation of the property over time.
  - A ratio greater than 1 means that cash flow from the property covers debt servicing costs adequately.
  - The higher the ratio, the lower the credit risk
- The **loan-to-value ratio** equals the loan amount divided by the appraised value of the property.
  - The lower the ratio, the lower the credit risk.

Basic CMBS Structure

- A credit-rating agency determines the level of credit enhancement required for the issue to attain the credit rating desired by the issuer.
- Different bond classes are created with each class having a different priority on cash flows. The various bond classes are retired sequentially with all principal repayments, prepayments, and proceeds from default (from selling repossessed properties) being used to repay the highest-rated tranche first.
- Losses from loan defaults are charged against the lowest-rated tranche first. If this tranche is not rated by credit-rating agencies, it is known as the **first-loss piece, residual tranche,** or **equity tranche.**
- The equity tranche typically has no specific interest rate (as it is the residual tranche). Investors price it based on the expected residual rate of return. Actual returns can be better or worse than expected depending on actual future interest rate movements and actual defaults.
- Interest payments are made to all tranches.
- Typically, CMBS investors have significant call protection, which actually results in these securities trading more like corporate bonds than like RMBSs.
  - Call protection at the loan level can come in form of prepayment lockouts, defeasance, prepayment penalties, and yield maintenance charges.
  - Call protection at the structure level comes from credit tranches.

- Most commercial loans that back CMBSs have balloon maturity provisions, i.e., they require a significant amount of principal to be repaid at maturity (as opposed to during the term of the loan). This exposes investors to **balloon risk**, which is more like extension risk as there is usually a **workout period** during which the borrower and lender try to modify the original terms of the loan to ensure eventual repayment.

Non-Mortgage Asset–Backed Securities

The collateral backing asset-backed securities can be classified as either amortizing or non-amortizing assets.

Amortizing loans:

- The periodic cash flows include interest payments, principal repayments (in accordance with an amortization schedule), and (if allowed) prepayments.
- Examples include residential mortgage loans and automobile loans.

Non-amortizing loans:

- These only require a monthly minimum payment with no scheduled principal payment.
- If the payment received is less than the interest amount due, the shortfall is added to the outstanding loan balance.
- If the payment is greater than the interest amount due, the excess serves to reduce the outstanding loan balance.
- Since there is no scheduled principal payment amount, the concept of prepayment does not apply to non-amortizing assets.
- Examples include credit card receivables.

The type of collateral (amortizing versus non-amortizing assets) has a significant effect on the structure of the securitization.

- When amortizing assets are securitized, the total face value (total amount outstanding) declines over time due to scheduled repayments and prepayments, and the number of outstanding loans (composition of the collateral) declines as a result of (1) defaults and (2) full principal repayments or full amortizations.
- On the other hand, securitizations of non-amortizing loans usually take the form of a **revolving structure**, where the composition of the collateral can change over the term of the securities. This is because principal repayments can either be (1) reinvested by purchasing additional loans, or (2) passed on to security holders.
  - During an initial **lockout** or **revolving period** (which immediately follows the origination of the transaction), all principal repayments are reinvested in additional loans with a principal amount equal to the total principal amount received. While this can result in a fewer total number of individual loans comprising the collateral, the total face value outstanding remains the same.
  - During the **principal amortization period** (which follows the lockout period), principal repayments are not used to purchase additional loans, but are distributed to security holders.

Auto Loan Receivable-Backed Securities

These securities are backed by auto loan and lease receivables. Cash flows for auto loan-backed securities consist of regularly scheduled monthly interest and principal payments and prepayments.

- Generally speaking, auto loan-backed securitizations come with some form of credit enhancement.
- Typically, the securitizations involve a senior/subordinate structure (to provide credit protection to the senior tranches). Further, some securitizations also involve reserve accounts, overcollateralization, and excess interest on the receivables.

Credit Card Receivable-Backed Securities

- The cash flow from a pool of credit card receivables includes (1) finance charges collected (interest charges on the unpaid balance after the grace period), (2) fees (for late payments and membership), and (3) principal repayment.
- Interest payments are made to security holders periodically (monthly, quarterly, or semiannually). The interest rate may be fixed or floating (typically with no cap).
- During the **revolving period** (also known as the **lockout period**), any principal repayments from the pool of receivables are used to purchase additional receivables to maintain the size of the pool. During this period, the cash flow passed on to security holders consists only of (1) finance charges and (2) fees collected from the pool of receivables. Principal repayments are only passed on to security holders once the **principal-amortizing period** sets in.
- Even though receivables in a revolving structure may not be prepaid (since there is no concept of prepayment here), all the bonds may be retired early if an **early** or **rapid amortization provision** is triggered.

Collateralized Debt Obligations

A CDO is a security that is backed by a diversified pool of securities.

- Like an ABS, a CDO also involves the creation of an SPV.
- A **CDO manager** (also known as **collateral manager**) is responsible for managing the collateral portfolio of assets (consisting of debt obligations).
- The funds used to purchase the collateral assets are raised from the issuance of bonds to investors. Bond classes may include **senior bonds**, **mezzanine bonds** (with credit ratings between senior and subordinated bonds), and **subordinated bonds** (also known as the **residual** or **equity class**).
- **Restrictive covenants** are placed on the manager to ensure that the credit ratings assigned to the various tranches at issuance are maintained during the term of the CDO.
- Cash flows from the underlying portfolio of assets include (1) coupon interest payments, (2) proceeds from maturing assets, and (3) proceeds from sale of assets. These cash flows are used to make interest and principal payments to the various bond classes.
- From the asset manager/issuer's perspective, the aim is to earn a rate of return on the collateral pool of assets that is higher than the interest costs of bonds issued. This excess return accrues to the equity holders and the CDO manager. Effectively, issuing a CDO is like undertaking a leveraged transaction where the idea is to use borrowed funds (raised from bonds issued) to generate a return that exceeds the funding cost.
- From the investors' perspective, each class of bonds entails a different level of risk. Senior/mezzanine bond investors may be able to earn a potentially higher return than on a comparably-rated corporate bond by gaining exposure to debt products that they may

not otherwise be able to purchase. Equity investors can earn an equity-type return by taking the (higher) risk associated with the subordinated class.

- Certain restrictions are placed on the manager (via various tests and limits) to ensure that the senior bond classes are adequately protected and the ratings issued to the bond classes are maintained. Failure to meet these tests may trigger an immediate payoff to the senior bond classes until the tests are satisfied. This payoff would have the effect of deleveraging the CDO (as the asset manager's reliance on its cheapest source of funding, i.e., senior bonds, would be reduced).

The major difference between an ABS and a CDO is that in an ABS the cash flows from the collateral pool are used to pay off bond holders without the active management of collateral. In a CDO, the manager buys and sells debt obligations (assets) to (1) generate the cash flow required to repay bond holders and to (2) earn a competitive return for the equity tranche.

Covered Bonds

Covered bonds are senior debt obligations that are backed by a segregated pool of assets (typically consisting of commercial or residential mortgages). They are different from ABS in the following ways:

- For covered bonds, the pool of assets remains on the originator's balance sheet, whereas in an ABS they are transferred from the originator to a bankruptcy-remote special legal entity.
- Covered bonds usually consist of one bond class per cover pool, whereas ABS often use credit tranching to create bond classes with different exposures to default risk.
- Any prepaid or non-performing loans in the cover pool must be replaced by the sponsor (to ensure sufficient cash flows until the maturity of the covered bond), whereas the pool of loans backing an ABS is typically static.

Types of Covered Bonds

- For **hard-bullet covered bonds**, if payments do not occur according to the original schedule, a bond default is triggered and bond payments are accelerated.
- On the other hand, **soft-bullet covered bonds** delay the bond default and payment acceleration of bond cash flows until a new final maturity date, which is usually up to a year after the original maturity date.
- **Conditional pass-through covered bonds** convert to pass-through securities after the original maturity date if all bond payments have not yet been made.

Because of their dual recourse nature, strict eligibility criteria, dynamic cover pool, and redemption regimes in the event of sponsor default, covered bonds usually carry lower credit risk and offer lower yields than otherwise similar ABS.

UNDERSTANDING FIXED-INCOME RISK AND RETURN
Cross-Reference to CFA Institute Assigned Reading #43

Sources of Return on a Fixed-Rate Bond

1. Receipt of promised coupon and principal payments.
2. Reinvestment of coupon payments.
3. Potential capital gains/losses if the bond is sold prior to maturity.

If a bond is purchased at a premium/discount, it adds another dimension to the total rate of return.

Horizon Yield, Carrying Value and Capital Gains and Losses

The **horizon yield** equals the YTM at issuance if the following two conditions hold:

- The bond is sold at its **carrying value**, i.e., at a price that lies on its **constant-yield price trajectory**.
- All coupon payments can be reinvested at a rate that equals the bond's YTM at issuance until date of sale.

Carrying value refers to the value of a bond (at any time between the purchase date and maturity date) that entails the same YTM as when the bond was purchased. The carrying value reflects amortization of any premium/discount since the time of purchase. **Capital gains/losses** arise if a bond is sold at a price different from its carrying value.

Interest Rate Risk

There are two types of **interest rate risk**, which offset each other:

- **Reinvestment risk.** The future value of any interim cash flows received from a bond (these could be coupon payments as well as principal repayments on amortizing bonds) increases when interest rates rise and decreases when interest rates decline.
- **Market price risk.** The selling price of a bond (at any point during its term or before maturity) decreases when interest rates rise and increases when interest rates decline.

Reinvestment risk matters more to a long-term investors, while market price risk matters more to short-term investors. Therefore, two investors who are holding the same bond can have different exposures to interest rate risk depending on their individual investment horizons.

Interest Rate Risk of Fixed-Rate Bonds

Duration

Duration measures the sensitivity or responsiveness of a bond's **full price** (including accrued interest) to changes in **its yield-to-maturity** (or market discount rate). Broadly speaking, duration can be classified as:

- **Yield duration**, which measures the responsiveness of a bond's price with respect to **its own yield-to-maturity**. Yield duration statistics include Macaulay duration, modified duration, money duration and the price value of a basis point.

- Curve duration, which measures the responsiveness of a bond's price with respect to **a benchmark yield curve** (e.g., government yield curve, forward curve, or government par curve). Coupon duration statistics include effective duration.

Macaulay Duration

Macaulay duration represents the weighted average of the time it would take to receive all the bond's promised cash flows, where the weights are calculated as the present value of each cash flow divided by the bond's **full price.**

Macaulay duration (in terms of periods) can also be computed using the following closed-form formula:

$$\text{MacDur} = \left\{ \frac{1 + r}{r} - \frac{1 + r + [N \times (c - r)]}{c \times [(1 + r)^N - 1] + r} \right\} - (t/T)$$

Macaulay duration is typically not used as a measure of the interest rate sensitivity of a bond's price. However, it does have has some useful applications, including measurement of the duration gap.

Modified Duration

Modified duration is calculated by dividing Macaulay duration by one plus the yield per period.

$$\text{ModDur} = \frac{\text{MacDur}}{1 + r}$$

Modified duration can be used to estimate the percentage price change for a bond in response to a change in its **yield-to-maturity**.

$$\%\Delta \text{PV}^{\text{Full}} \approx -\text{AnnModDur} \times \Delta \text{Yield}$$

- Modified duration only provides a linear estimate of the change in the price of a bond in response to a change in yields.
- It provides good estimates for bond prices in response to relatively small changes in yields, but its estimating accuracy fades with larger changes in yields as the curvature (convexity) of the price-yield profile becomes more pronounced.

If Macaulay duration is not already known, annual modified duration can be estimated using the following formula:

$$\text{ApproxModDur} = \frac{(\text{PV}_-) - (\text{PV}_+)}{2 \times (\Delta \text{Yield}) \times (\text{PV}_0)}$$

- This approximation basically estimates the slope of the line tangent to the price-yield profile for a bond at a particular yield level.
- The value for approximate modified duration obtained by applying this formula gives us the percentage change in the price of a bond in response to a 100 bps (1%) change in yields.

- The percentage price change if yields were to change by 50 basis points would be half the figure obtained from applying the formula.

We can also use the approximate modified duration (ApproxModDur) to estimate Macaulay duration (ApproxMacDur) by applying the following formula:

$$\text{ApproxMacDur} = \text{ApproxModDur} \times (1 + r)$$

Effective Duration

Effective duration (also known as **OAS duration**) measures the sensitivity of a bond's price to a change in **the benchmark yield curve.**

$$\text{EffDur} = \frac{(PV_-) - (PV_+)}{2 \times (\Delta\text{Curve}) \times (PV_0)}$$

Note that:

- Effective duration is a **curve duration** statistic that measures interest rate risk in terms of a change in the benchmark yield curve (Curve).
- Modified duration is a **yield duration** statistic that measures interest rate risk in terms of a change in the bond's own yield-to-maturity (Yield).

Effective duration is the appropriate measure of risk **for bonds with embedded call options**, including callable bonds (and mortgage-backed bonds).

- Modified or Macaulay duration (essentially, just one statistic) can be computed to estimate the percentage price change for a **traditional fixed-rate bond** in response to a change in the benchmark yield and/or credit spread.
- On the other hand, **for bonds with embedded options** (where there is no well-defined internal rate of return), a curve duration statistic must be computed to measure the effects of a change in benchmark yields, and a separate measure (e.g., credit duration) must be computed to measure the effects of a change in the credit spread.

Further, note that unlike modified duration, effective duration does not necessarily provide more accurate estimates for changes in a bond's price if we use a smaller change in benchmark rates.

Finally, although effective duration is the appropriate interest rate risk measure for bonds With embedded options, it is also used for traditional bonds to supplement the information provided by modified and Macaulay duration.

Key Rate Duration

Key rate duration (or partial duration) is a measure of a bond's (or bond portfolio's) sensitivity to a change in the benchmark yield for a given maturity. Key rate durations are used to assess **shaping** or **yield curve risk** for a bond, i.e., the bond's sensitivity to changes in the shape of the benchmark yield curve, or non-parallel shifts in the yield curve (e.g., the yield curve becoming steeper or flatter).

For parallel shifts in the benchmark yield curve, key rate durations will suggest the same interest rate sensitivity as effective duration.

Properties of Bond Durations

Fraction of the Coupon Period that has Elapsed (t/T):

All other things remaining the same, Macaulay duration falls as time passes through a coupon period, and then jumps after each coupon payment (creating a saw tooth-like pattern).

Time-to-Maturity

- For fixed-rate coupon bonds trading at par or premium to par, longer times-to-maturity correspond to a higher Macaulay duration.
    - However, Macaulay duration for these bonds never rises above a threshold level defined by MacDur $= (1 + r)/r$
- For fixed-rate coupon bonds trading at a discount, longer times-to-maturity generally correspond to a higher Macaulay duration.
    - Given a long enough time-to-maturity, Macaulay duration for discount bonds actually rises to a maximum level that lies above MacDur $= (1 + r)/r$.
    - However, after reaching its maximum level, as time-to-maturity further increases, Macaulay duration for discount bonds starts falling back towards $(1 + r)/r$ if the coupon rate is low relative to the yield-to-maturity.
- The Macaulay duration for a zero-coupon bond equals its time-to-maturity.
- For a non-callable **perpetuity** (or **consol**) i.e., a bond that pays a fixed coupon forever, Macaulay duration equals the threshold level MacDur $= (1 + r)/r$.

Coupon Rate

All other things remaining the same, a lower-coupon bond has higher duration and more interest rate risk than a higher-coupon bond.

Yield-to-Maturity

All other things remaining the same, a lower yield-to-maturity bond has higher duration and more interest rate risk than a higher yield-to-maturity bond.

Callable Bonds

- The price of a callable bond is always *lower* than the price of an otherwise identical non-callable bond. The difference represents the value of the embedded call option.

When interest rates are **high** relative to the coupon rate:

- It is highly unlikely that the issuer will call the bond, so the value of the embedded call option is relatively low.
- Therefore, the effective durations (slopes of the price-yield profiles) of the callable and non-callable bonds are very similar.

When interest rates are **low** relative to the coupon rate:

- It becomes more likely that the issuer will call the bond (and exercise the option to refinance at a lower cost of funds), so the embedded call option gains value for the issuer.
- As interest rates fall, the callable bond suffers "price compression."
- The effective duration (slope of the price-yield profile) of the callable bond is *lower* than that of an otherwise identical non-callable bond – its expected life shortens as the weighted average time to receipt of cash is reduced.

Putable Bonds

- The price of a putable bond is always greater than the price of an otherwise identical non-putable bond. The difference represents the value of the embedded put option.

When interest rates are **low** relative to the coupon rate:

- It is highly unlikely that the investor will put the bond back to the issuer, so the value of the embedded put option is relatively low.
- Therefore, the effective durations (slopes of the price-yield profiles) of the putable and non-putable bonds are very similar.

When interest rates are **high** relative to the coupon rate:

- It becomes more likely that the investor will put the bond back to the issuer, so the embedded put option gains value for the investor.
- As interest rates rise, the putable bond does not lose as much value as an otherwise identical non-putable bond. The put price effectively serves as a floor on its value.
- The effective duration (slope of the price-yield profile) of the putable bond is lower than that of an otherwise identical non-putable bond – its expected life shortens as the weighted average time to receipt of cash is reduced.

To summarize, the presence of an embedded option (be it a call or a put) *reduces* the duration of the bond and makes it less sensitive to changes in the benchmark yield curve, assuming there is no change in credit risk.

Computing the Duration of a Bond Portfolio

1. Compute the weighted average of time to receipt of the portfolio's aggregate cash flows.

Under this method, projected cash flows on all (1) traditional bonds and (2) bonds with embedded options held in the portfolio are aggregated to determine the portfolio's **cash flow yield** (i.e., internal rate of return based on those projected cash flows), which is then used to compute Macaulay and modified duration for the portfolio. While theoretically accurate, this method is difficult to implement in practice.

2. Compute the weighted average of the durations of the individual bonds held in the portfolio.

Under this method, Macaulay and modified duration statistics for a bond portfolio are computed as the weighted average of the statistics for the individual bonds that comprise the portfolio, where each bond's weight equals the proportion of the total portfolio's market value that it comprises (based on **full prices).**

$$\text{Portfolio duration} = w_1D_1 + w_2D_2 + \ldots + w_ND_N$$

Money Duration and Price Value of a Basis Point

Money duration (or **dollar duration**) is a measure of the *dollar* (or whichever currency the bond is denominated in) *price change* in response to a change in yields.

$$\text{MoneyDur} = \text{AnnModDur} \times \text{PV}^{\text{Full}}$$

The estimated (dollar) change in the price of the bond is calculated as:

$$\Delta PV^{Full} = -MoneyDur \times \Delta Yield$$

The **price value of a basis point (PVBP)** estimates the change in the full price of a bond in response to a 1 bp change in its yield-to-maturity.

$$PVBP = \frac{(PV_-) - (PV_+)}{2}$$

Bond Convexity

Duration *underestimates* the price increase caused by a reduction in yields, and *overestimates* the decrease in prices when yields rise. Therefore, price estimates of option-free bonds based on duration must be revised upwards to bring them closer to their actual values. This revision is performed via the **convexity adjustment**. The more the curvature or convexity of the price-yield relationship, the more significant the convexity adjustment becomes.

Annual convexity can be approximated using the following equation:

$$ApproxCon = \frac{(PV_-) + (PV_+) - [2 \times (PV_0)]}{(\Delta Yield)^2 \times (PV_0)}$$

The percentage change in a bond's full price can be estimated as:

$$\%\Delta PV^{Full} \approx (-AnnModDur \times \Delta Yield) + \left[\frac{1}{2} \times AnnConvexity \times (\Delta Yield)^2\right]$$

The **money convexity** of a bond is its annual convexity multiplied by the full price of the bond such that:

$$\Delta PV^{Full} \approx (-MoneyDur \times \Delta Yield) + \left[\frac{1}{2} \times MoneyCon \times (\Delta Yield)^2\right]$$

Factors that Affect Convexity

- The longer the term-to-maturity, the greater the convexity.
- The lower the coupon rate, the greater the convexity.
- The lower the yield-to-maturity, the greater the convexity.
- The greater the dispersion of cash flows, the greater the convexity.

Given the same price, yield-to-maturity and modified duration, a more convex bond will outperform a less convex bond in both bull and bear markets.

Convexity for Bonds with Embedded Options

For callable bonds (and other bonds with embedded options) the first-order effect of a change in the benchmark yield curve is measured by **effective** duration, and the second-order effect of a change in the benchmark yield curve is measured by **effective convexity**. Effective convexity is a **curve convexity** statistic.

$$\text{EffCon} = \frac{[(PV_-) + (PV_+)] - [2 \times (PV_0)]}{(\Delta\text{Curve})^2 \times (PV_0)}$$

Negative convexity (also known as **concavity**) is an important feature of callable bonds. When the benchmark yield is high, callable and non-callable bonds experience similar price changes to changes in benchmark yields. However, as benchmark yields decline, there comes a point where the callable bond moves into negative convexity territory, where the embedded call option holds significant value to the issuer and is highly likely to be exercised.

Putable bonds always have positive convexity.

Interest Rate Risk and the Investment Horizon

Yield Volatility

Changes in bond prices result from two factors:

1. The impact per basis point change in the yield-to-maturity. This factor is captured by duration and convexity; and
2. The number of basis points in the change in yield-to-maturity. This factor is captured by **yield volatility**.

Investment Horizon, Macaulay Duration, and Interest Rate Risk

Given a particular assumption about yield volatility, Macaulay duration indicates the investment horizon for which coupon reinvestment risk and market price risk offset each other. This is one of the applications of duration where "years-based" interpretation is meaningful and where Macaulay duration is used rather than modified duration.

When interest rates rise:

- Money duration measures the immediate decline in the value of the bond.
- Over time, the value of the bond is pulled up to par.
- The gain in future value of reinvested coupon starts out small, but increases at an increasing rate over time.
- At a certain point during the life of the bond, the gain on reinvested coupon and the loss on the sale of the bond offset each other. That point is the Macaulay duration of the bond.

When interest rates fall:

- Money duration measures the immediate increase in the value of the bond.
- Over time, the value of the bond is pulled down to par.
- The loss in future value of reinvested coupon starts out small, but increases at an increasing rate over time.
- At a certain point during the life of the bond, the gain on sale of the bond and the loss on the future value of reinvested coupon offset each other. That point is the Macaulay duration of the bond.

Important Takeaways

1. When the investment horizon is *greater* than the Macaulay duration of the bond, coupon reinvestment risk dominates market price risk. In this case, the investor is concerned about interest rates *falling*.

2. When the investment horizon is *less* than the Macaulay duration of the bond, market price risk dominates coupon reinvestment risk. In this case, the investor is concerned about interest rates *rising*.

3. When the investment horizon equals the Macaulay duration of the bond, coupon reinvestment risk and market price risk offset each other.

The difference between the Macaulay duration of a bond and the investment horizon is known as the **duration gap**.

$$\text{Duration gap} = \text{Macaulay duration} - \text{Investment horizon}$$

As time passes, (1) the investment horizon falls and (2) the Macaulay duration of the bond also changes, so the duration gap changes as well.

Credit and Liquidity Risk

For fixed-income securities, changes in the components of the overall yield-to-maturity do not occur in isolation i.e., there is interaction between changes in benchmark yields and spreads, between changes in the expected inflation rate and the expected real interest rate, and between changes in credit and liquidity risk. Therefore, for a fixed-rate bond, "inflation duration" or a "credit duration" all refer to the same number and we can use modified duration and convexity to estimate the change in the value of a bond in response to any change in the yield-to-maturity regardless of the source of the yield-to-maturity change.

Empirical Duration versus Analytical Duration

- **Analytical duration** assumes that government bond yields and spreads are independent variables that are uncorrelated with each other.
- **Empirical duration** uses historical data in statistical models that incorporate several factors that affect bond prices.

FUNDAMENTALS OF CREDIT ANALYSIS
Cross-Reference to CFA Institute Assigned Reading #44

Credit risk refers to the risk of loss resulting from a borrower's failure to make full and timely payments of interest and/or principal. It has two components:

- **Default risk** or **default probability** refers to the probability of a borrower failing to meet its obligations to make full and timely payments of principal and interest under the terms of the bond indenture.
- **Loss severity** or **loss given default** refers to the portion of the bond's value that an investor would lose if a default actually occurred. Loss severity equals 1 minus the recovery rate.

The **expected loss** is calculated as the probability of default multiplied by loss severity.

$$\text{Expected loss} = \text{Default probability} \times \text{Loss severity given default}$$

Spread risk refers to the risk of a widening of the yield spread on the bond. It encompasses:

- **Downgrade risk** or **credit migration risk**: This is the risk that the issuer's credit worthiness may deteriorate during the term of the bond, causing rating agencies to downgrade the credit rating of the issue.
- **Market liquidity risk**: This is the risk that an investor may have to sell her investment at a price lower than its market value due to insufficient volumes (liquidity) in the market. Two issuer-specific factors that affect liquidity risk are **the size of the issuer** and the **credit quality of the issuer**.

Seniority Ranking

Companies may issue debt with different rankings in terms of seniority, where the most senior or highest-ranking debt has the first claim on the issuer's cash flows and assets in case of an issuer default or restructuring. Debt may be classified as:

- **Secured debt**: Holders of secured debt have a direct claim on certain assets and their associated cash flows.
- **Unsecured debt** or **debentures**: Holders of unsecured debt only have a general claim on the issuer's assets and cash flow.

In the event of default, secured debt ranks higher than unsecured debt in the **priority of claims**.

Further, within each category of debt, there are sub-rankings.

Recovery Rates

All creditors at the same level in the capital structure are treated as one class irrespective of (1) the coupon rate offered on their bonds, and (2) when their bonds are maturing. This is referred to as bonds ranking **pari passu** (i.e., on an equal footing) in right of payment.

Recovery rates are highest for the senior-most class of debt in the priority of claims and fall with each lower rank of seniority. Therefore, the lower the seniority of the bond, the greater the credit risk and this is why investors demand a higher yield to invest in lower ranked debt instruments.

Apart from the relative seniority of a particular bond, recovery rates also vary (1) by industry and (2) depending on when the default occurs in a credit cycle.

Priority of Claims: Not Always "Absolute"

In practice, holders of junior and subordinated debt and even shareholders may recover some value on their interests without more senior creditors being paid in full.

Credit Ratings

Rating agencies issue credit ratings, which reflect an opinion on the potential risk of default of a particular (1) bond issue or (2) bond issuer.

Issuer versus Issue Ratings

Rating agencies usually provide credit ratings for the issuer (referred to as a corporate family rating) and for different issues (referred to as corporate credit rating) as well.

- The corporate family rating (CFR) is based on the overall creditworthiness of the issuer.
- The corporate credit rating (CCR) applies to a specific financial obligation of the issuer and is based on factors such as the issue's relative seniority ranking in the priority of claims and covenants.

The existence of cross-default provisions implies that the **probability of default** for all the different issues of a particular company is the same. However, different issues can be assigned different (higher or lower) credit ratings due to a ratings adjustment known as notching.

Generally speaking:

- For more risky issuers (with lower credit ratings), a larger notching adjustment is applied across seniority rankings. For these issuers, the probability of default is higher, so the potential difference in loss from a lower or higher seniority ranking is a bigger consideration in assessing the issue's credit risk.
- For less risky issuers (with higher credit ratings), the probability of default is lower, so there is less of a need to notch ratings to capture any potential difference in loss severity.

Risks in Relying on Agency Ratings

- Credit ratings can (and generally tend to) change significantly during a bond's term.
- Rating agencies also make mistakes.
- Certain risks (e.g., litigation risk faced by tobacco companies, environmental and business risks faced by chemical companies) cannot be anticipated in advance so rating agencies fail to capture these risks in assigned credit ratings.
- Ratings tend to lag market pricing of credit.

Further, credit ratings primarily focus on the risk of default, whereas (especially for low-quality credits) market price depends more on expected loss (i.e., default probability times loss severity). Therefore, two bonds with similar default risk, but different recovery rates will have similar ratings, but different market values.

The Four Cs of Credit Analysis

Capacity

Capacity refers to a borrower's ability to make its debt payments on time.

Industry Structure

Generally speaking:

- An industry that relies on just a few suppliers has greater credit risk than an industry that has multiple suppliers.
- Industries that rely heavily on just a few customers have greater credit risk than those that sell to a large number of customers.
- The higher the barriers to entry, the lower the level of competition in an industry, and the lower the credit risk of industry participants.
- Industries that offer products and services for which there are no good or cost-effective substitutes have greater pricing power and hence, lower credit risk.
- The greater the intensity of competition among companies in an industry, the lower the industry's profit potential, and the higher the credit risk.
- If an industry is characterized by high fixed costs (e.g., airlines and hotels), companies would find it difficult to cut down costs if they are unable to generate sufficient revenue.

Industry Fundamentals

Evaluation of industry fundamentals is based on:

- Industry cyclicality
- Growth prospects
- Published industry statistics

Company Fundamentals

Analysis of company fundamentals involves an examination of the company's:

- Competitive position
- Track record/operating history
- Management's strategy and execution
- Financial ratios

Collateral

Collateral refers to the quality and value of assets that are pledged against the issuer's debt obligations. Analysts focus more on assessing collateral when the probability of default is significantly high (as is the case with companies with low creditworthiness).

It is sometimes difficult to observe the value and quality of a company's assets directly so analysts should consider the following factors:

- The nature and amount of intangible assets on the balance sheet.
- The amount of depreciation an issuer takes relative to its capital expenditures.

Covenants

Covenants refer to the terms and conditions in a bond's indenture that place restrictions (**negative** or **restrictive covenants**) or certain requirements (**affirmative covenants**) on the issuer.

- While covenants protect bondholders by creating a binding framework for the repayment of debt obligations, they must offer management sufficient flexibility to run the business.
- Covenants provide only limited protection to investment-grade bondholders and slightly stronger protection to high-yield investors.
- Covenants tend to be stronger for bonds that are issued in weak economic times (to induce investors to purchase them).

Character

Character refers to the quality and integrity of management. When evaluating management's character, analysts should:

- Evaluate the suitability and reliability of management's strategy.
- Assess management's track record in executing strategies successfully, while keeping the companies they run clear of bankruptcy, restructuring and other distressed situations.
- Identify the use of aggressive accounting policies and/or tax strategies.
- Look for any history of fraud or malfeasance.
- Look for instances of poor treatment of bond holders in the past.

Ratios and Ratio Analysis

Profitability and Cash Flow Measures

- Earnings before interest, taxes, depreciation, and amortization (EBITDA)
- Funds from operations (FFO)
- Free cash flow before dividends
- Free cash flow after dividends

Leverage Ratios

- Debt / Capital
- Debt / EBITDA
- FFO / Debt

Coverage Ratios

- EBITDA / Interest expense
- EBIT / Interest expense

Issuer Liquidity

All other things remaining same, companies with ready access to liquidity represent lower credit risk. Generally speaking, issuer liquidity is a bigger factor when evaluating credit risk for high-yield companies than for investment grade companies.

Factors Affecting the Yield Spread on Corporate Bonds

This yield spread is composed of the liquidity premium and credit spread.

$$\boxed{\text{Yield spread} = \text{Liquidity premium} + \text{Credit spread}}$$

Yield spreads on corporate bonds are affected by the following:

- **Credit cycle:** Credit spreads widen (narrow) as the credit cycle deteriorates (improves). They are widest (tightest) at or near the bottom (top) of the credit cycle when financial markets believe that risk is high (low).
- **Broader economic conditions:** Investors demand a higher (lower) risk premium in relatively weak (strong) economic conditions.
- Credit spreads are narrow when broker-dealers bring sufficient capital to the market, but tend to widen when there is a reduction in broker-provided capital available for market-making purposes.
- **General market supply and demand:** Credit spreads tend to widen when there is an excess supply of new issues, and tend to narrow when there is excess demand for bonds.
- Financial performance of the issuer

Finally, note that yield spreads on low credit quality bonds tend to be wider that those on high credit quality bonds.

The Return Impact of a Change in the Credit Spread

For small, instantaneous changes in the yield spread, the return impact (i.e., the percentage change in price, including accrued interest) can be estimated using the following formula:

$$\boxed{\text{Return impact} \approx -\text{Modified duration} \times \Delta\text{Spread}}$$

For larger changes in the yield spread, we must also incorporate the (positive) impact of convexity into our estimate of the return impact:

$$\boxed{\text{Return impact} \approx -(\text{MDur} \times \Delta\text{Spread}) + (1/2 \times \text{Convexity} \times \Delta\text{Spread}^2)}$$

- Longer-duration bonds are generally more sensitive to changes in the yield spread.
- Longer-maturity bonds entail more uncertainly than shorter-maturity bonds This is why **spread curves** (also referred to as **credit curves**) are generally upward sloping.

Evaluating the Credit of High-Yield Corporate Debt

High-yield corporate bonds (also referred to as **non-investment-grade corporate bonds** or **junk bonds**) are those that are rated below Baa3/BBB- by the credit rating agencies. High yield bonds entail a greater risk of default than investment grade bonds. As a result, credit analysts pay more attention to recovery analysis (or loss severity in the event of default) when evaluating these bonds.

Special Considerations when Analyzing High Yield Corporate Bonds

- **Liquidity:** While having cash or the ability to generate cash is important for all debt issuers, it is absolutely critical for high-yield debt issuers. High-yield companies only have access to limited sources of liquidity.

- **Financial projections:** Analysts should forecast earnings and cash flows several years into the future to assess whether the issuer's credit profile will remain stable, improve, or deteriorate. Analysts should also incorporate required capital expenditures, changes in working capital, and realistic "stress" scenarios in their analysis to identify any vulnerabilities in the business.

- **Debt structure:** High-yield companies usually have many layers of debt in their capital structures, with each layer having a different seniority ranking and hence, entailing a different potential recovery rate in the event of default. To evaluate the credit risk of a high-yield issuer with many layers of debt in its capital structure, analysts must calculate leverage for each level of the debt structure.

  High-yield companies with a relatively high proportion of secured debt (typically bank debt) in their capital structure are said to be "top-heavy." It is generally difficult for such companies to take on more debt in the event of financial stress because of (1) the stringent covenants associated with bank debt and (2) the relatively short maturity of bank debt relative to other forms of debt. Both these factors contribute to a higher risk of default for these companies and lower recovery rates for less secured creditors.

- **Corporate structure:** High-yield investors need to assess whether debt has been issued by the parent or its subsidiary, and how cash can move between the two. They should compute leverage ratios for each of the debt-issuing entities individually, and on a consolidated basis.

- **Covenant analysis:** Analysis of covenants takes on even more significance for high-yield bonds than investment-grade bonds. Some of the important covenants for high-yield issuers are:
  - Change of control put
  - Restricted payments:
  - Limitations on liens and additional indebtedness
  - Restricted versus unrestricted subsidiaries

It is also important to analyze covenants in a high-yield issuer's bank credit agreements. Bank covenants can be more restrictive than bond covenants.

Equity-like Approach to High-Yield Analysis

An equity-like approach can be useful for analyzing high-yield bonds. One such approach is to calculate multiples (e.g., EV/EBITDA and debt/EBITDA) and compare them across several issuers. For a given issuer, if there is only a small difference between the EV/EBITDA and debt/EBITDA ratios, it indicates that the issuer has a relatively small "equity cushion," which means higher risk for bond investors.

Evaluating the Credit of Sovereign Debt

Sovereign debt refers to debt issued by national governments. Credit analysis of sovereign bonds entails an evaluation of the government's ability and willingness to service its debt. An assessment of willingness to service debt is particularly important for sovereign debt as bondholders typically have no legal recourse if a national government is unwilling to meet its debt obligations.

Credit rating agencies typically assign a local currency debt rating and a foreign currency debt rating to sovereign issuers. This is because defaults on foreign currency-denominated sovereign bonds have tended to exceed defaults on local currency-denominated sovereign bonds.

Evaluating the Credit of Municipal Debt

Non-sovereign (or **sub-sovereign**) government entities include local and state governments as well as various agencies and authorities created by them.

General Obligation (GO) Bonds

GO bonds are unsecured bonds issued with the full faith and credit of the issuing entity, and are supported by the taxing authority of the issuer. Credit analysis of GO bonds is quite similar to that of sovereign bonds.

Revenue Bonds

These are issued for financing a specific project (e.g., a toll road, bridge, hospital, etc.) and are serviced with revenues generated from the project. Therefore, analysis of revenue bonds is similar to analysis of corporate bonds. It focuses on the cash-generating ability of the particular project and on the economic base supporting the project (sources of finance).

A key ratio used to analyze revenue-backed municipal bonds is the **debt service coverage ratio (DSCR)**. The higher the ratio, the lower the credit risk of the bond.

STUDY SESSION 15: DERIVATIVES

DR

DERIVATIVE MARKETS AND INSTRUMENTS
Cross-Reference to CFA Institute Assigned Reading #45

A **derivative** is a financial contract or instrument that derives its value from the value of something else (known as the **underlying**). The underlying on which a derivative is based can be an asset (e.g., stocks and bonds), an index (e.g., S&P 500), or something else (e.g., interest rates).

Exchange-Traded versus Over-the-Counter Derivatives

Exchange-Traded Derivatives Markets

Exchange-traded derivatives (e.g., futures contracts) are traded on specialized derivatives exchanges or other exchanges.

- **Standardization** facilitates the creation of a more liquid market for derivatives. However, it comes at the cost of flexibility.
    - Liquidity is a function of (1) trading interest and (2) level of uncertainty. Little trading interest and a high level of uncertainty lead to low liquidity.
- **Market makers** and **speculators** play an important role in these markets.
    - Market makers stand ready to buy at one (low) price and sell at another (high) price in order to lock in small short-term profits (known as **scalping**).
    - Speculators are willing to take educated risks to earn profits.
- The exchange is responsible for clearing and settlement through its **clearinghouse**. The clearinghouse is able to provide a credit guarantee to market participants.
- Exchange markets also have transparency, i.e., information regarding all transactions is disclosed to regulatory bodies. This regulation does bring certain benefits, but also means a loss of privacy.

Over-the-Counter (OTC) Derivatives Markets

OTC derivatives (e.g., forward contracts) do not trade in a centralized market; instead, they trade in an *informal* market. OTC derivatives are customized instruments. Dealers (typically banks) play an important role in OTC markets as they buy and sell these customized derivatives to market participants, and then look to hedge (or lay off) their risks. Due to the customized nature of OTC derivatives, dealers are typically unable to find identical offsetting transactions. Therefore, they turn to similar transactions to lay off some of the risk, and use their specialized knowledge and complex models to manage any remaining exposure.

- Note that there is a tendency to think that the OTC market is less liquid than the exchange market. This is not necessarily true.
- OTC derivative markets are less regulated than exchange-traded derivative markets.
- OTC markets offer more privacy and flexibility than exchange markets.

Forward Commitments versus Contingent Claims

A **forward commitment** is a legally binding **obligation** to engage in a certain transaction in the spot market at a future date at terms agreed upon today. Forward commitments can be made on exchange-traded derivatives and over-the-counter derivatives.

- **Forwards** are customized and private contracts between two parties, where one party has an obligation to buy an asset, and the counterparty has an obligation to sell the asset, at a price and future date that is agreed upon signing of the contract.

- **Futures** are standardized derivative contracts where one party, the buyer, will purchase an underlying asset from the other party, the seller, at a later date at a price agreed upon contract initiation.
- A **swap** is an over-the-counter derivative contract in which two parties agree to exchange a series of cash flows whereby one party pays a variable series that will be determined by an underlying asset or rate, and the counterparty pays either 1) a variable series determined by a different underlying asset or rate or 2) a fixed series.

A **contingent claim** is a derivative in which the outcome or payoff is determined by the outcome or payoff of an underlying asset, conditional on some event occurring.

- **Options** are contingent claims because their payoffs depend on the underlying's value in the future. Options are derivative instruments that give their holders the choice (not the obligation) to buy or sell the underlying from, or to the seller (writer) of the option. Options can be customized, over-the-counter contracts, or standardized, exchange-traded contracts.
- A **credit derivative** is a contract that transfers credit risk from one party (the credit protection buyer) to another party (the credit protection seller), where the latter protects the former against a specific credit loss. Credit derivatives include credit default swaps (CDS), total return swaps, credit spread options, and credit-linked notes.
- An **asset-backed security (ABS)** is a derivative in which a portfolio of debt instruments is pooled, and claims are issued on the portfolio in the form of tranches, which have different priorities of claims on the payments that come in from the pool of debt securities.

Purposes and Benefits of Derivatives

- Risk allocation, transfer, and management
- Information discovery
- Operational advantages
- Market efficiency

Criticisms and Misuses of Derivatives

- Destabilization and systematic risk
- Speculation and gambling
- Complexity

Arbitrage

Arbitrage opportunities exist whenever similar assets or combinations of assets are selling for different prices. Arbitrageurs exploit these opportunities and trade on mispricings until they are eliminated and asset prices converge to their "correct" levels. Arbitrage plays an important role in the study of derivatives. It is an important feature of efficient markets because it helps:

1. Determine prices
2. Improve market efficiency

BASICS OF DERIVATIVE PRICING AND VALUATION
Cross-Reference to CFA Institute Assigned Reading #46

Pricing the Underlying

The **price** or **value** of a financial asset is determined as the present value of expected future price plus (minus) any benefits (costs) of holding the asset, discounted at a rate appropriate for the risk assumed.

$$S_0 = \left[\frac{E(S_T)}{(1 + r + \lambda)^T} \right] - \theta + \gamma$$

- The required rate of return includes the risk-free rate and a risk premium.

The Principal of Arbitrage

Arbitrage and Derivatives

When the underlying is combined with the derivative to create a perfectly hedged portfolio, all of the price risk is eliminated and the position should earn the risk-free rate.

Long asset + Short derivative = Long risk-free asset (lending)

Long asset + Short risk-free asset (borrowing) = Long derivative

Short derivative + Short risk-free asset (borrowing) = Short asset

Risk Aversion, Risk Neutrality, and Arbitrage-Free Pricing

- Derivative pricing models discount the expected payoff of the derivative at the risk-free rate rather than the risk-free rate plus a risk premium.
- Further, the expected payoff is calculated based on what are known as **risk-neutral probabilities** (not actual or true probabilities of possible outcomes).
- While the risk aversion of investors is relevant to pricing assets, it is not relevant to pricing derivatives. As such, derivatives pricing is sometimes called **risk-neutral pricing**.

Limits to Arbitrage

- Significant transaction costs
- Large capital requirements
- The possibility of additional capital being required down the line
- Some assets possibly difficult to short
- Modeling risk

Derivatives Pricing versus Valuation

- **Price**, as it relates to forwards, futures, and swaps (note that options are not a problem in this regard), refers to the fixed price (that is agreed upon at contract initiation) at which the underlying transaction will take place in the future. These securities do not require an outlay of cash at contract initiation, so there is no concept of a price being paid at the beginning.
- The **value** of these contracts fluctuate in response to changes in the price of the underlying.

Forward Contracts

A forward is a contract between two parties, where one (the long position) has the **obligation** to buy, and the other (the short position) has an **obligation** to sell an underlying asset at a fixed forward price (that established at the inception of the contract) at a future date.

- Typically, no cash changes hands at inception.
- The long position benefits when the price of the underlying asset increases, while the short benefits when the price of the underlying asset falls.
- If the party that is adversely affected by price movements defaults on its commitment, the counterparty with the favorable position faces default risk.
- Forwards are a zero-sum game—one party's gain is the other party's loss.

Pricing and Valuation of Forward Contracts

The price of a forward contract is the fixed price or rate at which the underlying transaction will occur at contract expiration. The forward price is agreed upon at initiation of the forward contract. Pricing a forward contract means determining this forward price.

The value of a forward contract is the amount that a counterparty would need to pay, or would expect to receive, to get out of its (already-assumed) forward position.

Valuing a Forward Contract at Expiration (t = T)

$$V_T(0,T) = S_T - F(0,T)$$

Forward Contract Payoffs at Expiration

	$S_T > F(0,T)$	$S_T < F(0,T)$
Long position	$S_T - F(0,T)$ (Positive payoff)	$S_T - F(0,T)$ (Negative payoff)
Short position	$-[S_T - F(0,T)]$ (Negative payoff)	$-[S_T - F(0,T)]$ (Positive payoff)

Valuing a Forward Contract at Initiation (t = 0)

$$V_0(0,T) = S_0 - [F(0,T)/(1+r)^T] = 0$$

No-Arbitrage Forward Price

$$F(0,T) = S_0(1+r)T$$

If the underlying asset entails benefits/costs:

$$F(0,T) = (S_0 - \gamma + \theta)(1+r)^T; \text{ or } F(0,T) = S_0(1+r)^T - (\gamma - \theta)(1+r)^T$$

- The risk premium on the asset does not directly appear in determining the price of a forward.
- Although the forward price is fixed for a particular forward contract, a new contract calling for delivery of the same asset at the same point in time will have a different forward price (depending on the current spot price).

Valuing a Forward Contract During its Life

$$V_t(0,T) = S_t - [F(0,T)/(1+r)^{T-t}]$$

If the underlying asset entails benefits/costs:

$$V_t(0,T) = S_t - (\gamma - \theta)(1+r)^t - [F(0,T)/(1+r)^{T-t}]$$

Value of a Forward Contract

Time	Long Position Value	Short Position Value
At initiation	Zero, as the contract is priced to prevent arbitrage	Zero, as the contract is priced to prevent arbitrage
During life of the contract	$S_t - \left[\dfrac{F(0,T)}{(1+r)^{T-t}}\right]$	$\left[\dfrac{F(0,T)}{(1+r)^{T-t}}\right] - S_t$
At expiration	$S_T - F(0,T)$	$F(0,T) - S_T$

Forward Contracts on Interest Rates (Forward Rate Agreements)

A **forward rate agreement (FRA)** is a forward contract where the underlying is an interest rate (usually LIBOR). Think about the long position in an FRA as the party that has committed to take a hypothetical loan, and the short as the party that has committed to give out a hypothetical loan, at the FRA rate.

- If LIBOR at FRA expiration is *greater* than the FRA rate, the long benefits.
- If LIBOR at FRA expiration is *lower* than the FRA rate, the short benefits.

A borrower (who would like to lock in a borrowing rate) would take a long position on an FRA, while a lender (who would like to lock in a rate of return) would take a short position on an FRA.

Pricing a Forward Rate Agreement

The price of an FRA (forward price) represents the interest rate at which the long (short) position has the obligation to borrow (lend) funds for a specified period (term of the underlying hypothetical loan) starting at FRA expiration.

- Pricing an FRA is a simple exercise of determining the forward rate consistent with two (given) spot rates.
- Essentially, taking the long position on an FRA is equivalent to holding a longer-term Eurodollar time deposit and at the same time shorting (or owing) a shorter-term Eurodollar time deposit.

Futures Contracts

Characteristics of Futures Contracts

- Futures contracts are **standardized**.
  - The futures price is the only term set by the two parties involved in the contract; all other terms are established by the exchange including the expiration date of the contract, the underlying, the mode of settlement, and contract size.

- In the futures market, the **initial margin** is the amount that must be deposited by each party—the long and the short, into her account to be able to trade in the market.
- The **maintenance margin** is the minimum balance that must be maintained in an investor's account to avoid a **margin call** (a call for more funds to be deposited in the account).
- **Marking-to-market** is the process of adjusting the balance in an investor's futures account to reflect the change in value of her futures position since the last mark-to-market adjustment was conducted.
- The **clearinghouse** is the counterparty to every trade on the exchange. It acts as the short for every long position, and as the long for every short position.
- Taking the position as the counterparty to every trade combined with the ability to enforce periodic mark-to-market adjustments for all market participants makes for a very efficient mechanism for controlling default risk.
- Some futures contracts have **price limits**. These limits are set by the exchange to restrict the change in the settlement price of a contract from one day to the next.

Forward Prices versus Futures Prices

- If underlying asset prices are positively correlated with interest rates, the futures price will be higher than the forward price.
- If underlying asset prices are negatively correlated with interest rates, the forward price will be higher than the futures price.
- If interest rates are constant, forwards and futures would have the same prices.
- If futures prices are uncorrelated with interest rates, forwards and futures would have the same prices.
- Forward and futures prices would be different if the volatility of the forward price is different from the volatility of the futures price.

Swaps

A swap is an agreement to exchange a series of cash flows at periodic **settlement dates** over a certain period of time (known as the **tenor** of the swap).

Plain-Vanilla Interest Rate Swaps

- A plain-vanilla interest rate swap involves the exchange of fixed interest payments for floating-rate payments.
- The party that wants to receive floating-rate payments and agrees to make fixed-rate payments is known as the **pay-fixed** side of the swap or the **fixed-rate payer/floating-rate receiver**.
- The party that wants to receive fixed payments and make floating-rate payments is the **pay-floating** side of the swap or the **floating-rate payer/fixed-rate receiver**.
- There is no exchange of notional principal at initiation or expiration of the swap. The notional principal is simply used to determine the interest payment on each leg of the swap.
- Interest payments are not exchanged in full at each settlement date. Interest payments are netted, and the party that owes more in interest at a particular settlement date makes a payment equal to the difference to the other.
- As with forward contracts, there is an element of counterparty credit risk in swaps as the party that owes the lower amount can default.
- The floating rate is usually quoted in terms of LIBOR plus a spread. The floating rate for any period is known at the beginning of the period, while the settlement payment is actually made at the end of each period.

$$\text{Net fixed} - \text{Rate payment}_t = [\text{Swap fixed rate} - (\text{LIBOR}_{t-1} + \text{Spread})] \times (\text{No. of days}/360) \times \text{Notional principal}$$

Pricing versus Valuation of Swaps

- At the initiation of the swap, the **swap fixed rate** is set at a level at which the present value of the floating-rate payments (based on the current term structure of interest rates) equals the present value of fixed-rate payments so that there is zero value to either party. This swap fixed rate therefore represents the **price** of the swap.
- Over the term of the swap, as there are changes in the term structure of interest rates, the **value** of the swap will fluctuate.
  - ○ If interest rates increase after swap initiation, the present value of floating-rate payments (based on the new term structure) will exceed the present value of fixed-rate payments (based on the swap fixed rate).
    - ■ The swap will have a positive value for the fixed-rate payer (floating-rate receiver).
    - ■ The swap will be an asset to the fixed-rate payer and a liability for the floating-rate payer.
  - ○ If interest rates decrease after swap initiation, the present value of floating-rate payments will be lower than the present value of fixed-rate payments.
    - ■ The swap will have a positive value for the floating-rate payer (fixed-rate receiver).
    - ■ In this case, the swap will be an asset to the floating-rate payer and a liability for the fixed-rate payer.

Swaps and Forward Contracts

A swap essentially combines a series of forward contracts into a single transaction. For example, a plain vanilla interest rate swap is a combination of FRAs, where one FRA expires on each settlement date over the tenor of the swap, and the FRA rate (forward price) for each FRA equals the swap fixed rate (swap price).

Swaps and Bonds

The payoffs of the pay-fixed side of an interest rate swap are similar to those of a strategy of issuing a fixed-rate bond (on which fixed payments must be made) and using the proceeds to purchase a floating-rate bond (which will return floating-interest payments). On the other hand, the payoffs of the pay-floating side are similar to issuing a floating-rate bond and using the proceeds to purchase a fixed-rate bond.

- If interest rates increase, the fixed-rate payer benefits as there is a positive difference between her (floating-rate) receipts and (fixed-rate) payments.
- If interest rates decrease, the fixed-rate payer loses out as there is a negative difference between (floating-rate) receipts and (fixed-rate) payments.

Options

European versus American Options

- A **European** option is one that can only be exercised at the option's expiration date.
- An **American** option can be exercised at any point in time up to, and including, the option's expiration date.

Moneyness and Exercise Value

Moneyness refers to whether an option is in-the-money or out-of-the-money.

- An option is in-the-money when immediate exercise of the option will generate a positive payoff for the holder.
- An option is out-of-the-money when immediate exercise will generate a negative payoff for the holder.
- An option is at-the-money when immediate exercise will result in neither a positive nor a negative payoff for the holder.

The intrinsic value or exercise value of an option is the amount an option is in-the-money by. It is the amount that would be received by the option holder if he were to exercise the option immediately. An option has zero intrinsic value if it is at- or out-of-the money.

Call Options

- A call option gives the **holder/buyer** the **right** to **buy** (or call) the underlying asset for the given exercise price at the expiration date of the option.
- A call option **writer/seller** has the **obligation** to **sell** the asset to the holder of the call option for the given exercise price, should the option holder choose to exercise the option.

Call Option Payoffs

Option Position	Descriptions	Payoff	
		$S_T > X$	$S_T < X$
		Option holder exercises the option	Option holder does not exercise the option
Call option holder	Choice to buy the underlying asset for X	$S_T - X$	0
Call option writer	Obligation to sell the underlying asset for X if the option holder chooses to exercise the option	$-(S_T - X)$	0

$$\text{Intrinsic value of call} = \text{Max}\,[0, (S_t - X)]$$

Moneyness and Exercise Value of a Call Option

Moneyness	Current Market Price (S_t) versus Exercise Price (X)	Intrinsic Value Max $[0, (S_t - X)]$
In-the-money	S_t is greater than X	$S_t - X$
At-the-money	S_t equals X	0
Out-of-the-money	S_t is less than X	0

Put Options

- A **put option** gives the **holder/buyer** the **right** to **sell** (or put) the underlying asset for the given exercise price at the option's expiration date.
- A put option **writer/seller** has the **obligation** to **buy** the asset from the put option holder at the option's expiration date for the given exercise price, should the holder choose to exercise the option.

Put Option Payoffs

Option Position	Descriptions	Payoff	
		$S_T < X$	$S_T > X$
		Option holder exercises the option	Option holder does not exercise the option
Put option holder	Choice to sell the underlying asset for X	$X - S_T$	0
Put option writer	Obligation to buy the underlying asset for X if the option holder chooses to exercise the option	$-(X - S_T)$	0

Intrinsic value of a put option = Max $[0, (X - S_t)]$.

Moneyness and Exercise Value of a Put Option

Moneyness	Current Market Price (S_t) versus Exercise Price (X)	Intrinsic Value Max $[0, (X - S_t)]$
In-the-money	S_t is less than X	$X - S_t$
At-the-money	S_t equals X	0
Out-of-the-money	S_t is greater than X	0

Put-Call Parity

$$c_0 + \frac{X}{(1 + R_F)^T} = p_0 + S_0$$

A **fiduciary call**, which is composed of (1) a call option on a stock and (2) a zero-coupon riskless bond that pays X at maturity (face value equals X) must have the same value as a **protective put**, which is composed of (1) a European put option on a stock and (2) a share of the same stock as long as:

- The call and put option, and the zero-coupon bond, have the same time to maturity/expiration (T).
- The exercise price of the call and the put, and the face value of the zero-coupon bond, are the same (X).
- The call and the put are options on the same underlying asset as the one held in Portfolio B (S). This asset makes no cash payments and has no carrying costs.
- The call and put can only be exercised at expiration i.e., they are European options.

Combining Portfolios to Make Synthetic Securities

Strategy	Consisting of	Value	Equals	Strategy	Consisting of	Value
Fiduciary call	Long call + Long bond	$c_0 + \dfrac{X}{(1 + R_F)^T}$	=	Protective put	Long put + Long underlying asset	$p_0 + S_0$
Long call	Long call	c_0	=	Synthetic call	Long put + Long underlying asset + Short bond	$p_0 + S_0 - \dfrac{X}{(1 + R_F)^T}$
Long put	Long put	p_0	=	Synthetic put	Long call + Short underlying asset + Long bond	$c_0 + S_0 - \dfrac{X}{(1 + R_F)^T}$
Long underlying asset	Long underlying asset	S_0	=	Synthetic underlying asset	Long call + Long bond + Short put	$c_0 + \dfrac{X}{(1 + R_F)^T} - p_0$
Long bond	Long bond	$\dfrac{X}{(1 + R_F)^T}$	=	Synthetic bond	Long put + Long underlying asset + Short call	$p_0 + S_0 - c_0$

Factors that Affect the Value of an Option

Value of the Underlying

- The greater (lower) the value of the underlying, the greater (lower) the exercise value of the call option, and the greater its price/value.
- The lower (greater) the value of the underlying, the greater (lower) the exercise value of the put option, and the greater its price/value.
- Note that the value of the underlying serves as an upper boundary on the price of American and European call options.

Exercise Price

- For call options, the higher the exercise price, the *lower* the exercise value of the option.
- For put options, the higher the exercise price, the *higher* the intrinsic value.
- The maximum value of a European put option equals the present value of its exercise price, $X/(1 + RFR)^T$.

Risk-Free Rate

- The value of a call option is *directly* related to the risk-free rate.
- The value of a put option is *inversely* related to the risk-free rate.

Time to Expiration

- The value of a European call option is *directly* related to the time to expiration.
- The value of a European put option can be either *directly* or *inversely* related to the time to expiration. Typically, the direct effect holds, but the inverse effect can prevail if a longer time to expiration comes with a higher risk-free rate, and if the option is deep in-the-money.

Volatility

- Greater volatility in the price of the underlying asset *increases* the value of both calls and puts.
- At any point in time before expiration, an option is worth at least as much as its exercise value. However, on top of its exercise value, there is also an element of speculative value in the option to account for the possibility that the underlying asset's price could move favorably over the remaining time to expiration and result in a payoff greater than the current exercise value. This speculative value is known as the time value of an option, which increases with volatility but decreases as the option nears expiration (known as time value decay). At expiration, no time value remains, and the option is worth its exercise value.

Payments from the Underlying and the Cost of Carry

- For call option holders, benefits from the underlying, which cause a decline in the value of the underlying, are a negative because they lead to a decline in the exercise value. For put option holders, on the other hand, benefits from the underlying are a positive (as the value of the underlying falls).
- Carrying costs have the opposite effect. They are a positive for call options, but a negative for puts.

Lowest Prices of European Calls and Puts

- The lowest value of a European call is the greater of (1) zero and (2) the value of the underlying minus the present value of the exercise price.
- The lowest value of a European put is the greater of (1) zero and (2) the present value of the exercise price minus the value of the underlying.

Put-Call Forward Parity

$$p_0 - c_0 = \frac{[X - F(0,T)]}{(1 + R_F)^T}$$

Assumptions

- The price of the forward contract on the underlying is given by $F(0,T)$.
- The put and the call options expire at the same time as the forward contract.
- X represents the exercise price of the call and put options.
- The options are European options.
- The options and the forward contract are based on the same underlying asset.

Payoffs

	Outcome at T	
	$S_T < X$ **Put Expires In-the-Money** **Call Expires Out-of-the-Money**	$S_T > X$ **Call Expires In-the-Money** **Put Expires Out-of-the-Money**
Protective put with forward contract		
Risk-free bond	$F(0,T)$	$F(0,T)$
Forward contract	$S_T - F(0,T)$	$S_T - F(0,T)$
Long put	$X - S_T$	0
Total	X	S_T
Protective put with asset		
Asset	S_T	S_T
Long put	$X - S_T$	0
Total	X	S_T
Fiduciary call		
Call	0	$S_T - X$
Risk-free bond	X	X
Total	X	S_T

The One-Period Binomial Model

In the one-period binomial model, the price of the underlying stock starts off at a given level, S, and can either:

- Move up by a factor of u to a new price, S^+, one period later with a probability of q; or
- Move down by a factor of d to a new price, S, one period later with a probability of $1 - q$.
- Note that q and $1 - q$ are actual or real probabilities of the up and down movements respectively.

$$S^+ = Su$$
$$c^+ = \text{Max}(0, S^+ - X)$$

$$S$$
$$c = ?$$

$$S^- = Sd$$
$$c^- = \text{Max}(0, S^- - X)$$

$$t = 0 \qquad t = T$$

Value of a Call Option

$$c = \frac{\pi c^+ + (1 - \pi)c^-}{(1 + r)}$$

where

$$\pi = \frac{(1 + r - d)}{(u - d)}$$

The value of an option under this approach is computed by discounting the expected value of the payoff (calculated using **risk-neutral probabilities**) at the risk-free rate.

American Option Pricing

- Minimum value of an American call option = Max $[0, (S_0 - X/(1 + RFR)^T]$
- Minimum value of an American put option = Max $[0, (X - S_0)]$

American Call Options

- There is no reason to exercise an American call option on an asset that offers no benefits before expiration.
- However, if the asset does offer benefits, early exercise of an American call option may be warranted.
- If there are significant costs of carry on the underlying, there is less of a reason to exercise the American call option early.

American Puts

- It would be beneficial to exercise an American put prior to expiration when a company is in or nearing bankruptcy, and its stock price is close to zero.
- Dividends and coupon interest discourage early exercise for American puts.
- Carrying costs on the underlying encourage exercise for American puts.

STUDY SESSION 16: ALTERNATIVE INVESTMENTS

AI

INTRODUCTION TO ALTERNATIVE INVESTMENTS
Cross-Reference to CFA Institute Assigned Reading #47

Methods of Investing in Alternative Investments

- **Fund investing** involves investors contributing assets to a fund, with management then selecting and managing fund assets.
- In **co-investing**, an investor contributes capital to the general fund but also has rights to purchase a position in the same assets.
- **Direct investing** describes an investor purchasing a stake in an asset without the benefit of a special vehicle such as a fund.

Investment and Compensation Structures

- Particularly in hedge funds and private equity funds, GPs do not earn a performance fee until the LPs have received the amount of their initial investment and the total return has exceeded the **hurdle rate** specified in the LPA.
- The LPA may include a **catch-up clause** allowing GPs to retain all profits above the hurdle rate until their performance fee has been received.
- Every dollar above the hurdle rate after the GPs earn their performance fee accrues to the GPs and LPs in some proportion.
- A **waterfall** represents the method in which LPs and GPs are compensated.
  - **American waterfall** describes a deal-by-deal process that allows the GP to receive compensation before the LPs have received back their investment and the hurdle rate of return.
  - **European waterfall** describes a whole-of-fund process where GPs do not receive compensation until investors have received return of their investment and the hurdle rate has been met.
- If the LPA contains a **clawback provision**, LPs will reclaim part of the GP's performance fee paid against performance that fails to materialize.

Hedge Fund Characteristics

- Hedge fund investors may be subjected to **extended lockup periods** (i.e., they may not sell the investment for some period) and minimum periods to serve notice of redemption.
- Low correlation with traditional assets makes it difficult to measure performance against a benchmark, frequently leading to use of custom benchmarks.
- Hedge fund risk is sometimes measured by maximum drawdown; that is, the period of largest negative returns.

Hedge Fund Strategies

- Equity hedge strategies
  - Market neutral
  - Fundamental L/S growth
  - Fundamental value
  - Short biased
  - Sector specific
- Event-driven strategies
  - Merger arbitrage
  - Distressed/restructuring

- o Special situations
- o Activist
- Relative value strategies
  - o Convertible bond arbitrage
  - o General fixed income
  - o Asset-backed, mortgage-backed, and high yield
  - o Volatility
  - o Multi-strategy
- Macro and CTA strategies

Private Equity

- **Leveraged buyout (LBO)** strategies typically involve taking a public company private or taking over an established private company. A significant amount of debt typically will be used, with assets of the target company serving as collateral for the loans to decrease the capital cost for the strategy.
- **Venture capital (VC)** describes investment in or financing for private growth companies ranging from idea inception to acquisition or initial public offering (IPO) launch.
- **Private investment in public equities (PIPEs)** describes publicly traded company use of private equity.

Natural Resources

Commodities

Futures price = Spot price $(1 + r)$ + Storage costs − Convenience yield

- **Contango** exists when convenience yield is low or does not exist, and futures prices may be higher than the spot price.
- **Backwardation** exists when convenience yield is high, and futures prices are lower than the spot price.
- Contango lowers the yield of a long investor and enhances the return to a short investor.

Timberland and Farmland

- Timberland includes land owned or leased to earn returns it generates from crops and timber.
- Farmland consists of planted and harvested crops and permanent crops that grow on trees (e.g., nuts) or vines (e.g., grapes).

Real Estate

- Residential real estate includes single-family detached homes and multi-family attached units.
- A residential unit leased to a tenant or otherwise leased for a non-residential purpose is considered commercial real estate.
- Commercial real estate also includes office buildings, shopping centers, and warehouses.

Characteristics

- Typically requires a large capital investment.
- Is generally considered illiquid.
- Prices are often undiscoverable.

Listed (i.e., public) REITs provide investors with much greater liquidity, lower trading costs, and better transparency than owning physical real estate.

Mortgage-Backed Securities

- MBS structures expose investors to reinvestment risk when interest rates fall.
- When interest rates rise, duration of MBS rises.

Infrastructure Assets

- **Economic infrastructure assets** include transportation, ICT and utility and energy assets.
- **Social infrastructure assets** involve providing, maintaining, and operating services directed toward human activities (i.e., medical care, education, social welfare housing).
- **Brownfield investments** refer to investments in existing investable infrastructure assets.
- **Greenfield investments** refer to investments in infrastructure assets that are to be constructed.

As with private equity, infrastructure assets tend to have higher return and risk in the pre-build or early stages of development versus investment in later-stage projects (i.e., brownfield) with a history of cash flow.

Issues in Appraising Alternative Asset Performance

- The **Sharpe ratio** and the **Sortino ratio** do not capture the effects of correlation with the target pool of assets to diversify. They also fail to capture the effects of leverage on portfolio results.
- The **Treynor ratio** makes use of historical beta in its computation.
- The **Calmar ratio** divides compound annual return by maximum drawdown (MDD) to establish a measure of return relative to risk.

Private Equity and Real Estate Performance Appraisal Issues

- **MOIC** is the sum of total distributions to date and residual values of assets still on the books, divided by total invested capital.
  - MOIC ignores the time value of cash flow receipts and outflows but provides an easy scoring mechanism.
- Real estate managers also may be judged by actual rental income divided by the initial purchase price (i.e., **the capitalization rate** or **cap rate**).
- **Downside risk** also may be captured in the capital loss ratio, which measures the deals realized below cost net of any recoveries divided by total invested capital.

Hedge Fund Performance Appraisal Issues

- Leverage often contributes to the larger returns or losses earned by hedge funds, making it important to consider when looking at performance.
- Valuations reported by hedge funds may use market values or may require manager estimates of asset value.
- Adverse market conditions tend to attract more investor redemptions, which can severely stress a portfolio of illiquid positions as in a hedge fund.

AI

Calculating Fees and Returns

- A **waterfall provision** in a limited partnership (LP) agreement specifies how distributions of funds from the partnership are prioritized to the LPs before they are split with the general partners (GPs).
- **Fund management fees** based on AUM or otherwise set out are typically deducted from the fund regardless of any profit or positive return.
- **Incentive fees** will generally be paid to a fund manager after investors earn a hurdle rate (i.e.,preferred return) on invested capital.
  - A **hard hurdle rate** means the manager applies the incentive against the return in excess of the hurdle rate.
  - A **soft hurdle rate** means the manager apples the incentive against the entire return.
- A **high-water mark (HWM)** is the highest fund net-of-fees value reported for an investor. Many fee structures require the fund to recover losses and return to the HWM before manager incentives may be paid, thus preventing investors from paying twice for the same performance.
- LPs should also have a **clawback provision** in their agreement specifying recovery of incentive fees or carried interest received by the GPs should there be future shortfalls in the return of LP capital contributions or preferred return.

STUDY SESSION 17: PORTFOLIO MANAGEMENT (1)

PORTFOLIO MANAGEMENT: AN OVERVIEW
Cross-Reference to CFA Institute Assigned Reading #48

Importance of the Portfolio Perspective

- Portfolios of securities may offer equivalent expected returns with lower volatility of returns (lower risk) compared to individual securities.
- A simple measure of the value of diversification is the diversification ratio. It is the ratio of the standard deviation of an equal-weighted portfolio to the standard deviation of a randomly selected component of the portfolio. The lower the diversification ratio, the greater the risk reduction benefits of diversification, and the greater the portfolio effect.
- The composition of the portfolio (weight of each security held in the portfolio) is an important determinant of the overall level of risk inherent in the portfolio. By varying the weights of the individual securities, investors can arrive at a portfolio that offers the same return as an equally weighted portfolio, but with a lower standard deviation (risk).

Types of Investment Management Clients

Summary of Investment Needs by Client Type[1]

Client	Time Horizon	Risk Tolerance	Income Needs	Liquidity Needs
Individual investors	Varies by individual	Varies by individual	Varies by individual	Varies by individual
Defined benefit pension plans	Typically long-term	Typically quite high	High for mature funds; low for growing funds	Varies by maturity of the plan
Endowments and foundations	Very long-term	Typically high	To meet spending commitments	Typically quite low
Banks	Short-term	Quite low	To pay interest on deposits and operations expenses	High to meet repayment of deposits
Insurance companies	Short-term for property and casualty; long-term for life insurance companies	Typically quite low	Typically low	High to meet claims
Investment companies	Varies by fund	Varies by fund	Varies by fund	High to meet redemptions
Sovereign wealth funds	Varies by fund	Varies by fund	Varies by fund	Varies by fund

[1]Exhibit 17, Volume 5, CFA Program Curriculum 2022

Steps in the Portfolio Management Process

Planning

The planning step involves understanding the client's needs and constraints and developing an investment policy statement (IPS). The IPS is a written document that describes the objectives and constraints of the investor.

Execution

Asset allocation: The asset allocation of a portfolio refers to the distribution of investable funds between various asset classes (e.g., equities, fixed-income securities, alternative investments, etc.).

Security analysis: Analysts use their knowledge of various companies and the industry to identify investments that offer the most attractive risk return characteristics from within each asset class.

Portfolio construction: After determining the target asset allocation and conducting security analysis, the portfolio manager will construct the portfolio in line with the objectives outlined in the IPS.

Feedback

Portfolio monitoring and rebalancing: The portfolio must be regularly monitored. Changes in fundamental factors and client circumstances may require changes in the portfolio's composition. Rebalancing may be required when changes in security prices cause a significant change in weights of assets in the portfolio.

Performance measurement and reporting: This step involves measuring the performance of the portfolio relative to the benchmark stated in the IPS and reporting portfolio performance to the client.

Buy Side versus Sell Side

- A buy-side firm uses (buys) the services of sell-side firms.
- A sell-side firm is a broker/dealer that sells securities and provides independent investment research and recommendations to their clients (i.e., buy-side firms).

Active versus Passive Management

- Active managers aim to use fundamental research, quantitative research, or a combination of both to outperform either predetermined performance benchmarks.
- Passive managers attempt to replicate the returns of a market index.

Traditional versus Alternative Asset Managers

- Traditional managers generally focus on long-only equity, fixed-income, and multi-asset investment strategies, generating most of their revenues from asset-based management fees.
- Alternative asset managers, however, focus on hedge fund, private equity, and venture capital strategies, among others, while generating revenue from both management and performance fees (or "carried interest").

Ownership Structure

- The majority of asset management firms are privately owned, typically by individuals who either established their firms or play key roles in their firms' management. Privately owned firms are typically structured as limited liability companies or limited partnerships.
- Publicly traded asset managers have substantial assets under management. A prevalent ownership form in the industry is represented by asset management divisions of large,

PM

diversified financial services companies that offer asset management alongside insurance and banking services.

Asset Management Industry Trends

- Growth of passive investing.
- Use of "big data" in the investment process.
- Robo-advisers are an expanding wealth management channel.

Pooled Investments

Pooled investments are investments in securities issued by entities that represent ownership in the underlying assets held by those entities. These include:

- **Mutual funds and exchange traded funds,** in which investors can participate with a relatively small initial investment.
- **Hedge funds and private equity funds,** which may require a minimum investment of US$1 million or more.

Mutual Funds

Mutual funds pool money from several investors and invest these funds in a portfolio of securities.

- **Open-end funds** accept new investment funds and issue new shares at a value equal to the fund's net asset value per share at the time of investment. These funds also allow investors to redeem their investment in the fund at the prevailing net asset value per share.
- **Closed-end funds** accept no new investment money into fund. Shares in the fund are traded in the secondary market so new investors invest in the fund by purchasing shares in the market, and investors liquidate their holdings by selling the shares in the market. Unlike open-end funds, shares of closed-end funds can trade at a discount or premium to the net asset value per share, depending on the demand and supply of shares in the market.

The structure of open-end funds makes it easy for them to grow in size, but it does pose the following problems:

- The portfolio manager needs to manage cash inflows and outflows.
- An inflow of new investment requires the manager to find new investments.
- Funds need to keep cash for redemptions.

Closed-end funds do not face these problems, but as mentioned earlier, they cannot accept new investments.

Mutual funds may also be classified into:

- **Load funds** that charge a percentage fee for investing in the fund and/or for redemptions from the fund on top of an annual fee.
- **No-load funds** that only charge an annual fee based on a percentage of the fund's NAV.

PM

Types of Mutual Funds

- **Money market funds:** These invest in high-quality, short-term debt instruments. Money-market mutual funds can be divided into tax-free and taxable funds.
- **Bond funds:** These invest in individual bonds and sometimes preference shares as well. Unlike money-market mutual funds, they usually invest in longer term instruments.
- **Stock funds:** These invest in equities and equity indices. Stock mutual funds can be actively or passively managed.
- **Hybrid or balanced funds:** These invest in both bonds and equities.

Other Investment Products Compared with Mutual Funds

Exchange Traded Funds (ETFs)

- Investors in index mutual funds purchase shares directly from the fund, while investors in an ETF purchase shares from other investors (just like buying or selling shares of stock). Investors are allowed to short ETF shares and even purchase them on margin.
- ETFs have lower costs, but unlike index mutual funds, investors do incur brokerage costs when trading ETFs.
- ETFs are constantly traded throughout the business day. Each trade occurs at the prevailing market price at that time. All purchases and redemptions for a mutual fund for a given day occur at the end of a trading day, at the same price.
- ETFs pay out dividends, while index mutual funds usually reinvest dividends.
- The minimum required investment is usually smaller for an ETF.
- Unlike mutual funds, in which no consideration is given to the tax position of the investor, transactions in SMAs take into account the specific tax needs of the investor.
- The required minimum investment for an SMA is usually much higher than for a mutual fund.

Hedge Funds

Hedge funds are private investment vehicles that typically use leverage, derivatives, and long and short investment strategies. Their salient features, including short selling, absolute returns, leverage, low correlations, and fee structures, are discussed at length in the alternative investments section.

Private Equity and Venture Capital Funds

Unlike most traditional asset managers that trade in public securities, private equity and venture firms often take a "hands-on" approach to their portfolio companies through a combination of financial engineering (e.g., realizing expense synergies, changing capital structures), installment of executive management and board members, and significant contributions to the development of a target company's business strategy.

As with most alternative funds, the majority of private equity and venture capital funds are structured as limited partnerships. These limited partnership agreements exist between the fund manager, called the general partner (GP), and the fund's investors, called limited partners (LPs). The funds generate revenue through management fees, transaction fees, carried interest, and investment income.

PORTFOLIO RISK AND RETURN: PART I
Cross-Reference to CFA Institute Assigned Reading #49

Measures of Return

Holding period return is simply the return earned on an investment over a single specified period of time.

$$R = \frac{P_T + D_T}{P_0} - 1$$

Holding period returns may also be calculated for more than one period by compounding single period returns:

$$R = [(1 + R_1) \times (1 + R_2) \times \ldots \times (1 + R_n)] - 1$$

The **arithmetic or mean return** is a simple average of all holding period returns.

- Arithmetic return is easy to calculate and has known statistical properties such as standard deviation, which is used to evaluate the dispersion of observed returns.
- The arithmetic mean return is biased upwards as it assumes that the amount invested at the beginning of each period is the same. This bias is particularly severe if holding period returns are a mix of both positive and negative returns.

$$R = \frac{R_{i1} + R_{i2} + \ldots + R_{iT}}{T} = \frac{1}{T} \sum_{t=1}^{T} R_{iT}$$

The **geometric mean return** accounts for compounding of returns, and does not assume that the amount invested in each period is the same.

- The geometric mean is lower than the arithmetic mean (due to the effects of compounding) unless there is no variation in returns, in which case they are equal.

$$R = \{[(1 + R_1) \times (1 + R_2) \times \ldots \times (1 + R_n)]^{1/n}\} - 1$$

The **money-weighted return** accounts for the amount of money invested in each period and provides information on the return earned on the actual amount invested.

- The money-weighted return equals the internal rate of return of an investment.
- A drawback of the money-weighted return is that it does not allow for return comparisons between different individuals or different investment opportunities.

The **time-weighted rate of return** measures the compounded rate of growth of an investment over a stated measurement period. In contrast to the money-weighted return, the time-weighted return:

1. Is not affected by cash withdrawals or contributions to the portfolio.
2. Averages the holding period returns over time.

- The time-weighted rate of return is preferred because it is not affected by the timing and amount of cash inflows and outflows.
- Decisions regarding contributions and withdrawals from a portfolio are usually made by clients. Since these decisions are not typically in investment managers' hands, it would be inappropriate to evaluate their performance based on money-weighted returns.
- If a manager does have discretion over withdrawals and contributions of funds in a portfolio, money-weighted return might be a more appropriate measure of portfolio performance.
- If funds are deposited into the investment portfolio prior to a period of superior (poor) performance, money-weighted return will be higher (lower) than time-weighted return.

If the portfolio experiences frequent addition and/or withdrawal of funds, the time-weighted rate of return can be estimated by valuing the portfolio at frequent, regular intervals, particularly if additions and withdrawals are unrelated to market movements.

If a portfolio is valued daily over the course of a year, the time-weighted rate of return can be calculated as:

$$(1 + r_1) \times (1 + r_2) \times \ldots \times (1 + r_{365}) - 1 \text{ where r} = \text{daily holding period returns.}$$

If we have annual returns data, the annualized time-weighted return can be calculated as the geometric mean of N annual returns, as follows:

$$rTW = [(1 + r_1) \times (1 + r_2) \times \ldots \times (1 + r_N)]^{1/N} - 1$$

Annualized returns are calculated to make comparisons across investment instruments with different maturities.

- It is assumed that returns earned over short investment horizons can be replicated over the year.

$$r_{annual} = (1 + r_{period})^n - 1$$

The **return on a portfolio** is simply the weighted average of the returns on individual assets. For example, the return of a two-asset portfolio can be calculated as:

$$R_p = w_1 R_1 + w_2 R_2$$

Other Return Measures and Their Applications

Gross versus Net Returns

- Gross returns are calculated before deductions for management expenses, custodial fees, taxes and other expenses that are not directly linked to the generation of returns.
- Net returns deduct all managerial and administrative expenses that reduce an investor's return. Investors are primarily concerned with net returns.

PM

Pre-Tax versus After-Tax Nominal Returns

- Pre-tax nominal returns do not adjust for taxes or inflation.
- After-tax nominal returns account for taxes. Most investors are concerned with returns on an after-tax basis.

Real versus Nominal Returns

- Nominal returns consist of the real risk-free rate of return, a premium for risk, and a premium for inflation.
- Investors calculate the real return because:
  - It is useful in comparing returns across time periods as inflation rates may vary over time.
  - It is useful in comparing returns among countries when returns are expressed in local currencies in which inflation rates vary between countries.
  - The after-tax real return is what an investor receives as compensation for postponing consumption and assuming risk after paying taxes on investment returns.

Leveraged Return

The leveraged return is computed when an investor uses leverage (by either borrowing money or using derivative contracts) to invest in a security. Leverage enhances returns, but also magnifies losses.

Variance and Covariance of Returns

The risk of an asset or a portfolio of assets can be measured by its standard deviation, which is the positive square root of variance.

Variance of a Single Asset

Variance equals the average squared deviation of observed values from their mean.

- A higher variance indicates higher volatility or dispersion of returns.

Standard Deviation of an Asset

The population and sample standard deviations are calculated as:

$$\sigma = \sqrt{\frac{\sum_{t=1}^{T} (R_t - \mu)^2}{T}}$$

$$s = \sqrt{\frac{\sum_{t=1}^{T} (R_t - R)^2}{T - 1}}$$

Variance of a Portfolio of Assets

The formula for the variance of a portfolio is:

$$\sigma_P^2 = \sum_{i,j=1}^{N} w_i w_j \text{Cov}(R_i, R_j)$$

$$\sigma_P^2 = \sum_{i=1}^{N} w_i^2 \text{Var}(R_i) + \sum_{i,j=1, i \neq j}^{N} w_i w_j \text{Cov}(R_i, R_j)$$

The standard deviation of a portfolio of two risky assets is calculated as:

$$\sigma_p = \sqrt{w_1^2 \sigma_1^2 + w_2^2 \sigma_2^2 + 2 w_1 w_2 \sigma_1 \sigma_2 \rho_{1,2}} \text{ or } \sqrt{w_1^2 \sigma_1^2 + w_2^2 \sigma_2^2 + 2 w_1 w_2 \text{Cov}_{1,2}}$$

Other Investment Characteristics

Distributional Characteristics

- **Skewness** refers to the asymmetry of a returns distribution.
  - When most of the distribution is concentrated on the left, it is referred to as right skewed or positively skewed.
  - When most of the distribution is concentrated to the right, it is referred to as left skewed or negatively skewed.
- **Kurtosis** refers to fat tails or higher than normal probabilities for extreme returns. This leads to an increase in an asset's risk that is not captured by the mean-variance framework.

Market Characteristics

Markets are not always **operationally efficient**. One limitation on operational efficiency in markets is liquidity. Liquidity has an impact on the bid-ask spread (illiquid stocks have a wider spread) and on the price impact of a trade (illiquid stocks suffer a greater price impact).

Informational efficiency is discussed in later readings on market efficiency.

The Concept of Risk Aversion

Risk-averse investors aim to maximize returns for a given level of risk, and minimize risk for a given level or return.

Risk-seeking investors get extra utility or satisfaction from the uncertainty associated with their investments.

Risk-neutral investors seek higher returns irrespective of the level of risk inherent in an investment.

Risk tolerance refers to the level of risk that an investor is willing to accept to achieve her investment goals.

- The lower the risk tolerance, the lower the level of risk acceptable to the investor.
- The lower the risk tolerance, the higher the risk aversion.

Utility Theory

In order to quantify the preferences for investment choices using risk and return, utility functions are used. An example of a utility function is:

$$U = E(R) - \frac{1}{2}A\sigma^2$$

"A" is a measure of risk aversion. It is higher for investors who are more risk averse as they require larger compensation for accepting more risk.

The utility function assumes the following:

- Investors are generally risk averse, but prefer more return to less return.
- Investors are able to rank different portfolios based on their preferences and these preferences are internally consistent.

We can draw the following conclusions from the utility function:

- Utility is unbounded on both sides— it can be highly negative or highly positive.
- Higher return results in higher utility.
- Higher risk results in lower utility.
- The higher the value of "A" the higher the negative effect of risk on utility.

Important Notes Regarding the Risk Aversion Coefficient, "A"

- "A" is positive for a risk-averse investor. Additional risk reduces total utility.
- It is negative for a risk seeking investor. Additional risk enhances total utility.
- It equals zero for a risk neutral investor. Additional risk has no impact on total utility.

Indifference Curves

The risk-return trade-off that an investor is willing to bear can be illustrated by an **indifference curve**. An investor realizes the same total utility or satisfaction from every point on a given indifference curve. Since each investor can have an infinite number of risk-return combinations that generate the same utility, indifference curves are continuous at all points.

1. They are **upward sloping**. This means that an investor will be indifferent between two investments with different expected returns only if the investment with the lower expected return entails a lower level of risk as well.
2. They are **curved**, and their slope becomes steeper as more risk is taken. The increase in return required for every unit of additional risk increases at an increasing rate because of the diminishing marginal utility of wealth.

The slope of an indifference curve represents the extra return required by the investor to accept an additional unit of risk.

- A risk-averse investor would have a relatively steep indifference curve (significant extra return required to take on more risk).
- A less risk-averse investor would have a flatter indifference curve (lower extra return required to take on more risk).
- A risk-seeking investor would have an indifference curve with a negative slope. Her utility increases with higher return and higher risk.

- A risk-neutral investor would have a perfectly horizontal indifference curve. Her utility does not vary with risk.

Application of Utility Theory to Portfolio Selection

Capital Allocation Line

$$E(R_p) = RFR + \sigma_{port} \frac{[E(R_i) - RFR]}{\sigma_i}$$

- The CAL has an intercept of RFR.
- The expression for the slope of the CAL is the extra return required for each additional unit of risk and is also known as the market price of risk.

The point of tangency between the CAL and an investor's indifference curve indicates the optimal risky asset portfolio that the investor should invest in.

Portfolio Risk

The formula for the standard deviation of a portfolio consisting of 2 risky assets is:

$$\sigma_p = \sqrt{w_1^2\sigma_1^2 + w_2^2\sigma_2^2 + 2w_1w_2\sigma_1\sigma_2\rho_{1,2}} \text{ or } \sqrt{w_1^2\sigma_1^2 + w_2^2\sigma_2^2 + 2w_1w_2Cov_{1,2}}$$

The first part of the formula for the 2-asset portfolio standard deviation $(w_1^2\sigma_1^2 + w_2^2\sigma_2^2)$ tells us that portfolio standard deviation is a *positive* function of the standard deviation and weights of the individual assets held in the portfolio. The second part $(2w_1w_2Cov_{1,2})$ shows us that portfolio standard deviation is also dependent on how the two assets move in relation to each other (covariance or correlation).

From the 2-asset portfolio standard deviation formula it is also important to understand that:

- The maximum value for portfolio standard deviation will be obtained when the correlation coefficient equals +1.
- Portfolio standard deviation will be minimized when the correlation coefficient equals −1.
- If the correlation coefficient equals zero, the second part of the formula will equal zero and portfolio standard deviation will lie somewhere in between.

Implications

- When asset returns are *negatively* correlated, the final term in the standard deviation formula is negative and serves to *reduce* portfolio standard deviation.
- If the correlation between assets equals zero, portfolio standard deviation is *greater* than when correlation is negative.
- When asset returns are positively correlated, the second part of the formula for portfolio standard deviation is also positive, and portfolio standard deviation is higher than when the correlation coefficient equals zero. With a correlation coefficient of +1 (perfect positive correlation) there are no diversification benefits.
- The risk (standard deviation) of a portfolio of risky assets depends on the asset weights and standard deviations, *and most importantly on the correlation of asset returns*. The *higher* the correlation between the individual assets, the *higher* the portfolio's standard deviation.

- A conservative investor can experience both a higher return and a lower risk by diversifying into a higher-risk, higher-return asset if the correlation between the assets is fairly low.
- When correlation equals +1, the risk-return combinations that result from altering the weights lie along a straight line between the two assets' risk-return profiles.
- As correlation falls, the curvature of this line increases.
- When correlation equals −1, the curve is represented by two straight lines that meet at the vertical axis. This point represents a zero-risk portfolio where portfolio return must equal the risk-free rate to prevent arbitrage.

Avenues for Diversification

- Investing in a variety of asset classes that are not highly correlated.
- Using index funds that minimize the costs of diversification and grant exposure to specific asset classes.
- Investing among countries that focus on different industries, are undergoing different stages of the business cycle and have different currencies.
- Choosing not to invest a significant portion of their wealth in employee stock plans as their human capital is already entirely invested in their employing companies.
- Only adding a security to the portfolio if its Sharpe ratio is greater than the Sharpe ratio of the portfolio times the correlation coefficient.
- Only adding a security to the portfolio if the benefit (additional expected return, reduced portfolio risk) is greater than the associated costs (trading costs and costs of tracking a larger portfolio).
- Adding insurance to the portfolio by purchasing put options or adding an asset class that has a negative correlation with the assets in the portfolio (e.g., commodities).

The Minimum-Variance and Efficient Frontiers, and the Global Minimum-Variance Portfolio

- Combining risky assets may result in a portfolio that has lower risk than any of the individual assets in the portfolio.
- As the number of assets available increases, they can be combined into a large number of different portfolios (each with different assets and weights), and we can create an **opportunity set** of investments.
- Combinations of these assets can be formed into portfolios that entail the lowest level of risk for each level of expected return. An envelope curve that plots the risk-return characteristics of the lowest risk portfolios is known as the **minimum variance frontier.**
  - No risk-averse investor would invest in any portfolio that lies to the right of the MVF as it would entail a higher level of risk than a portfolio that lies on the MVF for a given level of return.
- The **global minimum-variance portfolio** is the portfolio of risky securities that entails the lowest level of risk among all the risky asset portfolios on the minimum variance frontier.
- All portfolios on the MVF that lie above and to the right of the global minimum-variance portfolio dominate all portfolios on the MVF that lie below and to the right of the global minimum variance portfolio.
  - This dominant portion of the MVF (the one above and to the right of the global minimum variance portfolio) is known as the **Markowitz efficient frontier.** It contains all the possible portfolios that rational, risk-averse investors will consider investing in.

PM

347

A Risk-Free Asset and Many Risky Assets

- The risk-free asset has zero risk (so it plots on the y-axis), an expected return of RFR, and zero correlation with risky assets.
- The risk-return characteristics of portfolios that combine the risk-free asset with a risky asset or a portfolio of risky assets lie along a straight line.

As the investor combines the risk-free asset with portfolios further up the efficient frontier, she keeps attaining better portfolio combinations. Each successive portfolio on the efficient frontier has a steeper line (higher slope) joining it to the risk-free asset. The slope of this line represents the additional return per unit of extra risk. The steeper the slope of the line, the better the risk-return trade-off the portfolio offers. The line with the steepest slope is the one that is drawn from the risk-free asset to Portfolio M (which occurs at the point of tangency between the efficient frontier and a straight line drawn from the risk-free rate). This particular line offers the best risk-return trade-off to the investor. Any combination of the risk-free asset and Portfolio M dominates all portfolios below CAL_M.

The Two-Fund Separation Theorem

The two-fund separation theorem states that regardless of risk and return preferences, all investors hold some combination of the risk-free asset and an optimal portfolio of risky assets. Therefore, the investment problem can be broken down into two steps:

1. The investing decision, where an investor identifies her optimal risky portfolio.
2. The financing decision, where she determines where exactly on the optimal CAL, she wants her portfolio to lie. Her risk preferences (as delineated by her indifference curves) determine whether her desired portfolio requires borrowing or lending at the risk-free rate.

Optimal Investor Portfolio

- The line CAL_M represents the best portfolios available to an investor. The portfolios along this line contain the risk-free asset and the optimal portfolio, Portfolio M, with varying weights.
- An individual's optimal portfolio depends on her risk-return preferences, which are incorporated into her indifference curves. The point where her indifference curve is tangent to CAL_M indicates her optimal investor portfolio.

PORTFOLIO RISK AND RETURN: PART II
Cross-Reference to CFA Institute Assigned Reading #50

Review

- Risky assets can be combined into portfolios that may have a lower risk than each of the individual assets in the portfolio if assets are not perfectly positively correlated.
- An investor's investment opportunity set includes all the individual risky assets and risky asset portfolios that she can invest in.
- The minimum variance frontier reduces the investment opportunity set to a curve that contains only those portfolios that entail the lowest level of risk for each level of expected return.
- The global minimum variance portfolio is the portfolio of risky assets that entails the lowest level of risk among all portfolios on the minimum variance frontier.
- Investors aim to maximize return for every level of risk. Therefore, all portfolios above and to the right of the global minimum variance portfolio dominate those that lie below and to the right of the global minimum variance portfolio.
- The section of the minimum variance frontier that lies above and to the right of the global minimum variance portfolio is referred to as the Markowitz efficient frontier.

A risk-free asset has an expected return of RFR, a standard deviation (risk) of zero, and a correlation with any risky asset of zero. Once the risk-free asset is introduced into the mix:

- Any portfolio that combines a risky asset portfolio that lies on the Markowitz efficient frontier and the risk-free asset has a risk return trade-off that is linear (CAL is represented by a straight line).
- The point at which a line drawn from the risk-free rate is tangent to the Markowitz efficient frontier defines the optimal risky asset portfolio. This line is known as the optimal CAL.
- Each investor will choose a portfolio (optimal investor portfolio) that contains some combination of the risk-free asset and the optimal risky portfolio. The weights of the risk-free asset and the optimal risky portfolio in the optimal investor portfolio depend on the investor's risk tolerance (indifference curve).
- The optimal investor portfolio is defined by the point where the investor's indifference curve is tangent to the optimal CAL.

The CAL and the CML

A **capital allocation line (CAL)** includes all combinations of the risk-free asset and **any risky asset portfolio.**

The **capital market line (CML)** is a special case of the capital allocation line where the risky asset portfolio that is combined with the risk-free asset is the **market portfolio.**

Graphically, the market portfolio occurs at the point where a line from the risk-free asset is tangent to the Markowitz efficient frontier. The market portfolio is the optimal risky asset portfolio given homogenous expectations. All portfolios that lie below the CML offer a lower return than portfolios that plot on the CML for each level of risk.

Equation of CML:

$$E(R_p) = R_f + \frac{E(R_m) - R_f}{\sigma_m} \times \sigma_p$$

Capital Market Line

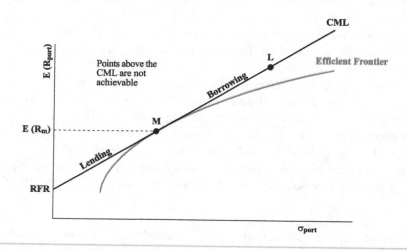

- At Point RFR, an investor has all her funds invested in the risk-free asset.
- At Point M, she has all of her funds invested in the market portfolio (which only contains risky securities).
- At any point between RFR and M, she holds both the market portfolio and the risk-free asset (i.e., she is lending some of her funds at the risk-free rate).

However, an investor may want to attain a higher expected return than available at Point M, where all her funds are invested in the market portfolio. Adding leverage to the portfolio by borrowing money at the RFR and investing it in the market portfolio will allow her to attain a risk-return profile beyond (to the right of, or above) Point M on the CML (e.g., Point L).

The particular point that an investor chooses on the CML depends on her utility function, which in turn is determined by her risk and return preferences.

Leveraged Positions with Different Lending and Borrowing Rates

Practically speaking, an investor's ability to repay is not as certain as that of the U.S. government, so the rate at which she would be able to borrow would be higher than the rate at which she would be able to lend. Given the disparity in borrowing and lending rates, the CML would no longer be a straight line.

- The slope of the CML to the left of Point M (when she invests a portion of her portfolio in the risk-free asset at R_f) would be:

$$\frac{E(R_m) - R_f}{\sigma_m}$$

- The slope CML to the right of Point M (where she is borrowing at R_b) would be:

$$\boxed{\dfrac{E(R_m) - R_b}{\sigma_m}}$$

Systematic and Nonsystematic Risk

When investors diversify across assets that are not perfectly positively correlated, the portfolio's risk is lower than the weighted average of the individual assets' risks. In the market portfolio, all the risk unique to individual assets comprising the portfolio has been diversified away.

- The risk that disappears due to diversification in the portfolio construction process is known as **unsystematic risk** (also known as unique, diversifiable or firm-specific risk).
- The risk inherent in all risky assets (caused by macro-economic variables) that cannot be eliminated by diversification is known as **systematic risk** (also known as non-diversifiable or market risk).

$$\boxed{\text{Total Risk} = \text{Systematic risk} + \text{Unsystematic risk}}$$

Complete diversification of a portfolio requires the elimination of all unsystematic or diversifiable risk. Once unsystematic risk has been eliminated and only systematic risk remains, a completely diversified portfolio would correlate perfectly with the market.

By adding assets to a portfolio that are not perfectly correlated with the assets already in the portfolio, we can reduce the overall standard deviation of the portfolio. However, we cannot eliminate the variability and uncertainty of macroeconomic factors that affect returns on all risky assets. We do not have to include all the assets in the market portfolio to diversify away unsystematic risk. Studies have shown that a portfolio consisting of 12–30 different stocks can diversify away 90% of unsystematic risk.

In capital market theory, taking on a higher degree of unsystematic risk will not be compensated with a higher return because unsystematic risk can be eliminated, without additional cost, through diversification. Only if an investor takes on a higher level of risk that cannot be easily diversified away (systematic risk) should she expect to be rewarded in the form of a higher return. Systematic risk is measured as the contribution of a security to the risk of a well diversified portfolio.

Return-Generating Models

A **return-generating model** is a model that is used to forecast the return on a security given certain parameters. A multi-factor model uses more than one variable to estimate returns.

- **Macroeconomic factor models** use economic factors (e.g., economic growth rates, interest rates and inflation rates) that correlate with security returns to estimate returns.
- **Fundamental factor models** use relationships between security returns and underlying fundamentals (e.g., earnings, earnings growth and cash flow growth) to estimate returns.
- **Statistical factor models** use historical and cross-sectional returns data to identify factors that explain returns and use an asset's sensitivity to those factors to project future returns.

The Market Model

The market model is an example of a single-index return generation model. It is used to estimate beta risk and to compute abnormal returns. The market model is given as:

$$R_i = \alpha_i + \beta_i R_m + e_i$$

First, the intercept α_i and slope coefficient β_i are estimated using historical asset and market returns. These estimates are then used to predict returns in the future.

Calculation and Interpretation of Beta

Beta is a measure of the sensitivity of an asset's return to the market's return. It is computed as the covariance of the return on the asset and the return on the market divided by the variance of the market.

$$\beta_i = \frac{\text{Cov}(R_i, R_m)}{\sigma_m^2} = \frac{\rho_{i,m}\sigma_i\sigma_m}{\sigma_m^2} = \frac{\rho_{i,m}\sigma_i}{\sigma_m}$$

Important Points Regarding Beta

- Beta captures an asset's systematic or non-diversifiable risk.
- A positive beta suggests that the return on the asset follows the overall trend in the market.
- A negative beta indicates that the return on the asset generally follows a trend that is opposite to that of the current market trend.
- A beta of zero means that the return on the asset is uncorrelated with market movements.
- The market has a beta of 1. Therefore, the average beta of stocks in the market also equals 1.

The market model described previously can also be used to compute beta.

The Capital Asset Pricing Model

The capital asset pricing model (CAPM) is a single-index model that is widely used to estimate returns given security betas. The CAPM is expressed as:

$$E(R_i) = R_f + \beta_i[E(R_m) - R_f]$$

Assumptions of the CAPM

- Investors are utility maximizing, risk-averse, rational individuals.
- Markets are frictionless, and there are no transaction costs and taxes.
- All investors have the same single period investment horizon.
- Investors have homogenous expectations and therefore, arrive at the same valuation for any given asset.
- All investments are infinitely divisible.
- Investors are price-takers. No investor is large enough to influence security prices.

The Security Market Line

The SML illustrates the CAPM equation. Its y-intercept equals the risk-free rate and its slope equals the market risk premium ($R_m - R_f$).

Recall that the CAL and the CML only applied to efficient portfolios; not to individual assets or inefficient portfolios. They used total risk on the x-axis, and since only systematic risk is priced, they could only be used for efficient portfolios (those with no unsystematic risk and whose total risk therefore was the same as their systematic risk).

The SML and the CAPM on the other hand, apply to any security or portfolio, regardless of whether it is efficient. This is because they are based only on a security's systematic risk, not total risk.

The CAPM equation tells us that the expected (required) rate of return for a risky asset is determined by the risk-free rate plus a risk premium. The risk premium for an asset is determined by the systematic risk of the asset (β_i), and the prevailing market risk premium ($R_m - R_f$).

Portfolio Beta

The CAPM can also be applied to portfolios of assets.

- The beta of a portfolio equals the weighted average of the betas of the securities in the portfolio.
- The portfolio's expected return can be computed using the CAPM:

$$E(R_p) = R_f + \beta_p[E(R_m) - R_f]$$

Applications of the CAPM

Estimate of expected return: The expected rate of return computed from the CAPM is used by investors to value stocks, bonds, real estate and other assets. In capital budgeting, where the NPV is used to make investing decisions, the CAPM is used to compute the required rate of return, which is then used to discount expected future cash flows.

Portfolio Performance Evaluation

The **Sharpe ratio** is used to compute excess returns per unit of total risk. It is calculated as:

$$\text{Sharpe ratio} = \frac{R_p - R_f}{\sigma_p}$$

Notice that the Sharpe ratio basically equals the slope of the CAL. A portfolio with a higher Sharpe ratio is preferred to one with a lower Sharpe ratio given that the numerator of the portfolios being compared is positive. If the numerator is negative, the ratio will be closer to zero (less negative) for riskier portfolios, resulting in distorted rankings. Two drawbacks of the Sharpe ratio are that it uses total risk as a measure of risk even though only systematic risk is priced, and that the ratio itself is not informative.

The **Treynor ratio** basically replaces total risk in the Sharpe ratio with systematic risk (beta). It is calculated as:

$$\text{Treynor ratio} = \frac{R_p - R_f}{\beta_p}$$

For the Treynor ratio to offer meaningful results, both the numerator and the denominator must be positive. Neither the Sharpe nor the Treynor ratio offer any information about the significance of the differences between the ratios for portfolios.

M^2 provides a measure of portfolio return that is adjusted for the total risk of the portfolio relative to that of some benchmark.

Ex ante:

$$M^2 = \left[E(R_p) - R_f\right]\frac{\sigma_m}{\sigma_p} + R_f = \text{SR} \times \sigma_m + R_f$$

Ex post:

$$M^{\tilde{2}} = \left(\overline{R}_p - \overline{R}_f\right)\frac{\dot{\sigma}_m}{\dot{\sigma}_p} + R_f = \overline{\text{SR}} \times \dot{\sigma}_m + R_f$$

- The equations show that M^2 can be thought of as a rescaling of the Sharpe ratio that allows for easier comparisons among different portfolios.
- M^2 and Sharpe ratios rank portfolios identically because both (1) the risk-free rate and (2) market volatility are constant across all comparisons. Only the Sharpe ratio differs, so it determines all rankings.

Jensen's alpha is based on systematic risk (like the Treynor ratio). It first estimates a portfolio's beta risk using the market model, and then uses the CAPM to determine the required return from the investment (given its beta risk). The difference between the portfolio's actual return and the required return (as predicted by the CAPM) is called Jensen's alpha. Jensen's alpha is calculated as:

$$\alpha_p = R_p - \left[R_f + \beta_p(R_m - R_f)\right]$$

Jensen's alpha for the market equals zero. The higher the Jensen's alpha for a portfolio, the better its risk adjusted performance.

Security Characteristic Line

The security characteristic line (SCL) plots the excess returns of a security against the excess returns on the market. The equation of the SCL is given as:

$$R_i - R_f = \alpha_i + \beta_i(R_m - R_f)$$

Note that Jensen's alpha is the y-intercept, and beta is the slope of the SCL.

Security Selection

- If the expected return using price and dividend forecasts is higher than the investor's required return given the systematic risk in the security, the security is undervalued and the investor should buy it.
- If the expected return using price and dividend forecasts is lower than the investor's required return given the systematic risk in the security, the security is overvalued and the investor should sell it.

Constructing a Portfolio

The CAPM tells us that investors should hold a portfolio that combines the risk-free asset with the market portfolio. Let's assume that we begin with the S&P 500 as our risky asset portfolio. The S&P 500 index only contains large-cap U.S. stocks, but does not encompass the entire global market. Therefore, we might want to consider a security not included in the S&P 500 for inclusion in the portfolio. The decision regarding whether the particular security should be included in our portfolio depends on the α_i of the security (based on the CAPM and the S&P 500 as the market portfolio). Positive α_i securities (even if they are correctly priced) should be added to the portfolio.

Further, within the set of securities included in the S&P 500, some may be undervalued (expected to generate positive alpha) and others may be overvalued (expected to generate negative alpha) based on investor expectations. The weight of undervalued securities should be increased and that of overvalued securities should be reduced.

The weight of each nonmarket security in the portfolio should be proportional to:

$$\frac{\alpha_i}{\sigma_{ei}^2}$$

where:

α_i = Jensen's alpha
σ_{ei}^2 = Nonsystematic variance of the security

> The information ratio $\left(\frac{\alpha_i}{\sigma_{ei}}\right)$ measures the abnormal return per unit of risk added by the security to a well-diversified portfolio. The larger the information ratio is, the more valuable the security.

Beyond the CAPM

Limitations of the CAPM

Theoretical limitations

- The CAPM is a single-factor model; only systematic risk is priced in the CAPM.
- It is only a single period model.

Practical limitations

- A true market portfolio is unobservable as it would also include assets that are not investable (e.g., human capital).
- In the absence of a true market portfolio, the proxy for the market portfolio used varies across analysts, which leads to different return estimates for the same asset (not permissible in the CAPM world).
- Using different periods for estimation results in different estimates of beta, leading to varying return expectations for the same asset.

PM

Extensions of the CAPM

Theoretical models like the arbitrage pricing theory (APT) expand the number of risk factors.

Practical models use extensive research to uncover risk factors that explain returns.

Study Session 18: Portfolio Management (2)

PM

BASICS OF PORTFOLIO PLANNING AND CONSTRUCTION
Cross-Reference to CFA Institute Assigned Reading #51

The Investment Policy Statement

An investment policy statement is an invaluable planning tool that adds discipline to the investment process. Before developing an IPS, an investment manager must conduct a fact finding discussion with the client to learn about the client's risk tolerance and other specific circumstances.

The IPS can be thought of as a roadmap which serves the following purposes:

- It helps the investor decide on realistic investment goals after learning about financial markets and associated risks.
- It creates a standard according to which the portfolio manager's performance can be judged.
- It guides the actions of portfolio managers, who should refer to it from time to time to assess the suitability of particular investments for their clients.

Major Components of an IPS

- An introduction that describes the client.
- A statement of purpose.
- A statement of duties and responsibilities, which describes the duties and responsibilities of the client, the custodian of the client's assets, and the investment manager.
- Procedures that outline the steps required to keep the IPS updated and steps required to respond to various contingencies.
- The client's investment objectives.
- The client's investment constraints.
- Investment guidelines regarding how the policy should be executed (e.g., whether use of leverage and derivatives is permitted) and specific types of assets that must be excluded.
- Evaluation and review guidelines on obtaining feedback on investment results.
- Appendices that describe the strategic asset allocation and the rebalancing policy.

Risk Objectives

- An example of an **absolute risk objective** would be that the client does not want to lose more than 5% of her capital over a particular period.
- **Relative risk objectives** relate risk to a certain benchmark that represents an appropriate level of risk.

Risk tolerance is a function of both, a client's ability to take risk as well as her willingness to take risk. The ability to take risk is a function of several factors including time horizon, expected income, and net worth. Generally speaking, a client with a longer time horizon, high expected income and greater net worth has a greater ability to bear risk. A client's willingness to bear risk, on the other hand, is based on more subjective factors including her psychological makeup, and level of understanding of financial markets.

Risk Tolerance

	Ability to Bear Risk	
Willingness to Take Risk	**Below Average**	**Above Average**
Below Average	Below-average risk tolerance	Resolution needed
Above Average	Resolution needed	Above-average risk tolerance

When there is a mismatch between a client's ability and willingness to take risk, the prudent approach is to conclude that the client's tolerance for risk is the lower of the two factors. Further, any decisions made must be documented.

Return Objectives

- **Absolute return objectives** state the percentage return desired by the client. The return may be expressed on a real or nominal basis.
- **Relative return objectives** express the required return relative to a stated benchmark. A good benchmark should be investable i.e., an investor should be able to replicate it.

The return objective may be stated before or after fees and on a pre- or post-tax basis. Further, it could also be expressed in terms of a required return i.e., the amount an investor needs to earn over the investment horizon to meet a specified future goal.

The portfolio manager must ensure that the client's return objective is realistic in light of her tolerance for risk.

Investment Constraints

Liquidity refers to the ability to readily convert investments into cash at a price close to fair market value. Investors may require ready cash to meet unexpected needs and could be forced to sell their assets at unfavorable terms if the investment plan does not consider their liquidity needs.

Time horizon refers to the time period between putting funds into an investment and requiring them for use. A close relationship exists between an investor's time horizon, liquidity needs and ability to take risk. The shorter the time horizon, the harder it would be for an investor to overcome losses.

Tax concerns play a very important role in investment planning because, unlike tax-exempt investors, taxable investors are really only concerned with after-tax returns on their portfolios.

Legal and regulatory factors: Investors also need to be aware of legal and regulatory factors. For example, some countries impose a limit on the proportion of equity securities in a pension fund's portfolio.

Unique circumstances: There may be a number of individual and unusual considerations that affect investors. For example, many investors may want to exclude certain investments from their portfolios based on personal or socially conscious reasons.

ESG Investing

- **Negative screening:** Excluding companies or sectors based on business activities or environmental or social concerns.

- **Positive screening:** Including sectors or companies based on specific ESG criteria, typically ESG performance relative to industry peers.
- **ESG integration:** Systematic consideration of material ESG factors in asset allocation, security selection, and portfolio construction decisions.
- **Thematic investing:** Investing in themes or assets related to ESG factors.
- **Engagement/active ownership:** Using shareholder power to influence corporate behavior to achieve targeted ESG objectives along with financial returns.
- **Impact investing:** Investments made with the intention to generate positive, measurable social and environmental impact alongside a financial return.

Portfolio Construction

Once the IPS has been compiled, the investment manager begins constructing the portfolio. How the portfolio funds are allocated across different asset classes is referred to as the portfolio's **strategic asset allocation (SAA)**. A portfolio's SAA is important because it is a portfolio's allocation across various asset classes (not its allocation across securities within those asset classes) that is the primary determinant of portfolio returns.

Capital Market Expectations

Capital market expectations refer to a portfolio manager's expectations regarding the risk and return prospects of various asset classes. Capital market expectations are quantified in terms of expected returns, standard deviation of returns, and correlations among asset classes.

The Strategic Asset Allocation

The strategic asset allocation defines how the investor's funds are divided across different asset classes. Traditionally, cash, equities, bonds, and real estate were defined as the major asset classes. Recently, hedge funds, private equity and commodities have been added to the list. Further, each asset class can be subdivided into several sub-classes.

The risk return characteristics of the strategic asset allocation depend on the expected returns and risk of the individual asset classes, and on the correlations between the asset classes. Typically, risk-averse investors will place a higher weight on government bonds and cash in their SAA's, while those with a higher risk tolerance will have a higher weight invested in equities.

Steps Toward an Actual Portfolio

1. **Risk budgeting:** This is the process of subdividing the desired level of portfolio risk (which has been determined in the IPS) across the different sources of investment returns i.e., the strategic asset allocation, tactical asset allocation and security selection.
2. **Tactical asset allocation:** This refers to an allocation where the manager deliberately deviates from the strategic asset allocation for the short term.
3. **Security selection:** A manager may be able to outperform the asset class benchmark by investing in particular securities within the asset class that she expects to do well (better than the benchmark).
4. **Portfolio rebalancing:** Changes in security prices will lead to changes in the weights of different asset classes in the portfolio and cause them to deviate or "drift" from policy weights. Therefore, the portfolio should be rebalanced periodically and brought in line with policy weights.

Alternative Portfolio Organizing Principles

The broad array of ETF offerings, covering the main equity and fixed income indices as well as commodities, enable retail investors to obtain fast, inexpensive, and liquid exposure to asset classes. Robo-advice has further reduced the costs for retail investors to create a well-diversified portfolio.

Risk parity investing is an approach to portfolio construction where asset classes are weighted according to risk contribution.

THE BEHAVIORAL BIASES OF INDIVIDUALS
Cross-Reference to CFA Institute Assigned Reading #52

Categories of Behavioral Bias

The major categories of individual behavioral bias are:

- Behavioral finance micro (BFMI): Individual investor (i.e., biases):
  - *Cognitive errors* (conscious)—Faulty analysis process resulting from memory, information processing, or statistical errors (e.g., using rules of thumb).
  - *Emotional biases* (unconscious)—Faulty reasoning resulting from feelings and impulses.
- Behavioral finance macro (BFMA): Market behavior (e.g., anomalies)

> **IMPORTANT:**
> Investors can identify the sources of and therefore overcome cognitive errors more easily than emotional biases.

Cognitive errors involve faulty reasoning; emotional biases result from pleasure seeking or pain avoidance.

Emotions include perceptions, beliefs, or feelings that arise spontaneously as a mental state without conscious effort. Emotions may be real or imagined, and individuals experiencing them may only be able to work around them rather than control them.

In some cases, market participants make cognitive errors that justify their emotional biases.

Cognitive Errors

Cognitive errors occur when investors fail to gather appropriate information, consider it carefully, and update probabilities.

Belief Persistence Biases

A **belief persistence bias** involves cognitive errors that reject contradictory new information:

- Selective exposure: Notice only information of interest.
- Selective perception: Ignore or modify contradictory information.
- Selective retention: Remember and consider only confirming information.

Conservatism bias results when financial market participants (FMPs) overweight initial observations or information and then fail to adequately update perceptions when new information arises.

This bias is related to the amount of effort involved in information acquisition, data processing, and updating existing projections (i.e., cognitive costs).

FMPs should consider new information and react decisively when a new conclusion arises.

Confirmation bias results when people only notice belief-confirming information, or disregard or fail to properly weight contradictory information.

FMPs may ignore negative information once they have decided, or may develop screening criteria that bolster positive information about the investment. In the process, good investments may be screened out.

Concentrated positions often result, especially if the investor's own company is involved.

FMPs should attempt to overcome confirmation bias by actively seeking opinions contradictory to their own. Investment ideas should be confirmed via third-party research before confirming the opinion via purchases.

Representativeness bias involves classifying new information based on meaning derived from past information, even if it doesn't fit:

- **Base-rate neglect** ignores the probability that new information matches existing information used for classification.
- **Sample-size neglect** uses isolated cases or small sample sizes to represent the general case.

FMPs may continue to apply existing methods of using information in classifying investment opportunities, or make investments based on small bits of information. Investors will fire their investment manager when supposed results don't occur, or sell a security when they cannot properly classify new information.

FMPs can avoid representativeness bias by proper asset allocation, making changes only when adequate information to support a change has developed, and using longer-term performance data.

To avoid representativeness bias, investors should ask whether an investment belongs to group A or is statistically more likely to belong to group B.

Illusion of control bias occurs when people believe they have more control or influence than they actually have.

Suffering from illusion of control bias leads to overconcentration in portfolio positions and frequent trading that increases costs and drives down returns compared to buy-and-hold strategies.

Detection of illusion of control bias requires understanding the complexity of capital markets with little prospect for control. Success depends on systematic factors (e.g., economic growth, market sentiment, etc.) rather than any investor skill.

FMPs should seek contrary opinions. Investors can remind themselves of their own fallibility by keeping transaction records, including the rationale for any trade.

Hindsight bias involves remembering only information that reinforces existing beliefs. This stems from a viewpoint that results in the past were inevitable rather than risky at the time. In part, this follows from filling in memory gaps with preferential information.

Suffering from hindsight bias leads to a false sense of confidence, and can lead investors to believe money manager performance should have been better than it was.

FMPs should keep transaction records, including the rationale for any trade. They should remind themselves that managers should invest according to their strategy and that this will result in ups and downs over time. Educating investors and measuring managers against benchmarks can help toward this end.

Information-Processing Biases

This category of cognitive biases results from irrational information use.

Anchoring and adjustment bias involves people developing an initial estimate (the anchor) and subsequently adjusting that estimate up or down.

Consequences of this bias are that people weight the anchor too heavily and then make insufficient adjustments that bias the final estimate regardless of the new information's importance.

Overcoming this bias involves discovery of whether the investor is sticking to the original anchor for legitimate reasons.

Investors should be advised that past prices contain little information about the future expectations for their investments.

Mental accounting bias occurs when people treat money differently depending on its source or expected use. Although money is inherently fungible (i.e., each currency unit is interchangeable with other units), people segregate these pools of funds from other uses, with some pools believed more important to protect than others.

Consequences of mental accounting bias include failing to consider correlation of returns among various pools. This can result in inefficient diversification. People may also chase income in their mental accounting scheme without considering potential losses, resulting in principal erosion.

Effective education about the drawbacks of engaging in this behavior can help overcome mental accounting bias. Combining all their assets can surprise investors about how much they have and what they can accomplish by allocating across all the pools. Using total return rather than pool-focused returns will also help them understand how wealth can grow while maintaining moderate income withdrawals.

> **IMPORTANT:** Investors may engage in offsetting positions (i.e., buying and selling the same security) as well as concentrated positions that move together with high correlation.

Framing bias occurs when people decide differently based on how the decision maker views the risks and returns of the choice as well as how the choice is formulated. This involves risk seeking in the domain of losses versus risk aversion in the domain of gains.

Narrow framing results when people decide a subset of the big picture such as return potential without due consideration of the risks.

Consequences of framing bias include identifying the same opportunity differently depending on whether it is stated in the domain of losses (e.g., probability of not achieving goal is 25%) or is the complementary statement in the domain of gains (e.g., probability of achieving goal is 75%).

Investors may also choose suboptimal investments depending on how they are framed, even with properly identified risk tolerances.

Excessive trading may also occur with short-term price fluctuations.

Investors should try to be neutral when analyzing investments (i.e., without loss or gain framing). This bias can be mitigated by determining whether a riskier investment was selected in the domain of losses rather than the domain of gains.

> **IMPORTANT:** Investors should always focus on expected risks and returns rather than past performance.

Availability bias uses shortcuts (i.e., heuristics) to investment outcomes based on how readily information comes to mind.

- **Retrievability**: The first thing to be recalled is considered the most likely.
- **Categorization**: Searches take place within perceived relevant sets of information.
- **Narrow range of experience**: More weight is attached to experiential observation.
- **Resonance**: People project their preferences onto others, and believe there is a higher probability of believing/liking what they do.

Consequences include being overly swayed by advertising, or restricting investments to familiar categories (e.g., domestic equities). Failure to diversify may result from retrievability and categorization, and will tend to cause inadequate diversification. Improper asset allocation can result from investments or companies that don't resonate.

Detection should focus on determining whether the investment selection results from what FMPs have heard recently or what they like, or whether it results from a disciplined approach—that is, a long-term focus, a proper strategic asset allocation, and thorough research and analysis of investment options.

Investors can also keep in mind the ultimate outcome of asset bubbles when other investors are caught up in a new bubble.

Emotional Biases

Fewer **emotional biases** have been identified, but they are harder to control for than cognitive errors because people are often invested in their feelings more than in cognitive processes. Individuals will often become defensive when faced with their own emotional biases.

Loss Aversion Bias

Loss aversion results from the declining marginal utility of wealth. People strongly prefer avoiding losses to scoring gains, and people will incur additional risk to avoid losses.

FMPs suffering from loss aversion bias may also trade excessively when selling winners, which results in higher costs and lower returns.

Loss aversion bias combines with framing bias to attract those in loss positions to attempt recoupment.

Myopic loss aversion is a special case in which people tend to use bonds for long-term funding (rather than a properly diversified portfolio) in the domain of gains, and use equities with an outsized risk profile for short-term gains in the domain of losses. Over time, this results in unjustifiably high equity risk premiums.

Loss aversion bias can be mitigated by a disciplined approach; it is impossible to completely eliminate the pain of an investment loss.

Overconfidence Bias

Overconfidence bias results when people overestimate their analytical abilities and judgment, as well as the usefulness of information they possess. Although showing aspects of both cognitive and emotional biases, it is included as an emotional bias because it is difficult to get people to revise self-perceptions:

IMPORTANT: The **disposition effect** describes how people will dispose of winners quickly, which limits upside potential, but will hold losing positions in hopes of avoiding losses on a position, which increases position risk.

IMPORTANT: The **house-money effect** describes investors with gains—especially unexpected gains—in an investment as believing that money to be different from other money, and engaging in more risk-seeking behavior with it.

IMPORTANT: A long-term investor will be more likely to accept portfolio risk than a short-term investor, so investments should be reviewed regularly but infrequently.

- **Prediction overconfidence.** Assigning unrealistically narrow confidence intervals to predictions, resulting in poorly diversified portfolios.
- **Certainty overconfidence.** Assigning unrealistically high probabilities to outcomes for which the investor is responsible, often resulting in excessive trading when investments fail to meet return predictions.

Overconfidence becomes intensified when combined with *self-attribution bias*, which is related to investor self-esteem:

- Self-enhancing—claiming responsibility for success
- Self-protecting—denial of responsibility of failure

FMPs with overconfidence bias:

- Underestimate risks and returns.
- Hold concentrated portfolio positions.
- Engage in excessive trading.
- Underperform the market.

To detect and mitigate overconfidence, traders should review trading records, understand the reasons for winners and losers, and calculate portfolio performance over at least a two-year period. This process disciplines the FMP against too much risk and excessive trading.

Self-Control Bias

Self-control bias results when people fail to act in their long-term interests and instead succumb to short-term satisfaction. This outcome may result from *hyperbolic discounting* in which people prefer smaller payoffs now to larger future payoffs.

Self-control bias can result in undersaving for the future. FMPs then attempt to make up the shortfall by accepting too much portfolio risk, which puts the asset base in jeopardy.

When combined with mental accounting, FMPs will overallocate to bonds for income. This further stretches the portfolios' ability to meet long-term goals due to lack of reinvested earnings as well as lack of capital appreciation. Risk-seeking FMPs are likely to invest in risky equity securities to make up the difference.

FMPs should integrate a written personal budget and investment plan.

Status Quo Bias

Status quo bias occurs when people prefer to do nothing rather than make a change (i.e., they maintain the status quo). While regret-aversion bias and endowment bias involve a reason not to change (although it may be emotional rather than rational), status quo bias requires no conscious decision. Try not to confuse the status quo bias (do nothing) with conservatism (slow to update new information).

FMPs with status quo bias—especially when paired with regret-aversion bias and endowment bias—will maintain inappropriate risk profiles and fail to explore outcome-improving alternatives.

Detection and mitigation involve educating FMPs on risk-reducing and return-enhancing diversification.

PM

367

Endowment Bias

Endowment bias occurs when FMPs value an asset in their possession more than if they were to buy it. This contrasts with rational economic man (REM), who would purchase a good for the same price at which he sells it.

The "endowment" of special importance to a security or an investment may result from inheritance from a loved one or simply from making the effort to buy it. On occasion, people cite disloyalty as the reason for not wishing to sell at an appropriate price.

FMPs suffering from endowment bias will continue to maintain an inadvisable asset allocation, refusing to diversify and preferring not to make changes (i.e., elements of status quo bias).

Detection and mitigation of endowment bias might include asking investors what they would invest in if they received the same amount of cash rather than the investment. It may be appropriate to ask the former owner's intention for the investment.

It may be appropriate to ease into a new investment before cashing out the endowed investment and risking investor disaffection.

Regret-Aversion Bias

Regret-aversion bias occurs when people avoid making decisions for fear they will be unsuccessful. While similar to status quo bias, regret aversion differs in that there is a reason (i.e., regret) they prefer not to decide rather than simply a lack of initiative as with status quo bias.

Regret aversion can cause FMPs to hold losing positions for fear they might rebound after the sale, or to exit and remain out of a market in which they just lost money when the prudent action would be to remain invested:

- Errors of commission—actions people take
- Errors of omission—actions people could have taken but did not

Consequences involve underperforming portfolios of low-risk securities and failing to reach investment goals. Well-known or popular companies are chosen rather than those equally likely to succeed.

FMPs can detect and mitigate the effects of regret-aversion bias by understanding diversification benefits. Advisors should illustrate how everyone makes mistakes and why bubbles can be as bad as downturns.

Asset Allocation and Investment Policy

Behavioral portfolio theory employs goals-based investing in which an optimized portfolio considers each goal separately as a layer of the composite asset structure. Risk management for the portfolio considers the probability and likelihood of losses.

This approach helps investors understand the appropriate level of risk for their goals, as well as satisfying loss aversion preferences.

In this approach, the base of the investments pyramid assigns low-risk investments to the client's obligations and needs. Moderate-risk investments fund priorities and desires, while higher-risk or speculative investments fund aspirational goals.

PM

Behaviorally Modified Asset Allocation

Rational portfolio allocation involves selecting from efficient portfolios that optimize risk and return identified via questionnaire and goal setting.

Behaviorally modified asset allocation distinguishes between cognitive biases and emotional biases to determine which preferences can be modified and which must be followed, and establishes a portfolio based on a modified asset allocation the investor will follow.

Two considerations determine whether an advisor should adapt to or moderate client biases:

1. Level of wealth: Greater wealth compared with needs allows greater adaptation because only high-impact events jeopardize the client's standard of living (i.e., standard of living risk [SLR]).
2. Type of behavioral bias:
   - Moderate cognitive biases with a high SLR.
   - Adapt to emotional biases with a low SLR.

As much as +/− 10% adaptation will be required for the high-SLR emotional bias situations, while low-SLR cognitive bias adjustments will be closer to +/− 2%.

> **IMPORTANT:** A behavioral portfolio may not be efficient from a mean-variance optimization standpoint because each layer has been optimized separately, but will be easily understood and followed by investors.

> **IMPORTANT:** Moderating a bias involves recognizing the bias and attempting to either eliminate or reduce the impact of the bias.

> **IMPORTANT:** A blended recommendation of moderating and adapting becomes appropriate when clients exhibit low-SLR emotional bias situations or high-SLR cognitive bias situations.

PM

INTRODUCTION TO RISK MANAGEMENT
Cross-Reference to CFA Institute Assigned Reading #53

Risk encompasses all of the uncertain environmental variables that lead unpredictability of outcomes. Taking risk is an integral part of conducting business and managing investment portfolios. While risk is generally seen in an unfavorable light, the challenge for companies/investment managers lies in carefully choosing, understanding, and managing the risks entailed by their decisions.

Risk Management Framework

A **risk management framework** refers to the infrastructure, process, and analytics required to support the risk management function in an organization.

Risk governance comes from the board. It is the top-down process and guidance, which directs risk management activities to align with the organization's goals and risk appetite.

Risk identification and measurement is an ongoing process that requires entails analyzing the business or portfolio to identify risk exposures, tracking changes in those risk exposures, calculating risk metrics to gauge the significance of those risks under various scenarios, as well as keeping an eye on the business environment for potential risk drivers.

- A **risk driver** refers to any fundamental underlying factor that gives rise to a risk that is relevant to the entity.

Risk infrastructure refers to the people, systems and technology required to track risk exposures and conduct quantitative risk analysis. It includes the process (known as **risk capture**) through which risk exposures are populated in the risk management system, as well as the databases, models, and skilled personnel needed to develop and maintain the risk framework.

Policies and processes translate risk governance into the organization's day-to-day operations and decision-making processes in order to ensure that risky activities kept in line with the entity's risk tolerance levels.

Risk monitoring, mitigation, and management requires pulling together risk governance, identification and measurement, infrastructure, and policies and processes and continually reviewing and reevaluating in the face of changing risk exposures and risk drivers. Further, it requires recognizing when the entity's risk exposure is not aligned with its predetermined risk tolerance, and then taking action to bring them back into alignment.

Communication of critical risk issues must happen continuously across all levels of the organization.

Note that:

- Risk management is not about minimizing risk. It is about actively understanding and embracing those risks that offer the best chance of achieving organization's goals with an acceptable chance of failure.
- Risk management is not even about predicting risks. It is about being prepared for (positive or negative) unpredictable events such that their impact would have already been quantified and considered in advance.

Risk Governance

An Enterprise View of Risk

The governing body, or board, plays the following roles within the risk management framework:

- It determines the organization's goals and priorities, which form the basis of enterprise risk management.
- It determines the organization's risk appetite/tolerance i.e., defines which risks are acceptable, which risks must be mitigated and to what extent, and which risks are unacceptable.
- It is responsible for overseeing risk management to continually ensure that it is functioning properly, and is consistent with the goal of maximizing value.

Desirable Properties of Good Risk Governance

- Good risk governance should provide a sense of the worst loss that the organization can manage in various scenarios.
- It should provide clear guidance, but at the same time leave enough flexibility for management to execute strategy.
- The focus should be on enterprise risk management (that focuses on the objectives, health and value of the organization as a whole).
- It should provide a regular forum (e.g., a risk management committee) where the risk framework and key risk issues are discussed at management level.
- It should provide for the appointment of a chief risk officer (CRO) who is responsible for building and implementing the risk framework for the enterprise and managing all related activities. Further, the CRO's insight should be used in making key strategic decisions.

Risk Tolerance

Risk tolerance identifies the extent to which the entity is willing to experience losses or opportunity costs and to fail meeting its objectives. At the governance level, the idea is not really to select activities that will maximize value or produce the highest returns given an acceptable level of risk (this duty falls on management), but to define the entity's risk appetite.

Defining an organization's risk tolerance calls for answering the following questions:

- What shortfalls within the organization would cause it to fail to achieve critical goals? This questions looks to address internal risk factors.
- What uncertain forces is the organization exposed to? This question focusses on outside risk factors.

Factors that Affect a Company's Risk Tolerance

- The more dynamic a company in its ability to respond to adverse events, the higher its risk tolerance.
- The greater the loss a company can bear without impairing its status as a going concern, the higher its risk tolerance.
- The stronger the company's competitive position, the higher its risk tolerance.
- The overall competitive landscape in the industry and the regulatory landscape also influence a company's risk tolerance.

Risk Budgeting

Risk budgeting focuses on how risk is taken by quantifying and allocating tolerable risk to various activities/investments based on their characteristics.

Risk budgets can be complex/multi-dimensional or simple/one-dimensional.

- **Single-dimension risk measures** include standard deviation, beta, value at risk (VaR) and scenario loss.
- **Multi-dimension risk approaches** include one where portfolio risk is evaluated based on the risk profiles of underlying asset classes (equity, fixed income, etc.), and another risk-factor approach where exposure to various risk factors is used to capture associated risk premiums (value stocks versus growth stocks).

The benefit of risk budgeting lies in the fact that it forces the organization into thinking about risk trade-offs and fosters a culture where risk is an important consideration in all key decisions.

Identification of Risks

Financial Risks

- **Market risk** arises from changes in interest rates, stock prices, exchange rates and commodity prices.
  - ○ Generally speaking, the underlying risk drivers of market risk are fundamental economic conditions or events in the overall economy, industry or the company itself.
- **Credit risk** (**default risk** or **counterparty risk**) is the risk of loss if one party fails to pay an amount owed on an obligation (e.g., bond or derivative).
  - ○ Generally speaking, the underlying risk drivers of credit risk tend to be fundamental weakness in the economy, industry or in demand for a company's products.
- **Liquidity risk** (or **transaction cost risk**) is the risk of a substantial downward valuation adjustment when trying to sell an asset.
  - ○ In several transactions, there is a bid-ask spread that is known at the time of purchase. This spread is simply a **transaction cost**. Liquidity risk would arise if this spread would widen when it the asset is being sold.
  - ○ Generally speaking, the primary drivers of liquidity risk are (1) changes in market conditions or the market for the individual asset and (2) the size of the position i.e., large positions are typically more difficult and costly to offload.

Non-Financial Risks

- **Settlement risk** (also known as **Herstatt risk**) is related to default risk, but has more to do with settlement of payments just before a default.
- **Legal risk** is of two types. First, there is the risk of being sued for something the entity does or fails to do. Second, there is the risk of the terms of a contract not being upheld by the legal system.
- **Compliance risk** encompasses **regulatory risk**, **accounting risk** and **tax risk**. It refers to the risk of the organization incurring significant unexpected costs, back taxes, financial restatements and penalties.
- **Model risk** is the risk of a valuation error resulting from using an incorrectly specified model or improperly using a valid model.

- ○ **Tail risk** is related to model risk, and can even be viewed as a form of model risk. It refers to the risk of events captured by the tail of a distribution occurring more frequently than expected by the model.
- **Operational risk** is used to describe all internal risks that arise from the people and processes that work together in an organization to produce its output. Examples include the risk of hackers breaking into the company's computer systems, its computers becoming infected with a virus, and programming errors and bugs.
- **Solvency risk** is the risk that the entity runs out cash, and is therefore unable to survive or succeed, even if it is otherwise solvent.

Interactions between Risks

It is very important for organizations to recognize that risks interact, and that the interaction is more 'toxic' in stressed market conditions. When different sources of risk come together, the combined risk is almost always non-linear in that the total risk faced is much greater than the simple sum of the individual risks, and this makes the situation even worse. Unfortunately, most risk models and systems do not directly account for risk interactions.

Measuring and Modifying Risks

Value at Risk (VaR)

Value at risk or **VaR** is a measure of the size of the tail of the distribution of profits on a portfolio or for an entity. A VaR measure is composed of (1) a currency amount, (2) a time period, and (3) a probability. If a bank states that its VaR is $4 million at 3% for one day, it means that bank expects to lose a minimum of $4 million in one day 3% of the time.

- VaR is a **minimum** extreme loss metric.
  - ○ There is no ultimate maximum loss that is stated in the measure. However, the statistics used to compute VaR can be used to estimate average extreme losses.
    - ▪ **Conditional VaR** or **CVaR** is calculated as the weighted average of all loss outcomes in a statistical distribution that exceed the VaR loss.
    - ▪ **Expected loss given default** (which is used to measure credit risk) measures the average expected loss if the underlying company defaults.
- VaR can be measured in several different ways, which results in highly diverse estimates.
- VaR is subject to model risk as well.
  - ○ VaR is based on a particular assumption about the probability distribution of returns or profits. If that assumption is incorrect, the VaR estimate will be incorrect.
  - ○ VaR also requires certain inputs. If those inputs are incorrect, the VaR estimate will be incorrect.
- VaR can understate actual risk. Under the normal distribution, extreme negative returns are accounted for, but they are offset by extreme positive returns. However, actual historical returns have exhibited a tendency for more extreme negative returns than assumed by the normal distribution (tail risk). In response, statisticians have developed **extreme value theory** to help them gauge the likelihood of outcomes that exceed those that would normally be expected.

Due to its shortcomings, critics have argued that naive users of VaR can be lulled into a false sense of security. A presumably tolerable VaR can give the illusion that risk is under control, even when it is actually not. Nonetheless, VaR is accepted as a risk measure by most banking regulators and is approved for disclosure purposes in accounting standards.

PM

Two measures in particular that are often used to complement VaR are scenario analysis and stress testing. Although scenario analysis and stress testing can provide useful information (and banks are required to perform them) they are also subject to model risk.

Methods of Risk Modification

Risk Acceptance: Self-Insurance and Diversification

- Self-insurance refers to retaining exposure to a risk that is considered undesirable but is too costly to eliminate by external means.
- Diversification is another form of accepting risk, but it does so in the most efficient manner possible. When it comes to portfolio risk management, diversification is the key to eliminating non-systematic risk, but other forms of risk management may be needed to mitigate other risks.

Risk Transfer is the process of passing on a risk to another party, usually in the form of an insurance policy.

Risk shifting refers to actions that change the distribution of risk outcomes. Risk shifting is associated with derivative contracts and risk modification vehicles. Risk shifting mechanism are used when the organization wants to modify the probability distribution of returns, or adjust the payoff diagram of its risk exposures.

How to Choose a Method for Modifying Risk

Generally speaking:

- For risks that lie outside the core competencies of the organization, management should try to avoid those risks. If the potential value added is too great to ignore, then management must at least take adequate precautions.
- Organizations that have large amounts of free cash flow should self-insure as much as possible because self-insurance reduces costs and enables the company to retain flexibility. At the same time, organizations should aim to diversify as much as possible.
- Insurance works best when risks can be pooled, but this is not the case for many types of risks, particularly those that can affect a large number of parties at the same time as premiums can be prohibitively high.
- For financial risks that exceed risk appetite, risk shifting is a very common choice. However, risk shifting tools such as derivatives may not be available for all types of risks.

TECHNICAL ANALYSIS
Cross-Reference to CFA Institute Assigned Reading #54

Technical analysis is a security analysis technique that involves the examination of past market trends (using data such as prices and trading volumes) to predict the future behavior of the overall market and of individual securities.

Technical analysis is based on the following:

- Supply and demand determine prices in real time.
- Changes in supply and demand cause changes in prices.
- Prices can be projected with charts and other technical tools.

Principles and Assumptions

- Technicians suggest that market trends and patterns reflect irrational human behavior.
- Technicians believe that the market reflects collective investor knowledge and sentiment.
- Technical analysis is the only tool available to investors to forecast future prices for assets that do not have underlying financial statements or associated income streams.
- Technicians believe that security price movements occur before fundamental developments occur or are reported.

Technical versus Fundamental Analysis

- Technical analysis uses only trading data, which includes market price and volume information. Fundamental analysis uses external information (e.g., financial reports, industry and macroeconomic analysis) and also incorporates social and political variables.
- The data used by technical analysts is more concrete and reliable. The financial statements used by fundamental analysts are subject to manipulation by management.
- Fundamental analysis is more conceptual as it aims to determine the theoretical long-term (intrinsic) value of a security. Technical analysis is more practical as it studies actual trading patterns to evaluate the market price of a security.
- Technical analysis has been in use for a longer period in investment decision-making. Fundamental analysis is a relatively new field.

Drawbacks of Technical Analysis

- Technicians only study market movements and trends, which can change without warning. Further, it may take some time for a clear, identifiable trend to emerge.
- Technicians expect trends to repeat themselves so a change in investor psychology may be missed by them.
- Application of technical analysis is limited in markets that are subject to significant outside manipulation and in illiquid markets.

Construction and Interpretation of Technical Analysis Charts

Charts

Charts are used to illustrate historical price information, which is used by technicians to infer future price behavior. The choice of charts is governed by the purpose of the analysis.

Line Charts

- A line chart is a simple graphical display of prices over time.
- Charts plot closing prices as data points, and have a line connecting these points.
- Time is plotted on the horizontal axis and prices are plotted on the vertical axis.
- Line charts provide a broad overview of investor sentiment, and the information they provide can be analyzed quickly.

Bar Charts

- A bar chart presents four pieces of information-opening price, highest and lowest prices, and the closing price for each time interval.
- A short bar indicates low price volatility, while a longer bar indicates high price volatility.
- For each time interval, the top of the line shows the highest price, while the bottom of the line shows the lowest price. The cross-hatch to the left indicates the opening price, while the cross-hatch to the right indicates the closing price.

Candlestick Charts

- A candlestick chart provides the opening and closing prices, and highs and lows during the period.
- Further, it also clearly illustrates whether the market closed up or down.
- The body of the candle is shaded if the closing price was lower than the opening price, and the body is clear if the closing price was higher than the opening price.

Point and Figure Chart

To construct a point and figure chart, a box size and a reversal size must first be determined.

- The box size refers to the minimum change in price that will be represented by a box on the chart.
- The reversal size determines when a new column will be created on the chart.
- The vertical axis measures discrete movements in price.
- Box and figure charts are useful as they highlight the prices at which trends change (when the columns change), as well as price levels at which the security most frequently trades (congestion areas).

Scale

The vertical axis on a charts can be constructed with a linear (arithmetic) scale or a logarithmic scale.

- A linear scale is more appropriate when the data fluctuate within a narrow range.
- In a logarithmic scale, percentage changes are plotted on the vertical axis. They are more appropriate when the range of data is larger.
- Time is plotted on the horizontal axis.

Volume

Volume is used by technicians as a barometer of the strength of a trend.

- If a security's price is increasing with increasing volumes, it shows that more and more investors are purchasing the stock at higher prices. This indicates that the trend is expected to continue as the two indicators "confirm" each other.

- If a security's price is rising with declining volumes (the two indicators are diverging), it suggests that the trend is losing momentum as fewer investors are willing to buy at higher prices.

Time Intervals

Short term investors may create charts with intervals less than a minute long, while longer term investors may use charts with intervals as long as one year.

Relative Strength Analysis

Relative strength analysis is used to evaluate the relative performance of a security compared to a stated benchmark by plotting the ratio of the security's price to the benchmark index over time.

- An upward-sloping line indicates outperformance.
- A downward-sloping line suggests underperformance.

Trend, Support, Resistance Lines, and Changes in Polarity

Trend analysis assumes that investors tend to behave in herds and that trends usually continue for an extended period of time.

An uptrend occurs when a security's price makes higher highs and higher lows.

- Higher highs occur when each high lies above the previous high, and when the price declines (there is a retracement) each subsequent low is higher than the prior low.
- To illustrate an uptrend, the technician connects all the lows on the price chart with a straight line.
- Major retracements (that drag the security's price significantly below the trend line) indicate that the uptrend is over and that the price may decline further.
- There are more ready buyers for a security than there are sellers and traders are willing to pay a higher price for the security over time.

A downtrend is indicated by lower highs and lower lows on the price chart.

- A technician connects all the highs on the chart to illustrate the downtrend.
- Major breakouts above the trend line may indicate that the downtrend is over and that the security's price could rise further.
- In a downtrend, sellers are willing to accept lower and lower prices for the security, which indicates negative investor sentiment regarding the asset.

During a sideways trend, there is a relative balance between demand and supply.

- Typically, options positions are more profitable than long or short positions on the security itself during a sideways trend.

Trend analysis involves the use of support and resistance levels.

- A support level is defined as the price at which there is sufficient buying interest in the stock to arrest the price decline.
- A resistance level is the price at which enough selling activity is generated to prevent any further increase in price.

PM

Support and resistance levels may be horizontal or sloped lines.

The change in polarity principle asserts that once the price rises above the resistance level, it becomes the new support level. Similarly, once the price falls below a support level, it becomes the new resistance level.

Chart Patterns

Chart patterns are formations on price charts that look like recognizable shapes. Recurring chart patterns can be used to predict future prices because these patterns essentially represent collective investor sentiment over a given time period.

Reversal Patterns

Reversal patterns indicate the end of a prevailing trend.

Head and Shoulders

A head and shoulders pattern follows an uptrend in the price of a security. It is composed of three parts:

- **Left shoulder**: The left shoulder consists of a strong rally with high volumes.
- **Head**: The price starts to rise again, and this time records a higher high than the one reached in the left shoulder. However, volumes in this rally are lower.
- **Right shoulder**: The right shoulder is similar to the left shoulder, but with lower volumes.

Note that the neckline may not always be a perfectly horizontal line.

Volume is very important in analyzing head and shoulders patterns. The fact that the high of the "head" is higher than the "high" of the left shoulder, but has lower volumes indicates that investor interest is waning.

When one indicator is bullish (rising price) while another is bearish (lower volumes) it is known as a divergence.

- Once a head and shoulders pattern has formed, prices are expected to decline (the uptrend that preceded the head and shoulders pattern is expected to reverse).
- Once the price falls below the neckline (which previously acted as a support level), it becomes the new resistance level (change in polarity principle).

Inverse Head and Shoulders

- A downtrend in prices precedes an inverse head and shoulders pattern.
- The price characteristics of each of the three segments of the head and shoulders pattern are reversed in an inverse head and shoulders pattern, but the volume characteristics are the same.

Setting Price Targets with Head and Shoulders Patterns

Once the neckline has been breached in the head and shoulders pattern, the price is expected to decline by an amount equal to the distance between the top of the head and the neckline.

$$\text{Price target} = \text{Neckline} - (\text{Head} - \text{Neckline})$$

Typically, the stronger the rally preceding the head and shoulders pattern, the more pronounced the expected reversal.

Setting Price Targets for Inverse Head and Shoulders Patterns

Inverse head and shoulders patterns are preceded by a downtrend. Therefore, prices are expected to rise or break out above the neckline after the right shoulder has been formed.

$$\text{Price target} = \text{Neckline} + (\text{Neckline} - \text{Head})$$

Double Tops and Bottoms

A double top occurs when an uptrend in prices reverses twice at approximately the same price level (two highs are recorded at roughly the same level). Usually, the first top has a higher volume.

For a double top, the price target (where the reversal will end) is established at a level that is lower than the valley (the low recorded between the two tops) by an amount that equals the distance between the tops and the valley.

The more significant the sell-off after the first top (deeper the valley) and the longer the time period between the two tops, the more significant the formation is considered to be.

A double bottom indicates the reversal of a downtrend. It occurs when, following a recent downtrend, prices fall to a certain level, rise for a bit, then fall back to the same level and rise again.

For double bottoms, the price is expected to rise above the peak between the two bottoms by approximately an amount equal to the distance between the bottoms and the peak.

Triple Tops and Bottoms

A triple top consists of three peaks at roughly the same level, while a triple bottom occurs when three troughs are formed at roughly the same price level.

- Triple tops and bottoms are rare, but when they occur, they indicate more significant reversals than double tops and double bottoms.
- Generally speaking, the greater the number of times the price reverses at a given price level, and the longer the period over which the pattern is formed, the more significant the expected reversal.

Continuation Patterns

A continuation pattern is used to confirm the resumption of the current market trend.

Triangle Patterns

A triangle pattern is formed when the range between highs and lows over a period narrows down on the price chart. The line connecting the highs over the period eventually meets the line connecting the lows, forming a triangle.

An ascending triangle is formed when the trend line connecting the highs is horizontal while the trend line connecting the lows is upward-sloping.

- Ascending triangles form during an uptrend.
- Eventually the share price is expected to rise.

PM

A descending triangle suggests that the stock price will continue to decline.

- The line connecting the highs is downward-sloping, while the line connecting the lows is horizontal.

In a symmetrical triangle, the line connecting the highs is downward-sloping, while the line connecting the lows is upward-sloping.

- Such a formation suggests that buyers are becoming more bullish as they continue to buy at higher prices than before, but sellers are becoming increasingly bearish as they sell at successively lower prices.
- After the formation, the trend ends up in the same direction as the trend that preceded the triangle formation.

More about Triangle Patterns

- The height of the triangle (also known as **measuring implication**) equals the distance between the two trend lines at the start of the formation.
- Once the price breaks through one of the trend lines, analysts expect the price to move further by roughly the measuring implication.
- Usually, the breakout from the triangle occurs between halfway and three-fourths of the way into the pattern; not at the end of the pattern.
- The longer the triangle pattern, the more significant and volatile the subsequent price movement is expected to be.

Rectangle Patterns

When the two trend lines (one that connects the highs and the other that connects the lows) are both horizontal, a rectangle pattern is formed. Once a breakout occurs, the trend in prices is the same as the trend that preceded the rectangle formation.

Flags and Pennants

Flags and pennants form over a much shorter time interval (usually on a daily price chart over a week) compared to triangles and rectangle patterns.

A flag is formed when two trend lines are parallel to each other (similar to country flags or parallelograms).

- Typically, the slope of the trend lines is opposite to that of the prevailing trend.

A pennant is basically a triangle that is formed over a relatively short span of time (typically over a week).

- For both flags and pennants, the expectation is that the trend that preceded the formation will continue after the pattern.
- The breakout beyond the trend line is expected to roughly equal the distance between the start of the trend and the flag or the pennant.

Common Technical Analysis Indicators

Price-Based Indicators

Price-based technical indicators incorporate current and historical market price information.

Moving Average

A moving average is the average of the closing price over a given number of periods. Moving averages smooth out short term price fluctuations and therefore, give a clearer picture of a market trend.

- A simple moving average uses the arithmetic mean, weighing each price equally in computing the average.
- An exponential moving average attaches a greater weight to recent prices in computing the average.

Applications of Moving Averages

- Generally, a stock that is in a downtrend tends to trade below its moving average, while one in an upward trend will typically trade above its moving average.
- Moving average trend lines can also act as support or resistance levels.
- When the short-term moving average intersects the long-term moving average from below, the formation is referred to as a *golden cross* and is a bullish sign.
- When the short-term moving average intersects the long-term moving average from above, it forms a *dead cross* which is a bearish signal.

Bollinger Bands

Bollinger bands consist of a simple moving average plus upper and lower bands that are calculated by adding and subtracting a specific number of standard deviations from the moving average.

Applications of Bollinger Bands

- A contrarian technical strategy based on Bollinger bands aims to sell the security when it reaches the upper band and purchase the security when it touches the lower band. The assumption here is that the security will continue to trade within the bands.
- A long-term investor may purchase the security once it has broken out significantly above the upper band, or short the security once it has fallen significantly below the lower band.

Momentum Oscillators

Momentum oscillators are used to identify changes in market sentiment. They are calculated in such a manner that they either fluctuate within a range (usually between 0 and 100) or hover around a number (such as 0 or 100).

- It is easy to identify extreme highs and lows on oscillators, and these extremes indicate that market buying/selling activity is more aggressive than historical levels.
- Technicians focus on whether oscillators and price data are moving in the same direction (convergence) or in different directions (divergence).
- When the price forms a new low, but the momentum oscillator is not at its lowest, the formation is a divergence. It implies that the downtrend is weakening and is expected to end soon.

Applications of Momentum Oscillators

- The oscillator range for a security can be used to determine the strength of a trend. Oversold conditions suggest that bearish market sentiment will end soon, while overbought conditions signal that the bullish market sentiment may soon change.

- They may signal a trend reversal when they reach historical highs or lows.
- They can be used to make short-term trading decisions in non-trending markets.

Momentum or Rate of Change Oscillator

A momentum oscillator (rate of change (ROC) oscillator) is calculated as follows:

$$M = (V - V_x) \times 100$$

where :
 M = momentum oscillator value
 V = last closing price
 V_x = closing price x days ago, typically 10 days

- When the momentum oscillator value crosses zero into positive territory in an uptrend (when prices are also rising) it is a bullish signal.
- When it crosses zero into negative territory in a downtrend (when prices are falling), it is a bearish signal.
- Crossovers that occur in the opposite direction of the trend are ignored because technicians who use oscillators first consider the general trend when making trading decisions.

The base value for an oscillator can also be set at 100. In this case, the oscillator is calculated as:

$$M = \frac{V}{V_x} \times 100$$

Relative Strength Index

A relative strength index (RSI) compares a security's gains with its losses over a given time period.

$$RSI = 100 - \frac{100}{1 + RS}$$

where $RS = \dfrac{\Sigma(\text{Up changes for the period under consideration})}{\Sigma(|\text{Down changes for the period under consideration}|)}$

- The RSI lies between the 0 and 100.
- A value above 70 typically represents an overbought situation, while a value below 30 usually indicates an oversold situation.
- Less volatile stocks may trade in a narrower range.
- The RSI range for any stock does not need to be symmetrical around 50.

Stochastic Oscillator

A stochastic oscillator is based on the assumption that in an uptrend, the stock price tends to close near the high of its recent range, while in a downtrend it tends to close around its recent low.

The stochastic oscillator lies between 0 and 100 and is usually calculated using 14-day price data. It is composed of two lines, %K and %D.

$$\%K = 100\left(\frac{C - L14}{H14 - L14}\right)$$

where :
C = last closing price
L14 = lowest price in last 14days
H14 = highest price in last 14days
%D (signal line) = Average of the last three %K values calculated daily.

Applications of Stochastic Oscillators

- Generally speaking, when the stochastic oscillator is greater than 80, it usually indicates that the security is overbought and should be sold. A value lower than 20 indicates that the security is oversold and should be purchased. However, analysts should consider the absolute level of the two lines in light of their historical range.
- Crossovers between the two lines can also give trading signals similar to crossovers of moving average lines. When the %K (smoothed line) crosses %D from below, it is a short-term bullish signal, and if it crosses %D from above, it is a bearish signal.

Moving Average Convergence/Divergence Oscillator

The moving average convergence/divergence oscillator (MACD) is the difference between the short term and long term moving average of a security's price. The MACD is composed of two lines:

- The MACD line, which is the difference between two exponentially smoothed moving average lines (typically over 12 and 26 days).
- The signal line, which is the exponentially smoothed moving average of the MACD line (typically over 9 days).

The MACD is compared with its historical levels to determine whether market sentiment regarding the security is different from what it usually is. The indicator itself moves around 0 and has no limits.

Applications of the MACD Oscillator

- Crossovers of the MACD line and the signal line may indicate a change in trend (similar to crossovers of moving averages and the stochastic oscillator).
- When MACD line moves outside its historical range, it indicates a weakening in the current trend.
- Convergence (which suggests that the trend will continue) occurs when the MACD and price move in the same direction, while divergence (which suggests that the trend will reverse) occurs when the MACD and price move in opposite directions.

Sentiment Indicators

Sentiment indicators evaluate investor activity looking for signs of bullishness or bearishness.

PM

Opinion Polls

A number of companies conduct regular polls of investors and investment professionals to gauge market sentiment. Technicians compare the data (which is also presented graphically) with recent market highs, lows and inflection points to establish relationships that might be useful in predicting future market direction.

Calculated Statistical Indexes

- A high **put-call ratio** indicates that the market is bearish, while a low ratio suggests that the market is bullish.
- The **VIX** rises when investors fear a market decline.
- **Margin debt levels** are very strongly correlated with the movement in the market.
- The **short interest ratio** may be interpreted in two ways. A high ratio may suggest that:
  - There is overall a negative outlook on the security and one should expect the price to decline.
  - The effect of short sales has already been factored into the current market price. When these short sellers cover their positions, the price of the stock will rise.

Flow of Funds Indicators

Technicians also look at the potential demand and supply for securities in making trading decisions.

Arms Index

$$\text{Arms Index} = \frac{\text{Number of advancing issues / Number of declining issues}}{\text{Volume of advancing issues / Volume of declining issues}}$$

- When the market is in balance, the arms index is close to 1.
- Values above 1 indicate that there is more activity in declining stocks, and that the market is in a selling mood.
- Values below 1 indicate that there is more activity in advancing stocks and that market sentiment is currently bullish.

Margin Debt

Margin loans may increase stock purchases, while declining margin balances may force the selling of stocks.

Mutual Fund Cash Positions

- Contrarians buy when mutual funds' cash positions are high and sell when their cash positions are low.
- The average cash percentage of mutual funds has historically hovered around 6.8%.

New Equity Issuance

When the new equity issuance indicator is high, the market is usually near its peak and is likely to decline in the future.

Secondary Offerings

While these offerings do not increase the number of shares outstanding, they do increase the number of shares available for trading (the free float). Therefore, secondary offerings affect the supply of shares just like IPOs.

Cycles

Over time, technicians have observed recurring cycles in the markets, only some of which can be logically explained. By identifying different cycles, technicians look to predict the market's future direction.

Kondratieff Waves

Nikolai Kondratieff suggested that economies went through a 54-year economic cycle. His theory was mainly derived from economic cycles and commodity prices, but similar cycles have also been seen in equity prices during the time of his work.

18-year Cycle

The 18-year cycle is usually mentioned in real estate markets though it can also be observed in equities and other markets.

Decennial Pattern

The decennial pattern traces the average annual stock returns (based on the DJIA) according to the last digit of the year. The DJIA has historically performed poorly in years ending with a 0, while the best ones have been years that end with a 5.

Presidential Cycle

Historically, it has been observed that the third year (of the four-year U.S. Presidential term) boasts the best stock market performance. The stock market has done reasonably well in the fourth year as well. One explanation for this is that politicians up for re-election inject stimuli into the economy to increase their popularity.

Intermarket Analysis

Intermarket analysis refers to the technique of combining analysis of different markets to identify trends and reversals of trends. It is based on the principle that markets for different categories of securities (stocks, bonds, currencies, commodities, etc.) are interrelated and influence each other, and asserts that these relationships are strengthening with increasing globalization. Some of the relationships that have been observed between different asset classes are:

- Stock prices and bond prices tend to move in the same direction. Therefore, rising bond prices are a positive for stocks.
- Declining bond prices are a signal of commodities prices possibly rising.
- A strong dollar usually results in lower commodity prices.

Applications of Intermarket Analysis

- Technicians often use relative strength analysis to identify inflection points in a particular market and then look for a change in trend in a related market.

- Given technical observations regarding the business cycle at any time, relative strength analysis can be used to identify potentially lucrative investments from within the equity market.
- Intermarket analysis can also be used to identify which countries one should invest in.

Technical Analysis Applications to Portfolio Management

A **top-down approach** to portfolio management focuses on how the overall economy affects different sectors or industries.

In **bottom-up investing**, the investor focuses her attention on a specific company's technicals rather than on the industry or index in which that company is classified.

The key value-add of technical analysis in fundamental portfolio management is in the form of timing of the purchase or sale of that security.

FINTECH IN INVESTMENT MANAGEMENT
Cross-Reference to CFA Institute Assigned Reading #55

Fintech refers to the use of technology-based innovations that are changing the way financial services and products are being designed and delivered to clientele.

Big Data refers to the massive amounts of data produced by financial markets, businesses, governments, individuals, and sensor networks.

- Structured data can be stored in database tables.
- Unstructured data cannot be stored in tables.
- Semi-structured data can have both characteristics.

Artificial Intelligence(AI) is designed to perform cognitive or decision-making tasks in a comparable or superior manner to human intelligence.

Machine learning (ML) consists of computer programs that use algorithms to learn how to complete tasks over time so that greater experience translates into better performance.

Analysts must they to ensure that they select appropriate input data and appropriate data analysis techniques. They must always be wary of overfitting data (which occurs when the program learns inputs and targeted outputs too precisely) and underfitting data (which occurs when a program is too simplistic, precluding the ML program from identifying relationships and patterns when training with a dataset). Finally, they must be wary of their programs becoming "black box" approaches, which can create results that are inexplicable or hard to understand.

Types of Machine Learning

- **Supervised learning** involves labeling or identifying inputs and outputs to the algorithm so that it can be trained to identify relationships for labeled data and work with other data sets.
- **Unsupervised learning** does not involve giving programs labeled data, but instead requires algorithms to describe the data and its structure on its own.
- **Deep learning** (or **deep learning nets**) is a technique that uses neural networks to perform multistage, nonlinear processing to identify patterns and relationships in data through a supervised or unsupervised approach.

Data Science

Data science is an interdisciplinary field that uses advances in computer science (including machine learning), statistics, and other disciplines for the purpose of extracting information from Big Data (or data in general). Data-processing methods include data capture, curation, storage, search, and transfer.

Data visualization refers to how the data will be formatted, displayed, and summarized in graphical form. Traditional structured data can be visualized using tables, charts, and trends, while non-traditional unstructured data require new techniques of data visualization. Some of these newer techniques that can be applied to textual data include tag clouds and mind maps.

Common programming languages used in data science include Python, R, Java, C/C + + , and Excel VBA. Common databases include SQL, SQLite, and NoSQL.

PM

Fintech Applications in Investment Management

- **Text analytics** is the use of programs to retrieve and analyze information from unrelated sources to conduct predictive analysis and find indicators of future performance.
- **Natural language processing (NLP)** is the analysis and interpretation of language using artificial intelligence, including translation, speech recognition, and text mining.
- **Robo-advisory services** aim to provide cost-effective and easily accessible investment solutions through the Internet without the interaction of human financial advisers.
- **Risk analysis** applications include stress-testing financial institutions, identifying adverse near-term market trends, detecting declining corporate earnings, analyzing real-time trading patterns, portfolio scenario analysis and back-testing, and assessing alternative data quality.
- **Algorithmic trading** involves computerized buying and selling based on prespecified rules and guidelines for lowering costs, improving execution speed, and providing anonymity for investment managers. **High-frequency trading (HFT)** is a form of algorithmic trading that uses real-time, granular market data to execute trades in fractions of a second through ultra-high-speed networks when certain conditions are met.

Distributed Ledger Technology

Distributed ledger technology (DLT) is a new form of financial recordkeeping that allows entities to share database information through networks. A DLT network consists of a digital ledger and a consensus mechanism that involves networked computers (or nodes) validating transactions and agreeing on updates to create unchangeable records that are easily accessible to participants on a near-real-time basis. To provide security for networks and database integrity, DLTs use **cryptography** (or algorithms) to encrypt data so that it is unusable to any unauthorized parties.

Blockchains are digital ledgers where information is sequentially recorded in "blocks" that are "chained" together using cryptography. This means transactions are grouped together into blocks that are linked to previous blocks through a secure link (or "hash").

- In **permissioned** networks, members might have restrictions on their activities and level of access to the ledger, such as adding transactions, viewing transactions, and seeing limited details of transactions.
- In a **permissionless** (or open) DLT network, all users can see every blockchain transaction and have the ability to perform all network functions.

Challenges to the Adoption of DLT by the Investment Industry

- Lack of DLT network standardization.
- Not be financially competitive with existing solutions.
- Substantial storage and power requirements.
- Accidental trades can only be undone by submitting offsetting trades (due to immutability of transactions).
- Regulatory approaches typically differ by jurisdiction.

ETHICS AND TRUST IN THE INVESTMENT PROFESSION
Cross-Reference to CFA Institute Assigned Reading #56

Ethics describes a system of principles, beliefs, and values that guide (or society believes should guide) our behavior. **Principles** are fundamental truths that form the basis for a chain of reasoning leading to beliefs about cause and effect and the way things should and shouldn't be.

Standards of conduct serve as benchmarks for the minimally acceptable behavior required of members of a group. They serve to clarify the organization's **code of ethics**, which lays out its beliefs regarding obligatory and forbidden conduct.

Professionals use specialized knowledge and skills in service to others. A profession's code of ethics publicly communicates the shared principles and expected behaviors of a profession's members. It helps foster confidence in members of the profession.

Challenges to Ethical Behavior

- **Overconfidence bias**: People being more likely to overestimate the morality of their own behavior, particularly in situations that they have not faced before.
- **Situational influences**: External factors, such as environmental or cultural elements, that shape a person's thinking, decision making, and behavior such as the **bystander effect** (where people are less likely to intervene in an emergency when others are present).
- Focusing on the immediate rather than long-term outcomes or consequences of a decision.

Some ethical behavior may be illegal. New laws designed to reduce or eliminate conduct that adversely affects the markets can create opportunities for different, but similarly problematic, conduct.

Ethically sound decisions are almost always better than law from an equity standpoint, but almost always require good judgment and active consideration of stakeholders' interests from the stakeholder perspective.

Ethical Decision-Making Frameworks

An ethical decision-making framework is a tool for analyzing the potential alternative actions and consequences of a decision. It raises awareness of different perspectives, improves decision-making, and helps avoid unanticipated ethical consequences.

A general ethical decision-making framework is shown below:

- **Identify:** Facts of the situation, ethical/legal obligations to stakeholders, and potential conflicts of interest.
- **Consider:** Potential alternatives, situational influences, and guidance external to the situation.
- **Decide and act.**
- **Reflect:** Why did or why didn't the decision yield the expected result?

CODE OF ETHICS AND STANDARDS OF PROFESSIONAL CONDUCT; GUIDANCE FOR STANDARDS I–VII
Cross-Reference to CFA Institute Assigned Readings #57 & #58

All CFA Institute members and candidates enrolled in the CFA Program are required to comply with the Code of Ethics and the Standards of Professional Conduct (Code and Standards). The CFA Institute Bylaws and Rules of Procedure for Proceedings Related to Professional Conduct (Rules of Procedure) form the basic structure for enforcing the Code and Standards.

The Rules of Procedure are based on the following two principles:

1. Fair process.
2. Maintaining confidentiality of process.

The CFA Institute Board of Governors is responsible for implementing the Professional Conduct Program (PCP) through the Disciplinary Review Committee (DRC).

The CFA Institute Designated Officer, through the Professional Conduct staff, carries out professional conduct inquiries. Circumstances which can initiate an inquiry include:

- Information disclosed on the annual Professional Conduct Statement.
- Written complaints received by Professional Conduct staff.
- Questionable conduct as publicized by the media or any other source.
- A violation report submitted by a CFA examination proctor.

Once an inquiry is initiated, the Professional Conduct staff undertakes an investigation which can include:

- Requesting a written explanation.
- Interviewing related person(s).
- Collecting any supporting documents.

The information collected is reviewed by the Designated Officer, who may conclude that:

1. No disciplinary action is needed
2. A cautionary letter needs to be issued
3. Proceedings need to be continued

If it is concluded that there has been a violation of the Code and Standards, the Designated Officer can propose a disciplinary sanction. The member or candidate has the right to accept or reject the decision. A rejection would require the matter to be referred to a hearing by a panel of CFA Institute members. Sanctions by CFA Institute may include condemnation by peers, consequences for current or future employment or suspension from the CFA program.

The adherence of investment professionals to ethical practices benefits all market participants.

- Clients are reassured that investment professionals they hire prioritize their interests.
- Investment professionals benefit from the more efficient and transparent operation of the market that promotes integrity.

Sound ethics is fundamental to capital markets and the investment profession as it increases investors' confidence in global financial markets. Ethics is also of paramount importance because of the interconnectedness of global financial markets, which gives rise to the issue of market sustainability. It is imperative that top management foster a strong culture of ethics not just among CFA charter holders and candidates but among all staff members who are involved directly or indirectly with client relations, the investment process, record keeping, and beyond.

However, new challenges continually arise for members and candidates in applying the Code and Standards. This is because ethical dilemmas are not unambiguously right or wrong and require a bit of judgment.

The CFA Institute Code of Ethics plays an integral role in maintaining the integrity of CFA Institute members and upholding professional excellence. All CFA Institute members and CFA candidates must abide by this code and are encouraged to notify their employers of any violations. Violations may result in disciplinary sanctions by CFA Institute, which may include revocation of membership, candidacy in the CFA program and the right to use the CFA designation.

The Code of Ethics requires all members and candidates to:

- Act with integrity, competence, diligence, respect, and in an ethical manner with the public, clients, prospective clients, employers, employees, colleagues in the investment profession, and other participants in the global capital markets.
- Place the integrity of the investment profession and the interests of clients above their own personal interests.
- Use reasonable care and exercise independent professional judgment when conducting investment analysis, making investment recommendations, taking investment actions, and engaging in other professional activities.
- Practice and encourage others to practice in a professional and ethical manner that will reflect credit on themselves and the profession.
- Promote the integrity of, and uphold the rules governing, capital markets.
- Maintain and improve their professional competence and strive to maintain and improve the competence of other investment professionals.

Standards of Professional Conduct:

I. **Professionalism**
   A. Knowledge of the Law
   B. Independence and Objectivity
   C. Misrepresentation
   D. Misconduct

II. **Integrity of Capital Markets**
   A. Material Nonpublic Information
   B. Market Manipulation

III. **Duties to Clients**
   A. Loyalty, Prudence, and Care
   B. Fair Dealing
   C. Suitability
   D. Performance Presentation
   E. Preservation of Confidentiality

IV. **Duties to Employers**
   A. Loyalty
   B. Additional Compensation Arrangements
   C. Responsibilities of Supervisors

ET

V. **Investment Analysis, Recommendations, and Actions**
   A. Diligence and Reasonable Basis
   B. Communication with Clients and Prospective Clients
   C. Record Retention
VI. **Conflicts of Interest**
   A. Disclosure of Conflicts
   B. Priority of Transactions
   C. Referral Fees
VII. **Responsibilities as a CFA Institute Member or CFA Candidate**
   A. Conduct as Participants in CFA Institute Programs
   B. Reference to CFA Institute, the CFA Designation, and the CFA Program

The best way to prepare for Ethics is to thoroughly read the Standards themselves, along with related guidance and examples.

INTRODUCTION TO THE GLOBAL INVESTMENT PERFORMANCE STANDARDS (GIPS®)
Cross-Reference to CFA Institute Assigned Reading #59

Individual and institutional investors typically use past investment performance to gauge a fund manager's ability and to make investment decisions. Questions relating to the accuracy and credibility of the data used to present investment performance make comparisons difficult.

The GIPS standards aim to provide clients and prospective clients with comparable and representative investment performance data. They establish an industry-wide, standard approach for calculation and presentation of investment performance. This forces complying firms to avoid misrepresentation and to communicate all relevant information that prospective clients should know to make informed investment decisions. Compliance with GIPS standards for any firm is *voluntary* and not required by any legal or regulatory authorities. However, only investment management firms that actually manage assets can claim compliance. Plan sponsors and consultants cannot claim to comply with GIPS if they do not manage any assets. They can only endorse the standards or require their investment managers to comply with them. Further, compliance is a firm-wide process that cannot be achieved on a single product or composite. In order to claim compliance, the firm needs to comply with all requirements of GIPS standards; there is no such thing as partial compliance to GIPS.

The GIPS standards benefit two main groups—investment management firms and prospective clients.

The GIPS standards require the use of composites. A composite is formed by combining discretionary portfolios into one group that represents a particular investment objective or strategy. A composite representing a particular strategy, must include **all** discretionary portfolios managed according to that strategy.

To ensure that the firm does not include only its best performing funds when presenting its investment performance, the GIPS standards require that the criteria for classifying portfolios into composites be decided before performance is known (i.e., on an ex-ante basis), not after the fact.

Firms that claim compliance with GIPS standards are responsible for ensuring that they really are compliant and that they maintain their compliant status going forward. After claiming compliance, firms may hire an independent third party to verify that they are compliant to add credibility to their claim.

Verification assures that the investment manager is compliant with GIPS standards on a firm-wide basis. Verification needs to be performed on the entire firm rather than specific composites. Verification tests:

- Whether the investment firm has complied with all the composite construction requirements on a firm-wide basis; and
- Whether the firm's processes and procedures calculate and present performance information according to GIPS standards.

Verification is optional, and it cannot be performed by the firm itself.

ET

Objectives of GIPS

- Promote investor interests and instill investor confidence.
- Ensure accurate and consistent data.
- Obtain worldwide acceptance of a single standard for calculating and presenting performance.
- Promote fair, global competition among investment firms.
- Promote industry self-regulation on a global basis.

Who Can Claim Compliance?

- Any firm that actually manages assets may choose to comply with the GIPS standards.
- Compliance is a firm-wide process that cannot be achieved on a single product or composite.
- Complying with the GIPS standards is voluntary.

Who Benefits from Compliance?

- Asset management firms
- Investors
- Asset owners
- Oversight bodies

Composites

- A **composite** must include all actual, fee-paying, discretionary portfolios managed in accordance with the same investment mandate, objective, or strategy.
- The requirement to create, use and maintain composites is designed to prevent firms from cherry-picking—using the best-performing accounts to represent the performance of an investment strategy.
- A claim of compliance requires that all fee-paying discretionary accounts managed by the firm be included in at least one composite.

Verification

Verification needs to be performed on the entire firm rather than specific composites. Verification tests:

- Whether the investment firm has complied with all the composite construction requirements on a firm-wide basis; and
- Whether the firm's processes and procedures calculate and present performance information according to GIPS standards.

Verification is optional, and it cannot be performed by the firm itself.